MW00961362

INTERPRETER

A JOURNAL OF LATTER-DAY SAINT FAITH AND SCHOLARSHIP

VOLUME 41 · 2020

THE INTERPRETER FOUNDATION

OREM, UTAH

THE INTERPRETER FOUNDATION

ISSN 2372-1227 (print)
ISSN 2372-126X (online)

Mission Statement

Supporting The Church of Jesus Christ of Latter-day Saints through scholarship.

The Interpreter Foundation supports the Church in the following ways:

- **Promotion:** We provide tools to encourage and facilitate personal learning by study and faith, and disseminate accurate information to the public about the Church.

- **Explanation:** We make the results of relevant scholarship more accessible to non-specialists.

- **Defense:** We respond to misunderstandings and criticisms of Church beliefs, policies, and practices.

- **Faithfulness:** Our leadership, staff, and associates strive to follow Jesus Christ and be true to the teachings of His Church.

- **Scholarship:** Our leadership, staff, and associates incorporate standards of scholarship appropriate to their academic disciplines.

The Interpreter Foundation is an independent organization that supports but is not owned, controlled by, or affiliated with The Church of Jesus Christ of Latter-day Saints. The material published by the Interpreter Foundation is the sole responsibility of the respective authors and should not be interpreted as representing the views of The Interpreter Foundation or of The Church of Jesus Christ of Latter-day Saints.

This journal compiles weekly publications. Visit us online at InterpreterFoundation.org
You may subscribe to this journal at https://interpreterfoundation.org/annual-print-subscription/

TABLE OF CONTENTS

Two Essays on Sustaining
and Enlarging the Doctrine

Daniel C. Peterson

Abstract: *In a pair of recent books, Patrick Mason and Terryl and Fiona Givens seek to revitalize, reinvigorate, and deepen our understanding of basic terms and concepts of the Restoration. I welcome such efforts, convinced (even where I sometimes quibble) that the conversations they will engender among faithful and committed believers can be very healthy. Now that "the times of refreshing [have] come from the presence of the Lord" (Acts 3:18), it is imperative, both for ourselves and for a world that needs to hear the news, that we not lose sight of the radical freshness of the divine gift and of its comprehensively transforming power. My hope for The Interpreter Foundation is that — while joyfully recognizing, indeed celebrating, the fact that prophets and apostles lead the Kingdom, not academics and intellectuals — it will contribute not only to the defense of the Restoration but to the explication of Restoration doctrines and enhanced understanding and appreciation of their riches.*

A few weeks ago, the remarkably prolific, learned, and always interesting Latter-day Saint thinkers Terryl and Fiona Givens kindly sent me a copy of a brief new book they had just published. It's entitled *All Things New: Rethinking Sin, Salvation, and Everything in Between.*[1]

I've enjoyed it very much. Twice. I'm in deep sympathy with the fundamental project, and I recommend the book enthusiastically. Like Patrick Mason's soon-to-be published *Restoration: God's Call to the 21st-Century World*, which I read in manuscript before it went to press, it is a book that will challenge faithful Latter-day Saint readers in a good and

---

1. Fiona and Terryl Givens, *All Things New: Rethinking Sin, Salvation, and Everything in Between* (Meridian, ID: Faith Matters Publishing, 2020).

positive way and that deserves to be widely discussed.[2] Indeed, in my view, discussing these books would benefit us considerably as a community.

Discussing such matters can be not only beneficial, but truly part of the "sweet work" of the Kingdom. As the prolific English minister and hymnist Isaac Watts (1674–1748) reminds us,

> Sweet is the work, my God, my King,
> To praise thy name, give thanks and sing,
> To show thy love by morning light,
> And talk of all thy truths at night.[3]

We benefit not only because it *is* genuinely sweet to talk of "poems and prayers and promises and things that we believe in,"[4] but because through such conversations we might become better equipped to defend, commend, and build the Kingdom. We might be more effective in sharing the Gospel and serving the Saints and the world in which we live.

Terryl and Fiona see us as being harmed by a kind of disease, and I'm inclined to agree:

> We believe that ... many ... struggling Saints are suffering as a consequence of what scripture calls "the traditions of the fathers, which [are] not correct" (Alma 21:17). ... The philosopher Friedrich Schleiermacher describes the situation well. He wrote that one can believe and teach that "everything is related to the redemption accomplished by Jesus of Nazareth" and yet that redemption can be "interpreted in such a way that it is reduced to incoherence." His diagnosis is the subject of this book.[5]

Now, please don't jump to the conclusion that Terryl and Fiona Givens are apostate heretics, calling out The Church of Jesus Christ of Latter-day Saints and stepping forward to steady the ark. They are energetic believers in the Restoration.[6] But they also believe that the

---

2. See Patrick Q. Mason, *Restoration: God's Call to the 21st-Century World* (Meridian, ID: Faith Matters Publishing, 2021).

3. "Sweet is the Work," *Hymns*, no. 147.

4. The phrase comes, of course, from the 1971 John Denver song named, precisely, "Poems, Prayers and Promises."

5. Givens and Givens, *All Things New*, 3.

6. See Nathaniel Givens, Jeffrey Thayne, and J. Max Wilson, "Latter-day Saint Radical Orthodoxy: A Manifesto," a late-2020 document to which — along with a number of others, including me — Terryl Givens and Fiona Givens are original signatories, https://latterdayorthodoxy.org/.

Restoration is ongoing, and that, while the Saints have been given (among many other divine blessings) great doctrinal gifts, our understanding of those gifts is still limited in some important ways, even stunted, by the language in which we speak and write about them, which has been corrupted by centuries of misunderstanding and apostasy.

> [W]e offer here what we hope may provide bases for an ongoing conversation about the language of the Restoration. … Here are a few caveats about what this sketch is and is not. We are neither offering dogmatic definitions nor offering a comprehensive treatment. We are trying to model and inspire fresh ways of thinking through the religious vocabulary that pervades our wounded world and particularly our Church that is still emerging from the wilderness.[7]

They want to get back to what they believe to have been the original Christian vision, and they set that vision out in their first chapter:

> We will discuss two doctrines that were part of Christian self-understanding in the early years: the eternal nature of our souls, extending back beyond the formations of the world, and the parenthood of God taken as more than mere metaphor. These two sacred truths — the eternal nature of men and women, and the loving, selfless, devoted love of a parental God — were the lifeblood of a vibrant Christian community that saw the purpose of life as an educative experience in the school of love.[8]

> These two doctrines — our premortal life with the plans there set in motion and the true parental nature of God — are the foundations of the Restoration and are unique in the current Christian world.[9]

They cite a beautiful passage from the 1997 book *Sanctuary*, by the late Chieko Okazaki (1926–2011), who served as first counselor in the general presidency of the Relief Society between 1990 and 1997:

> At the end of this process, our Heavenly Parents will have sons and daughters who are their peers, their friends and their colleagues.[10]

This essay wasn't really intended to be a review of *All Things New*, let alone of Patrick Mason's *Restoration*, but it's clearly evolved as I've written it beyond what I had planned. Consequently, before I use them as a platform

---

7. Givens and Givens, *All Things New*, 78, 79.
8. Ibid., 5.
9. Ibid., 27.
10. Cited at ibid., 81.

from which to make the one simple point that I intended to make with the present article, I want to say a few more things about the Givens' book.

Throughout the book, they cite "many beautiful and God-touched voices,"[11] ancient and medieval and modern, both Latter-day Saint and mainstream Christian, and occasionally Jewish. "Latter-day Saints," they correctly point out, "can find much to applaud and much to learn from earnest God- and Truth-seekers across the spectrum."[12] "God-touched souls have recurrently provided pinpricks of light amid the greater darkness."[13] A significant number of these are the voices of women — enough to suggest that including them was a deliberate choice. I enthusiastically welcome this choice.[14]

At many places in *All Things New*, I found myself exclaiming "Yes!" Sometimes this was because they had just made a point that I myself have made somewhere or other. (I've always loved this definition from Ambrose Bierce's minor 1906 masterpiece *The Devil's Dictionary*: "Admiration, n. Our polite recognition of another's resemblance to ourselves.") At other places, though, it was because of a fine insight that crystallized something for me that I had maybe not seen before.

Here is just one of a large number of examples:

> We might venture a definition of *salvation*: to be *saved* is to become the kind of persons, in the kinds of relationships, that constitute the divine nature. ... If salvation is about what we are to become as individuals, heaven is the name given to those relationships in which individuals find fulness of joy. That may not be a complicated idea, but its implications are far-reaching.

---

11. Ibid., 5.

12. Ibid., 21.

13. Ibid., 31.

14. I'm very pleased to see them draw several times on thoughts from Francine Bennion, a friend who belongs to a monthly reading group in which both my wife and I have participated for something on the order of three decades now. I believe that there is much to be learned from different voices generally, and specifically from women's theological reflections. A case in point: When I was first writing the article recently republished in more accessible form than hitherto as "Notes on Mormonism and the Trinity" (the title of the article dates back to long before President Russell M. Nelson's admonitions regarding the terms *Mormon* and *Mormonism*), I was delighted to discover that the readings I found most rich in profitable insights came, to a large extent, from liberation theologians and feminist theologians. See Daniel C. Peterson, "Notes on Mormonism and the Trinity," *Interpreter: A Journal of Latter-day Saint Faith and Scholarship* 41 (2020): 87–130, https://journal.interpreterfoundation.org/notes-on-mormonism-and-the-trinity/.

> For one thing, it clarifies why neither salvation nor heaven are rewards that God can dispense, or that we can earn.[15]

> Heaven, as Joseph taught, is not a matter of reward or position or place but a particular kind of sociability.[16]

Significantly, the title of their Chapter 6 is "Heaven: From 'Where' to 'with Whom.'" I find that profound. Moreover, it gives serious meaning to a witticism from Joseph Smith that is often treated as a mere joke:

> [L]et me be resurrected with the Saints, whether I ascend to heaven or descend to hell, or go to any other place. And if we go to hell, we will turn the devils out of doors and make a heaven of it.[17]

Ultimately, to be saved is to become like Christ, who is like the Father:

> And ye shall be even as I am, and I am even as the Father; and the Father and I are one. (3 Nephi 28:10)

This is, as *All Things New* expressly recognizes, a daunting prospect:

> Restoration theology is, from the first word, far more ambitious, presumptuous, and gloriously aspirational than we may recognize. Restoration theology goes far beyond the current Christian hope of personal redemption from death and hell. Our faith tradition aspires to make us into the likeness of our Heavenly Parents. Our sin, as Saints, may be in thinking that such an endeavor could be anything other than wrenching, costly, inconceivably difficult, and at times unimaginably painful. We do not become, in C. S. Lewis's phrase, "little Christs" by a couple of well-spent hours ministering to our assigned families and abstaining from tea and coffee. ... We are still very much in the morning of an eternity of striving.[18]

There are no shortcuts to Christlikeness. If God were able to make us Christlike with a simple wave of a magical divine wand, he could and presumably would — and certainly should — already have done so, long before there had ever been Adolf Hitlers, Jeffrey Dahmers, Joseph Stalins, Colombian drug lords, mass murdering terrorists, abusive husbands,

---

15. Givens and Givens, *All Things New*, 82, 86.

16. Ibid., 142.

17. Joseph Smith, *History of the Church of Jesus Christ of Latter-day Saints*, 7 vols., edited by B. H. Roberts, 5:517.

18. Givens and Givens, *All Things New*, 84.

abused children, dishonest accountants, and cheating spouses. Long before our own fumbling attempts at righteousness, our own acts of selfishness and thoughtlessness, our repeated failures at acting as we know we should.

But — and until you read *All Things New* for yourself, you'll have to take my word for it — despite the intimidating, bracing character of the Givens's message, this book is resoundingly hopeful, deeply reassuring, and encouraging. God, they remind us, is a loving Father, not a hanging judge, who wants to share with us all that he possesses.

Or, in the spirit of the book itself, perhaps I should say that God are — note the purposeful plural — a loving Father and Mother who want to share with us everything that they have and are, and who sent God the Son, Jesus Christ, as our divine healer.

One of the most striking aspects of *All Things New* is its common practice of using plural verbs and pronouns to refer to God. As others no doubt will, I found this grammatically jarring. (I'm a grammarian, not only in English, and I spend much of my daily time writing and editing, and grading student papers. Verb-subject agreement is one of my particular small and pedantic obsessions.) But I also found it stimulating and exhilarating.

After saying, early in the book, that "a change in pronoun usage may be in order" with respect to the word *God*, they proceed to make the change.[19] And for such a change, unaccustomed to it as we are by either official Church usage or our own folk habits out in the pews, there is certainly doctrinal justification in Latter-day Saint tradition:

> Elder John A. Widtsoe wrote: "The glorious vision of life hereafter … is given radiant warmth by the thought that … [we have] a mother who possesses all the attributes of Godhood." The Apostle Erastus Snow went further: "Deity consists of man and woman. … I have another description: There never was a God, and there never will be in all eternities, except they are made of these two component parts: a man and a woman; the male and the female." If this is true, then when we employ the term *God*, it will often be the case that two divine Beings are behind the expression. The writer of Genesis employed the name Adam to refer to a fully collaborative couple; *Adam* is effectively their surname (Gen. 5:2; Moses 6:9). Just as Adam can refer to both Adam and Eve, there will … be instances when *God* is rightly followed by the pronoun *They*. Brigham Young taught that "we were created … in the image of our father and

---

19. Ibid., 25.

our mother, the image of our God." His statement indicates that calling Heavenly Mother "God" is consistent with the biblical account of the creation of both the "male and female" being in "the image of God" (Gen. 1:26–27).[20]

But let's get back to the hopeful, optimistic, encouraging character of *All Things New*. As the epigraph to their introduction, the Givenses quote William Tyndale:

> Evangelion (that we call the gospel) is a Greek word and signifieth good, merry, glad, and joyful tidings, that maketh a man's heart glad, and maketh him to sing, dance, and leap for joy.[21]

And that is very much the spirit in which they write. It is all about healing, love, and the hope that all might ultimately be saved — a universalistic or at least quasi-universalistic position to which I have also long been inclined.

So, it may seem churlish on my part to acknowledge that at some points in *All is New*, I quibbled with what they had to say.

Although, for instance, I think that their criticism of the renewed influence of St. Augustine in the Reformation is well-aimed and worthy of serious consideration, I'm a bit more inclined than they evidently are to see positive developments from the Reformers and the Reformation, as well. (In other words, I'm somewhat more traditionally Latter-day Saint in my attitudes here, while believing that the traditional Latter-day Saint attitude needs their correction.)[22]

Moreover, while I think their criticism of "penal substitution" models for the atonement of Christ is entirely justified — I'm inclined to agree with them that "Brokenness, not sinfulness, is our general condition; healing from trauma is what is needed"[23] — I'm not sure that I understand exactly what it is that they're putting in its place.[24] It isn't clear to me, in their model, why our salvation demanded that Jesus absolutely had to suffer in Gethsemane and be crucified on the cross at Golgotha. And yet, evidently, he did. And as to why he did, the "penal substitution" theory has the great advantage of clarity, even if it

---

20. Ibid., 27.

21. Ibid., 1, citing David Daniell, *William Tyndale: A Biography* (New Haven, CT: Yale University Press, 1994), 123.

22. See, for example, the discussion at Givens and Givens, *All Things New*, 43–50.

23. Ibid., 105.

24. See the discussion in Chapter 13, "Atonement: From Penal Substitution to Radical Healing," in Givens and Givens, *All Things New*, 131–50.

lacks the advantages of truth and of suitably depicting the nature of God. Nor is it apparent to me what role the performance of vicarious temple ordinances for the dead can play in their conception of Jesus as Savior and of the healing role of his sacrificial offering. And yet we're repeatedly told that such ordinances are absolutely necessary — they don't dispute this — and we devote great effort and expense to seeking out our dead and performing the required rituals on their behalf.

For a much smaller issue, I was struck by the fact that in one passage they approvingly cite the theologian David Bentley Hart as saying that "Paul speaks of … sin as a kind of contagion, disease with which all are born; … but never as an inherited condition of criminal culpability."[25] And then, three pages later, they observe, with what I take to be disapproval, that "In the Christian past, sin was equated with a contagion."[26] I think that I can see a way to reconcile the two statements, but perhaps I'm wrong.

And, while I myself have come to the view (which is plainly also theirs) that our eternal progress to Godlikeness will, at best and if we make it at all, require eons of time and learning beyond the grave, I would have appreciated some engagement with such passages as Alma 34:32, which seem (at least at first and second glance) to run counter to such a viewpoint:

> For behold, this life is the time for men to prepare to meet God; yea, behold the day of this life is the day for men to perform their labors.[27]

Furthermore, I would very much like to discuss with them their continual use of the term *woundedness* to describe the human condition. It is, in crucial ways, fundamental to their project (with which, I stress again, I am deeply sympathetic).

I worry about it not because I disagree with the idea of the word. I happen to find it extraordinarily apt and insightful, and it's crucial to the way in which I myself have tried to act when I've been entrusted with stewardships in the Church (e.g., as a bishop) that involved pastoral counseling. I see wounded souls (in everyone, very much including myself) that need education, coaching, encouragement, and healing more than they require punishment. What caught my attention, though, was the way, in *All Things New*, the word went from being a textual variant to being the foundation for discussion:

---

25. Givens and Givens, *All Things New*, 105.

26. Ibid., 108.

27. Alma 34:32. See, too, Alma 34:31–36.

In 1 Nephi 13, the Lord's messenger characterizes the modern world's inhabitants as being in a state of "awful woundedness" (1830 edition) or in an "awful state of blindness" (1837 edition).[28]

The 1837 and present editions replace "state of awful woundedness" with "awful state of blindness." The common point of both descriptive words is telling: woundedness and blindness alike describe a condition for which we are not responsible; the injury is due to the agency of others who have removed "plain and precious" things from the scriptural record.[29]

Those two passages, one on the third page of *All Things New* and the other its accompanying chapter endnote, represent essentially the last mentions of the fact that *woundedness* might not be the actual, accurate word at 1 Nephi 13:32. Elsewhere — for example, in these passages — no doubt about the word is apparent at all:

- "what Nephi called 'the state of awful woundedness' that we inhabit"[30]
- The book's ninth chapter, entitled "Sin," bears the subtitle "From Guilt to Woundedness."[31]
- "[T]he most pervasive image the New Testament and Book of Mormon employ in reference to our condition is woundedness. The angel uses that word to describe the human condition to Nephi."[32]
- "When the angel referred to the world of today as being in a "state of awful woundedness," he provided a term, *woundedness*, that is accurate and is a catalyst to love."[33]

It is true that 1 Nephi 13:32 reads "state of awful woundedness" in the Original Manuscript of the Book of Mormon. Next, when Oliver Cowdery copied the Original Manuscript onto the Printer's Manuscript, he initially transposed those words, writing "awful state of woundedness" before correcting them back to the Original Manuscript's "state of awful woundedness." And accordingly, that is the way that the passage reads in the Book of Mormon's 1830 first edition. However, in his preparation

---

28. Givens and Givens, *All Things New*, 3.
29. Ibid., 6n2. For Terryl Givens's thoughts on the phrase, see also https://bookofmormonstudynotes.blog/2019/11/13/what-is-awful-woundedness.
30. Givens and Givens, *All Things New*, 21–22.
31. Ibid., 103.
32. Ibid., 104.
33. Ibid., 108.

for publishing the 1837 edition of the Book of Mormon, Joseph Smith went back to the original word order of the *Printer's Manuscript* while changing *woundedness* to *blindness*. Thus, in the 1837 edition, the relevant passage reads "awful state of blindness." Subsequently, this has remained the reading of all of the official editions of the Book of Mormon published by The Church of Jesus Christ of Latter-day Saints ever since.

So, should "state of awful woundedness" be the preferred reading? I readily acknowledge that such a reading is attractive and that it might afford — indeed, *does* afford — a rich basis for theological, soteriological, and anthropological reflection. However, I have to point out that Royal Skousen's critical Yale edition of the Book of Mormon, based on decades of meticulous study of Book of Mormon textual history and language, reads "state of awful wickedness" — in contradiction not only to the Original Manuscript, the Printer's Manucript, Joseph Smith's 1837 revision, and the current official edition published by the Church. Although I genuinely like "awful woundedness," I'm persuaded by Skousen's reasoning that "awful woundedness" may have been a dictation or scribal error, and that "state of awful wickedness," although conjectural, is very possibly the proper reading. At a minimum, it must be said that "awful woundedness" is very far from a sure thing.[34]

My concern is that if we try to base ourselves on how we *think* scripture should have been worded rather than the way it *actually* was worded, we risk cutting ourselves loose from our mooring into untethered subjectivism. Happily, though, in this case I judge the damage to be minimal (if, indeed, there is any damage at all).

But, as I approach my peroration, I want to stress that I like *All Things New* very much. I like the ambition, even the audacity, of it. The Restoration and its vision of human destiny are audacious — radical — and that should not be forgotten. Years ago, a rather distant relative, intending to say something nice about the place where I had just accepted a faculty teaching position, described Provo, Utah, as a pleasant little religious town. He meant well, and I responded in kind. But the last thing I want is to be associated with a quaint and sentimentalized "Old Time Religion." I love, and have always loved, the sheer adventurousness, the revolutionary ambition, the radicality and expansiveness, the cosmic

---

34. See Royal Skousen, ed., *The Book of Mormon: The Earliest Text* (New Haven and London: Yale University Press, 2009), 36; also the argument given in Royal Skousen, *Analysis of Textual Variants of the Book of Mormon*, Volume 4 of the Critical Text of the Book of Mormon, *Part One: Title Page, Witness Statements, 1 Nephi 1–2 Nephi 11*, 2d ed. (Provo, UT: FARMS and *BYU Studies*, 2017), 295–97.

vision, of the doctrines of the Restoration, and that's what I like so very much about both the Givens' new book and Patrick Mason's *Restoration: God's Call to the 21st-Century World.*

Not surprisingly — I love these passages, too — *All Things New* happily quotes the stirring words of "the visionary member of the Seventy, B. H. Roberts":

> Mental laziness is the vice of men, especially with reference to divine things. Men seem to think that because inspiration and revelation are factors in connection with the things of God, therefore the pain and stress of mental effort are not required; that by some means these elements act somewhat as Elijah's ravens and feed us without effort on our part. ... "[W]hy then should man strive and trouble himself to understand? Much study is still a weariness of the flesh." So men reason; and just now it is much in fashion to laud "the simple faith;" which is content to believe without understanding, or even without much effort to understand.[35]

The Givenses say — and I strongly concur — that we need to be continually rethinking the doctrines we have received, to receive them afresh and to teach them in ever fresh ways. Admittedly in a unique way, the Reformation formula *Ecclesia semper reformanda est* — "the church must always be reformed" — applies to the Restored Church of Jesus Christ every bit as much as it applies to the churches of Protestantism. *Semper reformanda.* It is true, of course, that we have the distinct advantage of being led by living prophets and apostles, and intellectuals and scholars should not — nay, must not —attempt to usurp their authority. But that's no excuse for laziness on our part. We must escape traps of tiredness, stale routine, irrelevance to real, contemporary concerns.

> B. H. Roberts foresaw this need and hoped for its fulfillment in our day. He found his inspiration in the writings of the eminent American philosopher Josiah Royce. Disciples, Royce said, "are of two sorts. There are, first, the disciples pure and simple. ... They expound, and defend, and ward off foes, and live and die faithful to one formula. ... On the other hand, there are disciples of a second sort. ... The seed that the sower strews upon [his] fields springs up in [his] soil, and bears fruit — thirty, sixty, an hundredfold. ... Disciples of the second sort cooperate in the works of the Spirit ... [and] help lead ... *to a truer expression*"

---

35. Givens and Givens, *All Things New*, 70. The description of B. H. Roberts comes from page 72.

(our emphasis). B. H. Roberts read these words and built them into a prophecy and a call to action. "Mormonism," he said, "calls for [these disciples of the second sort,] disciples who will not be content with merely repeating some of its truths, but will develop its truth; and enlarge it by that development. The disciples of 'Mormonism,' growing discontented with the necessarily primitive methods which have hitherto prevailed in sustaining the doctrine, ... will cast them in new formulas; cooperating in the works of the Spirit, until they help to give to the truths received a more forceful expression."[36]

Patrick Mason and Terryl and Fiona Givens have given us examples of "second-sort" discipleship. Whatever flaws may exist in their books, I honor and respect them for that.

The Interpreter Foundation, you might think — along with this, its flagship journal — is dedicated to discipleship of that first sort, to defending what we've received and to warding off foes. It is certainly true that doing so is one of our principal missions. But it's my devout hope that we can also contribute to the second sort of discipleship, to developing enlarged and more forceful expressions of the Restoration.

Of course, as the author of Ecclesiastes recognized, "to every thing there is a season, and a time to every purpose under the heaven" (Ecclesiastes 3:1). In a letter to his wife, Abigail, the American Founder John Adams wrote

> The Science of Government it is my Duty to study, more than all other Sciences: the Art of Legislation and Administration and Negotiation, ought to take Place, indeed to exclude in a manner all other Arts. — I must study Politicks and War that my sons may have liberty to study Mathematicks and Philosophy. My sons ought to study Mathematicks and Philosophy, Geography, natural History, Naval Architecture, navigation, Commerce and Agriculture, in order to give their Children a right to study Painting, Poetry, Musick, Architecture, Statuary, Tapestry and Porcelaine.[37]

I thank all of those who have brought the Interpreter Foundation to where it is today, and who will carry it yet further. Without the time and effort and financial support offered by a large number of generous people, there would be nothing. Specifically, now, I'm grateful for those

---

36. Givens and Givens, *All Things New*, 72.

37. John Adams, "John Adams to Abigail Adams, 12 May 1780," https:// founders.archives.gov/documents/Adams/04-03-02-0258.

who *have* written the articles and reviews in this issue of *Interpreter: A Journal of Latter-day Saint Faith and Scholarship.* They do their work without financial compensation. I'm grateful to the source checkers, the copy editors, the anonymous peer reviewers, and all those who make the production of the *Journal* possible — and especially to Allen Wyatt and Jeff Lindsay, who have been assigned that ceaselessly demanding task, week after week after week. To all, my sincere and deep appreciation.

Daniel C. Peterson *(PhD, University of California at Los Angeles) is a professor of Islamic studies and Arabic at Brigham Young University and is the founder of the University's Middle Eastern Texts Initiative, for which he served as editor-in-chief until mid-August 2013. He has published and spoken extensively on both Islamic and Mormon subjects. Formerly chairman of the board of the Foundation for Ancient Research and Mormon Studies (FARMS) and an officer, editor, and author for its successor organization, the Neal A. Maxwell Institute for Religious Scholarship, his professional work as an Arabist focuses on the Qur'an and on Islamic philosophical theology. He is the author, among other things, of a biography entitled* Muhammad: Prophet of God *(Eerdmans, 2007).*

"We May Not Understand Our Words": The Book of Abraham and the Concept of Translation in *The Pearl of Greatest Price*

John S. Thompson

Review of Terryl Givens with Brian Hauglid, *The Pearl of Greatest Price: Mormonism's Most Controversial Scripture* (New York: Oxford University Press, 2019). 285 pages. $34.95 (hardback).

Abstract: *In recent years there has been an effort among some scholars to make sense of the historical sources surrounding Joseph Smith's claims to be a translator of ancient records. Terryl Givens, with some assistance from Brian Hauglid, has explored the evidence surrounding the Book of Abraham and suggests that, in this case, Joseph Smith may not have translated an ancient record of Abraham's writings into English as typically believed in the Latter-day Saint community. Consequently, Givens provides four alternative ways the work of "translating" may have been understood or practiced by the Prophet and his scribes. This essay highlights some evidence that was overlooked, misunderstood, and glossed by Givens, calling into question his fourfold attempt at redefining what it meant for Joseph Smith to translate this ancient record.*

Somewhat perplexing about Jared's remark to his brother in the Book of Mormon's account of the Tower of Babel is his reasoning that if their language is confounded, they might not understand their own words: "Cry unto the Lord, that he will not confound us that we may not understand our words" (Ether 1:34). Traditional interpretation of the Tower of Babel story posits that the confounding of languages was a sudden multiplying of spoken dialects, making it difficult for one person or group to understand the words of another. Jared's concern that they might not understand their own words, however, suggests something deeper.

Perhaps this story, as others have suggested, is less about a miles-high building and the sudden onset of the world's spoken dialects and more about a ritual ascent to "heaven" via a false temple and the confounding of God's word through subtle changes to its terminology and meaning based on the reasonings of mortals.[1] Small changes may seem innocuous at first but might lay the foundations for rifts, divisions, and the fragmenting of religious "languages" over time. Joseph Smith lamented about this kind a confounding when he said "the teachers of religion of the different sects understood the same passage of Scripture so differently as <to> destroy all confidence in settling the question by an appeal to the Bible."[2] In such multiplicity of religious languages, people may use words such as "baptism" or "priesthood" or "God" in their rhetoric, but they may not understand their unadulterated meaning.

In recent years, there has been an effort among some scholars to make sense of the historical sources surrounding Joseph Smith's claims to be a "translator."[3] Some of the evidence they highlight appears to call into question the typical understanding of that title in the Latter-day Saint community — an understanding based on 1) the Prophet's own claims that he was revealing in English some texts that were originally written in ancient languages, such as the Book of Mormon, the Book of Abraham, and some lost biblical narratives, and 2) the community's scriptural declaration that seers, like Joseph Smith, can "translate all records that are of ancient date; … a seer can know of things which are past" (Mosiah 8:13, 17). These claims are understood to be miraculous and are generally accepted by faith in the Latter-day Saint community.

Recently, the popular and gifted writer Terryl Givens (with some assistance from Brian Hauglid) addressed some of the controversy surrounding Joseph Smith's translation of the Book of Abraham in his

---

1. E.g., see Hugh Nibley, *Lehi in the Desert, The World of the Jaredites, There Were Jaredites, The Collected Works of Hugh Nibley 5* (Salt Lake City: Deseret Book, 1988), 172-73.

2. Joseph Smith, "History, 1838-1856, volume A-1 [23 December 1805-30 August 1834]," p. 2-3, *The Joseph Smith Papers*, https://www.josephsmithpapers.org/paper-summary/history-1838-1856-volume-a-1-23-december-1805-30-august-1834/2.

3. For the most recent collection of articles dealing with this issue, see *Producing Ancient Scripture: Joseph Smith's Translation Projects in the Development of Mormon Christianity*, eds. Michael Hubbard MacKay, Mark Ashurst-McGee, Brian M. Hauglid (Salt Lake City: University of Utah Press, 2020).

commentary on the Pearl of Great Price, a Latter-day Saint scriptural collection containing, in part, a few of Joseph Smith's revealed translations.[4] As is typical of Givens' works generally, the book makes accessible some of Joseph Smith's cultural and theological contexts and provides balanced textual and reception histories of the Pearl of Great Price's various components. His writing style is approachable and engaging and gives readers much to ponder.

In his chapter on the Book of Abraham, Givens briefly explores 1) Joseph Smith's title as "seer," including the role that the Urim and Thummim and translation play in defining that title; 2) an assumption that Joseph Smith believed the original ancient Adamic language, being pure, provided one the ability to fully access and express God's word unhampered, and that recovering this concrete dialect was ultimately a part of the Restoration in its fullest sense; 3) Joseph Smith's personal connection to, and the broader antebellum American fascination with, all things Egyptian and the events leading up to Joseph Smith's acquisition of mummies and papyri; 4) the relationship of the Book of Abraham to Joseph Smith's temple theology; and 5) the reception-history of the Book of Abraham by both critics and defenders, with a focus on the controversy surrounding Joseph Smith's translation of it.

As will be shown, Givens' attempt at a balanced portrayal of some of the difficulties and controversies surrounding the Book of Abraham eventually gives way to his ultimate conclusion that, at least in this case, it does not appear that Joseph Smith provided an English translation of an ancient text written by Abraham after all. Rather, for Givens, the evidence demonstrates that the Prophet mistakenly thought he was translating an ancient writing of Abraham from characters that were actually part of an ancient Egyptian text known as a Book of Breathings, while simultaneously creating a modern story of Abraham in his own fertile, if not divinely inspired, mind.

---

4. Terryl Givens with Brian M. Hauglid, *The Pearl of Greatest Price: Mormonism's Most Controversial Scripture* (New York: Oxford University Press, 2019). While my comments herein are directed at Givens, since he is the author of this volume, this should not diminish the fact that Hauglid's views are also represented and are thus being reviewed as well. Hauglid's views can more clearly be seen in his recently published article: Brian M. Hauglid, "Translating an Alphabet to the Book of Abraham" *Producing Ancient Scripture: Joseph Smith's Translation Projects in the Development of Mormon Christianity,* eds. Michael Hubbard MacKay, Mark Ashurst-McGee, and Brian M. Hauglid (Salt Lake City: University of Utah Press, 2020), 363-89.

After outlining some problems surrounding Joseph Smith's explanations of the Egyptian vignettes and other evidence that appears to demonstrate the Prophet used the Book of Breathings as his source for "translating" the Book of Abraham, Givens concludes:

> Smith certainly believed that he was successfully rendering the actual Egyptian symbols into their English counterparts. In the case of the facsimiles he was apparently wrong, and in the case of the Book of Abraham narrative he may have been as well.[5]

Accepting the possibility that Joseph Smith was wrong in spite of what he "certainly believed" himself to be doing, Givens attempts to give the Prophet some margin of piety and sensibility by choosing to "broaden or complicate reductive ways" of viewing what it might have meant for Joseph Smith to "translate."[6]

In his last section entitled "From Mummies to Scripture: Rethinking Translation," Givens proposes four different ways to view "translating" in the context of the Book of Abraham, providing more nuanced and creative ways to frame this word than what Latter-day Saints have typically understood. This recasting of the term can appear to make sense of the evidence that Givens presents and seems like an earnest attempt to mollify the difficulties surrounding Joseph Smith's claims in light of contrary evidence. However, there is evidence that was overlooked, glossed, or misunderstood that seriously questions the conclusions that spurred Givens' fourfold reframing in the first place. Reviewing this evidence and Givens' four-fold proposal allows for some discussion, again, of the main controversies surrounding Joseph Smith's translation of the Book of Abraham as well as an opportunity to clarify what Joseph Smith is doing with illustrations on the papyri he possessed.

There are, as usual, insightful perspectives about the Restoration movement that Givens brings to the table in his work. However, due to his and Brian Hauglid's associations with Brigham Young University and because of the high consumption of Givens' works in the Latter-day Saint faith community, it is important to raise awareness of the evidence that contradicts their attempt to alter the language of that community in this moment. This is not to cast a shadow over everything else these fine scholars have done, but it is important to demonstrate that the conclusions that these and other scholars make with respect to the Book of Abraham translation are not as inevitable as they portray.

---

5. Givens with Hauglid, *The Pearl of Greatest Price*, loc. 180 of 285, Kindle.
6. Ibid., 184.

I. Symbolic/Esoteric Translation

In his first attempt to recast Joseph Smith's "translation" efforts, Givens proposes that the Prophet, like others of his day, may have erroneously viewed the individual Egyptian characters on the Book of Breathings papyri as packed full of esoteric and symbolic meaning, not as the uni-, bi-, multi-literal phonemes and classifiers that form the pronunciation and meaning of actual words and sentences conveying Egyptian thought. Consequently, Joseph Smith may have thought he was mystically unpacking paragraphs of Abrahamic text from single characters on the Book of Breathings papyrus based on a mistaken belief that Abraham, the Egyptians, or some other ancient had embedded sentences and paragraphs of ideas related to Abraham into each character via their mystical ability.

"That Smith fully embraced this cultural preconception seems manifest in the earliest manuscripts of the Book of Abraham," Givens declares.[7] The Kirtland era manuscripts to which Givens refers include multiple copies of an "Egyptian Alphabet" (EA), a single "Egyptian Counting" document, a single "Grammar and Alphabet of the Egyptian Language" (GAEL) and multiple manuscript copies of the Book of Abraham along with a few other documents. All were recently published in the Joseph Smith Papers collection.[8] Some characters from the Egyptian Book of Breathings that Joseph Smith possessed appear in the left margins of the EA, GAEL, and the Book of Abraham manuscripts. On the EA and GAEL, many of the characters have what appears to be a name or pronunciation and additional English words and phrases written to their right, including many words and phrases found in the Book of Abraham. Further, in the EA/GAEL, some of the left-margin characters will repeat, with earlier repetitions having simple words or phrases in the English text on the right, while later repetitions seem to expand the words or phrases into fuller sentences or paragraphs, many found in the Book of Abraham. This can give an appearance that Joseph Smith and his scribes "fully embraced" the idea of extracting expanding layers of meaning from the character in the left margin.

In spite of Givens agreeing that "the relationship between the Abraham/Egyptian Papers and the Book of Abraham is far from settled ... ," stating that "this is not to say that we know how these two projects were related to each other in the minds of Joseph Smith and his contemporaries

---

7. Ibid., 188.

8. Robin Scott Jensen and Brian M. Hauglid, eds., *Revelations and Translations, Volume 4: Book of Abraham and Related Manuscripts* (Salt Lake City: Church Historian's Press, 2018).

and, therefore, exactly how the translation of the Book of Abraham came about," and mentioning that "the possibility that he dictated the text in a flow of oracular inspiration cannot be entirely ruled out,"[9] he contradicts himself in the final analysis by asserting that the EA/GAEL documents are Joseph Smith's intellectual and collaborative effort with his scribes to derive esoteric meaning and an Egyptian grammar from the Book of Breathing characters "en route" to producing the Book of Abraham, and that the Book of Abraham was not a free-flowing text given to him by revelation in likeness of the Book of Mormon:

> The Book of Abraham manuscripts, unlike their Book of Mormon counterpart, bear clear evidence of reworking, revising, and editing. This was no spontaneous channeling of a finished product by any stretch … What the surviving documents reveal is a remarkably complex, multilayered grammar that Smith constructed en route to deciphering the hieroglyphics.[10]

Since Givens appears to have adopted the view that Joseph Smith and his scribes ultimately derive the Book of Abraham from Egyptian characters that make up an ancient Egyptian Book of Breathings, not from characters that make up a text about Abraham, Givens further asserts that

> His system has no basis in linguistics and does not pass the muster with any Egyptologist; but the considerable labor and sheer inventiveness evident in the project provide a remarkable window into his methodology and imagination."[11]

Asserting the idea that Joseph Smith used the EA/GAEL as working papers for creating the Book of Abraham manuscripts appears reasonable at first glance, but it is a highly problematic theory when all the evidence is considered and carefully weighed. The following five sections offer a sample of the many evidences not addressed or glossed over by Givens that seriously question the viability of such a theory.

The 1835 Sources

Givens states, "What seems clear from the 1835 historical record and an analysis of the 1835 Abraham manuscripts and the grammar and alphabet manuscripts is that they were created roughly at the same time."[12] An exacting look at the 1835 sources, however, demonstrates

---

9. Givens with Hauglid, *The Pearl of Greatest Price*, loc. 173-74, 188.
10. Ibid., 201.
11. Ibid.
12. Ibid., 173.

that this statement is not accurate. According to these sources, Joseph Smith began providing the text of the Book of Abraham in the first days he obtained the papyri in early July 1835, before any mention of an EA/GAEL.[13] Text from the first chapter of the Book of Abraham is used by Oliver Cowdery in a preface to a blessing he recorded in September 1835,[14] and the late August 1835 edition of the Doctrine and Covenants uses unique material from Book of Abraham chapter 3.[15]

13. In a July 20, 1835 letter to his wife Sally, William W. Phelps explained that some mummies and papyri were brought to Kirtland a few weeks earlier and "[a]s no one could translate [the Egyptian papyri] they were presented to President Smith. He soon knew what they were and said they, the 'rolls of papyrus,' contained a sacred record kept by Joseph in Pharoah's [sic] Court in Egypt, and the teachings of Father Abraham." (Leah Y. Phelps, "Letters of Faith from Kirtland," *Improvement Era* 45 [August 1942]: 529, https://archive.org/details/improvementera4508unse/page/n49/mode/2up; see also Bruce A. Van-Orden, "Writing to Zion: The William W. Phelps Kirtland Letters (1835-1836)," *BYU Studies Quarterly* 33, no. 3 [1993]: 554, https://scholarsarchive.byu.edu/byusq/vol33/iss3/9/). Earlier in the same letter, Phelps mentions that that he had just received her letter the prior evening and that Joseph Smith said his emotion was the same reading her letter "as it was when reading the history of Joseph in Egypt" (Ibid., 555). It is not clear to what history Joseph Smith was referring, but the context does not rule out the possibility that he was referencing the writings of Joseph claimed to be on the papyri. A later Sept. 11, 1835 letter from Phelps to his wife mentioned that "[n]othing has been doing in the translation of the Egyptian Record for a long time," suggesting that some translation had occurred earlier (Ibid., 563). O. Cowdery's letter to William Frye, published in the Dec. 1835 Messenger and Advocate, indicates that on the first day that Michael Chandler met with Joseph Smith about the papyri: "Being solicited by Mr. Chandler to give an opinion concerning his antiquities, or translation of some of the characters, bro. S[mith] gave him the interpretation of some few for his satisfaction" (Oliver Cowdery, "Egyptian Mummies" *Latter Day Saints' Messenger and Advocate* II, no. 3 [Dec. 1835]: 235).

14. Oliver Cowdery's preface includes the following seeming paraphrase from the Book of Abraham: "we diligently saught for the right of the fathers, and the authority of the holy priesthood, and the power to admin in the same: for we desired to be followers of righteousness and the possessors of greater knowledge," (Dan Vogel, ed., *Early Mormon Documents Vol. 2* [Salt Lake City: Signature Books, 1999], 451-54, https://www.josephsmithpapers.org/site/priesthood-restoration?p=1&highlight=we%20diligently%20saught%20for%20the%20right%20of%20the%20fathers).

15. The proper name Shinehah from the Book of Abraham appears as a code word in Doctrine and Covenants (1835) 98:9 ("Doctrine and Covenants, 1835," p. 243, *The Joseph Smith Papers*, https://www.josephsmithpapers.org/paper-summary/doctrine-and-covenants-1835/251).

These sources suggest that Joseph Smith may have revealed text into Abraham 3 by the end of the summer of 1835.[16]

In contrast, the first mention in the 1835 sources of an EA or GAEL being created is an October 1835 entry in Joseph Smith's journal.[17] Significantly, the entry mentions that William Phelps, Joseph Smith, and Oliver Cowdery worked on an EA, and the three EA documents in the Joseph Smith Papers collection are in their handwriting. There are no other EA papers in the collection. This is strong evidence that these documents are the very ones mentioned in the October 1835 entry and should be dated to that month. The GAEL is likely of later date as it appears to copy from the EA and expand it.[18]

This same October 1835 entry mentions that "The system of astronomy was unfolded." But the source is not clear on what is meant and could have multiple interpretations:

  a) It could be indicating that the system of astronomy found in Abraham 3 was first revealed on October 1, but this would require dismissing the evidence that suggests Abraham 3 was revealed earlier.

  b) Brian Hauglid suggests that since the unfolding of a system of astronomy was mentioned in the same entry that mentions the creation of the EA, then the EA itself may be the revealed unfolding of the system and Abraham 3 was

---

16. Later 1835 sources, including some Abraham 3 material in the EA/GAEL themselves and a Dec. 1835 entry in Joseph Smith's journal that mentions he showed the Egyptian records to Brigham Young, William E. McLellin, and Jared Carter and "explained many things to them concerning the dealings of God with the ancient <s> and the formation of the planetary System," can all be viewed as corroborative evidence supporting the idea that Abraham 3, which outlines a system of astronomy, had already been revealed by Joseph Smith. For more evidence of Abraham 3 being translated in 1835 see Kerry Muhlestein and Megan Hansen, "'The Work of Translating': The Book of Abraham's Translation Chronology," in *Let Us Reason Together: Essays in Honor of the Life's Work of Robert L. Millet*, eds. J. Spencer Fluhman and Brent L. Top (Provo, UT: Religious Studies Center; Salt Lake City: 2016), 139-62. Hauglid's argument that the unique Abraham 3 material in the August 1835 Doctrine and Covenants could have been discerned independent of the Book of Abraham is only conjecture and glosses a crucial source (see Hauglid, "Translating an Alphabet to the Book of Abraham," 370n35).

17. Joseph Smith, "Journal, 1835-1836," p. 3, *The Joseph Smith Papers*, https://www.josephsmithpapers.org/paper-summary/journal-1835-1836/4.

18. Portions of "the Egyptian Alphabet documents were later copied into the Grammar and Alphabet volume" (Jensen and Hauglid, introduction to *Revelations and Translations: Volume 4*).

"translated" later in Nauvoo and based on the EA/GAEL.[19] However, no system of astronomy appears in the EA. There is a mention of Kolob and a few other astronomical terms that also appear in the Book of Abraham, again suggesting that chapter 3 had already been translated, but certainly no "system" is explained or outlined in the EA. The GAEL contains some passages that attempt to explain astronomical relationships, but this document is created later. On the difference between the system in the GAEL and the system in Abraham 3, see below.

---

19. Hauglid, "Translating an Alphabet to the Book of Abraham," 370. Hauglid asserts that everything beyond Abraham 2:18 of the current versification, the extent of the verses found on the Kirtland era copies of the missing original Book of Abraham translation document, was translated on the two days (Mar. 8-9) between the first and second published installments of the Book of Abraham in Nauvoo 1842 (Ibid., 372-75). These journal entries mention he both translated and revised during this interim. Contrary to Hauglid's view, the following timeline makes more sense of the evidence as it currently stands: Due to material from Abraham 3 referenced in 1835 and later sources, Joseph Smith appears to have translated at least into Abraham 3 prior to Aug. 1835. Additional translation occurred in or beyond Abraham 3 in the days between Oct. 1 and late Nov. 1835 when the last entry indicating that he translated that year appears in Joseph Smith's journal. How far they went in the story of Abraham during 1835 cannot be determined. When the Prophet returns to translating and also revising after the first installment is published in Nauvoo in 1842, some of the material he translates appears to have been prepared for the second installment as stated in his journal: "Commenced Translating from the Book of Abraham, for the 10 No of the Times and Seasons" ("Journal, December 1841-December 1842," p. 89, *The Joseph Smith Papers*, https://www.josephsmithpapers.org/paper-summary/journal-december-1841-december-1842/20). Nothing precludes material from the later end of the published chapters (e.g., Abraham 5) to have been translated during this time, contra Gee as well as Muhlestein and Hansen's leanings, since it is difficult to know how far they got in 1835. Such would satisfy the above journal entry's claim. But nothing in the sources require Abraham 3 to be translated at this time as Hauglid asserts. It makes more sense of the sources to conclude that Abraham 3 had already been translated but was part of the revision work that Joseph Smith also said he did prior to publication of the second installment in the Mar. 15, 1842 issue. Revisions that could have allowed Joseph Smith to incorporate addition clarifications and understanding from his Hebrew studies, etc. In other words, Joseph both translated and revised for the Mar. 15, 1842 just as his journal claims. Hauglid, "Translating an Alphabet to the Book of Abraham," 369 also attempts to make the EA part of Joseph Smith's prophetic mission by suggesting that the "unfolding" of the system of astronomy means that the Egyptian Alphabet in the previous line of the Oct. 1 entry was an unfolding revelation also, but this is not what the text actually says.

c) It could indicate that the astronomical material in Abraham 3 was translated in the summer of 1835 but an additional astronomical system was "unfolded" on October 1. This additional material could be an understanding of the astronomy in the vignette for Facsimile #2, or it could be the additional astronomical material promised in the Book of Abraham narrative itself:

> "But the records of the fathers, even the Patriarchs, concerning the right of Priesthood, the Lord my God preserved in mine own hands, therefore a knowledge of the beginning of the creation, and also of the planets, and of the stars, as they were made known unto the fathers, have I kept even unto this day, and I shall endeavor to write some of these things upon this record, for the benefit of my posterity that shall come after me."[20]

A system of astronomy as "made known unto the fathers" was already in the records that Abraham possessed, but the system of astronomy he learned in Abraham 3 came by means of a revelation through the Urim and Thummim.[21] Abraham, however, promised to write what the fathers understood concerning the planets and stars. Additionally, the narrative indicates that Abraham received his revelation concerning astronomy (Abraham 3) *before* he entered Egypt, but Joseph Smith's caption for Facsimile #3 indicates that Abraham also taught astronomy *later* when in Egypt. If this October 1 entry is referring to some later system of astronomy in the narrative, this would insinuate that a great deal more of the Book of Abraham was translated by October 1 than was ever published, but such a proposition is unlikely given that we do not have record of many days spent translating prior to this date.

d) Perhaps the simplest interpretation is that although Joseph Smith appears to have revealed the English text of the Book of Abraham into chapter 3 sometime

---

20. "Book of Abraham and Facsimiles, 1 March–16 May 1842," p. 705, *The Joseph Smith Papers*, https://www.josephsmithpapers.org/paper-summary/book-of-abraham-and-facsimiles-1-march-16-may-1842/3.

21. Ibid., 719, https://www.josephsmithpapers.org/paper-summary/book-of-abraham-and-facsimiles-1-march-16-may-1842/5.

prior to September 1835, their understanding of this system of astronomy was "unfolded" on October 1 in a way that Joseph Smith began to understand better its meaning or, as John Gee suggests, an understanding of astronomy relative to Facsimile #2 may have been unfolded.[22]

Almost a decade later, one entry in the Manuscript History of the Church suggests that the EA/GAEL was started in July 1835, but this is not consistent with the contemporary 1835 written evidence. Further, the source of this entry is unknown and seems to have been a later generalization, as it was appended to the end of all the July entries without a specific date. These and other factors[23] make the actual timing of this entry suspect at best without corroborative evidence. Givens and others rely on this much later source, not those from 1835, to assert that the EA/GAEL were created at roughly the same time as the Book of Abraham or that the EA/GAEL were the working papers for creating the Book of Abraham. Giving priority to or uncritically accepting a roughly decade-later, single entry of unknown origin over clearer, more contemporary sources is not sound methodology.

Later 1835 journal entries indicate that Joseph Smith continued to translate more passages of the Book of Abraham after the EA was started in early October, but if one follows the 1835 evidence strictly, the Book of Abraham phrases that actually appear in the EA/GAEL were already revealed prior to their appearance in these documents. Consequently, any theory that the EA/GAEL were started at the same time or were part of the production of the Book of Abraham text based on the 1835 sources is straining the evidence.

---

22. See John Gee, *An Introduction to the Book of Abraham* (Provo, UT: Religious Studies Center, Brigham Young University, 2017), loc. 247, 268-76 of 2126, Kindle.

23. It is believed that Joseph Smith did not review or edit this volume of the *History of the Church* for accuracy (see "History, 1838-1856, volume B-1 [1 September 1834-2 November 1838]," *The Joseph Smith Papers*, https://www.josephsmithpapers.org/paper-summary/history-1838-1856-volume-b-1-1-september-1834-2-november-1838/1). Also, William Phelps' known involvement in projects similar to the EA/GAEL prior to the acquisition of the Egyptian papyri (discussed below) could potentially cause confusion in later recollections of the exact timing of the EA/GAEL, so preference should be given to contemporary records.

Relationships between Documents

Givens notes the truism that similar texts shared between the EA/GAEL and Book of Abraham manuscripts "suggests some relationship between the production of both sets of documents" and "in the most conspicuous instance, there is a clear correspondence between Abraham 1:1–3 and the grammar and alphabet book."[24] There is certainly a relationship between the EA/GAEL and the Book of Abraham manuscripts, but it is the nature of this relationship that is far from clear. But in spite of this lack of clarity, Givens asserts the EA/GAEL demonstrate that Joseph Smith was "attacking the task [of translating the Book of Abraham] as an amateur linguist and working cooperatively with colleagues,"[25] providing "a remarkable window into his methodology and imagination" as noted above.

Whatever relationship the EA/GAEL have to the currently existing Book of Abraham manuscripts, it is important to highlight a very critical point that Givens neglects to mention: the extant manuscripts of the Book of Abraham are widely recognized as copies of an earlier original manuscript that is now lost.[26] The 1835 evidence recommends that the lone three verses that Phelps wrote on one of the manuscripts (Abraham 1:1–3) were the earliest translated. Sources indicate that he (along with Oliver Cowdery, whose hand does not appear on any of the extant Abraham manuscripts) was an initial scribe to the Prophet for his earliest translation efforts of the Book of Abraham in July.[27] The other extant Book of Abraham manuscripts from the Kirtland era are in the hand of Joseph Smith's later Kirtland scribes, Frederick G. Williams and

---

24. Givens with Hauglid, *The Pearl of Greatest Price*, loc. 173.

25. Ibid.

26. "Textual evidence suggests that these Book of Abraham texts were based on an earlier manuscript that is no longer extant" ("Book of Abraham Manuscript, circa July-circa November 1835-A [Abraham 1:4-2:6]," Historical Introduction, *The Joseph Smith Papers*, https://www.josephsmithpapers.org/paper-summary/book-of-abraham-manuscript-circa-july-circa-november-1835-a-abraham-14-26/1; "The earliest surviving manuscript of the Book of Abraham, probably written in early October 1835 in the handwriting of Frederick G. Williams, contains a long dittography (a repetition of part of the manuscript), which is characteristic of copied manuscripts — not dictated ones" (Gee, *An Introduction to the Book of Abraham*, loc. 399 of 2126, Kindle).

27. It is not out of the realm of possibility that these three verses are "the interpretation of some few" that Joseph Smith gave to Chandler in early July according to Oliver Cowdery's recollection in his December 1835 letter to William Frye (Cowdery, "Egyptian Mummies").

Warren Parrish, and start at Abraham 1:4 where Phelps had left off. The evidence strongly indicates that Williams' manuscript appears to have been copied from an earlier manuscript now missing, and Parrish then copies and corrects William's manuscript.[28] Parrish then makes another copy of these verses onto the manuscript that Phelps had begun, creating a single document of the verses in this set of manuscripts.[29]

Since the manuscripts are mostly, if not completely, copies of a missing original, Givens' claim that they give one insight into Joseph Smith's

---

28. John Gee, "Fantasy vs. Reality," *Interpreter: A Journal of Latter-day Saint Faith and Scholarship* (forthcoming).

29. The Phelps/Parrish manuscript could be understood as an effort to produce a "printer's manuscript." Phelps had mentioned in his July 20, 1835 letter to his wife their intention of publishing the Book of Abraham even at that early date, so it is not unreasonable to think that a printer's copy may have been started in Kirtland, though never published at that time (Van-Orden, "Writing to Zion," 9-10). That they were attempting to publish the record long before Nauvoo is clear from a Nov. 5, 1837 meeting wherein the church voted to "sanction the appointment of the Presidents in authorizing Brother [Willard] Richards & Brother Hadlock [Reuben Hedlock], to transact the business of the Church in procuring the means to translate & print those records taken from the chatacombs of Egypt, now in the temple." ("Minute Book 1," p. 259, *The Joseph Smith Papers*, https://www.josephsmithpapers.org/paper-summary/minute-book-1/263). Having an original translation manuscript and separate copy for printing would be in keeping with the pattern that Joseph Smith and his scribes followed before with the Book of Mormon. In this framework, the editing and markups in the surviving Abraham manuscripts would not be indicative of a struggling, collaborative, intellectually fluid *translation* process as Givens asserts — such could only be determined by viewing the original manuscript — but of editorial preparations for publication. This would explain why the Phelps/Parrish copy of the extant manuscripts covers the same verses published in the first installment of the Book of Abraham when it was finally printed in Nauvoo — not because that was necessarily all they had translated (again only the missing original manuscript could reveal the true extent) but because this was as far as they got in their effort to create a printer's copy while in Kirtland. The Phelps/Parrish manuscript was likely used to make a cleaner final copy for the printer in Nauvoo for the first installment of its publication in the Times and Seasons newspaper. If the Kirtland manuscripts were part of a preparation for printing, then the editorial insertions clearly made on Richard's manuscript copy (see ("Book of Abraham Manuscript, circa July-circa November 1835-A [Abraham 1:4-2:6]," 2-3) that refer the reader to the images of the altar and gods placed "at the commencement of this record" and "at the beginning" (Abraham 1:12, 14) should be understood as the editor, not Abraham, directing the readers to an image at the commencement of the planned publication ("this record"), not at the commencement of Abraham's record. Facsimile #1 was indeed placed at the commencement of the Book of Abraham text when it was published.

"methodology and imagination" for producing the original Book of Abraham text is highly problematic. Sound scholarship dictates that one should not assume that whatever relationship the EA/GAEL have to the extant manuscript copies of the Book of Abraham is indicative of their relationship to the original translation manuscript, and thus reveal the methodology by which Joseph Smith "translated." That is not a controlled interpretation of the evidence. Further, the supposed dependence of Phelps' original creation of Abraham 1:1–3 on the GAEL that Givens cites in his footnote is much too speculative and problematic to use as a basis for this conclusion; it is certainly not "clear."[30] Does the missing original manuscript also have Egyptian characters in its margin? Can it be shown to have a demonstrable dependence on the EA or GAEL? Without this original manuscript, there is no way to test the assumptions that Givens can only assert throughout his chapter.

Direct Revelation vs. Collaborative Intellectual Effort

Since Givens assumes that the EA and the GAEL are an integral part of Joseph Smith's effort to produce the original Book of Abraham manuscript, he stresses that "the process by which [Joseph Smith] produced the Book of Abraham was of a different category altogether from that of his 1829 production of the Book of Mormon."[31] The Prophet "wrestled with the Book of Abraham, using seer stones or not, on and off for seven years,"[32] and "his approach was one that combined prolonged and collaborative intellectual effort along with 'direct inspiration of Heaven,' as one transcriber noted."[33]

Givens' footnote about this transcriber, Warren Parrish, states: "Parrish's is the only contemporary, firsthand account of Smith's translation method, and it gives no details other than the quoted expression."[34] Actually, Parrish provides additional, even crucial, detail that Givens left out in this moment. The full testimony is thus: "I have set by his side and penned down the translation of the Egyptian

---

30. Jeff Lindsay, "A Precious Resource with Some Gaps," *Interpreter: A Journal of Latter-day Saint Faith and Scholarship* 33 (2019): 71–76.
31. Givens with Hauglid, *The Pearl of Greatest Price*, loc. 173.
32. Ibid.
33. Ibid., 201.
34. Ibid., 221.

Hieroglyphicks as he claimed to receive it by direct inspiration of Heaven."[35]

As the only scribal witness reporting how Joseph Smith translated the Book of Abraham, Parrish's testimony should not be so glossed over. Writing down the translation "as" Joseph Smith received it "direct" from heaven does not sound like there was any "prolonged and collaborative intellectual effort" in this process. Contrary to Givens' belief that the Book of Abraham translation "was no spontaneous channeling of a finished product by any stretch," Parrish's testimony, one of the principal sources that really matters, does indeed sound like the Book of Abraham was produced in much the same way Joseph Smith brought forth the Book of Mormon — by simply dictating, or spontaneously channeling, the translation as he received it from heaven. Note the similarities (highlighted with italics) between Parrish's testimony above and Oliver Cowdery's, who was scribe for the spontaneous channeling of the Book of Mormon:

> These were days never to be forgotten — to *sit under* the sound of a voice dictated by the *inspiration of heaven*, awakened the utmost gratitude of this bosom! Day after day I continued, uninterrupted, *to write* from his mouth, *as he translated*, ...[36]

As an aside, it is important to also note that Parrish claims Joseph Smith was translating "the" hieroglyphics, suggesting that, at the time, Parrish assumed that the Prophet was bringing forth the Book of Abraham from actual text on the papyri, not catalyzed thereby.

Givens himself notes other historical sources that refute his own claim that Joseph Smith translated the Book of Abraham through "prolonged and collaborative intellectual effort." Regrettably, Givens glosses over this evidence as well, stating, "That Smith employed the Urim and Thummim, or seer stone, is entirely likely. However, his employment of such a device should in no way obscure *the fact* that the process by which he produced the Book of Abraham was of a different category altogether from that of his 1829 production of the Book of Mormon."[37] Asserting this "fact," however, requires Givens to dismiss all the contemporary

---

35. Warren Parrish, letter to the editor, *Painesville Republican*, 15 February 1838, http://www.sidneyrigdon.com/dbroadhu/OH/painerep.htm#021538.

36. Oliver Cowdery to William W. Phelps, 7 Sept. 1834, *LDS Messenger and Advocate,* October 1834, 1:14, https://archive.org/details/LDSMessengerAndAdvocate18341837/page/n13/mode/2up, emphasis added, except "inspiration" is italicized in the original.

37. Givens with Hauglid, *The Pearl of Greatest Price*, loc. 173, emphasis added.

evidence that explicitly states otherwise and to ignore the problem of having no evidence that explicitly supports his claim.

The Relationship of the Margin Characters

On the surface, the affiliations between the EA/GAEL and Book of Abraham text appear to demonstrate that the EA/GAEL were Joseph Smith's and his collaborators' effort to extract — through a pseudo-intellectual and inspirational exercise — expanding degrees of meanings from the Egyptian characters on the papyri and then use these expanding meanings to ultimately create their final meanings in the Book of Abraham manuscripts. The marginal characters and their name/pronunciation in the EA/GAEL can be shown to repeat and the English text next to each repetition does seem to expand and become more elaborate. However (and this is an important distinction), the same margin-character is *not* carried over and associated with a similar text in the Book of Abraham manuscripts as one would expect if Givens' assumptions are to be followed logically. In fact, only one of the 170 characters in the left margin of the EA/GAEL having English text next to it loosely matches the same character and accompanying text on the Book of Abraham manuscript copies.[38] In other words, any similar English words or passages shared between the EA/GAEL and the Book of Abraham manuscripts actually have different Egyptian and other characters in the left margin. Conversely, any similar marginal characters between the EA/GAEL and the Book of Abraham manuscripts do not have English texts that relate next to them. Further, the Egyptian characters in EA/GAEL are generally from one fragment of papyri (JSPI), but those in the Abraham manuscripts are from a different fragment (JSPXI). Givens has not provided any logical explanation for these major disconnects between the EA/GAEL and Book of Abraham manuscripts — disconnects that seriously call into question the kind of relationship he suggests they have to one another.

Further, many of the margin characters in EA/GAEL are not even Egyptian, and in the Egyptian Counting document, *none* of the margin characters are Egyptian, despite its title. Some of the characters are known

---

38. See Kerry Muhlestein, "Assessing the Joseph Smith Papyri: An Introduction to the Historiography of their Acquisitions, Translations, and Interpretations," *Interpreter: A Journal of Latter-day Saint Faith and Scholarship* 22 (2016): 34. Final details noted by John Gee and Kerry Muhlestein, "The Translation of the Book of Abraham," *Interpreter: A Journal of Latter-day Saint Faith and Scholarship* (forthcoming).

from standard masonic ciphers typically used to cryptographically encode meaning into symbols that one could later decode if they had the key.[39] Additionally, not all the English texts in the EA/GAEL that Joseph Smith is supposedly "translating" in that moment relate to the Book of Abraham; some of the text appears to draw from revelations that Joseph Smith produced earlier, including D&C 76 and 88.[40] This strengthens the case that the Book of Abraham passages in the EA/GAEL were likely pre-existing texts as well, just as the 1835 sources suggest.

In fact, before Joseph Smith even acquired the Egyptian papyri, William Phelps had created documents like the EA/GAEL and sent a sample to his wife in a May 1835 letter.[41] This document was organized with non-Egyptian characters on the left, a name or pronunciation to its right, and non-Abrahamic ideas/texts in English next to them just like the EA/GAEL. Later, Phelps copies these same non-Egyptian characters that he sent his wife, in their exact same sequence, into the EA, but in that document he gives them different names/pronunciations and connects them to passages from the Book of Abraham.[42] If Joseph Smith was supposedly translating the Book of Abraham from the Egyptian characters on the Breathing papyri, why are passages from the Book of Abraham associated with non-Egyptian characters in the EA that Phelps

---

39. Noted in William Schryver, "The Kirtland Egyptian Papers" (presentation, 2010 FairMormon Conference, August 5 and 6, 2010, Sandy, UT), https://www.fairmormon.org/conference/august-2010/the-meaning-of-the-kirtland-egyptian-papers-part-i.

40. In the EA four margin-characters appear in immediate sequence with the names/pronunciations "Ebeth=ka," "Kah tu ain tri eth," "Kah tu ain," and "Dah tu Hahdess Hahdees" (EA, 2). These same characters and names are repeated and described throughout the GAEL as "Ebethka. The celestial Kingdom where God dwells" (GAEL, 29); "Kahtu ain trieth: an other Kingdom. govrned by different laws. a second king. or governed by another, or second person not having been exalted" (GAEL, 27); Kahtu=aim: Another Kingdom governed by different laws, composed of subjects who receive their place at a future period, and governed by those who are under the directions of another; a kingdom whose subject differ one from another <in glory>; who come not into the pres behold not the face of of God" (GAEL, 23), and "Dah tu Hah dees: Hell another Kingdom; the least kingdom, or kingdom without glory; the whole kingdom and dom[a]in of darkness, with all its degrees and parts. governed by the Doagrass him who is an enemy to G<o>od" (GAEL, 33), following the sequence and some phraseology relative to the three degrees of glory and kingdom of no glory in D&C 76 & 88 (see, e.g., D&C 76:98 which shares the same phrase "differ(s) one from another in glory"). Noted in Schryver, "The Kirtland Egyptian Papers."

41. William W. Phelps to Sally Waterman Phelps, 26 May 1835, William W. Phelps Papers, Brigham Young University.

42. Schryver, "The Kirtland Egyptian Papers."

had used previously, having the same sequence and format but with different names and English texts? Givens provides no explanation for this evidence that calls into question his assertions.

The above has led some to conclude that the EA/GAEL documents may be better understood as cipher keys, with Phelps leading a project to encode ideas from Joseph Smith's revelations into the various characters, including some from the papyri and some from masonic ciphers, among others.[43] The use of Masonic cipher characters would not be unusual since Phelps had been a Master Mason prior to his involvement with the papyri.[44]

Though this theory is a more logical view of the evidence than what Givens promotes, as it explains the use of masonic ciphers and other non-Egyptian characters in the EA/GAEL as well as non-Book of Abraham material, it also falls short of explaining the relationship of the EA/GAEL to the extant Book of Abraham manuscripts. Why would the two seemingly related sets of documents not use the same character for encoding similar texts?

Examining Astronomical Systems

The astronomical system described in the GAEL is different than the astronomical system described in Abraham 3. It appears that some of Joseph Smith's contemporaries may have misunderstood and misinterpreted Abraham 3 and Facsimile #3, assuming that they reflected a model where lesser bodies orbited and thus were governed by greater more central bodies — e.g., the sun, earth, moon, and other "moving" planets orbited and were governed by "central," "fixed" bodies, and

---

43. Ibid.

44. "having been regularly initiated, passed and raised to the degree of Master Mason, I hereby withdraw myself from any connection with masonic lodges, and renounce the self-organized institution of freemasonry" (W. W. Phelps, "Renunciation," *The Lake Light*, January 14, 1828, http://www.olivercowdery.com/ smithhome/Phelps/PhelpsIndex.htm; and reprinted in the *Seneca Farmer, and Waterloo Advertiser* V, no. 28 [February 6, 1828]).

everything orbited Kolob and God at the center of the "Mormon Solar System."[45] The GAEL reflects such a post-Copernican-influenced view.[46]

In contrast, the Book of Abraham text is more reflective of a pre-Copernican geocentric model, more in keeping with the views of

---

45. My thanks to Derek Jensen for pointing this out. See his "'One of Them Was Nearest unto the Throne of God': Nineteenth-Century Cosmologies and the Book of Abraham," *Archive of Restoration Culture: Summer Fellows Paper 2000-2002*, ed. by Richard L. Bushman (Provo, UT: Brigham Young University, 2005). James G. Bennett "More Prophecy," *New York Herald*, Apr 5, 1842; used the phrase "Mormon Solar System" to describe the "curious map" of Facsimile #2; reprinted in the *Times and Seasons* (2 May 1842), 773-74 (thanks to Derek Jensen for this reference). See also Dan Vogel and Brent Lee Metcalfe, "Joseph Smith's Scriptural Cosmology" in *The Word of God*, ed. by Dan Vogel (Salt Lake City: Signature Books, 1990), 187-212; however, their ability to discern the ancient geocentric cosmology in the Book of Abraham is obscured due to their reliance on 19th century sources, including the GAEL, to interpret the text.

46. The GAEL describes a system with three "grand central" stars, along with 12 other "fixed" stars (15 total), governing another set of 15 "moving" planets/stars, which included the earth, sun, and moon: "The earth under the governing <powers > of oliblish, Enish go on dosh, and Kae-e van rash, which are the grand governing key or in other words, the governing power, which governs the fifteen fixed stars <(twelve *[2 words illegible]*)> that belong governs the earth, sun, & moon, (which have their power <in> one,) with the other twelve moving planets of this system. Oliblish=Enish go on dosh, and Kaii , en rash, are the three grand central stars which powers that govern all the other creations, which have been sought out by the most aged of all the fathers, since the begining of the creation, by means of the urim and Thummim: The names of the other twelve of the fixed stars are: ..." (p. 24). The GAEL also speaks of these fixed stars having light at the "centre" from which all the other heavenly bodies draw their light: "The gover[n]ing principle of light Because God has said Let this be the centre for light, and let there be bounds that it may not pass. He hath set a cloud round about in the heavens, and the light of the grand govering of <15> fixed stars centre there; and from there its is drawn, by the heavenly bodies according to their portions;" (p. 25). "The King of day or the central moving planet, from which the other governing moving planets receive their light.— having a less motion— slow in its motion— The earth's chief Joy." (p. 31). The central bodies appear to be "slow" in their motion when compared to those heavenly bodies immediately orbiting them. Since the explanations published with Facsimile #2 identifies the central character as Kolob, it is understandable that some might interpret this, and thus the Book of Abraham text, to reflect a Kolob/God-is-at-the-center view of the universe (see, for example, Kerry Muhlestein, "Encircling Astronomy and the Egyptians: An Approach to Abraham 3," *Religious Educator: Perspectives on the Restored Gospel* 10, no. 1 [2009], 38-43), but since two of the outer, non-central, characters in Facsimile #2 are identified as "God on his throne," such an interpretation overlooks evidence that questions the conclusion made.

ancient civilizations of Abraham's day, such as Egypt.[47] This suggests that the principal author of the GAEL, William W. Phelps, may have misinterpreted the astronomical system outlined in the Book of Abraham when he created this document due to the modern scientific context of his day. This contradicts somewhat the idea that the GAEL and its system of astronomy was a basis for the Book of Abraham astronomy.

The above examples are a small selection of evidence to demonstrate that Givens' assertion that the EA/GAEL reveal Joseph Smith's "methodology and creativity" for translating the Book of Abraham from the Egyptian papyri is much too simplistic a view. It leaves many problems unexplained and overlooks crucial evidence that contradicts the "facts" as he presents them.

II. Bricolage

Givens likens Joseph Smith's effort to "translate" the Book of Abraham to bricolage. *Bricolage* is the art of repurposing objects into a new interpretation or new creation of the present — a modern example is the genre of art known as "junk art" or "found art." As such, bricolage abandons any effort to understand the used object's original setting or purpose. Such is not necessary, for bricolage is an appropriation and new creation, an improvisation loosely based on the shape or color of the object, not what the object actually is. Givens declares that bricolage "was the very basis of [Joseph Smith's] methodology of Restoration."[48]

Since the original setting and purpose of objects are of no concern in bricolage, Givens proposes that the Book of Abraham may have been a sort of improvisation based on what the papyri merely suggested, not what they really were. Consequently, he suggests that the Book of Abraham may not have been an actual "restored" or "preserved" text from antiquity, rather:

> Smith's transposition of the Egyptian papyri into the Book of Abraham may model [a] "produced" type of text ... Both the notion of bricolage and Elior's textual transformation seem in keeping with David Bokovoy's hypothesis of the Book of Abraham as "inspired pseudepigrapha," ... [where] one "need not believe that the Book of Abraham is a supernatural, though traditional, translation of an ancient text written by

---

47. John Gee, William J. Hamblin, and Daniel C. Peterson, "'And I Saw the Stars': The Book of Abraham and Ancient Geocentric Astronomy," in *Astronomy, Papyrus, and Covenant*, eds. John Gee and Brian M. Hauglid (Provo, UT: Foundation for Ancient Research and Mormon Studies, Brigham Young University, 2005), 1-16.

48. Givens with Hauglid, *The Pearl of Greatest Price*, loc. 193.

the patriarch Abraham, nor the translation of a Hellenized pseudepigraphic book of Abraham originally written in the first century bc." Instead, he [Bokovoy] explains, "it can make even more sense that by engaging the ancient papyri, the Prophet Joseph was inspired to produce this book of scripture as author, or in his vernacular, 'seer/translator.'"[49]

Givens is proposing in this section that the Egyptian papyri and their vignettes may have inspired Joseph Smith to produce a modern work that he *falsely attributes* (the meaning of the term pseudepigrapha) to Abraham. He did not render into English an ancient story written *by* Abraham. Consequently, the meaning and purpose of the papyri in their original setting is not important, for this is a modern bricolage inspired by fragments that merely suggest antiquity but were wholly repurposed for a contemporary creation.

Based on what we know from the surviving fragments and copies of now missing papyri, it is evident that the three vignettes that Joseph Smith used to illustrate the Book of Abraham were not originally drawn on their respective papyri to illustrate a story about Abraham. Rather, their immediate use was to illustrate texts and/or represent ideas in the ancient Egyptian religion. These three vignettes were drawn on two different papyri, for two different owners, and likely came from two different burials. The original vignette for Facsimile #1 currently exists and is on a papyrus, now in fragments, that also contains a text belonging to a genre that Egyptologists call the Book of Breathings. Apart from being on the same papyrus, the vignette's actual relationship to the text is uncertain since there are no other Book of Breathing texts with a similar vignette illustrating it, nor does the text seem to fully describe this vignette. It is possible that this picture represented some other aspect of the Egyptian religion entirely, rather than serving as an illustration for the Book of Breathings specifically.

The vignette for Facsimile #3 is currently missing but similar illustrations are attested in the Book of Breathings genre of ancient Egyptian religious texts.[50] This, coupled with the fact that the owner's proper name written in Facsimile #3 is the same as the owner's name in this Book of Breathings text, suggests that the vignette for Facsimile #3 was

---

49. Ibid.

50. Marc Coenen, "An Introduction to the Document of Breathing Made by Isis," *Revue D'egyptologie* 49 (1998): 39-40. Quinten Barney, "The Neglected Facsimile: An Examination and Comparative Study of Facsimile No. 3 of the Book of Abraham," (master's thesis, Brigham Young University, 2019), 65-70.

likely an illustration originally made to illustrate the Book of Breathings that Joseph Smith possessed. Although the vignettes for Facsimile #1 and #3 were on the same papyrus, they may have already been separated when Joseph Smith first acquired them due to the fragmented condition of this papyrus. The fragment containing the vignette for Facsimile #1 was glued onto paper by itself in Joseph Smith's day.[51]

The source for Facsimile #2 was a different papyrus of a larger vertical size and of a different shape and style compared to the Book of Breathings papyrus.[52] It was created anciently for a different owner and is a document that Egyptologists call a hypocephalus due to its typical placement under or near the head of the deceased's corpse in burial.

The captions and texts within these three facsimiles express ideas and name gods relative to the ancient Egyptian religion. None mention Abraham nor details in the story of Abraham that Joseph Smith published.

In spite of an obvious difference in style, shape, and size between the hypocephalus papyrus and the other two vignettes that appeared on the Breathing papyrus, Joseph Smith published the facsimiles of all three as illustrations for the Book of Abraham text he was revealing. That he appears to have published all three facsimiles true to the size of their originals, with #2 much bigger than #1 and #3, indicates that Joseph Smith made no attempt to make them look as though they were copied from a common source.

Some of the original illustrations on the papyri were damaged and missing portions, so when Joseph Smith published their facsimiles, he or his scribes appear to have filled in some of these holes by copying texts or figures from elsewhere in the collection or drawing fillers themselves. Some of the Egyptian texts were even copied upside down, likely due to their inability to read the Egyptian on these papyri.

Why Joseph Smith had texts or figures copied from elsewhere in the papyri collection in order to fill holes in these three illustrations is not given in the historical sources. Some may assume that Joseph Smith was attempting to restore how the ancient Egyptians would have

---

51. "Source Note" for "Egyptian Papyri, circa 300 BC-AD 50," *The Joseph Smith Papers*, https://www.josephsmithpapers.org/paper-summary/egyptian-papyri-circa-300-bc-ad-50/1.

52. The facsimiles appear to have been created and published in the *Times and Seasons* true to their relative size. The hypocephalus was published on an insert much bigger than the two illustrations from the Book of Breathings papyrus. See "Book of Abraham and Facsimiles, 1 March–16 May 1842," p. 703, https://www.josephsmithpapers.org/paper-summary/book-of-abraham-and-facsimiles-1-march-16-may-1842/1.

originally depicted the missing portions, but this is conjecture. It is just as plausible, since he merely had texts and figures copied from elsewhere in the collection and did not pretend to restore anything unique where these holes exist, that his main purpose was to fill the holes for aesthetic or functional purposes relative to publishing, not to restore the original ancient Egyptian religious iconography.

Joseph Smith's published explanations for these illustrations associate many of the details in the facsimiles to the story and religious context of Abraham's life that he was revealing, but why he made those connections is not clear from the historical sources. Some may assume that Joseph Smith attempted to identify all the characters as they were originally understood by the ancient Egyptians, but this is mostly conjecture, though there are some notable exceptions discussed below. It is just as plausible that Joseph Smith was simply reinterpreting the ancient Egyptian iconography to fit the story of Abraham. Reinterpreting iconography or texts of one tradition to represent the figures or concepts in another tradition is an age-old practice among most cultures from antiquity to the present. For example, Christians in antiquity reinterpreted winged solar disks as representing God in their own religious worldview even though it was not originally created or understood that way by the Egyptians.[53] However, no scholar of antiquity would state that the Christians were wrong or ludicrous for reinterpreting the iconography that way, unless, of course, they assumed that the Christians were trying to explain how the Egyptians viewed winged solar disks.

Many of the explanations for the figures in the facsimiles published with the Book of Abraham are actually declared to be "representative," so one should take care not to assume that Joseph Smith was stating what they all originally meant to the Egyptians: "*represent* the pillars of heaven,"[54] "*signifying* expanse,"[55] "Is made to *represent* God,"[56] "*representing* also the grand Key-words of the Holy Priesthood,"[57] "the stars *represented* by numbers 22 and 23,"[58] "*represents* this earth,"[59]

---

53. László Kákosy, "A Christian Interpretation of the Sun-Disk," in *Studies in Egyptian Religion: Dedicated to Professor Jan Zandee* (Leiden: E.J. Brill, 1982), 72–75.

54. "Book of Abraham and Facsimiles, 1 March–16 May 1842," 703.

55. Ibid.

56. Ibid., insert.

57. Ibid.

58. Ibid.

59. Ibid.

"*represents* God,"[60] "*representing* the priesthood, as *emblematical* of the grand Presidency of Heaven,"[61] "*Signifies* Abraham."[62]

In light of all the above, the simplest and probably best reason that these particular facsimiles and their explanations were published with the Book of Abraham is that Joseph Smith himself removed these three illustrations from their immediate Egyptian religious context and reinterpreted them to fit the story of Abraham he revealed. Nothing in the historical sources requires one to conclude, even if they are a believer in Joseph Smith's prophetic calling, that such were ever used anciently — whether in Abraham's day or in the Greco-Roman time period in which the Joseph Smith papyri were created — as illustrations for an Abrahamic tradition.

The immediate context, identifying labels and captions, and much of the meaning for these three facsimiles in their ancient Egyptian religious setting is relatively known, though additional particulars are still being discovered and understood about them, and Joseph Smith appears to have taken them out of that context (though, again, some seemingly contrary details must still be dealt with as discussed below) and reinterpreted them. This seems to support, somewhat, Givens' use of the term bricolage. However, there are two major problems with fully using that term.

Repurposing vs. Syncretizing the Egyptian Illustrations

Consistent with the definition of the term, classifying what Joseph Smith did as *bricolage* insinuates that he completely repurposed the vignettes from the papyri, creating something entirely new with no regard for the original context out of which those objects came. However, this does not quite fit the evidence. While Joseph Smith's explanations appear to mostly reinterpret the figures as representative of details in the Abrahamic tradition he was revealing, he simultaneously attempts to explain some of the symbolic meaning of a few details in their ancient Egyptian context: "as understood by the Egyptians,"[63] "the Egyptians meant it to signify,"[64] "which is called by the Egyptians,"[65] "called by the

---

60. Ibid.
61. Ibid., 784.
62. Ibid.
63. Ibid., 703.
64. Ibid.
65. Ibid., insert.

Egyptians,"[66] "in Egyptian, signifying,"[67] "Is called in Egyptian,"[68] "is said by the Egyptians to be."[69]

Additionally, Joseph Smith explains that some of the details in the vignettes have corollary meanings to the ancient Hebrews as well. For example, in regard to Facsimile 1, Fig. 12, the explanation states that "the Egyptians meant it to signify Shaumau, to be high, or the heavens, answering to the Hebrew word, Shaumahyeem."[70] Likewise, the Egyptian symbol in Facsimile 2, Fig. 4 "answers to the Hebrew word Raukeeyang, signifying expanse, or the firmament of the heavens; also a numerical figure in Egyptian signifying one thousand."[71]

If Joseph Smith is reinterpreting the facsimiles with no regard for their original context as a term like bricolage suggests, then these attempts to recover some original ancient context and meaning needs to be explained but are mostly overlooked by Givens. If, on the other hand, Joseph Smith is reinterpreting the facsimiles through the typical practice of syncretism, then his efforts to simultaneously recover some original ancient meaning of the illustrations in their Egyptian context as well as reinterpret them into the Abrahamic context makes sense. It is often the case that when one culture reinterprets the iconography or text of another, they do it because a detail in one culture is similar to a detail in the other, thus the two similar ideas become syncretized.

The evidence suggests that the explanations published with the facsimiles have two functions that are present at the same time: 1) most of the explanations appear to be Joseph Smith syncretizing a detail in the story of Abraham to a "representative" figure in the vignette, and 2) some of the explanations are Joseph Smith telling his readers, assumedly through his claims to the power of God, the ancient Egyptian (and Hebrew parallel) symbolic meaning of a few of the figures which provides his basis for the syncretism. Because Joseph Smith uses both kinds of explanations, it can sometimes be difficult to tell which he is employing. The best approach is simply to take cues from Joseph Smith himself. When his explanation explicitly declares that this is what the ancient Egyptians thought about or called one of the details in the vignette, then he is supposing his readers will recognize that he is claiming to use his

---

66. Ibid.
67. Ibid.
68. Ibid.
69. Ibid.
70. Ibid., 703.
71. Ibid., insert.

powers as a seer, as defined in the Book of Mormon, to "know of things which has [sic] past" (Mosiah 8:17). Only these specific instances are fair game for scholars to inspect the plausibility of his claims in the field of ancient studies generally and Egyptology specifically.

However, these specific instances do not require the reader to view *every* explanation as conveying original Egyptian thought, as most have assumed. For example, to say that Joseph Smith's identification of Osiris as Abraham in both Facsimile #1 and #3 is wrong because that is not what the text labels in the vignettes or Egyptian religion in general says about the figure is a strawman argument, because Joseph Smith actually never specifically claimed that the Egyptians, or Egyptian religion in general, identified this character as Abraham. Only Joseph Smith himself identified the character as Abraham, but he does not tell us why he does. Consequently, that he could be simply reinterpreting the figure based on some perceived relationship he sees is just as plausible as claiming he erroneously identified what the ancient Egyptian meant this to be. It is important to note in this regard that when the explanations connect a detail from the Book of Abraham to a figure in the facsimiles, the explanations either simply label the figure with the Abrahamic detail or says that the figure "represents" a detail in the Abraham story. But in those instances when Joseph Smith specifically says this is what the Egyptian thought or said about the figure, his explanation never reflects a detail that is specific to Abraham.

Once these distinctions and boundaries of the evidence are clear, scholars are free to explore whether or not any of the connections Joseph Smith made has precedence. Ancient Egyptians, ancient Jews, ancient Christians, and others have syncretized Abrahamic traditions to the Egyptian religion in their day which seem to have interesting parallels to some of the connections that Joseph Smith made between the facsimiles and the Abrahamic tradition in his day.[72] But finding such parallels does not mean necessarily that Joseph Smith restored an ancient Egyptian, Jewish, or Christian view of these specific vignettes. All it means is that Joseph Smith made a connection between the Book of Abraham text and the Egyptian vignettes because he discerned some relationship between the two, and it just so happens that others in antiquity had made similar connections between these two ancient traditions as well.

---

72. See Pearl of Great Price Central (website), https://www.pearlofgreatpricecentral.org, for examples.

In a few instances as noted above, Joseph Smith not only states what the meaning of a figure in the Egyptian context might be, but he also states that it has corollary meaning or is "answering to" a Hebrew word or idea, suggesting that the Prophet was not really focused on recovering Egyptian religion specifically. Rather his focus appears to be recuperating broader, though ancient, symbolic ideas that he believes the Egyptian figures might convey.

That recovering the Egyptians' religion specifically does not appear to be his main purpose with the vignettes is supported by the fact that he does not actually attempt to translate any of the ancient Egyptian texts in the vignettes. Why would he skip actually translating (whether in the traditional view of that word or in Givens' view) the texts in the vignettes that he spent so much time explaining if he thought they all pertained to Abraham? Might it be that Joseph Smith did not believe that the finer details of the Egyptian culture that these texts would likely contain was his purpose?

With respect to the texts in Facsimile #2, Joseph Smith's explanations simply say "Contains writings that cannot now be revealed unto the world; but is to be had in the Holy Temple of God;" "Ought not to be revealed at the present time;" "will be given in the own due time of the Lord;" however, "if the world can find out these numbers, so let it be. Amen."[73] Based on these descriptions, Joseph Smith seems content to just let the world figure out the actual meaning of these Egyptian texts, he sees no reason in making them known for his present purpose.

Contrary to Givens' assertion, Joseph Smith does not actually translate any of the text in Facsimile #3 either. For example, he interprets Fig. 5 as "Shulem, one of the king's principal waiters, as *represented by* the characters above his hand," but Joseph Smith does not actually tell us what the characters say, only that they are representative.[74]

---

73. "Book of Abraham and Facsimiles, 1 March–16 May 1842," p. 784.

74. Ibid. To be consistent with his general use of the vignettes, it is reasonable to believe that Joseph Smith may have simply viewed the Shulem of Abraham's day as symbolically "represented by" both the character and its caption in Facsimile #3, not that the Egyptians themselves would call this figure Shulem. Similarly, Joseph Smith indicates that the name for the figure that he reinterprets as Pharaoh is "given in the characters above the head" but does not actually translate the text above the head. Notably, there actually is a name given above the head, and the name and character in this moment is Isis who indeed does symbolically "represent" pharaoh in the ancient Egyptian religion. She represents the pharaoh so deeply that her name actually means and is spelled with the hieroglyph for the seat or throne of pharaoh.

Since the texts in the facsimiles were mostly ignored, restoring any voids in the fragments with text from another fragment and even placed upside down in the published version, would likely not have mattered to Joseph Smith. What these texts might actually say appears to be of little concern to him. He does, however, make one off-handed remark that the temple is the framework for truly understanding them, and this has certainly proven to be true in the field of Egyptology.

Indeed, as the original ancient setting of these facsimiles relative to Egyptian temple and tomb theology is better understood, Joseph Smith's use of them to "represent" the life of Abraham becomes more plausible, because the life of Abraham itself arguably follows a temple initiation progression.[75] In fact, Joseph Smith connected Abraham's binding of Isaac in Genesis 22 to the moment when Abraham was initiated into the highest order of the priesthood through the oath of God, providing an explicit temple context to Abraham's life story.[76] The Prophet may have viewed the flow of Abraham's entire narrative through the lens of a temple progression and so adopted and ordered the facsimiles to reflect that. An altar scene (Facs. #1), a cosmic scene (Facs. #2), and a throne scene (Facs. #3) follow the general flow and symbolic purposes of 1)

---

75. John S. Thompson, "The Story Cycles of the Patriarchs and Temple Progression" (2016 Temple on Mount Zion Conference, November 5, 2016, Provo, UT), https://www.youtube.com/watch?time_continue=12&v=MAfApISOUM0 &feature=emb_logo. Abraham's near-sacrifice in his younger years can relate to initial sacrifices at temple courtyard altars, Abraham's covenant and vision of the heavens/Creation relate to the expanded sight entering temples proper give, and the Abrahamic trials and sacrifice of Isaac lead to the oath of God and covenant blessings being made sure as indicative of temple throne rooms in the holy of holies. See also Hugh W. Nibley, "The Three Facsimiles from the Book of Abraham" (Provo, UT: FARMS, 1980) and "Abraham's Temple Drama," *Eloquent Witness: Nibley on Himself, Others, and the Temple, The Collected Works of Hugh Nibley* (Salt Lake City: Deseret Book, 2008), 17:445-82.

76. "That of Melchisedec who had still greater power even power of an endless life of which was our Lord Jesus Christ which also Abraham obtained by the offering of his son Isaac which was not the power of a Prophet nor apostle nor Patriarch only but of King & Priest" in Andrew Ehat and Lyndon Cook, *Words of Joseph Smith* (Grandin Book, 1991), 245 (Franklin D. Richards notes of August 27, 1843 sermon); John S. Thompson, "The Sacrifice of Isaac: Abraham's Initiation into the Highest Order of the Priesthood," *Genesis 22: Latter-day Saint Perspectives on the Binding of Isaac* (Foundation for Ancient Research and Mormon Studies and the Religious Studies Center Conference, Brigham Young University, March 2004).

courtyard altars, 2) holy places or hypostyle halls, and 3) holy of holies or sanctuaries in both Israelite and Egyptian temples.[77]

The point here is that in spite of Joseph Smith's overall use of the facsimiles as "representative," this is no mere bricolage with a lack of consideration for original meaning or context as the term suggests. Joseph Smith explicitly provides, as noted above, what the ancient Egyptian's thought about a few of the figures, and he also appears to draw connections between the figures and the story of Abraham based on ancient symbolism he perceives in both traditions that allow for a syncretism to occur. Both seem more like efforts to restore the "ancient order of things," not create a modern bricolage.[78]

Production of the Text

Beyond the facsimiles, Givens goes much further with this term and suggests to his readers that the entire Book of Abraham text can be viewed as bricolage as well. He admits that this amounts to calling the Book of Abraham a modern pseudepigrapha as David Bokovoy has done. In other words, the Book of Abraham is a modern, thus fictional, creation of Joseph Smith's own mind, and "falsely attributed" to Abraham.

Since Mormon Studies advocates are required to view all of Joseph Smith's "revelations" and "translations" as the inspiration and creativity of his own mind, bricolage would not be an inappropriate metaphor for them to adopt. As noted earlier, Givens believes that bricolage "was the very basis of [Joseph Smith's] methodology of Restoration."

The appeal of this idea is that it resonates somewhat with Latter-day Saints' experiences with personal revelation generally. Studying out a problem in their own minds and coming to a conclusion based on that study coupled with quiet feeling, roughly speaking. However, to assume that Joseph Smith's revealed "translations" are mostly the product of his

---

77. On the similarities between Israelite and Egyptian temple progression see "The Context of Old Testament Temple Worship: Early Ancient Egyptian Rites" in *Ascending the Mountain of the Lord: Temple, Praise, and Worship in the Old Testament*, eds. David R. Seely, Jeffrey R. Chadwick, and Matthew J. Grey (Provo, UT and Salt Lake City: Brigham Young University's Religious Studies Center and Deseret Book, 2013), https://rsc.byu.edu/ascending-mountain-lord/context-old-testament-temple-worship-early-ancient-egyptian-rites.

78. "And now as the great purposes of God are hastening to their accomplishment and the things spoken of in the prophets are fulfilling, as the kingdom of God is established on the earth, and the ancient order of things restored, the Lord has manifested to us this duty and privilege, ... " (Joseph Smith, "Baptism for the Dead," *Times and Seasons* 3, no. 12 (15 April 1842): 761.

own creative mind and inspiration, limited by his own actual knowledge and abilities, is to deny the uniqueness of his gifts and the miraculous role that Joseph Smith plays in the Latter-day Saint community. For them, he is not just a prophet, but a seer. And in the Latter-day Saint community a seer

> is greater than a prophet ... a seer is a revelator and a prophet also; and a gift which is greater can no man have, except he should possess the power of God, which no man can; yet a man may have great power given him from God. But a seer can know of things which are past, and also of things which are to come, and by them shall all things be revealed, or, rather, shall secret things be made manifest, and hidden things shall come to light, and things which are not known shall be made known by them, and also things shall be made known by them which otherwise could not be known. Thus God has provided a means that man, through faith, might work mighty miracles; therefore he becometh a great benefit to his fellow beings.[79]

Such powers enter the realm of miraculous and go beyond personal inspiration and creative genius that is tempered by one's own natural ability, knowledge, language, and thought processes.

Givens suggests to his readers that the Book of Abraham might be better viewed as a product of something similar to personal inspiration, wherein Joseph Smith pondered over the ancient Egyptian papyri but formulated in his own mind some kind of response that was filled with creativity and divine truth, rather than miraculously translating an actual ancient writing by the power of God as he claimed.[80] Contrary to actual scriptural definitions,

---

79. "Book of Mormon, 1830," p. 173, *The Joseph Smith Papers*, https://www.josephsmithpapers.org/paper-summary/book-of-mormon-1830/179, [Mosiah 8:15-18].

80. This is not to say that Joseph Smith did not himself often engage in regular personal revelatory experiences. He certainly noticed things in his environment, pondered their truth and considered their purpose, and made daily decisions based upon his impressions and inspiration. However, Joseph Smith did not claim that he was solely recreating or repurposing noticed fragments into a new movement, born uniquely of his own mind and experience, but he and his followers thought he was actually restoring ancient truths that had their own pedigree and an ancient context in which they were born. They believed these ancient truths were revealed to him in miraculous ways, somewhat different than the day to day inspirations needed for life or for the Church. Joseph certainly had to fit his recovered antiquities into the present construction he was revealing through a process of trial and error and daily

Givens confounds the title "seer" to mean "writer of pseudepigrapha" and asserts that the "very basis" of Joseph Smith's methodology for "restoring" truth is not actually restoring, but creating bricolage.

III. Modern Translation Theory

Givens discusses briefly some standard modern translation theory, which states essentially that no one can truly translate the full intended meaning of one language (with all the unique cultural and personal context that goes into it) into another with its own different set of cultural and personal norms. Since every word has been immersed in a cultural context, theoretically it takes one submerged in that same context to understand all the nuances of the word. Consequently, the translator must engage in a kind of construction that goes beyond the strict words and syntax of the text she is translating and coerces either the sender closer to the receiver's mode of thinking or the receiver closer to the sender's.

> And for Smith, that meant not [bringing God closer to the reader,] defamiliarizing the wonderful or domesticating the sacred but leading the reader into new modes of perception and comprehension that would enable an initiation into eternal realms and perspectives. In practice, this could entail something as simple as the implementation of a diction borrowed from sacred discourse (the King James Version) or as complicated as reconstituting a source document [the Egyptian Book of Breathings] into an inspired and inspiring temple text [the Book of Abraham], of which the original would then appear as a pale reflection.[81]

---

inspiration, but the foundational truths seemed to come to him in ways beyond his own natural ability and thoughts. For example, a Mormon Studies scholar might be interested in women's benevolent societies of the nineteenth century and how these were an inspiration for Joseph Smith's creation of the Female Relief Society; however, Joseph Smith apparently taught that this organization was a restoration of an ancient order that existed in the primitive church: "Although the name may be of modern date, the institution is of ancient origin. We were told by our martyred prophet that the same organization existed in the church anciently" (Eliza R. Snow, "Female Relief Society," *Deseret News*, Apr. 22, 1868, 1; punctuation standardized). So is the Women's Relief Society bricolage, a purely modern creation based on a response to modern benevolent societies, or is it a restoration of an ancient order? Those who study antiquities are in a far better position to answer that question, but an inquiry into any claims of recovered antiquity by Joseph Smith is taboo these days and ignored as "apologetic."

81. Givens with Hauglid, *The Pearl of Greatest Price*, loc. 196.

While modern translation theory acknowledges the difficulties in conveying the ideas of one civilization into another, Givens takes this to an extreme by suggesting that Joseph Smith is not merely attempting to traverse the cultural, linguistic barrier between an ancient and modern language, but he is attempting to "translate" across the huge cultural divide between the masses and God. Consequently, Joseph Smith's "translations" bridge such a vast differential that the original is likely to be a "pale reflection" of the actual product. In other words, the Book of Abraham is a pale reflection of the Book of Breathings text and the illustrations, because it is not really an attempt to translate any mundane words on an actual ancient text into mundane English, but rather he is attempting to "translate" the masses themselves into higher or divine modes of thinking, bringing the reader into the cultural context of God. Thus the produced text is so much higher than its supposed source that it is hard for mortals to see the connection.

This is very eloquent, but such a theory disconnects the Book of Abraham from reality so much as to render any discussion of its relationship to the papyri, the ancient world, or pretty much anything rather pointless. More importantly, it is contrary to Joseph Smith's own revelations which state that God is more than willing to condescend to the more plainer languages and modes of thinking of the masses to help them understand his truths:

> For my soul delighteth in plainness: for after this manner doth the Lord God work among the children of men. For the Lord God giveth light unto the understanding: for he speaketh unto men according to their language, unto their understanding.[82]

> And then shall ye know that I have seen Jesus, and that he hath talked with me face to face, and that he told me in plain humility, even as a man telleth another in mine own language, concerning these things.[83]

> Behold I am God & have spoken it these are commandments are of me & were given unto my Servents in their weakness after the manner of their Language that they might come to understanding.[84]

---

82. "Book of Mormon, 1830," p. 118, *The Joseph Smith Papers*, [2 Nephi 31:3].

83. Ibid., 565 [Ether 12:39].

84. "Revelation, 1 November 1831-B [D&C 1]," p. 126, *The Joseph Smith Papers*, https://www.josephsmithpapers.org/paper-summary/revelation-1-november-1831-b-dc-1/2, [D&C 1:24].

Earlier in his chapter, Givens assumes, based on the work of Samuel Brown and others, that Joseph Smith was on a quest to recover the actual language that Adam spoke, for such, ostensibly, would allow the conveyance of ideas between God and the masses with no friction of misunderstanding. Recovering this ancient spoken language was part of Joseph Smith's Restoration, Givens asserts, and his efforts to learn Hebrew and Greek, and presumably Egyptian, got him closer to that original language.[85]

While some sort of "pure language" project does appear in Joseph Smith's contemporary orbit, assuming that it was part of the Prophet's spiritual mission is mostly conjecture. The pure language project is more likely William Phelps', and though Joseph Smith gets entangled from time to time, there is no explicit statement from him or anyone else that recovering the actual dialect of Adam was part of the Restoration of the gospel of Jesus Christ.[86]

Givens references Moses 6:5–7 as evidence that it was:

> And a book of remembrance was kept, in the which was recorded, in the language of Adam, for it was given unto as many as called upon God to write by the spirit of inspiration; And by them their children were taught to read and write, having a language which was pure and undefiled. Now this same Priesthood, which was in the beginning, shall be in the end of the world also.

He asserts that these verses "significantly but cryptically" refer to the language of Adam as "Priesthood"[87] (which on the surface appears plausible given the vague structure of the English) and since the text claims that this priesthood "which was in the beginning, shall be in the end of the world also," then this means that the Adamic language, which

---

85. Samuel Brown, "Joseph (Smith) in Egypt: Babel, Hieroglyphs, and the Pure Language of Eden," *Church History: Studies in Christianity and Culture* 78, no. 1 (Mar. 2009): 26-65; is a standard on this view, but it is also so full of unproven assertions as to require a separate review.

86. For the latest effort to connect Joseph Smith to this see David Golding, "'Eternal Wisdom Engraven Upon the Heavens:' Joseph Smith's Pure Language Project" in *Producing Ancient Scripture: Joseph Smith's Translation Projects in the Development of Mormon Christianity*, eds. Michael Hubbard MacKay, Mark Ashurst-McGee, Brian M. Hauglid (Salt Lake City: University of Utah Press, 2020), 331-62.

87. Givens with Hauglid, *The Pearl of Greatest Price*, loc. 113.

was in the beginning, shall be in the end of the world also. Scripturally then, recovering Adam's dialect is part of the Restoration.

While Givens' reading of Moses 6 is plausible, a more contextually sensitive reading recommends that it is not likely. It is more probable that "priesthood" here is referring to the lineage of priesthood bearers mentioned in these verses and the verses immediately preceding:

> And then began these <3/> men to call upon the name of the Lord; And the Lord blessed them; And a Book of rememberance was kept, in the which was recorded in the language of Adam. For it was given unto as many as called upon God, to write with <by> the finger <spirit> of insparation; And by them their children were taught to read & write, Having a language which was pure & undefiled. </> <4 <1>/> Now this <same which presthood which> was in the begining, which shall be in the <continue> end of the world <als>.[88]

In other words, the priesthood lineage of these men who "call upon the name of the Lord" and their children, whom they taught, will be in the end of the world also.

That the priesthood is a promised lineage of children or seed whom God would "call upon" until the end of the earth is highlighted later in this text when God speaks an "unalterable decree" to Enoch:

> the Lord could not withold and he covenented with Noah[89] and swore unto him with an oath that he would stay the floods that he would call upon the children of Noah and he sent fourth an unaltarable decree tha[t] a remnent of his seed should always be found among all nations while the earth should stand.[90]

This is made most clear in the Book of Abraham wherein the text explicitly calls Abraham's seed "priesthood":

> and in thee and in (that is in thy priesthood.) and in thy seed, (that is thy pristhood) for I give unto the[e] a promise that this right shall continue in thee, and in thy seed after thee, (that

---

88. "Old Testament Revision 2," p. 14, *The Joseph Smith Papers*, https://www.josephsmithpapers.org/paper-summary/old-testament-revision-2/18. The later published phrase this "same priesthood which" does not appear in "Old Testament Revision 1," *The Joseph Smith Papers*, https://www.josephsmithpapers.org/paper-summary/old-testament-revision-1/1; nor originally in this version but was added here as a superscript presumably to provide some clarity.

89. Corrected to "Enoch" in "Old Testament Revision 2", 23.

90. "Old Testament Revision 1," 18.

is to say thy literal seed, or the seed of thy body,) shall all the families of the earth be blessed.[91]

God's oath assured Enoch and Noah that their priesthood bearing seed would continue so the earth would never be flooded again, and the token of God's promise was the rainbow. John the Revelator's twenty-four elders in a continuous circle around the throne of God in the midst of a rainbow that also encircled the throne is the New Testament's echo of this same unalterable decree.[92] In other words, the circle-shaped rainbow is equated to the continuous priesthood seed (the circle of elders around God's throne) that God would call and ensure that they administer the gospel among all nations to the end of the world so that a flood would not occur again.

A modern revelation of Joseph Smith's also references this understanding of a promised seed being the priesthood that would be found in the end of the world:

> Therefore thus saith the Lord unto you with whom the priesthood hath continued through the lineage of your fathers: For ye are lawful heirs according to the flesh & have been hid from the world, with Christ in God. Therefore your life & the priesthood hath remained & must needs remain through you & your lineage untill the resteration of all things, spoken by the mouth of all the holy prophets since the world began.[93]

In some of his personal teachings, Joseph Smith himself spoke of this unalterable decree or promise that a remnant of the priesthood seed would always continue:

> Zachariah having no children, knew that the promise of God must fail, consequently he went into the Temple to wrestle with God according to the order of the priesthood to obtain a promise of a son, and when the Angel told him that his promise was granted he because of unbelief was struck dumb.[94]

---

91. "Book of Abraham Manuscript, circa July-circa November 1835-C [Abraham 1:1-2:18]," p. 8, *The Joseph Smith Papers*, https://www.josephsmithpapers. org/paper-summary/book-of-abraham-manuscript-circa-july-circa-november-1835-c-abraham-11-218/8, [Abraham 2:11].

92. See Revelation 4:2-4.

93. "Revelation Book 1," p. 177, *The Joseph Smith Papers*, https://www. josephsmithpapers.org/paper-summary/revelation-book-1/165, 177 [D&C 86:8-10].

94. Joseph Smith, *The Words of Joseph Smith: The Contemporary Accounts of the Nauvoo Discourses of the Prophet Joseph*, eds. Andrew F. Ehat and Lyndon W. Cook (Salt Lake City: Bookcraft, 1980), 196, https://rsc.byu.edu/ words-joseph-smith/23-july-1843-sunday-afternoon.

> The election of the promised seed still continues, and in the last days, they shall have the priesthood restored unto them, and they shall be the "Saviors on mount Zion" the "ministers of our God," if it were not for the remnant which was left, then might we be as Sodom and as Gomorah.[95]

Reading "priesthood" in the Book of Moses passage as a covenant seed or lineage that will be in the end of the world also is more fully supported in the teachings and revelations of Joseph Smith than Givens' proposal that the Adamic language will be in the end of the world also. There is simply nothing that explicitly demonstrates Joseph Smith believed or taught that recovering the Adamic language was part of his spiritual mission. To assert that he did is to engage in a kind of modern cultural parallelomania, wherein scholars see some ideas in the culture surrounding Joseph Smith (like "pure language" quests) that may have some broad points of connection to his revelations but then making logical leaps and assumptions that everything is the same without any real explicit evidence to back up such claims. While parallelomania is often a concern among those who study antiquity, Americanists in Mormon Studies generally would do well to learn to avoid similar trappings when things look similar between Joseph Smith's doings and his greater American context. The details are often more complicated than the simple assertions that he borrowed (or plagiarized) something from his environment.

Likewise, the role of language in the Restoration is a little more complicated than the simple assertion that Joseph Smith was swept up in common quests for pure language in his day. Language is certainly a medium through which the priesthood Joseph Smith restored operates. Priesthood and language are closely linked, but not necessarily in the way Givens asserts. The revelations of Joseph Smith do not claim that Adam's actual dialect, pronunciation and syntax, was the operative power and means by which God and the masses could best communicate. The verses in Moses discussed above suggest that the pure and undefiled language of Adam, recorded in the Book of Remembrance, was to "write by the spirit of inspiration." Speaking words that are filled with the spirit of truth, regardless of whether the words formed are in Hebrew, English, Chinese, Arabic, or Adam's actual spoken dialect, is a central teaching of Joseph Smith's revelations and is, thus, more likely the meaning of "pure language":

---

95. "Discourse, 16 May 1841, as Reported by *Times and Seasons*," p. 430, *The Joseph Smith Papers*, https://www.josephsmithpapers.org/paper-summary/discourse-16may-1841-as-reported-by-times-and-seasons/2.

> Do ye not remember that I said unto you, that after ye had received the Holy Ghost, ye could speak with the tongue of Angels? And now, how could ye speak with the tongue of Angels, save it were by the Holy Ghost? Angels speak by the power of the Holy Ghost; wherefore, they speak the words of Christ. — Wherefore, I said unto you, feast upon the words of Christ. (2 Nephi 32:2–3)

The thrust of these verses from the Book of Mormon is that speaking the words of Christ with the power of the Holy Ghost is what constitutes angelic language, not the recovering of some ancient dialect that has power only when tongue and mouth are shaped just right to make the right sounds, and not the recovering of some actual angel-ese.

An earlier passage in the Book of Mormon indicates that the words of the Jews in a book went forth from the apostles to the Gentiles "in purity." This was not a reference to their having recovered the Adamic language, rather, the book was pure because it "contained the plainness of the Gospel of the Lord, of whom the twelve apostles bear record; and they bear record according to the truth which is in the Lamb of God."[96] It was the fullness of truth that made their words pure, even though their records were likely of multiple languages such as Hebrew, Aramaic, and Greek. Eventually, however, the words were perverted because the Gentiles removed some things plain and precious.

The notion of ancient magical or hidden words certainly exists in the world's traditions and modern fantasies, with their quests to discover and use such words to open secret doors, transform objects, or affect other change. While such traditions and fantasies can be interesting, and captured the attention of Latter-day Saints from Joseph Smith's day to the present, due to the echoes of truth they contain, care should be taken not to assert that Joseph Smith made questing for the original primeval dialect central to the Restoration without real explicit evidence. To do so is to conflate the real with the counterfeit. While Joseph Smith certainly lamented about the inherent weakness in the spoken languages of today, as one might do about any weakness of mortality, the revelations of Joseph Smith indicate that such can be overcome with the Holy Ghost, not by recovering some lost ancient language. Joseph Smith's revelations assert that it is through the medium of the Holy Ghost that God and the masses can communicate now and be edified and understand one

---

96. "Book of Mormon, 1830," p. 30, *The Joseph Smith Papers*, [1 Nephi 13:24-25]. "Plainness" was changed to "fulness" in subsequent versions.

another, no Adamic dialect or complex view of "translation" is necessary. It is the Holy Ghost that can take any mortal language, as also any mortal body, and make it pure and undefiled. It is the spirit-infused words of truth that are the true "language of Adam."

> Therefore, why is it that ye cannot understand and know that he that receiveth the word by the spirit of truth, receiveth it as it is preached by the spirit of truth, wherefore he that preacheth and he that receiveth understandeth one another and both are edified and rejoice together.[97]

IV. "Authoritative" Writing

Givens argues that the sudden onslaught of a variety of literature and merging of genres leading up to Joseph Smith's world created a climate where

> rampant destabilization of narrative authority had a relevant, if indirect, bearing on matters of translation. For this destabilization historicized and complicated the question of who was speaking, with what authority, and how the answers to these questions were to be known ... As a result, many of the era's works grounded their appeal to authority in ways that today would be seen as dishonest, irresponsible, implausible, and self-contradictory. In this new world, authentic sentiment and moral fervor, not credentials or documentary evidence, became the supreme ground of moral authority.[98]

In such a climate, titles including "memoirs" or "autobiography" or content that included copies of "sworn affidavits" could all be purely fictional but still carry the weight of "truth" or moral authority. In other words, Joseph Smith's environment was a place and time where "authorship and authority acquire new and contradictory meanings."[99]

How Givens relates this to the translation of the Book of Abraham is not explicitly stated. But having explored the ideas that Joseph Smith may have thought he was "translating" the Book of Abraham from characters on the Book of Breathings, that the EA and GAEL appear to

---

97. "Revelations printed in *The Evening and the Morning Star*, June 1832-June 1833," p. [1], *The Joseph Smith Papers*, https://www.josephsmithpapers.org/paper-summary/revelations-printed-in-the-evening-and-the-morning-star-june-1832-june-1833/6, [D&C 50:17-22].

98. Givens with Hauglid, *The Pearl of Greatest Price*, loc. 4392 of 6929.

99. Ibid., loc. 4465 of 6929.

reveal his methodology, and that the papyri likely served as a catalyst for Joseph Smith to create, from his own imagination, a pseudepigraphal work having no real relationship to Abraham, Givens needs to explore what to do with Joseph Smith's actual claim that he was revealing an ancient text written by Abraham. The thrust of this final subsection of his chapter seems to suggest that although the Prophet's actual claims and efforts appear to be factually incorrect, having no basis in historical or scholarly reality, they might still be considered genuine in his day. Since fictional memoirs and affidavits in 19th century dime novels were used as actual evidence in courts of law (as Givens highlights), then certainly it would have been culturally acceptable for Joseph Smith to present the Book of Abraham as "authentic" in his day, even if it wasn't.

Even if "authentic sentiment and moral fervor, not credentials or documentary evidence" was acceptable to some in Joseph Smith's day, the reader should not suppose that such was acceptable to Joseph Smith. One need merely look to the great extent to which the Prophet credentialed and documented everything to recognize that a factual basis and real evidence for his claims, not mere sentiment or fervor, were important to him. He obtained three, and then eight more, official witnesses of the golden plates from which he translated the Book of Mormon,[100] sought or obtained scholarly certification for his Book of Mormon and Book of Abraham characters and translations,[101] claimed to receive angelic restorations of both the Aaronic and Melchizedek Priesthoods and various keys in the presence of another witness,[102] told the newly minted Church in its first revelation "Behold there Shall a Record be kept among you" and employed countless scribes to keep records,[103] received the vision of heaven and hell with another witness in the vision with him while others watched and heard them speaking what they saw,[104] established a whole religious system

---

100. "Book of Mormon, 1830," p. 589-90, *The Joseph Smith Papers*.

101. "History, 1838-1856, volume A-1 [23 December 1805-30 August 1834]," 9; "Certificate from Michael Chandler, 6 July 1835," p. [72], *The Joseph Smith Papers*, https://www.josephsmithpapers.org/paper-summary/certificate-from-michael-chandler-6-july-1835/1.

102. "Appendix 5, Document 6. Blessing to Oliver Cowdery, 2 October 1835," p. 12, *The Joseph Smith Papers,* https://www.josephsmithpapers.org/paper-summary/appendix-5-document-6-blessing-to-oliver-cowdery-2-october-1835/1;   Smith, "Journal, 1835-1836," 191-92.

103. "Revelation Book 1," 28, [D&C 21:1].

104. "Vision, 16 February 1832 [D&C 76]," p. 1, *The Joseph Smith Papers*, https://www.josephsmithpapers.org/paper-summary/vision-16-february-1832-dc-76/1, [D&C 76].

based on covenant/contract relationship and teaching the importance of keeping actual records of such covenants, for such records would be used in the final judgment.[105]

The first sermon Joseph Smith gave to the newly formed Quorum of the Twelve Apostles is a strong witness of his desires to keep records and witness everything, so that all things have a basis in documented, recorded fact for the benefit of the Church and the whole world:

> I have something to lay before this council, an item which they will find to be of great importance to them. I have for myself learned — a fact by experience which on reflection gives me deep sorrow. It is a truth that if I now had in my possession every decision which has been given had upon important items of doctrine and duties since the rise of this church, they would be of incalculable worth to the saints, but we have neglected to keep records of such things, thinking that prehaps that they would never benefit us afterwards, wh[i]ch had we now, would decide almost any point that might be agitated; and now we cannot bear record to the church nor unto the world of the great and glorious manifestations that have been made to us with that degree of power and authority wh[i]ch we otherwise could if we had those decisions to publish abroad.

> Since the twelve are now chosen, I wish to tell them a course which they may pursue and be benefitted hereafter in a point of light of which they, prehaps, are not now aware. At all times when you assemble in the capacity of a council to transact business let the oldest of your number preside, and let one or more be appointed to keep a record of your proceedings, and on the decision of every important item, be it what it may, let such decision be noted down, and they will ever after remain upon record as law, covenant and doctrine ...

> Here let me prophecy the time will come when if you neglect to do this, you will fall by the hands of unrighteous men. Were you to be brought before the authorities and accused of any crime or misdemeanor and be as innocent as the angels of God unless you can prove that you were somewhere else, your enemies will prevail against you: but if you can bring twelve

---

105. "Letter to the Church, 7 September 1842 [D&C 128]," p. 1, *The Joseph Smith Papers,* https://www.josephsmithpapers.org/paper-summary/letter-to-the-church-7-september-1842-dc-128/1, [D&C 128].

men to testify that you were in some other place at that time you will escape their hands. Now if you will be careful to keep minutes of these things as I have said, it will be one of the most important and interesting records ever seen. I have now laid these things before you for your consideration and you are left to act according to your own judgments.[106]

Indeed, the evidence is overwhelmingly against any idea that Joseph Smith merely let "authentic sentiment and moral fervor, not credentials or documentary evidence" become the basis for his moral authority.

In his closing remarks for this chapter on the Book of Abraham, Givens asserts that Joseph Smith never claimed the Book of Abraham was scripture, and he probably had no intention of canonizing it either:

> He [Joseph Smith] did not refer to this work as something he was called of God to do or as "a branch of his calling," as was true of his other translations. Neither did he, as in those other cases, claim scriptural status for the resulting product. Canonization was never likely in his conceiving, either.[107]

Givens does not elaborate on his sweeping declarations, for they are merely a side note as he wraps up his chapter, and it is not fully clear what he means by "scriptural status" and "canonization" or how those terms would have been understood in Joseph Smith's day; however, the Prophet certainly claimed the Book of Abraham was the writing of an ancient patriarch and recognized servant of God. While that is not formal canonization, is it a claim to scriptural status? Probably.

Fortunately, Joseph Smith provided more explicit insight into how he regarded the Book of Abraham when he prepared a forward for its publication. This forward was never published, but it provides an appropriate response to Givens' assertion:

> In future. I design to furnish much original matter, which will be found of enestimable advantage to the saints, — & to all who — desire a knowledge of the kingdom of God. — and as it is not practicable to bring forthe the new translation. of the Scriptures. & varioes records of ancint date. & great worth to this gen[e]ration in book <the usual> form. by books. I shall prenit [print] specimens of the same in the Times & Seasons

---

106. "Record of the Twelve, 14 February-28 August 1835," p. 1, *The Joseph Smith Papers*, https://www.josephsmithpapers.org/paper-summary/record-of-the-twelve-14-february-28-august-1835/7.

107. Givens with Hauglid, *The Pearl of Greatest Price*, loc. 201.

as fast. as time & space will admit. so that the honest in heart may be cheerd & comforted and go on their way rejoi[ci]ng. — as their souls become exp[an]ded. — & their undestandig [understanding] enlightend, by a knowledg of what Gods work through the fathers. in former days, as well as what He is about to do in Latter Days — To fulfil the words of the fathers.[108]

It appears that the Prophet would rather have published the Book of Abraham, along with the Joseph Smith Translation of the Bible and other records in the "usual form" of "books," but it was not practical in the moment. He speaks of them all as providing "a knowledge of the kingdom of God" and being of "great worth," soul expanding, and enlightening, because they are "Gods work through the fathers. in former days." Additionally, God's work includes fulfilling the words of these ancients in the "Latter Days." If this does not indicate that the Book of Abraham had the status of scripture in Joseph Smith's mind, then Givens will need to be more specific about what does.

Although Joseph Smith did have members formally bind themselves to the Bible and Book of Mormon on the day the Church was organized on April 6, 1830 as a form of institutional or communal canonization, it is difficult to tell what his intentions were with the Book of Abraham since he never finished publishing the project. But mentioning that he would have published it with the other forthcoming records in the "usual" form of books can suggest he anticipated a day when it was part of the standard works of the Church.

Conclusions

In order to fully engage the academy, historians and theologians in the field of Mormon Studies, like Givens, must write under the premise that Joseph Smith's revelations reflect his own natural understanding, creativity, and development. The Book of Mormon and Bible expansions, for example, can only be indicative of the Prophet's own 1829–1831 theological understanding and culture (the time period when he produced these texts) and thus are to be examined and interpreted within that specific period to ascertain meaning. The idea that some of Joseph Smith's revelations might actually be, as he claimed, divinely-aided translations of records from ancient prophets who may have had a more complex

---

108. "Editorial, circa 1 March 1842, Draft," p. [1], *The Joseph Smith Papers*, https://www.josephsmithpapers.org/paper-summary/editorial-circa-1-march-1842-draft/1. Thanks to Stephen Smoot and Matthew Roper for this reference.

theology than his own, or that his revelations might actually be, as he claimed, the words of a divine being whose ways and thoughts are higher than his own are not admissible. To work within any of these parameters is deemed "apologetic," and it is currently trendy to simply dismiss or ignore such approaches, even among scholars within the Church.

While some good may come from Mormon Studies and its natural evolutionary approach to Church history and theology — from "bracketing faith" and gaining admittance thereby to the world's dialogue concerning the Church and its members, to discussing the Book of Mormon or Book of Abraham only within their own internal limits or within the cultural environments of Joseph Smith's day, or interpreting all of Joseph Smith's revelations within their immediate religious, political, or social context — we must put a bright spotlight on some problematic outcomes that naturally follow such methodologies when they begin to be embraced within the Latter-day Saint faith community.

If Joseph Smith's revelations do indeed include translations of ancient sources or the thoughts of higher beings, as he claimed, then strictly interpreting these revelations in the modern religious contexts of Joseph Smith's natural mind and environment as the Mormon Studies movement demands will lead to different conclusions about terminology and meaning compared to those who examine the translations in the context of their claimed antiquity. Priesthood orders and inheritance laws, for example, functioned differently in antiquity than in antebellum protestant America. Interpreting priesthood or inheritance passages of ancient texts within modern contexts is bound to distort the meaning of the words and potentially lead to false constructs about the nature and historical development of priesthood or inheritance, if they are indeed ancient.

In a natural and gradual way, Latter-day Saints examining Joseph Smith's translations from a Mormon Studies perspective, in contrast to other approaches, such as ancient studies, will eventually define and understand the same words in the text so differently as to destroy all confidence in settling questions by an appeal to the sources. Like the Brother of Jared feared, we are arriving at a point where "we may not understand *our* words."

This modern confounding became most clear to me several years ago when I submitted a paper for publication on priesthood development in the Church, which demonstrated that Joseph Smith's teachings in Nauvoo concerning the highest order or fullness of the priesthood in relation to the temple — something that most Mormon Studies scholars assume is a late development in Joseph Smith's priesthood theology

— already appear fully developed in the Book of Mormon, Bible expansions, and other early revelations of Joseph Smith. One reviewer scoffed at such a possibility:

> There is no timeline or sense of historical development. It appears that Smith's ministry is caught within a time warp where the 1829 BoM is comparable to and possibly addressing an 1843 speech of Smith. Current terminology is applied and used so clumsily that seemingly clever BoM analysis is left fruitless and unconvincing. By the end terms like Holy Order are synonymous to other orders and new terminology like Fullness of the priesthood are never differentiated from the previous idea of Melchizedek priesthood.[109]

This reviewer clearly believes, or at least works from the premise, that the Book of Mormon must reflect an earlier less-developed theology of Joseph Smith's 1829 mind concerning priesthood that is fundamentally different from Joseph Smith's "new terminology" and complexity of his later periods. This is a tacit rejection of the possibility that the Book of Mormon might already contain a more fully developed priesthood and temple theology and terminology of an ancient people that might actually reflect Joseph Smith's later teachings concerning priesthood and temple in Nauvoo. The natural explanations that Mormon Studies demands will undoubtably create a version of priesthood development and terminology that is fundamentally different from those who allow the revelations and translations of Joseph Smith to have more complex ancient ideas, independent from or above his own. These fundamental differences in premise are preventing us from understanding one another.

Elder Jeffrey Holland's remarks to the Maxwell Institute, where Terryl Givens is currently a Fellow, are appropriate here:

> In the spirit of full disclosure, you should know that initially I was against any proposal to do at BYU what was called *Mormon studies* elsewhere because I knew what Mormon studies elsewhere usually meant. However, over time I have come to see merit in a Latter-day Saint studies effort at BYU *if you are willing to make it significantly different from the present* …. "Bracketing your faith" is what those in the field call it. … On this I stand with Levenson and Stephen Prothero, who has recently become a friend. Stephen said fifteen years ago

---

109. Anonymous email communication sent to author, June 7, 2017; as standard feedback.

that bracketing one's personal faith, its truth claims, and moral judgments has cost scholars credibility with readers because, as he says, no one knows exactly where authors are coming from ideologically. Elder Maxwell was more direct. He said that we are not really "learned" if we exclude the body of divine data that the eternities place at our disposal through revelation and the prophets of God. He also said, "The highest education, therefore, includes salvational truths," thus the invitation to include in your scholarly backpack the body of "divine data" that the eternities have placed at our disposal. We are to use salvational truths whenever and wherever we can.[110]

Givens began his complicating of the term "translate" by reminding his readers that the "Book of Mormon Wars" — i.e., scholarly debate concerning the possible authenticity of that book as an ancient record — has been superseded by scholarship which ignores questions of historicity and focuses more on internal textual analysis and its impact on individuals, communities, and cultures since its publication. Givens suggests that scholarship concerning the Book of Abraham, with its controversial claims to antiquity, might benefit from a similar transformation:

> Evaluating [Joseph Smith's] production in the light of modern Egyptological expertise may tell us something about his linguistic abilities — or lack thereof; it will reveal nothing about the religious world out of which the Book of Abraham came or the mind that rendered it in ways that came to profoundly shape the religious values and precepts of an entire people.[111]

Indeed, Givens points out that Joseph Smith's supposed attempt to translate a Book of Abraham from an ancient Egyptian Book of Breathings has a silver lining, because one can now view the Book of Abraham as a modern imaginative or creative work made within the Prophet's own inspired mind, rather than an English translation of an actual ancient text, and such a view

> brackets the questions of historicity and accuracy altogether and enables a new range of questions to emerge. Instead of evaluating

---

110. Jeffrey R. Holland, "The Maxwell Legacy in the 21st Century," *BYU Neal A. Maxwell Institute for Religious Scholarship Annual Report 2018* (lecture, Brigham Young University, Provo, UT, November 10, 2018), 15-17, https://byumiuploads.s3.amazonaws.com/uploads/2019/06/2018-Maxwell-Institute-Annual-Report-small.pdf.

111. Givens with Hauglid, *The Pearl of Greatest Price*, loc. 4067 of 6929.

Smith's work by looking back through the lens of contemporary Egyptology, we may learn the workings of Smith's prophetic imagination and his own unique cultural moment by entering more fully into his nineteenth-century context.[112]

This last quote needs a little more context and clarification as it is contributing to some confounding in the moment.

Just prior to this quote, Givens discusses the Church's Gospel Topics essay on the "Translation and Historicity of the Book of Abraham" and claims that it admits Joseph Smith may have mistakenly thought he was translating the Book of Abraham text from the Book of Breathings characters while, at the same time, it catalyzed a story about Abraham in Joseph Smith's mind: "the church now acknowledges on its website that prophetic misunderstanding and prophetic inspiration may coexist in the same person even at the same moment."[113]

However, the Church essay, though a little ambiguous, does not actually state this. The part of the essay in question, quoted by Givens, says that "Joseph's translation was not a literal rendering of the papyri as a conventional translation would be. Rather, the physical artifacts provided an occasion for meditation, reflection, and revelation. They catalyzed a process whereby God gave to Joseph Smith a revelation about the life of Abraham, even if that revelation did not directly correlate to the characters on the papyri."[114] This statement does not state that Joseph Smith mistakenly thought he was translating the Book of Abraham from characters on the papyri that were not the Book of Abraham. It merely acknowledges a theory that suggests the Book of Abraham may have been given to Joseph Smith by direct revelation as he contemplated the papyri and its vignettes generally.

Most adherents of the "catalyst theory" suggest that if the Book of Abraham text was not on any of the papyri that Joseph Smith possessed, then maybe the papyri inspired the Prophet to miraculously perceive the actual ancient text of Abraham, which he revealed in English, similar to the Parchment of John which Joseph Smith never possessed physically but perceived and translated into English anyway as recorded in Doctrine and Covenants 7. Consequently, this version of the catalyst theory still qualifies as a translation (an ancient text was rendered into

---

112. Ibid., loc. 4049 of 6929.

113. Ibid.

114. "Translation and Historicity of the Book of Abraham," The Church of Jesus Christ of Latter-Day Saints (website), https://www.churchofjesuschrist.org/study/manual/gospel-topics-essays/translation-and-historicity-of-the-book-of-abraham.

English, even if by the gift and power of God) and it does not "bracket the questions of historicity and accuracy altogether." Since it assumes the Book of Abraham was a real ancient writing that the Prophet revealed in its English translation by the gift and power of God, applying ancient studies to test its historicity and explore its meaning is still fair game. While there are historical problems with this theory, given Joseph Smith's and his contemporaries' claims that he translated the Book of Abraham from characters on the papyri he possessed,[115] nevertheless, adherents of this theory still assume the text is ancient.

In contrast, Givens' version of the catalyst theory assumes that the papyri did not inspire an actual, though miraculous, English translation of an ancient writing of Abraham, but rather the papyri sparked a modern, uniquely created, story about Abraham in the inspired, imaginative mind of Joseph Smith himself. Of course, such a view does not just "bracket" questions of historicity and accuracy, it nullifies them, effectively canceling the "Book of Abraham Wars." In this framework, anyone desiring to do Book of Abraham research can do so unhampered by Joseph Smith's claims of its antiquity, "entering more fully into his nineteenth-century context," just as many scholars have done with Book of Mormon.

While abandonment of the controversial elements surrounding the Book of Mormon (e.g., claims that it is a divinely enabled translation of an actual ancient record) has allowed for a flowering of Book of Mormon studies in the Mormon Studies movement generally, and the same could happen for the Book of Abraham as well, what is the cost for championing such efforts and downplaying the role and work of those who explore the antiquity of these records as Joseph Smith claimed?

It should be apparent that a narrowing of effort and marginalizing or bracketing the possible antiquity of the Book of Mormon and Book of Abraham not only might confound the terminology of the text (as modern constructs are imposed on potentially ancient documents), but

---

115. To be clear, Joseph Smith did claim 1) that he was providing a "translation of some ancient records," the "writings of Abraham," "written by his [Abraham's] own hand," "Book of Abraham and Facsimiles, 1 March-16 May 1842," p. 704 and 2) that he had learned specific things mentioned in the Book of Abraham "by translating the papyrus now in my house" (Smith, *Words of Joseph Smith*, 380). Noted in Gee, *An Introduction to the Book of Abraham*, 923). Additionally, the Book of Abraham itself claims to be a first-person record written by Abraham, not a third person story from the mind of Joseph Smith: "I [Abraham] shall endeavor to write some of these things upon this record, for the benefit of my posterity that shall come after me" "Book of Abraham and Facsimiles, 1 March-16 May 1842," p. 705 [Abraham 1:31]).

it may effectively silence any voices who may be "crying from the dust." It negates any real authentic testimony of those who have seen, heard, felt, and written about Jesus Christ in antiquity. Further, it prevents any richness of meaning or greater understanding that can be gained from studying these texts in their claimed ancient provenance. If Latter-day Saint Americanists persist in hyper-contextualizing every revelation and translation of Joseph Smith into the 19th century, then the unique terminology and meaning any ancient records might hold will surely be distorted, and the miraculous claims of Joseph Smith must continue to be watered-down and explained away, as is becoming more prevalent. The plain language of the Latter-day Saint community will grow in complication until we can no longer understand our words.

John S. Thompson *obtained his BA and MA in Ancient Near Eastern Studies from BYU and UC Berkeley respectively and completed a PhD in Egyptology at the University of Pennsylvania. He has been a full-time employee of the Church's Seminaries & Institutes of Religion for more than 25 years and currently serves as a Coordinator and Institute Director for the Boston/Cambridge, Massachusetts, area. He is married to Stacey Keller from Orem, Utah, and they have nine children and two grandchildren.*

A Priesthood Restoration Narrative for Latter-day Saints Believers

Brian C. Hales

Review of Michael Hubbard MacKay, *Prophetic Authority: Democratic Hierarchy and the Mormon Priesthood* (Urbana, IL: University of Illinois Press, 2020). 184 pages. $22.95 (paperback).

Abstract: *With ready access to all the documents acquired by the Joseph Smith Papers project, Michael Hubbard MacKay, co-editor of the Joseph Smith Papers' Documents, Volume 1: July 1828–June 1831, presents a new historical reconstruction of the priesthood restoration in* Prophetic Authority: Democratic Hierarchy and the Mormon Priesthood. *MacKay summarizes how Joseph Smith's initial authority was based primarily on charisma drawn from the Book of Mormon translation and his revelations. The transition next to apostolic authority — derived from priesthood keys restored by Peter, James and John — is also detailed. MacKay contextualizes the priesthood as part of Smith's efforts to offer "salvation to humankind and [bind] individuals to Christ" (37–38). Historical controversies are handled with frankness and depth. This study constitutes an important upgrade in the historiography of this controversial topic.*

While serving in Venezuela years ago, we missionaries taught investigators that the priesthood was restored by John the Baptist, and thereafter the Apostles Peter, James, and John appeared with higher ordinations. If additional questions arose regarding authority, we related accounts of the subsequent visits of Moses, Elias, and Elijah. It was a neat chronological package, orderly and easily defended.

Over the ensuing decade I learned that the priesthood restoration narrative was far more complex. Eventually, I encountered important works by Michael Quinn and Gregory Prince that examined significant questions regarding the establishment of the priesthood among the

Latter-day Saints.[1] Multiple differences of opinion among historians were evidently due to the absence of clarifying historical documentation, along with the presence of some contradictory data.

Despite these limitations, imagine a new historical reconstruction that describes the restoration of the priesthood written by a skilled author who is a fan of the Prophet Joseph Smith and who has access not only to all the previously published studies but also to every original document tied to Joseph Smith known to exist. Michael Hubbard MacKay, co-editor of the Joseph Smith Papers' *Documents, Volume 1: July 1828–June 1831*, used his remarkable researching abilities and access to voluminous resources to piece together a new narrative. His *Prophetic Authority* represents a significant advancement in our understanding of the unfolding priesthood in the early days of the Church.

Prophetic Authority uses seven chapters along with an introduction and an epilogue to explore and clarify this complex subject. The few excerpts from the book on key topics, included below, show the texture of this new dialogue about priesthood restoration. Chapter 1 starts not with ordinations but by a discussion of the importance of Joseph Smith's establishing a connection with the past: "Smith did not simply act like a prophet: he used material implements to bind himself successfully to a perceived ancient world from which he produced an ancient text" (12). Smith's authority began with the Book of Mormon translation: "Like a royal coronation, the plates and the Urim and Thummim crowned Smith as a religious leader" (14).

Besides the Book of Mormon, Smith's authority flowed from his revelations, which "were more than just text; they were visions, angelic experiences, physical expressions, embodied realities, all of which were demonstrated alongside and through objects" (21). Those around Joseph "were familiar with his human frailty and imperfections. Still, they believed he spoke for God when he was divinely directed to do so" (19). This God-connection presaged claims to priesthood authority, but communicated divine approval that set Joseph apart from other devotees.

After describing the religious milieu into which Joseph Smith was able to introduce and perpetuate priesthood leadership and power, *Prophetic Authority* identifies the overriding priority for the entire process: "To Smith and his early converts, sacramental ordinances identified Mormonism as a church that offered salvation to humankind and bound

---

1. See D. Michael Quinn, *The Mormon Hierarchy: Origins of Power* (Salt Lake City: Signature Books, 1994) and Gregory A. Prince, *Power from on High: The Development of Mormon Priesthood* (Salt Lake City: Signature Books, 1995).

individuals to Christ" (25). MacKay consistently positions Joseph Smith's efforts to establish priesthood ordinances as Christ-centric and salvific. Joseph's "high-ranking position was only valuable insofar as it offered the saints the ability to find certainty of their own salvation" (103).

Prophetic Authority recounts how Smith and his followers "were not ordained by other clergymen or by an inner calling from God" (31). That is, "Smith did not assume the authority to baptize. Rather, he constructed that authority through complex restoration narratives in which God delivered and authorized his power, a pattern that would hold true for future issues as well, such as the establishment of priesthood and apostleship" (30). *Prophetic Authority* points out how "the narratives, commandments, and translations did the heavy lifting of the Mormon construction project" (126).

From the beginning, the Christian denominationalists struggled with Smith's claims. "Joseph Smith's angelic visitations were harder for clergy to swallow," explains *Prophetic Authority*, "because they were wrapped in his claims to exclusive authority and prophetic responsibility" (31). Steeped in the culture that placed the Bible as the sole source of authorized teachings, Smith's declarations that the heavens were newly opened were easily rejected by traditionalists but embraced by his followers. "Placing aside *sola scriptura*, Smith's converts clung to the principle of *sola propheta*, in which the prophet was the supreme authority in all matters of doctrine and practice" (66).

Accepting the official date of May 15, 1829 for John the Baptist's visit, *Prophetic Authority* acknowledges that "Smith's understanding of this visitation by John evolved over time" (34). MacKay explains: "The role of the prophet was not just to receive new revelation, but to continue to seek and receive better understanding of older revelations" (49). "Reinterpretation happened frequently with Smith's revelations, to the extent that it formed a consistent pattern. Small pieces from earlier revelations appeared to be part of much larger initiatives that came into focus only years later" (36).

Prophetic Authority describes how Joseph Smith initially founded his authority on his prophetic calling in general — his charisma: "When Smith was constructing his own historical narrative in his official history ... he left the Peter, James, and John story out of his account to emphasize charisma and the construction of the Church of Christ" (54). But MacKay recognizes that "a sustainable and manageable priesthood hierarchy was not possible until he grounded his tradition within an official church where ordinations could be performed and ordinances carried out with the legitimating force of the institution" (53).

MacKay confronts head-on the controversial timing of Melchizedek Priesthood restoration: "Why did some eyewitnesses use language that claimed that the Melchizedek priesthood was restored in the 1831 conference when other equally reliable sources also claimed that Peter, James, and John had restored the Melchizedek priesthood in either 1829 or 1830?" (76). Following these ordinations from Peter, James, and John, *Prophetic Authority* describes how God's voice in the "chamber of Father Whitmer" authorized the first ordinations (128; see D&C 128:21): "Smith's history explains that with that authority given to them, he and Cowdery were commanded to ordain each other elders (thus officially connecting this ordinance to an ecclesiastical office) but to delay that ordinance until later" (59).

Eventually, priesthood authority was "established theologically and ecclesiastically … on the metaphor of keys, so all that was left to do was to turn the key and open the door" (117). The emphasis of keys required a different supportive narrative: "Once quorums received the keys of the priesthood from the president of the high priesthood, the narrative of Peter, James, and John became very relevant" (92-93). However, "The Peter, James, and John restoration narrative did not emerge immediately or even as a cohesive whole, but it has had the longest-lasting effect of all of Smith's restoration narratives" (101). Responding obliquely to critical assertions regarding the timeline of reports of these ordinations, *Prophetic Authority* notes: "Although there are no direct statements that claim the complaints from Missouri caused Smith and Cowdery to begin talking about the visit of Peter, James, and John, it is interesting that it was during this period that the two leaders began to include the narrative in private blessings, histories, and eventually a public revelation in the Doctrine and Covenants" (90).

Prophetic Authority identifies "three main historical milestones" for the development of apostolic authority as the presiding authority within the Church: "1829 (when the three ancient apostles apparently came), 1835 (when twelve modern apostles were chosen), and the 1839-46 Nauvoo period (which culminated with the modern apostles becoming the official administrators for the whole church)" (100-01). Smith's death on June 27, 1844 created a leadership void wherein the 1829 narrative of the visit of Peter, James, and John restoring Melchizedek priesthood keys and the apostleship became paramount. Simplifying that story created a more easily understood and defended narrative: "The succession crisis caused the twelve to describe Smith's priesthood restoration as an individual event rather than a process of angelic visits, progressive revelations, and ongoing struggles" (98).

In the Epilogue, MacKay "briefly opens the door to the next phase of authority in Mormon history [by] tracing the development of Mormon liturgy in five key areas" (119):

- "First, Smith's concern for the fate of those who died before baptism" (119).
- "Second, Smith's goal of binding the human family did not stop at baptism for the dead but extended to eternal marriages and sealings" (120).
- "Third, Smith expanded the priesthood through the exploration of Freemasonry in Nauvoo" (121).
- "Fourth, and related to the Quorum of the Anointed's panoptic prayer, Smith created Mormonism's most extensive ritual — the endowment — during the Nauvoo period" (122).
- "Once women were also participating in the ceremony and receiving their own endowment, Smith introduced the fifth innovation, which he termed the fullness of the priesthood: the notion of human deification" (124).

Apparently, we will have to wait for volume two to gain MacKay's insights regarding this unfolding of these priesthood-related rituals and blessings.

As a point of criticism, it is unfortunate that the author would use the descriptor "Mormon" nearly 500 times in a book published two years after the Church asked that writers avoid using that term in reference to the Church or its members. Also, the final section discusses the highest of all temple ceremonies, a topic only recently and briefly acknowledged in official Church venues, undoubtedly due to the sacredness attributed to such ordinances.[2]

Prophetic Authority comprises a unique blend of scholarship, research, and historical retelling that goes well beyond accounts that detail who, what, and where. By portraying Joseph Smith as reacting to external pressures, but equally responding to the ongoing heavenly flow of revelation, MacKay's reconstruction can easily sustain the fabric of faith. Even for those who disagree with how MacKay connects the dots, *Prophetic Authority* constitutes required reading for anyone interested in this controversial subject.

---

2. See "Nauvoo Journals, May 1843–June 1844," *The Joseph Smith Papers*, https://www.josephsmithpapers.org/intro/introduction-to-journals-volume-3?p=1&highlight=second%20anointing#8909556251496237924.

Brian C. Hales *is the author of six books dealing with polygamy, most recently the three-volume,* Joseph Smith's Polygamy: History and Theology *(Greg Kofford Books, 2013). His* Modern Polygamy and Mormon Fundamentalism: The Generations after the Manifesto *received the "Best Book of 2007 Award" from the John Whitmer Historical Association. He has presented at numerous meetings and symposia and published articles in* The Journal of Mormon History, Mormon Historical Studies, *and* Dialogue *as well as contributing chapters to* The Persistence of Polygamy *series. Brian works as an anesthesiologist at the Davis Hospital and Medical Center in Layton, Utah, and has served as the President of the Utah Medical Association.*

The Great Isaiah Scroll (1QIsaᴬ)— Catalogue of Textual Variants

Donald W. Parry

Abstract: *In this erudite survey of textual variants in the "Great Isaiah Scroll" from Qumran, Donald W. Parry lays out the major categories of these differences with illustrative examples. This significant description of the most significant book of Old Testament prophecy provides ample evidence of Parry's conclusion that the "Great Isaiah Scroll" "sets forth such a wide diversity and assortment of textual variants that [it] is indeed a catalogue, as it were, for textual criticism."*

[**Editor's Note:** Part of our book chapter reprint series, this article is reprinted here as a service to the LDS community. Original pagination and page numbers have necessarily changed, otherwise the reprint has the same content as the original.

See Donald W. Parry, "The Great Isaiah Scroll (1QIsaᴬ)—Catalogue of Textual Variants," in *"To Seek the Law of the Lord": Essays in Honor of John W. Welch,* ed. Paul Y. Hoskisson and Daniel C. Peterson (Orem, UT: The Interpreter Foundation, 2017), 247–65. Further information at https://interpreterfoundation.org/books/to-seek-the-law-of-the-lord-essays-in-honor-of-john-w-welch-2/.]

The Qumran caves, located near the northwestern area of the Dead Sea, yielded twenty-one copies of the book of Isaiah—two from Cave 1, eighteen from Cave 4, and one from Cave 5. An additional copy (making a total of twenty-two copies) of Isaiah was discovered south of Qumran in a cave at Wadi Murabbaʿat. All twenty-two copies of Isaiah are written in Hebrew. Most of these scrolls are severely damaged and fragmented, owing to long-term exposure to the elements. Altogether, the Isaiah scrolls represent about 10 percent of all biblical scrolls discovered at Qumran. This statistic alone indicates that Isaiah held a prominent place in the Qumran community, but other indications also reveal Isaiah's significance. Isaiah's book is treated as an authoritative work by the Qumran covenanters; in their sectarian writings, they cite, paraphrase, and allude to Isaiah more than any other prophet. These Isaiah quotations and allusions are located in legal, eschatological, and poetic contexts of the sectarian writings and reveal ideological and theological positions of the Qumran community. In addition to the twenty-two Isaiah scrolls themselves and the sectarian writings that include quotes and allusions to Isaiah, the Qumran discoveries included six Isaiah *pesharim* (commentaries).

The twenty-two copies of Isaiah represent significant archaeological finds. These Isaiah texts, discovered between the years 1947 and 1952, have impacted our understanding of the textual history of the Bible, and translators have utilized them for modern translations of the Bible.

The most significant of the twenty-two copies of Isaiah is called the Great Isaiah Scroll, or 1QIsaᵃ. This scroll is virtually complete, containing all sixty-six chapters. It is the only complete biblical scroll discovered in the eleven Qumran caves; as such, it presents a view of what biblical manuscripts looked like at the end of the Second Temple era, around the first century CE. Unlike the Masoretic Text (MT) with its consonantal and vocalization framework and system of notes, accents, and versification, 1QIsaᵃ features a handwritten manuscript without vocalization or accents. Additionally, 1QIsaᵃ contains interlinear or marginal corrections, scribal marks and notations, a different paragraphing system, and special morphological and orthographic features.

With regard to the topic of this present paper, 1QIsaᵃ contains such an assortment of textual variants versus the readings of MT, that this Qumran scroll may be considered a catalogue of textual variants. By *catalogue*, I refer to a "complete list of items." But unlike most catalogues, which generally present items in a systematic manner (such as alphabetical order), the textual variants of 1QIsaᵃ are not so systematized.

Scribal Activity in 1QIsaᵃ Produces Textual Variants

The scribe(s) who copied 1QIsaᵃ from a master copy had somewhat of a free approach to the text, characterized by exegetical or editorial pluses, morphological smoothing and updating, harmonizations, phonetic variants, and modernizations of terms. There is also evidence that a well-intended scribe simplified the text for an audience that no longer understood certain classical Hebrew forms. His editorial tendencies resulted in a popularization of certain terms, some from Aramaic that reflected the language of Palestine in his time period. This free approach, together with errors that occurred during the transmission of the text (e.g., haplography, dittography, graphic similarity, misdivision of words, interchange of letters, transposition of texts), occasionally produced textual variants.

These textual variants may be divided into four categories:

(1) inadvertent errors that have occurred during transmission of the text

(2) intentional changes of the text on the part of the scribes and copyists of either MT Isaiah or 1QIsaª

(3) synonymous readings

(4) scribes' stylistic approaches and conventions to the text

Not all variant readings, of course, fit neatly into one of these four categories; some readings are indeterminate.

It should be understood that examples of textual variants do not exist solely because of the scribal activity of one single witness or its ancestors, but because of the scribal activity of one or more of the major witnesses. Most of these scribal errors may easily be categorized according to the rules of textual criticism. A single type of reading does not dominate the deviations between MT Isaiah and 1QIsaª. The following examples, which serve to illustrate the variety of such variant readings listed above, demonstrate that 1QIsaª is indeed a catalogue of sorts of textual variants.

(1) Inadvertent Errors

Various publications that reveal the nature of textual criticism refer to mishaps that occur during the transmission of texts.[1] These include

---

It is a privilege to dedicate this article to my friend and colleague John Welch for his many contributions to studies of import to Latter-day Saints.

1   The most complete and up-to-date study of biblical Hebrew textual criticism is Emanuel Tov's *Textual Criticism of the Hebrew Bible* (Minneapolis: Fortress Press, 1992). See also Christian D. Ginsburg, *Introduction to the Massoretico-Critical Edition of the Hebrew Bible* (London: Trinitarian Bible Society, 1897; reprinted with prolegomenon by Harry M. Orlinsky, New York: Ktav, 1966); J. Weingreen, *Introduction to the Critical Study of the Text of the Hebrew Bible* (Oxford: Oxford University Press, 1982). Compare also the more brief treatments of the subject by Julio T. Barrera, *The Jewish Bible and*

pluses (e.g., dittography, conflate readings), minuses (e.g., haplography, *homoioteleuton*,[2] *homoioarcton*), changes (e.g., misdivision of letters or words, ligatures, graphic similarity), and differences in sequence (interchange of letters or metathesis and transposition of words). All of these major categories of accidental errors are present in both of the Hebrew witnesses MT Isaiah and 1QIsaᵃ.

Pluses—Minor Readings

• 1QIsaᵃ הארץ | MT ארץ 1:2

Most pluses that exist in either MT Isaiah or 1QIsaᵃ consist of function words or common words, such as *and, the, all, one, to, for, in, like*, et cetera. In Isaiah 1:2, 1QIsaᵃ has the plus of the article on אר-ץ, thus reading הארץ; but the article is lacking on MT Isaiah.

• 1QIsaᵃ אצבעותיכם בעאון | 4QIsaᶠ MT > 1:15

A well-known example of a plus in 1QIsaᵃ is located in Isaiah 1:15, בעאון אצבעותיכם (*your fingers with iniquity*). This plus is lacking in MT 4QIsaᶠ. אצבעותיכם בעאון serves to fill out the parallelism, thus, מלאו אצבעותיכם בעאון ידיכמה דמים ("your hands are full of blood, your fingers with iniquity"). It is possible that this plus is a primary reading, which dropped out of the proto-Masoretic text during its transmission history. Watts writes, "The addition [of 1QIsaᵃ] is parallel to the previous stich and would be a metrical improvement on MT."[3] So, too, Burrows states regarding 1QIsaᵃ's plus that "a fourth stichos would undoubtedly improve the metrical structure."[4] Cohen provides a compelling argument in favor of the originality of the plus belonging to 1QIsaᵃ, presenting four reasons as to why the scroll is to be preferred. Not only does he produce Ugaritic parallels, but he points out that "the parallelism in the first two clauses makes the possibility of parallelism in the second half of the verse more likely."[5]

---

the *Christian Bible*, trans. W. G. E. Watson (Brill: Leiden, 1998), 367–421 and Ernst Würthwein, *The Text of the Old Testament*, trans. Erroll F. Rhodes; Eerdmans (Grand Rapids, MI, 1995), 107–22.

2   Ginsburg, *Introduction to the Massoretico-Critical Edition*, 171–82, features a methodical examination of minuses caused by homoioteleuton.

3   John D. W. Watts, "Isaiah 1–33," in *Word Biblical Commentary*, Vol. 24, ed. David Hubbard and Glenn Barker (Waco, TX: Word, 1985), 14.

4   M. Burrows, "Variant Readings in the Isaiah Manuscript," *Bulletin of the American Schools of Oriental Research (BASOR)* 111 (Oct. 1948): 19.

5   Chaim Cohen, "A Philological Reevaluation of Some Significant DSS Variants of the MT in Isaiah 1–5," in *Diggers at the Well: Proceedings of a Third International*

Or, as some textual critics maintain, 1QIsa[a] features a harmonization, a word or phrase that has been drawn from a similar context or parallel passage, either from Isaiah itself or from another biblical book. This harmonization may have been created from the scribal school that produced 1QIsa[a] or from its *Vorlage*. This particular plus, some critics claim, was adapted from 59:3, which reads כפיכמה נגאלו בדם ואצבעותיכמה בעו.. For other passages where *blood* is paired with *iniquity*, see 26:21; Ezekial 3:18. For examples of other harmonizations in the scroll, see also 34:4 (cf. Micah 1:4); 51:3 (cf. 35:10; 51:11; 51:6 (cf. 40:26); 52:12 (cf. 54:5); and 60:4 (cf. 66:12).[6]

Conflations

Some deviant readings between the witnesses are conflated readings. Although conflated readings are not always clear-cut, one or more textual critics have identified a conflated element in the deviations. In Isaiah 11:9, the reading of 1QIsa[a] (תמלאה) is a hybrid verbal form, a conflation, possessing elements of a perfect feminine singular verb (= MT מלאה) and also the imperfect feminine prefix.[7] See also the conflated/hybrid form in Isaiah 63:3 (אגאלתי·). In Isaiah 14:2, MT reads אֶל־מְקוֹמָם, but 1QIsa[a] has a plus, אל אדמתם ואל מקומם; from whence came אל אדמתם? The scroll's scribe was possibly impacted by the double manifestation of אדמה in the immediate context, first attested in verse 1 and then again later in verse 2. Or, 1QIsa[a]'s reading may be a conflation, based either on its *Vorlage* or another manuscript that read אל אדמתם.

Dittography

• 1QIsa[a] השמיע השמיע | MT וְהִשְׁמִיעַ 30:30

וְהִשְׁמִיעַ—1QIsa[a]'s duplication of השמיע serves no rhetorical purpose; rather, it is a dittography.

Symposium on the Hebrew of the Dead Sea Scrolls and Ben Sira, ed. Takamitsu Muraoka and John F. Elwolde, Studies on the Texts of the Desert of Judah (STDJ) 36 (Leiden: Brill, 2000), 47.

6 For an additional discussion on harmonizations, see J. Koenig, *L'herméneutique analogique du judaïsme antique d'après les témoins textuels d'Isaïe*, Vetus Testamentum, Supplements 33 (Leiden: Brill, 1982).

7 See Shemaryahu Talmon, "Aspects of the Textual Transmission in the Light of Qumran Manuscripts," in *Qumran and the History of the Biblical Text*, ed. Frank Moore Cross and Shemaryahu Talmon (Cambridge, MA: Harvard University Press, 1975), 248.

Haplography

• 1QIsaᵃ < | Mic 4:2 (אל הר] יהוה]) MT 4QIsaᵉ אֶל־הַר־יְהֹוָה 2:3

אֶל־הַר־יְהֹוָה—For an example of a haplography, see Isaiah 2:3 where 1QIsaᵃ omitted the expression אֶל־הַר־יְהֹוָה by means of haplography, triggered by the prepositions אֶל . . . אֶל.

• 1QIsaᵃ שש כנפים | MT שֵׁשׁ כְּנָפַיִם שֵׁשׁ כְּנָפַיִם 6:2

שֵׁשׁ כְּנָפַיִם שֵׁשׁ כְּנָפַיִם—The copyist of 1QIsaᵃ wrote down שש כנפים and then skipped the second שש כנפים, another example of haplography.

Homoioteleuton

וְעָשָׁן וְגֹנַהּ אֵשׁ לֶהָבָה לָיְלָה כִּי עַל־כָּל־כָּבוֹד חֻפָּה: וְסֻכָּה תִּהְיֶה לְצֵל־יוֹמָם 4:5–6
MT 4QIsaᵃ ([ונגה אש להבה לז••• כי על כל כבוד חפה וסוכה [תהיה] לצל יומ֗ם]
• 1QIsaᵃ < |

Verses 5b–6a dropped out of 1QIsaᵃ through *homoioteleuton*, when the scribe's eye went from יומם to יומם. The reading of MT is supported by both 4QIsaᵃ and other versions.

Confusion of Letters or Graphic Similarity[8]

Graphically similar readings account for a small number of the readings of 1QIsaᵃ, where either the copyists of MT or the Qumran scroll incorrectly copied the text by using graphically similar characters.

• 1QIsaᵃ סער | MT בער 4:4

בער—The variant of 1QIsaᵃ (וברוח סער, "and by the whirlwind") has no contextual significance in this passage; it is likely that a copyist slipped by writing *samek* rather than *bet*, an error that pertains to the graphic similarity of the two characters. Or he was impacted by the expression רוח סערה ("whirlwind" or "stormy wind.") in Ezekial 1:4; 13:11, 13; Psalms 107:25; 148:8. For support of MT's reading of בער, see also Jeremiah 21:12 which also collocates the words משפט and √בער in the context of the execution of judgment.

• 1QIsaᵃ וידעו | MT וידעו 9:8[English v. 9]

וידעו—The variants between MT (וידעו) and 1QIsaᵃ (וירעו) most likely arose because of the confusion of the letters *dalet/resh* in the Assyrian square script. For other instances of the *dalet/resh* interchange in MT

---

8 See Weingreen, *Introduction to the Critical Study*, 38–45, for examples of graphically similar letters together with examples of variants in the HB.

and 1QIsaᵃ, see also Isaiah 16:14; 17:6, 12; 22:5; 23:10; 27:2; 33:8; 40:20; 41:19, and others. But it is also possible that the 1QIsaᵃ scribe (or his *Vorlage*) intentionally rendered the verb וירעו (via √רעע), thus reading, "And all the people will do evil (וירעו), even Ephraim and the inhabitants of Samaria, who say in pride and arrogance of heart…" There is one additional possibility, set forth by Kutscher.[9] He reminds us that the √ירע ("to tremble"; see Isa. 15:4) may have been the scroll's intended meaning.

• 1QIsaᵃ קדשו | MT קר ושוע 22:5

1QIsaᵃ reads קדשו. According to Weingreen, this is an example of graphic similarity: קדשו = קר ושוע. The *ayin* may have lost its guttural sound late in antiquity and a scribe read the *dalet* for the *resh*.[10] Consequently, the same scribe or a subsequent copyist changed the preposition אל to על in order to make sense of the passage. Contrast Weingreen with Blenkinsopp,[11] who prefers the reading of 1QIsaᵃ. He writes that verse "5b [of MT] defies translation and has probably been seriously damaged in the transmission; the present translation depends on 1QIsaᵃ (*mqrqr qdšv 'lhhr*), which makes better though by no means perfect sense and which MT (*mqrqr qr všv' 'l hhr*) may represent a damaged version." Blenkinsopp, therefore, translates verse 5b, "with crying out for help to his holy place on the mountain."

Misdivision of Words

• לו MTqere | (לוא) 1QIsaᵃ MTket לא [9:2[English v. 3

הגוי לא — For other occasions where לוא reads "to him" (versus "no, not"), see Isaiah 3:11. Ginsburg proposes that the original reading was הגילא = הגילה ("the rejoicing"); this word experienced an improper misdivision of words and subsequently the *waw* was incorrectly added.[12] הגילה fits the context and also corresponds with השמחה in the parallelism: "You have increased the rejoicing, you have magnified the joy."

9   E. Y. Kutscher, *The Language and Linguistic Background of the Isaiah Scroll (1QIsaᵃ)*, STDJ 6 (Leiden: Brill, 1974), 246.

10   Weingreen, *Introduction to the Critical Study*, 53.

11   Joseph Blenkinsopp, *Isaiah 1–39*, Vol. 19 of Anchor Bible (New York: Doubleday, 2000), 332.

12   Ginsburg, *Introduction to the Massoretico-Critical Edition*, 161.

Interchange of Letters or Metathesis[13]

• 1QIsaᵃ שלמה | MT שמלה 3:7

שַׂמְלָה) and 1QIsaᵃ (שלמה) exhibit two different words for— (שְׂמָלָה) MT שְׂמְלָה
garment or *clothing*. In the Hebrew Bible, שמלה (31 times) is attested
approximately twice as often as שלמה (16 times). Both carry the same
meaning. Kutscher produces a body of evidence "that שלמה is the original
form and שמלה of later vintage"; at some point through the transmission
of the word, שלמה came about by means of metathesis.[14] Based on the fact
that the previous verse (3:6) is part of the same pericope and that verse
attests שמלה for both MT and 1QIsaᵃ, then שלמה in 1QIsaᵃ 3:7 signifies an
error, an example of metathesis of the *mem* and *lamed*. Or, alternatively,
the scribe's *Vorlage* already contained the reading of שלמה. Compare also
the variant of ושמלתנו and ושלמתנו in 4:1.

Possible Ligature

• 1QIsaᵃ נסמך | MT נָסְנוּ 20:6

נוס MT and 1QIsaᵃ produce two different verbal roots, √נוס ("to— נָסְנוּ
flee") and √סמך ("to lean, support") respectively. MT has the primary
reading, because √נוס is often collocated with שם (e.g., Gen. 19:20; Exod.
21:13; Num. 35:6), an adverbial particle that follows the verb in both
MT and 1QIsaᵃ in the verse under discussion. √סמך followed by שם (=
1QIsaᵃ) is unprecedented in the Bible and achieves an awkward reading.
It is possible that the scroll's scribe changed the verbal root to reflect
his particular historical understanding regarding the pericope under
discussion, the Conquest of Ethiopia and Egypt: Isaiah's Dramatization
(Isa. 20:1–6). Thus Pulikottil has written, "The scribe wanted to make it
clear that the people of the coastland did not flee to Egypt for help, which
never happened; they only relied on the military assistance of Egypt."[15] It
is more probable, owing to the graphic similarities of נסנו and נסמך (both
forms begin with *nun* and *samek*, plus a ligatured *nun* and *waw* share the
appearance of a *mem*), that the scribe simply misread or miscopied the
verb that was in his *Vorlage*.

---

13 For additional examples of metathesis in the Hebrew Bible, see H. Junker,
"Konsonantenumstellung als Fehlerquelle und textkritisches Hilfsmittel im AT,"
Beihefte zur Zeitschrift für die alttestamentliche Wissenschaft (*BZAW*) 66 (1936): 162–74.

14 Kutscher, *The Language and Linguistic Background of the Isaiah Scroll*, 288.

15 Paulson Pulikottil, *Transmission of Biblical Texts in Qumran: The Case of the
Large Isaiah Scroll 1QIsaᵃ* (Sheffield: Sheffield Academic Press, 2001), 132.

Word Order[16]

• 1QIsaᵃ אין מים | (מׁיׁםׁ] אין]) MT 4QIsaᶠ מֵיִם אֵין **1:30**

אֵין מֵיִם—These terms are syntactically variegated (or transposed) in MT versus 1QIsaᵃ. Both מים אין (= MT and 4QIsaᶠ; see also Num. 20:5) and אין מים (= 1QIsaᵃ; see also Exod. 17:1; Num. 21:5; Deut. 8:15; Isa. 50:2; Jer. 38:6; Zech. 9:11) exist in the Bible, although אין מים is more common. Because of the multiple examples of such variations, Talmon has written that the "widely encountered textual phenomenon of inter-Version variations in the form of syntactical inversion cannot be judged to be merely an indication of ordinary scribal laxity."[17] Instead, Talmon sees many examples of such variations as "evidence for the existence of equally valid text-traditions which cannot be reduced to one common archetype, and/or scribal manifestations of stylistic conventions."[18] For other examples of syntactical variations between MT and 1QIsaᵃ, see Isaiah 23:9; 36:12; 37:1, 7, 32–33; 38:19; 43:3; 49:6, 25; 52:7; 55:13; 60:7; 61:7; 62:8; 63:9, 17. For syntactical variations between MT and for 1QIsaᵇ, see 52:13 and 62:8. And for an example of a syntactical variation between MT and 4QIsaᶠ, see 8:7.

אדוניכמה | (הַעַל אֲדֹנֶיךָ וְאֵלֶיךָ) MT 2 Kings 18:27 הַאֶל אֲדֹנֶיךָ וְאֵלֶיךָ **36:12** האליכמה ועל 1QIsaᵃ

הַאֶל אֲדֹנֶיךָ וְאֵלֶיךָ—1QIsaᵃ (האליכמה ועל אדוניכמה) presents a different word order than MT's. For a discussion of syntactical inversions or variations between MT and 1QIsaᵃ, see 1:30 above.

• 1QIsaᵃ רוח בוא | MT 2 Kings 19:7 בׄוׄ רׄוׄחׄ **37:7**

בׄוׄ רׄוׄחׄ—MT and 1QIsaᵃ (רוח בוא) have a different word order for these two words. Note that the scribe often spelled בו with the *alep* (cf. also כיא = כי; לוא = לו).

(2) Intentional Changes

Scribes and copyists of either MT or 1QIsaᵃ intentionally made changes to the Isaiah text. These changes include exegetical pluses or late editorial

---

16   It is not always easy to determine if the category "Word Order" belongs to "Inadvertent Errors" or to "Intentional Changes." Unless there is evidence to the contrary, I am placing "Word Order" in the grouping of "Inadvertent Errors."

17   Shemaryahu Talmon, "Textual Study of the Bible—A New Outlook," *Qumran and the History of the Biblical Text*, ed. Frank Moore Cross and Shemaryahu Talmon (Cambridge, MA: Harvard University Press, 1975) 370–71.

18   Ibid.

additions, harmonizations (when a scribe blends one reading with a second reading that is located in the immediate or greater context, or with a parallel text), morphological smoothing, morphological updating, updating the vocabulary, euphemistic changes, orthographic variants, and phonetic differences.

Exegetical Plus

44:3 אצק² MT | אצק¹ prec 1QIsaᵃ •

אצק²—The adverbial particle כ (*thus, so*) is an exegetical plus in 1QIsaᵃ that was inserted interlinearly, probably to assist in the flow of reading between two clauses in the verse.

Harmonizations

34:4 > MT | והעמקים יתבקעו 1QIsaᵃ •

והעמקים יתבקעו—This plus of 1QIsaᵃ, listed by scholars in verse 4, actually belongs to verse 3. Brownlee declares the plus of 1QIsaᵃ to be a harmonization, derived from Micah 1:4 (והעמקים יתבקעו). He further argues that the reading of MT (v. 3), minus the plus of 1QIsaᵃ, comprises a tristich as follows: "Their slain shall be flung out, and from their corpses their own stench shall rise — the mountains melting down with blood!" (translation by Brownlee). The third line of this tristich, writes Brownlee, serves as a "climax or conclusion" to the parallelistic structure, and that such a configuration is quite acceptable by modern scholars.[19] While the reading of MT is acceptable, the following two bicolons that are attested in the Qumran scroll also comprise a satisfactory structure, with "the valleys will be split" filling out the second bicolon: "Their slain will be cast down, and the stench of their corpses will rise, mountains will melt with their blood, the valleys will be split." The plus of the scroll may have been derived from Micah 1:4 (or vice versa) or from a source that is common to both the book of Micah and the Isaiah Scroll or its *Vorlage*.

---

19   W. H. Brownlee, *The Meaning of the Qumran Scrolls for the Bible. With Special Attention to the Book of Isaiah* (New York: Oxford University Press, 1964), 184–85.

Morphological Smoothing[20]

לוא תנחומים לוא | (ואשלמה נחמים לו) MT 1QIsa[b] וַאֲשַׁלֵּם נִחֻמִים לוֹ 57:18
• 1QIsa[a] ואשלם

1QIsa[a] doubles the dative pronoun (וא ש לם לוא תנחומים) via conflation. With regard to the MT reading נחמים, 1QIsa[b] and 1QIsa[a] has תנחומים, which is the Mishnaic Hebrew form.[21] This is direct evidence that the scroll's scribe has modernized this word.

The deviation between MT (לוֹ "to him") and 1QIsa[a] (לוא "to him") is not a variant reading, but an orthographic difference. Often the scroll writes "to him" with an *alep* (compare also בו = בוא; כי = כיא). For other examples of לוא ("to him"), see Isaiah 5:26; 9:2 (MT[qere] = לוֹ; MT[ket] = לא); 31:8; 36:22; 44:7; 57:18 (*bis* in the scroll); 59:16; 63:9.

62:1 אֶחֱשֶׁה MT | אחריש 1QIsa[a] •

אֶחֱשֶׁה—Following the negative particle לא are variant verbal roots, √חשה in MT and √חרש in 1QIsa[a]. These verbs are employed as synonymous readings in at least two parallelistic structures (see Isa. 42:14; Ps. 28:1), but here they are deviations in the first bicolon of verse 1. The reading of 1QIsa[a] may have been assimilated from one of these two parallelisms (Isa. 42:14 or Ps. 28:1); or, according to Talmon, the Qumran scroll "presumably perpetuated an established reading."[22] The theory held by Kutscher[23] that a scribe of 1QIsa[a] modernized the reading from the relatively rare √חשה (16 occurrences in the Hebrew Bible) to the more popular √חרש (47 occurrences in the Hebrew Bible) may be questioned because √חשה was *not* modernized in other verses of 1QIsa[a], i.e., 42:14; 57:11; 62:6; 64:11, and 65:6.

---

20 Smoothing, together with archaizing and modernizing, are "three related skewing processes which are involved in text production and preservation." Bruce K. Waltke and M. O'Connor, *An Introduction to Biblical Hebrew Syntax* (Winona Lake, IN: Eisenbrauns, 1990), 11. For examples of smoothing from the Samaritan Pentateuch, see 13. Morphological smoothing is a scribal activity that seeks to remove textual unevenness or inconsistencies through leveling out the text. Such inconsistencies may pertain to morphological, phonological, or syntactical structures.

21 Marcus Jastrow, *Dictionary of the Targumim, the Talmud Babli, and the Yerushalmi, and the Midrashic Literature* (Peabody, MA: Hendrickson, 2005), 1681.

22 Shemaryahu Talmon, "Observations on Variant Readings in the Isaiah Scroll (1QIsa[a])," in *The World of Qumran from Within: Collected Studies* (Leiden: Brill, 1990), 128.

23 Kutscher, *The Language and Linguistic Background of the Isaiah Scroll*, 34, 239.

Morphological Updating

13:10 יָהֵלּוּ MT | יאירו 1QIsaᵃ •

יָהֵלּוּ—MT יָהֵלּוּ (via √הלל, "to shine") sets forth the difficult reading, because √הלל occurs only four times in the Bible (Isa. 13:10; Job 29:3; 31:26; 41:10) and this verb does not exist in Rabbinic Hebrew. The scribe of 1QIsaᵃ replaced the rare יהלו with the common יאירו (via √אור), thus updating the text to a common biblical and Rabbinic Hebrew root.

37:13 וְעֵוָּה MT 2 Kings 19:9 | + ושומרון 1QIsaᵃ •

וְעֵוָּה—37:11–13 refers to nations, kingdoms, and city-states that Assyria had destroyed, including Gozen, Haran, Rezeph, Telassar, Hamath, Arpad, Sepharvaim, Hena, and Ivvah. At the end of the list of names of nations and city-states, 1QIsaᵃ adds "and Samaria" (ושומרון). Scholars generally agree that the invasion of Sennacherib into the kingdom of Judah (36:1–21) and Hezekiah's reaction (36:22–37:20) occurred after Samaria's destruction in 722 BCE. The 1QIsaᵃ scribe therefore added "and Samaria" to the text with the intent of updating the list of kingdoms and city-states. But this addition is unnecessary because the list of names in verses 11–13 was not meant to be comprehensive, but representative. *Samaria* was not listed simply because Hezekiah would have already been painfully aware of its destruction, for Samaria was his northern neighbor.

Updating the Vocabulary[24]

33:7 צָעֲקוּ MT | זעקו 1QIsaᵃ

צָעֲקוּ—In the Bible, √זעק and √צעק have the same meaning ("to cry out"). In Isaiah 14:31; 15:4–5; 26:17; 30:19; 57:13, both MT and 1QIsaᵃ attest √זעק; in Isaiah 19:20, both MT and 1QIsaᵃ have √צעק. But in Isaiah 33:7; 42:2; 46:7; 65:14, these two witnesses have deviations—MT reads √צעק and the scroll has √זעק. In other words, of the eleven occurrences of √זעק/√צעק in Isaiah, the Qumran scroll has √זעק ten times, but uses √צעק only once. Inasmuch as the √זעק is used more often in later biblical books,[25] it appears that the scroll's copyist updated the vocabulary from √צעק to √זעק in 33:7; 42:2; 46:7; 65:14. The versions cannot shed light on these readings.

---

24 Occasionally scribes from the Hebrew witnesses of Isaiah have updated the vocabulary, replacing archaic and outdated words with contemporary usage.

25 See the discussion in Kutscher, *The Language and Linguistic Background of the Isaiah Scroll*, 233.

Euphemistic Changes

Biblical scholars provide examples of indelicate words or anthropomorphisms that have been removed from the Hebrew Bible and replaced with euphemisms[26] or dysphemisms. Yeivin, for example, cites TB Megilla 25b, "Wherever the text is written indelicately, we read it delicately" and posits, "In 16 cases in the Bible, the *qere* form presents a euphemism."[27] Ginsburg maintains that "authoritative redactors of the Sacred Scriptures"[28] removed indelicate words and anthropomorphisms.

• MT^qere צוֹאָתָם | 2 Kings 18:27 (חריהמה) 1QIsa^a MT^ket חַרְאֵיהֶם 36:12
M^qere מֵימֵי רַגְלֵיהֶם | 2 Kings 18:27 MT^ket (שיניהמה) 1QIsa^a MT^ket שֵׁינֵיהֶם
2 Kings 18:27^qere •

חַרְאֵיהֶם—This word (cf. 2 Kings 18:27) belongs to the list of words in Megilla 25b that are considered to be indelicate expressions; צוֹאָתָם ("filth") is to be its euphemistic substitution. Hence the MT^ket/ MT^qere reading here.

• Tg בית שמש דעתידא למחרב | 1QIsa^a 4QIsa^b החרס | MT הַהֶרֶס 19:18

הַהֶרֶס—MT reads "the city of destruction" and two Qumran scrolls attest "the city of the sun." On the one hand, the variants between the Qumran scrolls and MT may be represented by a simple copyist error, writing *he* instead of *het*, or vice versa.[29] On the other hand, critics have argued that a redactor/editor of MT made a tendentious change to the text, or what McCarthy calls "a secondary dysphemism."[30] This textual change came about, according to one theory, to protect the legitimacy of the Jerusalem temple against a Jewish temple that was believed to have existed in Heliopolis.[31] HOTTP, Kutscher, and Wildberger support "City of the Sun" as the original reading.[32]

---

26   On euphemisms in the Bible, see the study of Abraham Geiger, *Urschrift und Übersetzungen der Bibel in ihrer Abhängigkeit von der inneren Entwicklung des Judenthums* (Breslau: Hainauer, 1857; repr., Frankfurt: Madda, 1928), 267–68.

27   Israel Yeivin, *Introduction to the Tiberian Masorah*, trans. E. J. Revell (Missoula, MT: Scholars Press, 1980), 56.

28   Ginsburg, *Introduction to the Massoretico-Critical Edition*, 346–347; see also 347–404.

29   For other examples of *he/het* confusion, see Kutscher, *The Language and Linguistic Background of the Isaiah Scroll*, 506.

30   Carmel McCarthy, *The Tiqqune Sopherim and Other Theological Corrections in the Masoretic Text of the Old Testament* (OBO, Freibureg and Göttingen, 1981), 239.

31   M. Delcor, "Le Temple d'Onias en Egypte," *Revue Biblique (RB)* 75 (1968):188–205.

32   See Hebrew Old Testament Text Project (HOTTP) Vol. 4, 45; Kutscher, *The Language and Linguistic Background of the Isaiah Scroll*, 116, and Hans Wildberger,

Phonetic Differences

40:11 מְלָאִים MT | טלים 1QIsa[a] •

מְלָאִים—1QIsa[a]'s טלים deviation of מְלָאִים is an orthographic deviation, based on phonetics.[33]

16:1 מִסֶּלַע MT | מסלה 1QIsa[a] •

מִסֶּלַע—*Sela* in this verse may refer to a proper name of a site in Moab, which some lexica suggest is Petra; or Sela may signify a cliff.[34] Elsewhere in the Bible, סלע means "rock" or "cliff." 1QIsa[a]'s סלה may be an alternate spelling found in the scribe's *Vorlage* or known to the scribe; or more likely, סלה indicates a phonetic error.[35]

(3) Synonymous Readings[36]

A few of the textual variants in MT Isaiah and 1QIsa[a] consist of synonymous readings. According to Talmon, synonymous readings are characterized as follows:

> a) They result from the substitution of words and phrases by others which are used interchangeably and synonymously with them in the literature of the OT. b) They do not affect adversely the structure of the verse, nor do they disturb either its meaning or its rhythm. Hence they cannot be explained as scribal errors. c) No sign of systematic or tendentious emendation can be discovered in them. They are to be taken at face value…If, as far as we can tell, they are not the product of different chronologically or geographically distinct linguistic strata."[37]

Isaiah 13–27, Continental Commentaries (Minneapolis: Fortress, 1997), 727.

33 For additional examples on variants based on phonetics, see G. R. Driver, "Hebrew Scrolls," *Journal of Theological Studies* 2 (1951): 18.

34 *The Brown-Driver-Briggs Hebrew and English Lexicon* (BDB), 701.

35 See also M. Burrows, "Variant Readings in the Isaiah Manuscript." *BASOR* 113 (1948): 25.

36 See Shemaryahu Talmon, "Synonymous Readings in the Textual Traditions of the Old Testament," *Scripta hierosolymitana* 8 (1961): 335–83. See also Tov, *Textual Criticism of the Hebrew Bible*, 260–61; and F. Díaz Esteban, *Sefer Okhlah we-Okhlah* (Madrid 1975), 193-94, on the interchange of synonymous expressions "and he spoke" versus "and he said" in the manuscripts.

37 Talmon, "Synonymous Readings," 336. Sanderson defines synonymous readings as "those variants for which no preferable reading can be determined even with probability. They are different legitimate ways of expressing the same idea."

Representative examples of synonymous readings include the following.

• 1QIsaᵃ האדמה | MT 4QIsaᶜ הָאָרֶץ 24:1

הָאָרֶץ—MT and 4QIsaᶜ set forth הָאָרֶץ, versus 1QIsaᵃ's synonymous reading of האדמה. Two items support the reading of הארץ: the pericope, consisting of 24:1–12, features ארץ eight times (but never אדמה); and verse 3a (הבוק תבוק הארץ, "the earth is completely made empty") rhetorically develops the reading of verse 1a (יהוה בוקק הארץ, "the LORD makes the earth empty"); that is, both expressions collocate ארץ with √בקק.[38]

• 4QIsaᶠ מצוד | 1QIsaᵃ מצודות | MT מְצָרֹת 29:3

מְצָרֹת—MT and 1QIsaᵃ attest readings that are graphically similar and that have synonymous meanings: MT has מְצָרֹת ("fortresses") and 1QIsaᵃ sets forth מצודות ("strongholds"). Inasmuch as both words work well in the context, it is not easy to settle on a primary reading. These two readings may point to a *vario lectio*, but it is more probable that a scribe of either Hebrew witness (or tradition, i.e., the proto-MT or 1QIsaᵃ) misread his *Vorlage* and wrote a *resh* in place of a *dalet*, or vice versa. See also the variants ומצדתה and ומצרתה in Isaiah 29:7. Another possibility, set forth by Kutscher, is that the words מצרה and מצדה "changed places" between verses 3 and 7.[39]

• 1QIsaᵃ ולוא | 4QIsaᵇ לְֹא² • 1QIsaᵃ לוא + | MT 4QIsaᵇ בַּל 35:9

בַּל—The double negative in 1QIsaᵃ (בל לוא), unknown in the Hebrew Bible, is probably the result of a error. The scribe first wrote בל, which is the primary reading, and then duplicated the לוא from verse 8, vertically located on the line above on the scroll (see col. xxviii, line 25). The vertical borrowing explains why MT and 4QIsaᵇ lack the double negative. Other possibilities, however, exist. בל לוא may be a conflated reading; or לוא may be the primary reading and בל a synonymous reading acquired from another text-type.[40]

• 1QIsaᵃ ממלכתו | MT 2 Kings 20:13 מֶמְשַׁלְתּוֹ 39:2

מֶמְשַׁלְתּוֹ—The nouns מֶמְשַׁלְתּוֹ and ממלכתו are synonymous or near synonymous readings. Tov refers to synonymous readings as

J. E. Sanderson, *An Exodus Scroll from Qumran* (Atlanta: Scholars Press, 1986), 41; see also 109–10.

38 For other examples of synonymous substitutions in 1QIsaᵃ, see Burrows, "Variant Readings in the Isaiah Manuscript," *BASOR* 113 (1948): 27.

39 Kutscher, *The Language and Linguistic Background of the Isaiah Scroll*, 260.

40 Talmon, "Aspects of the Textual Transmission of the Bible," 242–43.

"interchangeable words [that] entered the manuscript tradition at all stages of the transmission, both consciously and unconsciously."[41]

(4) Scribes' Stylistic Approaches and Conventions to the Text

The scribes' stylistic choices, conventions, or idiosyncrasies account for a number of variant readings that exist in the Hebrew witnesses of Isaiah. Examples of scribal stylistic preferences include the following:

Changes to Proper Names

• 1QIsa[a] חזקיה | MT יְחִזְקִיָּהוּ • 1QIsa[a] עוזיה | MT עֻזִּיָּהוּ 1:1

עֻזִּיָּהוּ—During the Second Temple era, theophoric names customarily featured shorter forms, that is, יחזקיה and עוזיה 1QIsa[a] generally employs the shorter forms throughout Isaiah, but with a few exceptions the longer form is used. In verse 1, for example, the scroll attests ישעיהו instead of ישעיה. See also the theophoric names listed in Isaiah 36:1, 14–16, 22; 37:1–3, 6, etc.[42]

Division of Letters

• 1QIsa[a] 1QIsa[b] ואיזה . . . איזה | וְאֵי־זֶה . . . אֵי־זֶה 66:1

וְאֵי־זֶה . . . אֵי־זֶה—The deviations here are not textual variants, but stylistic differences.

Filling Out a Parallelism

• 1QIsa[a] ילכו | MT < 35:6

ילכו—The plus of 1QIsa[a], having no support from other witnesses, may be an attempt to fill out the parallelism, with ילכו corresponding to נִבְקְעוּ. Tov attributes the plus of 1QIsa[a] to a scribal contextual change, derived "from the copyist's stylistic feelings"[43] and points out that all nouns in this verse, except for וּנְחָלִים ("streams"), are "assigned specific verbs. The scroll sensed the lack of a verb in this last clause and supplied

---

41 Tov, *Textual Criticism of the Hebrew Bible*, 260; see also Talmon, "Synonymous Readings," 335–83.

42 For a discussion of the forms of the name *Hezekiah* in 1QIsa[a], see Beegle, D. M. "Proper Names in the New Isaiah Scroll," *BASOR* 123 (1951): 28–9.

43 Tov, *Textual Criticism of the Hebrew Bible*, 263. See also Pulikottil, *Transmission of Biblical Texts in Qumran*, 79.

it, thus filling a conceptual void."[44] But Blenkinsopp prefers this plus of 1QIsaᵃ, and thus translates the bicolon as "Yes, water will burst forth in the desert, wadis flow (ילכו) in the wilderness."[45] MT, followed by the versions, has the primary reading.

Particles איך and איכה

• 1QIsaᵃ היכה | MT אֵיכָ֫ה 1:21

אֵיכָ֫ה—The particles אֵיךְ (61x in MT), אֵיכָה (17x in MT), אֵיכָכָה (4x in MT), and הֵיךְ (2x in MT) are exclamatory interrogatives meaning "how." In the verse under discussion, 1QIsaᵃ's unique reading היכה is a derivation of הֵיךְ, which appears only in late BH texts (Dan. 10:17, 1 Chron. 13:12). 1QIsaᵃ's היכה may have been influenced by Aramaic[46] or it is a hybrid of איכה and הי.[47] See also Isaiah 14:12, where the scroll reads היכה, versus MT's אֵיךְ. Elsewhere in Isaiah, MT has אֵיךְ where 1QIsaᵃ reads איכה (Isa. 14:4; 36:9 [MT = 2 Kings 18:24]; 48:11 [MT = 4QIsaᵈ]). Only twice does MT and the scroll have the equivalent reading of the particle אֵיךְ (Isa. 19:11; 20:6).

Orthographic Variants

• 1QIsaᵃ יהיליל | MT יְיֵלִיל 15:3

יְיֵלִיל—The deviation between MT (= יְיֵלִיל) and 1QIsaa (= יהיליל) is orthographic. The root letters are ילל for both words and both have the same translational values. Note that in Isaiah 52:5, MT sets forth יְהֵילִ֫ילוּ with the infixed he, as it is found in 1QIsaᵃ in the verse under discussion. For two textual variants of √ילל that exist between these two Hebrew witnesses, see 23:1 and 52:5.

Presentative Exclamations

• 4QIsaᵃ הן | 1QIsaᵃ MT הִנֵּה 20:6

הִנֵּה—הן and הִנֵּה are presentative exclamations that serve to give emphasis to "the immediacy, the here-and-now-ness, of the situation."[48]

---

44 Paulson Pulikottil, *Transmission of Biblical Texts in Qumran: The Case of the Large Isaiah Scroll 1QIsaa* (Sheffield: Sheffield Academic Press, 2001), 79.

45 Blenkinsopp, *Isaiah 1–39*, 455.

46 See Michael Sokoloff, *A Dictionary of Jewish Babylonian Aramaic of the Talmudic and Geonic Periods* (Ramat-Gan, Israel: Bar Ilan University Press, 2002), 377.

47 Kutscher, *The Language and Linguistic Background of the Isaiah Scroll*, 390.

48 T. O. Lambdin, *Introduction to Biblical Hebrew* (New York: Scribner, 1971), 168.

In the Bible, הנה is ten times more common than הן (approximately 1,060 occurrences of הנה versus 100 attestations of הן), with הן found most often in the books of Job (32 times) and Isaiah (27 times). There is no difference in meaning or use between the two presentatives.[49] MT and 1QIsaᵃ deviate with הן and הנה in the following verses: 23:13; 32:1; 38:17; 41:24, 29; 42:1; 44:11; 49:16, 21; 50:1–2, 9 bis, 11; 54:15–16 (MTqere הִנֵּה); 55:4–5; 56:3; 58:4; 59:1; 64:4, 8. With the exception of 38:17, MT reads הן versus 1QIsaᵃ, which has הנה. In 38:17, MT attests הנה and 1QIsaᵃ reads הן. These deviations (a) indicate a different scribal school; (b) that the *Vorlage* of the scroll read הנה; or (c) the 1QIsaᵃ scribe had a tendency to popularize הן to read הנה.

Abbreviated Form מני

• 1QIsaᵃ ממני | MT מני 22:4

ממני—מני is a common form in the Bible, occurring approximately one hundred eighty times. Contrast ממני with the abbreviated מני (vocalized as מֶנִּי), which is found only in Isaiah 22:4; 30:1; 38:12; Psalms 18:23; 65:4; 139:19; Job 16:6; 21:16; 22:18; and 30:10. For MT's three occurrences of מני in Isaiah, 1QIsaᵃ reads ממני in 22:4 and 30:1, but equals MT with its reading of מני in Isaiah 38:12. The translational value of מני and ממני are the same, as indicated by Ibn Ezra in his commentary to Isaiah 30:1.

Prepositions עַד and עדי

• 1QIsaᵃ עדי . . . עדי | ([עד] . . . עד) MT 4QIsaᶜ עַד . . . עַד 26:5

עַד . . . עַד—For this preposition that is attested in MT and 4QIsaᶜ, 1QIsaᵃ has the older form עדי.[50] The translational value is the same for both עַד and עדי, although suffixed forms (וְעָרֶיךָ, עָרֶיהָ, עָרֵיכֶם, etc.) of the preposition were built upon עדי. For the reading עדי ארץ in 1QIsaᵃ 26:5, compare Psalms 147:6 (עֲדֵי־אָרֶץ).

Morphological Forms בעורה and בעורנה

• 1QIsaᵃ בעורנה | MT בְּעוֹדָהּ 28:4

בְּעוֹדָהּ—Both MT (= בְּעוֹדָהּ) and 1QIsaᵃ (= בעורנה with an unetymological letter *nun*) are legitimate morphological forms, with both having the same translational value. Watts remarks that בעורנה is "a seemingly

49 See C. J. Labuschagne, "The Particles הן and הִנֵּה," *Oudtestamentische Studiën* 18 (1973): 1–14.

50 See Waltke and O'Connor, *An Introduction to Biblical Hebrew Syntax*, 215.

meaningless *nun* epenthetic before the suffix."[51] For the form בעורנה, see also 1 Kings 1:22.

Conclusion

1QIsa[a] contains a great number of textual variants, which may be categorized as follows: (1) accidental errors; (2) intentional changes; (3) synonymous readings; and (4) scribes' stylistic approaches. These four categories include multiple examples of haplography, homoioteleuton, dittography, confusion of letters (graphic similarity), conflation, pluses, minuses, misdivision of words, interchange of letters (metathesis), transposition of word order, possible ligature, exegetical or editorial pluses, synonymous readings, changes to proper names, improper division of letters, filling out a poetic parallelism, morphological smoothing and updating, euphemistic changes, harmonizations, phonetic variants, peculiar orthographic variants, and modernizations of terms. The textual variants of 1QIsa[a] sets forth such a wide diversity and assortment of textual variants that this scroll is indeed a catalogue, as it were, for textual criticism.

Donald W. Parry, *Professor of Hebrew Bible Studies, holds the Abraham O. Smoot Professorship at Brigham Young University. He is a member of the International Team of Translators of the Dead Sea Scrolls and author or (co)editor of a number of books and articles on the scrolls and the Hebrew Bible.*

---

51   Watts, *Isaiah 1–33*, 360.

Count Your Many Mormons: Mormon's Personalized and Personal Messages in Mosiah 18 and 3 Nephi 5

Nathan J. Arp

Abstract: *The present work analyzes the narrative art Mormon employs, specifically Mormon's unique strategies for personalized and personal messaging, which can be seen in how Mormon connects the narration of the baptism at the waters of Mormon in Mosiah chapter 18 with his self-introductory material in 3 Nephi chapter 5. In these narratives, Mormon seems to simultaneously present an overt personalized message about Christ and a covert personal connection to Alma$_1$ through the almost excessive repetition of his own name. Mormon discreetly plants evidence to suggest his intention for the careful re-reader to discover that Mormon was a 12th generation descendant of the first Alma. Mormon's use of personalizing and personal messages lends emotive power to his narratives and shines a light on Mormon's love for Christ's church.*

As "Another Testament of Jesus Christ," the narratives of the Book of Mormon of course focus on Christ; however, the strategies its authors use to direct our attention to Christ also shed light on these authors. Remarkably, our attention on the authors doesn't distract us from Christ but actually proffers the unique view of Christ as can only be seen through a personal lens. In contrast to the Bible, which "exhibits such a rage for impersonality as must lead to the conclusion that its writers actively sought the cover of anonymity,"[1] Mormon, like the other

---

1. Meir Sternberg, *The Poetics of Biblical Narrative: Ideological Literature and the Drama of Reading* (Bloomington: Indiana University Press, 1985), 65. This paper is heavily influenced by Sternberg's approach; however, I would not have known about Sternberg's work without the influence of Heather and Grant Hardy's publications, in particular "Another Testament of Jesus Christ: Mormon's

Book of Mormon narrators, has a different approach. He personalizes his messages — enters into the text as a person — for the reader through the use of the first person pronoun ("I" and "we")[2] and his own name to punctuate key theological points for the reader. Brant Gardner calls this interaction with the future reader Mormon's "author-voice," as opposed to the "narrator-voice," which he uses when "writing about the past."[3] In this paper, I am magnifying Gardner's concept of the "author-voice" to distinguish between two similar but distinct voices: a *personalized* and a *personal* voice. In the connected passages in Mosiah 18 and 3 Nephi 5, Mormon uses the repetition of his own name as part of a powerfully personalized message to the reader about Christ. Mormon makes use of his personal presence in the text to teach the reader about Christ — what I call a *personalized* message. In these same chapters (Mosiah 18 and 3 Nephi 5), Mormon also uses the repetition of his name as a key to unraveling a more subtle, personal message, not necessarily a message focused on Christ, but a message primarily about the person Mormon. This is what I call a *personal* message — a message about the person, Mormon. This paper presents the idea that Mormon discreetly leads the careful reader towards a personal message about a genealogical connection between himself and Alma$_1$[4] under his more overt message about Christ. Mormon's careful narrative strategies seem to suggest that he intended the reader to discover that Mormon was a 12th generation descendant of Alma. Mormon's personal and personalized messages align to maintain a continued focus on Christ and speak to the reader with unique, emotive power that Jesus is the Christ.

Poetics," *Journal of Book of Mormon Studies 16, no. 2 (2007)* and *Understanding the Book of Mormon: A Reader's Guide* (New York: Oxford University Press, 2010). I was impressed by Grant Hardy's acknowledgement of his wife's role in unofficially co-authoring *Understanding the Book of Mormon* on page IX, and so I refer to the Hardys as authors of that work throughout this article.

2. Some examples: Mosiah 8:1, Mosiah 23:23, Alma 24:30, Alma 30:60, Alma 43:3, Alma 53:10, Helaman 3:27, Helaman 12:2–3, 3 Nephi 5:12–20, 3 Nephi 7:1, 3 Nephi 26:12, 3 Nephi 28:24, and 4 Nephi 1:23.

3. Brant A. Gardner, "Labor Diligently to Write: The Ancient Making of a Modern Scripture" in *Interpreter: A Journal of Latter-Day Saint Faith and Scholarship* 35 (2020), 68, https://journal.interpreterfoundation.org/labor-diligently-to-write-the-ancient-making-of-a-modern-scripture-2/.

4. I am following the Hardys and others in the use of subscripts to help distinguish characters in the Book of Mormon who share the same name. Hardy and Hardy, *Understanding Book of Mormon*, 295–96n5.

What Counting 12 Mormons in Mosiah 18
Could Mean in Connection to 3 Nephi 5

The baptisms at the waters of Mormon are a watershed moment in the history of the people of Nephi. It was in "the land of Mormon," where "Alma did establish the church among the people" (3 Nephi 5:12). This church is the most precious possession the Nephites passed down through their lineage. Righteous Nephites gave everything else they had to preserve it. The significance of this place and this moment is emphasized through Mormon's personal approval. As our narrator, Mormon is the authority for most of the messages of the Book of Mormon. In the description of the baptisms of Alma's covert converts in the 18th chapter of Mosiah, Mormon employs some of his most direct engagement with the text — in an engagement both unique and personally powerful, he repeats his name. Through repeating his name a staggering 12 times in 26 verses (Mosiah 18:4–30), Mormon the person becomes the setting, the authorized witness condoning the event, and connects himself to its agent, Alma₁.⁵ Mormon's presence rises to its most salient in verse 30, where the reader can almost hear Mormon calling to us through the ink.

> And now it came to pass that all this was done in Mormon,
> yea, by the waters of Mormon,
> in the forest that was near the waters of Mormon,
> yea, the place of Mormon, the waters of Mormon, the forest
> of Mormon.
> How beautiful are they to the eyes of them
> who there came to the knowledge of their Redeemer!
> Yea, and how blessed are they,
> for they shall sing to his praise forever. (Mosiah 18:30)⁶

5. "The narrator's participation ensures the appearance of one member whose reliability is beyond doubt — an authorized reference-point to which we may safely appeal in order to sort out and motivate the versions originating in the other participants." Sternberg, *Poetics of Biblical Narrative*, 413. Mormon's presence, via his repeated name, in Mosiah 18 signifies Mormon presenting Alma to the reader as his authorized voice.

6. All quotes from the Book of Mormon are from *The Book of Mormon: The Earliest Text*, ed. Royal Skousen (New Haven, CT: Yale University Press, 2009). I have used this version of the Book of Mormon because it is currently "the definitive scholarly version of the Book of Mormon," as defined by Grant Hardy in its introduction. Skousen, *The Earliest Text*, xvii.

The Hardys note that this passage's "mesmerizing, almost incantatory repetition" is "uncharacteristically effusive" for Mormon.[7] Generally, Mormon's narrative is so characteristically terse that any deviation from the norm, like what we see here, should arrest the reader's attention.[8] Such blatant repetition invites the reader to hypothesize possible reasons that would prompt Mormon to resort to this level of personal engagement. In fact, the excessive repetition of his own name in this narrative is as personalizing for Mormon as his use of "I" or "I, Mormon." After this excessive repetition, Mormon employs an opposing strategy for communicating with the reader: silence. Mormon does not explain the overwhelming presence of his name in Mosiah 18 until 3 Nephi 5:12, a textual gap of some 200 pages.[9] Although Mormon as a setting appears a few more times between these two passages, Mormon, as a self-reference, is absent.[10] Both the excess and the absence of Mormon's name are circumstantial pieces of evidence that support this paper's

---

7. Hardy and Hardy, *Understanding Book of Mormon*, 96.

8. Sternberg observed, "[T]he Bible's verbal artistry, without precedent in literary history and unrivaled since, operates by passing off its art for artlessness, its sequential linkages and supra-sequential echoes for unadorned parataxis, its density of evocation for chronicle-like thinness and transparency" (Sternberg, *Poetics of Biblical Narrative*, 53). The Bible's narratives, according to Robert Alter, make use of a "striking artistic economy," where "the specification of external circumstances, setting, and gesture is held to a bare minimum" (Robert Alter, *The Art of Biblical Narrative* [New York: Basic Books, 2011], 42). Alter further suggests that as modern readers, "we have to readjust our habits … in order to bring an adequate attentiveness to the rather different narrative maneuvers that are characteristic of the Hebrew Bible" (Alter, *Art of Biblical Narrative*, 162). Readers of the Book of Mormon must also adjust their approaches, otherwise we can miss important and intended messages.

9. Mormon's excessive repetition of his name in Mosiah 18 occurs on pages 181–83, and his commentary on his name doesn't occur until 3 Nephi 5:12 on page 416, according to a 1995 print version of *The Book of Mormon: Another Testament of Jesus Christ* (Salt Lake City: The Church of Jesus Christ of Latter-day Saints, 1995).

10. 3 Nephi 5 is likely the first time Mormon introduces himself in our current Book of Mormon because of the loss of the 116 pages. The 116 manuscript pages were the actual beginning of Mormon's abridgment of the Book of Mormon. The book, the Words of Mormon, in which Mormon does introduce himself by name, which precedes the book of Mosiah in our current Book of Mormon, was originally at the end of the record attached to the small plates. Mormon's first introduction was likely in the beginning of his abridgment and part of the lost manuscript pages. Therefore, without having his first hypothetical introduction, 3 Nephi is his first introduction. For a discussion on some puzzling phenomena concerning the Words of Mormon, please see Gardner, "Labor Diligently to Write," 129–32.

claim that Mormon intentionally marked these passages with his name and their content to connect them. When Mormon finally resorts to using his name, he uses it to explain a connection to the establishment of the church and Alma₁ in Mosiah 18:[11]

> ... I am called Mormon,
> being called after the land of Mormon,
> the land in which Alma did establish the church among this
> people. (3 Nephi 5:12)

Mormon also manifests a "strikingly personal connection to history"[12] when he demonstrates to the reader his awareness of his sacred role in Nephite history, a role he is emphasizing by his personal presence:

> And it hath become expedient
> that I, according to the will of God
> —that the prayers of those who have gone hence,
> which were the holy ones,
> should be fulfilled according to their faith—
> should make a record of these things which have been done
> (3 Nephi 5:14)

After more than 400 years, Mormon *the setting* becomes *the person* determined to ensure that the legacy of the waters of Mormon makes it to the future. Mormon expounds upon his sacred role as record keeper in preserving these records for the future by referencing the promises made to the seed of Joseph and Jacob (Israel), that they will be brought back to a knowledge of the Lord their God. The promises made to the seed of Joseph are emphasized in the Book of Mormon because the Nephites and Lamanites were descendants of Joseph through Manasseh. And like those at the waters of Mormon "who there came to the knowledge of their Redeemer" (Mosiah 18:30) because of the person Mormon, who passed on the Nephite record, the seed of Jacob shall also come

---

11. Mormon interrupts the narrative to comment directly to the reader in multiple places, but he does not name drop ("I, Mormon") between these two places (Mosiah 18 and 3 Nephi 5) — a divide of more than 200 pages. The extreme repetitions of the name *Mormon* in Mosiah 18 and Mormon's extreme delay in inserting his name again in the narrative are tangentially related, but in concert with the connection in content — the land of Mormon — suggests an intentional, purposeful link between the two passages. 3 Nephi 5:12 is the only place in the extant Book of Mormon where Mormon calls the reader's attention to the origin of his name explicitly. Mormon's name as a setting appears in Mosiah 25:18, Mosiah 26:15, Alma 5:3, and Alma 21:1.

12. Hardy and Hardy, *Understanding Book of Mormon*, 94.

to "know their Redeemer, who is Jesus Christ" (3 Nephi 5:26). This is Mormon's personalized message of Christ. It is part of his sustained message throughout the Book of Mormon, for which Mormon speaks to us directly, so we cannot misunderstand.[13] He wants his message about Christ to carry forth and reconvert the children of Israel, particularly the descendants of Lehi (the remaining Lamanite and Nephite descendants).[14]

In both 3 Nephi 5 and Mosiah 18, Mormon likely inserts his name into the record to unlock a personal message as well. Like his repetitions of his name in Mosiah 18, Mormon uses his name in 3 Nephi 5:12 to again connect himself to Alma$_1$ and the church: "I am called Mormon, being called after the land of Mormon, the land in which Alma did establish the church." He also employs his name to add significance to his ancestry: "I am Mormon and a pure descendant of Lehi" (3 Nephi 5:20). Regarding 3 Nephi 5:20, Brant Gardner observed that "the reference to being a 'pure descendant of Lehi' is interesting from a genealogical/historical viewpoint" and posited that "perhaps [Mormon] could have traced descendance through one thousand years."[15] But interestingly, he does not provide a full account of his genealogy, apart from saying his father was also named Mormon (Mormon 1:5). These two instances of Mormon's name in 3 Nephi 5, and the 12 times his name appears in Mosiah 18 are meant to mark an aspect of Mormon he means for us to connect: his genealogical relationship to Alma$_1$.

Mormon provides information about Alma and his own ancestry in a uniquely binding way, and likewise he gives Alma's age with a reference to Nephite chronology, something Mormon also allows for few others besides himself. I propose that Mormon's excessive repetition of his name (12 times) in Mosiah 18 is a numerical key for identifying Alma and Mormon's relationship in terms of generations — they are 12 generations apart.

---

13. The concept of foolproof messaging was inspired by Sternberg, *Poetics of Biblical Narrative*, 50.

14. This same purpose is described in the title page of the Book of Mormon.

15. Gardner, "Labor Diligently to Write," 335, https://journal. interpreterfoundation.org/labor-diligently-to-write-the-ancient-making-of-a-modern-scripture-7/. Anita Wells, in discussing the Book of Mormon's archival tradition, also noted the oddity in the lack of lineage in the Book of Mormon in her article "Bare Record: The Nephite Archivist, The Record of Records, and the Book of Mormon Provenance," *Interpreter: A Journal of Mormon Scripture*, 24 (2017): 113–16, https://journal.interpreterfoundation.org/bare-record-the-nephite-archivist-the-record-of-records-and-the-book-of-mormon-provenance/.

A Descendent of Nephi: Alma and Mormon Connect

When Mormon introduces Alma$_1$ to the reader during the unjust trial of the prophet Abinadi, he makes an interesting interjection: "But there was one among them whose name was Alma, he also being a descendent of Nephi" (Mosiah 16:2).[16] The use of "also" here seems to be a personalized reference to Mormon. There is no one else in this particular account that Mormon describes as a descendent of Nephi. Given that Alma is a part of a Nephite colony in Nephite ancestral lands, Mormon's description of Alma as "also being a descendant of Nephi" (Mosiah 17:2) is unnecessary unless he was making a personal connection.[17] Mormon is telling us that both he and Alma are descendants of Nephi. This would not be such a unique designation if Mormon had not wanted it to be. Mormon describes only two people in the Book of Mormon specifically as descendants of Nephi — Alma and himself (see Mormon 1:5).[18] In a work detailing largely the history of the descendants of Nephi and a people who called themselves Nephites, it is significant that Mormon limits the epithet of "descendant of Nephi" to only Alma and himself. It is more common for a person to be designated as a descendant of Mulek or Zarahemla; this is expected, as these connections provide a more useful identification. The description unique to Alma and Mormon points to an intentionality on Mormon's part to make sure the reader could connect him with Alma as kin. They both descended from the same primogenitor.

---

16. Note that Mormon's introduction of Alma, "there was one among them whose name was …" is identical to Mormon's introduction of Zeezrom (Alma 10:31). Mormon also uses the exact phrase "there was one among them" to introduce Aminadab (Helaman 5:35–39). Similarly, Mormon uses the phrase "there was a man among them whose name was … " to introduce Abinadi (Mosiah 11:20) and Gideon (Mosiah 19:4). I don't think that this is coincidence.

17. Daniel L. Belnap, "The Abinadi Narrative, Redemption, and the Struggle for Nephite Identity," in *Abinadi: He Came among Them in Disguise*, ed. Shon D. Hopkins (Provo, UT: Religious Studies Center, Brigham Young University and Salt Lake City: Deseret Book, 2018), 27–66.

18. Amulek identifies himself as a descendant of Nephi in one of his speeches to the people, but this was not a description Mormon gave him (see Alma 10:2-3). In addition, the original title heading to the Third Book of Nephi includes the genealogy of the record keepers after Alma$_1$. Moroni also emphasizes Mormon's lineage to Nephi in Mormon 8:13. It is interesting to note that Moroni only references Mormon's ancestral connection to Nephi and not his own. It is possible that Moroni knew of his father's personal message and didn't want to confuse it with his own personal messages.

Counting Years in Nephite Chronology:
Alma and Mormon Connect Again

Mormon's connection to Alma is also evident in his choice to include Alma and his own age in relationship to the chronology in the Nephite record. In the first year of the reign of the judges, which was "five hundred and nine years from the time Lehi left Jerusalem," or about 91 BC, Alma died at the age of 82 years old; therefore, Alma was born around 173 BC (see Mosiah 29:45–46). In around 321 AD, Mormon was 10 years old and received his commission from Ammaron to be the next Nephite record keeper (see 4 Nephi 1:48–49 and Mormon 1:1–5). Consequently, Mormon was born approximately in 311 AD. Although Alma and Mormon are not the only people Mormon allows a connection between recorded ages and the Nephite chronology, this connection is still limited and, therefore, possible evidence of an intended signal from Mormon to the reader.[19] Mormon and Alma are connected to history as well as to each other.

Because of Mormon's interest in sharing these connections with Alma in both genealogy and chronology, Mormon's seemingly hyperbolic repetition of his name (12 times) in Mosiah chapter 18 may also be connected to chronology. That is, Mormon might be subtly revealing that he is a 12th generation descendant of Alma and that this relationship may also be linked in chronology. Because we know when Alma was born and when Mormon was born, we know these births were approximately 484 years apart, which almost exactly matches an interval of 40 years for each generation (12 generations x 40 years= 480 years). A 40-year interval between generations is credible seeing that it is used in the ancient Near East, the world of the Hebrew Bible and the original setting of the Book of Mormon. K.A. Kitchen explains, "The 40-year full generation comprises 20 years for one group to grow up to childbearing age, and then 20 years for their children to reach the same age (this lies behind Numbers 14:33)."[20]

---

19. Another example is Mosiah$_2$, whose age is memorialized in Nephite chronology in Mosiah 29:46. Moroni1 is given an age when he started as the Chief Captain of the Nephite's military, but his age is not set in chronology (see Alma 43:16–17).

20. K. A. Kitchen, *On the Reliability of the Old Testament* (Grand Rapids, MI: William B. Eerdmans Publishing, 2003), 307.

Alma, Alma and Mormon, Mormon:
Yet Another Possible Connection

Furthermore, when Mormon announces that he is a descendant of Nephi, he interjects that his father's name was Mormon too (Mormon 1:5). This extraneous interjection is unnecessary to the storyline and may signify Mormon's interest in an additional literary connection between himself and Alma$_2$ who, like Mormon, was named after his father Alma$_1$. This connection would be significant considering the fact that Mormon chooses Alma$_2$ as the preferred voice for the gospel preached in the Book of Mormon.[21] In the same way that Mormon is the setting for the first Alma's baptisms, the second Alma is the voice for Mormon. According to Michael F. Perry, the second Alma's voice is key to Mormon's strategy to show the word of God was more powerful "than the sword, or anything else" (Alma 31:5).[22] Alma's preaching dominates the Book of Mormon's ecclesiastical landscape so fully that the only other voice in the Book of Mormon as prevalent is that of Nephi$_1$, who is a first-person author of two books within the Book of Mormon.[23] One can get a sense of why Mormon may have chosen the second Alma as his preferred preacher by the literary quality of his sermons. It is Alma who recorded a chiasmus in Alma chapter 36 that John W. Welch has described as "a masterpiece of composition, as good as any other use of chiasmus in world literature, and it deserves wide recognition and appreciation."[24]

---

21. The Hardys note Mormon's admiration of Alma$_2$ in *Understanding the Book of Mormon*, 94 and 105. Michael F. Perry also highlights Alma's dominance in the Book of Mormon in "The Supremacy of the Word: Alma's Mission to the Zoramites and the Conversion of the Lamanites," *Journal of Book of Mormon Studies* 24 (2015): 119–37.

22. Perry, "Supremacy of the Word", 119–37.

23. John L. Hilton, "On Verifying Wordprint Studies: Book of Mormon Authorship," in *Book of Mormon Authorship Revisited: The Evidence for Ancient Origins* (Provo, UT: Foundation for Ancient Research and Mormon Studies), 225–54.

24. John W. Welch, "A Masterpiece: Alma 36," in *Rediscovering the Book of Mormon*, ed. John L. Sorenson and Melvin J. Thorne (Salt Lake City: Deseret Book, 1991), 116. In response to criticism leveled against the existence of a chiasmus in Alma 36, Noel B. Reynolds not only defended its existence using Hebrew rhetorical principles, but also concluded that the "powerful conjunction of rhetorical form, personal transformation, and doctrinal teaching establishes Alma 36 as one of the greatest literary gems of the Book of Mormon." See Reynolds's "Rethinking Alma 36," *Interpreter: A Journal of Latter-day Saint Faith and Scholarship* 34 (2020): 279–312, https://journal.interpreterfoundation.org/rethinking-alma-36/.

Conclusion

In tandem with his primary message, which is already personal, Mormon divulged more details about himself that he may not have wanted to interfere with his strategy for a more direct and "foolproof composition"[25] to preach of Christ. As proposed in this paper, Mormon may have felt that his own genealogy was not the primary message, so he chose to submerge these details underneath the main narrative. This way he could still express his connection with Alma but without distracting the reader from his primary message about Christ. These narrative techniques lend an air of authenticity to Mormon's narrative presence in the Book of Mormon. Mormon's own authenticity witnesses to the authenticity of the work that bears his name and strengthens his argument for a Christ.

As Mormon's readers, we can come to Christ not only through the doctrine Mormon taught through the history of his people but also through learning more about Mormon, someone who loved Christ and spent his whole life in Christ's service. Mormon's method of combining his personalized message about Christ with personal details speaks powerfully to us from the dust, as prophesied (Isaiah 29:4).[26] On a personal note, Mormon and the other narrators' personal engagement with me, as a reader, combined with personal spiritual witnesses convinced me of their reality and prepared me to eventually accept the reality of God and his son, Jesus Christ.

[*Author's note: The title of this article makes a play on the popular hymn, "Count Your Many Blessings," found at https://www.churchofjesuschrist.org/music/library/hymns/count-your-blessings. In the spirit of counting blessings, I am grateful to my friend Katherine and my brother David for their efforts in wordsmithing my first drafts and my rewrite. Similarly, thank you to the* Interpreter's *peer reviewers for their helpful suggestions that guided this paper to be the best it could be. Additionally, I express a heart-felt thank you to Leslie Reynolds, whose constant encouragement brought this paper to life. And finally, thank you to my friend Spencer, who first introduced me to the academic world of The Church of Jesus Christ of Latter-day Saints two decades ago.*]

Nathan J. Arp *graduated from Brigham Young University with a BA in Chinese language and literature. As a member of The Church of Jesus Christ of Latter-day Saints, Nathan has been enamored by the Church's*

---

25. Sternberg, *Poetics of Biblical Narrative*, 50.
26. See Isaiah 29:4; 2 Nephi 26:15; 2 Nephi 27:13; 2 Nephi 33:10; Mormon 8:26.

scriptures for decades. He has been a longtime consumer of scholarly publications about the scriptures and is grateful for this opportunity to participate in the process of production. When not in an office cubicle, he can be found laughing with his wife, wrestling with their children, or playing with words.

Notes on Mormonism and the Trinity

Daniel C. Peterson

Abstract: *With "awe, humility, and circumspection," Daniel C. Peterson provides a useful summary and discussion of Latter-day Saint beliefs as they relate to traditional Christian conceptions of the Trinity. In particular, his discussions reveals the many nuances of the questions raised, including the precise nature of the unity of the three persons of the Godhead and how the overall conception relates to doctrines of salvation and practical discipleship, which continued to be a controversial issue in both the Eastern and Western Churches for centuries. Peterson argues that the Latter-day Saint doctrine affirms both biblical precedents and, to a degree, some modern theological trends such as social theories of the Trinity.*

[**Editor's Note:** Part of our book chapter reprint series, this article is reprinted here as a service to the LDS community. Original pagination and page numbers have necessarily changed, otherwise the reprint has the same content as the original.

See Daniel C. Peterson, "Notes on Mormonism and the Trinity," in *"To Seek the Law of the Lord": Essays in Honor of John W. Welch,* ed. Paul Y. Hoskisson and Daniel C. Peterson (Orem, UT: The Interpreter Foundation, 2017), 267–316. Further information at https://interpreterfoundation. org/books/to-seek-the-law-of-the-lord-essays-in-honor-of-john-w-welch-2/.]

I approach this topic humbly, both because I am by no means an expert in the dauntingly complex area of trinitarian theology — St. Augustine, it is said, once quipped that anybody who denied the Trinity risked losing salvation, but that anybody who tried to understand the Trinity risked losing his mind — and because, of all subjects, the nature and character of God *should* be approached with awe, humility, and circumspection. Augustine also advised those who enter into this subject to "remember who we are, and of Whom we speak."[1] In this context, Alister McGrath's caution is worth taking to heart: "There is," he says,

> a tendency on the part of many—especially those of a more philosophical inclination—to talk about God as if he was some sort of *concept*. But it is much more accurate to think of God as someone we *experience* or *encounter*. God isn't an idea we can kick about in seminar rooms—he is a living reality who enters into our experience and transforms it.[2]

Nonetheless, we now proceed.

LDS Rejection of the Trinity?

It is often said, by both advocates and detractors of Mormonism, that The Church of Jesus Christ of Latter-day Saints rejects the doctrine of the Trinity.[3] After all, didn't Joseph Smith claim to see two distinct

---

This paper was originally written for (partial) presentation at a conference on Mormon theology held at the Divinity School of Yale University, in New Haven, Connecticut, in March 2003. It benefited from suggestions from Carl Griffin, Benjamin Huff, and Marc-Charles Ingerson, as well as from a pre-publication reading of Barry R. Bickmore's essay "Of Simplicity, Oversimplification, and Monotheism," a review of Paul Owen, "Monotheism, Mormonism, and the New Testament Witness," in *The New Mormon Challenge: Responding to the Latest Defenses of a Fast Growing Movement*, ed. Francis J. Beckwith, Carl Mosser, and Paul Owen (Grand Rapids: Zondervan, 2002), 271–314, that eventually appeared in the *FARMS Review* 15, no. 1 (2003): 215–58. Bickmore's discussion is highly relevant to the topic treated here. It then appeared, in somewhat different form, in the journal of the Society for Mormon Philosophy and Theology, *Element* 3, no. 1–2 (Spring and Fall 2007).

1   Augustine, *Sermons on Selected Lessons of the New Testament*, Sermon 2, "Of the Words of St. Matthew's gospel, chap. 3:13, 'Then Jesus cometh from Galilee to the Jordan unto John, to be baptized of Him,' Concerning the Trinity," trans. R. G. MacMullen, NPNF First Series (Peabody, MA: Hendrickson, 1994), 6:262. See Roger E. Olson and Christopher A. Hall, *The Trinity* (Grand Rapids: Eerdmans, 2002), on Augustine's insistence that intellectual ability must be accompanied by holiness of character when seeking spiritual and theological insight.

2   Alister E. McGrath, *Understanding the Trinity* (Grand Rapids: Zondervan, 1988), 13 (italics in the original).

3   That Latter-day Saints reject the Trinity is so uncontroversial that the claim even shows up, rather casually mentioned, in such places as Wayne Grudem, *Systematic Theology: An Introduction to Biblical Doctrine* (Leicester and Grand Rapids: InterVarsity and Zondervan, 1994), 407. In what follows, I have used *Latter-day Saint* and *Mormon* interchangeably. I have also used *Holy Spirit* in preference to *Holy Ghost*, although *Holy Ghost* is the standard locution of English-speaking Latter-day Saints, in deference to

personages in his 1820 First Vision?[4] Didn't he produce, in his Book of Abraham, a creation narrative that frankly speaks not of a singular God but of "the Gods" as the agents of creation?[5] "In the beginning," he taught in his most famous sermon, "the head of the Gods called a council of the Gods; and they came together and concocted a plan to create the world and people it."[6] Didn't he, in a sermon delivered less than two weeks before his martyrdom, deny the divine unity in unmistakably clear language? "I will preach on the plurality of Gods," he announced in Nauvoo, Illinois, on 16 June 1844.

> I wish to declare I have always and in all congregations when I have preached on the subject of the Deity, it has been the plurality of Gods. It has been preached by the Elders for fifteen years.

> I have always declared God to be a distinct personage, Jesus Christ a separate and distinct personage from God the Father, and that the Holy Ghost was a distinct personage and a Spirit: and these three constitute three distinct personages and three Gods. If this is in accordance with the New Testament, lo and behold! we have three Gods anyhow, and they are plural: and who can contradict it?[7]

On the basis of such passages, critics routinely proceed to argue that alleged Latter-day Saint rejection of the Trinity reveals Mormons to be tritheists (a charge that may or may not disturb the objects of the criticism) and even that Mormonism is therefore not Christian (a claim absolutely certain to disturb).

But this is all too simple. Although Latter-day Saints tend not to use the term *Trinity*, some Mormon authorities *have* employed the word to describe their belief in a Godhead of three persons. Thus, for example, here is Brigham Young, speaking of "the Father of us all, and the God and Father of our Lord Jesus Christ" at the Salt Lake Tabernacle in 1871:

---

what I take to be predominant usage in the wider Anglophone Christian world. Unless otherwise specified, all biblical quotations are from the New English Bible.

4   Joseph Smith – History 1:17. Joseph Smith – History is part of the canonical Latter-day Saint work known as the Pearl of Great Price.

5   Abraham 4–5. The Book of Abraham is also to be found in the Pearl of Great Price.

6   *Teachings of the Prophet Joseph Smith*, ed. Joseph Fielding Smith (Salt Lake City: Deseret Book, 1972), 349.

7   Joseph Smith, *History of the Church of Jesus Christ of Latter-day Saints* (Salt Lake City: Deseret Book, 1978), 6:474.

"Is he one? Yes. Is his trinity one? Yes."[8] Similarly, Apostle James E. Talmage's quasi-canonical treatise on *The Articles of Faith* contains several references to Godhead as a "trinity."[9] Furthermore, canonical texts peculiar to Mormonism assert the unity of Father, Son, and Holy Spirit at least as strongly as does the Bible itself. An April 1830 revelation to Joseph Smith, for instance, affirms that "Father, Son, and Holy Ghost are one God, infinite and eternal, without end."[10] The Book of Mormon concurs, declaring (with an interesting use of the singular verb) that "the Father, and...the Son, and...the Holy Ghost...*is* one God, without end."[11] The impressive testimony of the Three Witnesses to the Book of Mormon, published in every printing of the book since the 1830 first edition, concludes by ascribing "honor...to the Father, and to the Son, and to the Holy Ghost, which is one God."[12] "I am in the Father," says the Lord to Joseph Smith in an 1833 revelation, "and the Father in me, and the Father and I are one."[13] "Monotheism," explained the late apostle Bruce R. McConkie in his influential and oft-reprinted 1958 work *Mormon Doctrine,*

> is the doctrine or belief that there is but one God. If this is properly interpreted to mean that the Father, Son, and Holy Ghost — each of whom is a separate and distinct godly personage — are one God, meaning one Godhead, then true saints are monotheists.[14]

The question is, therefore, not whether Father, Son, and Holy Spirit are one in Mormon thought, but what the nature of their unity is.[15]

---

8   Brigham Young, "The One-Man Power—Unity—Free Agency—Priesthood and Government, Etc.," *Journal of Discourses* 14:92.

9   James E. Talmage, *The Articles of Faith* (Salt Lake City: The Church of Jesus Christ of Latter-day Saints, 1919), 38–47.

10   Doctrine and Covenants (D&C) 20:28

11   2 Ne. 31:21 (emphasis mine). Compare 3 Ne. 28:10.

12   In all Latter-day Saint editions of the Book of Mormon for many decades, the testimonial statement, endorsed by Oliver Cowdery, David Whitmer, and Martin Harris, has been included in the front matter.

13   D&C 93:3. Compare 3 Ne. 11:27, 36; John 17:21; 10:30.

14   Bruce R. McConkie, "Monotheism," in *Mormon Doctrine* (Salt Lake City: Bookcraft, 1958), 511, emphasis deleted.

15   Grudem, *Systematic Theology*, 248, is probably fairly typical in explaining that "Tritheism denies that there is only one God." If Grudem is correct, Latter-day Saints cannot be dismissed—in any simple way, at least—as tritheists, since they manifestly affirm the oneness of God.

The One and the Many

However, Latter-day Saints scarcely face this question alone. The precise nature of the divine unity is almost unanimously admitted to be unspecified, or underdetermined, in the New Testament.[16] The writers of the New Testament clearly affirm a relationship between Father, Son, and Holy Spirit. The Father's relationship to the Son is, obviously, paternal in some sense. And the Son's relationship to the Father is, plainly, in some sense filial. But in *what* sense? Is it literal, merely metaphorical, or something in between? Is the Father temporally prior to the Son, or not? Is the Father logically prior to the Son? What would that mean? Is the Son fully divine, or only derivatively so? And what are we to make of the Holy Spirit, which (or who) doesn't seem to be related to the Father as a Son or to the Son as a "brother"?

Alister McGrath contends that trinitarianism emerged inevitably out of reflection on the biblical data—"All that theologians have really done is to draw out something which is already there," he writes. "The doctrine of the Trinity wasn't *invented*—it was *uncovered*"—and there is little question that, in a certain sense at least, he is right.[17] But what kind of trinitarianism should it be? Certainly the developed Nicene doctrine of the Trinity is not to be found in the Bible. As the Jesuit theologian John Courtney Murray pointed out,

> The Christology of the New Testament was, in our contemporary word for it, functional. For instance, all the titles given to Christ the Son—Lord, Saviour, Word, Son of God, Son of man, Prophet, Priest—all these titles, in the sense that they bear in the New Testament, are relational. ... They do not explicitly define what he *is*, nor do they explicitly define what his relation to the Father is.[18]

The doctrine of the Trinity—the nature of the relationship between Father, Son, and Holy Spirit—has accordingly been among the most contentious issues in Christian history. "This most enigmatic of all Christian doctrines," Alister McGrath calls it.[19] Various accounts of that unity can be, and have been, constructed that accord more or

---

16 As will appear below, I disagree.

17 McGrath, *Understanding the Trinity*, 148, emphasis in original; compare pages 115–118, 130.

18 John Courtney Murray, *The Problem of God: Yesterday and Today* (New Haven: Yale University Press, 1964), 40, emphasis in original.

19 McGrath, *Understanding the Trinity*, 109 (compare page 93).

less with the biblically-imposed obligation to think monotheistically while simultaneously asserting the deity of three divine persons. For this reason, the story of trinitarianism is a tale of struggle, and often of mutual recrimination. Critics have dismissed mainstream trinitarian theology as "cosmic numerology" and classed it with astrology and other occult pseudo-sciences. Serious arguments have been mounted to demonstrate that classical trinitarianism is, in the strictest sense, logically incoherent.[20]

The mainstream Christian doctrine of the Trinity arises out of the strongly felt need to reconcile a strong commitment to the oneness of God—perhaps felt by sophisticated Hellenistic thinkers little less than by committed Jews (who had been struggling against circumambient pagan polytheism since at least their days in the Sinai)—with an equally strong sense of Jesus as a uniquely full earthly manifestation of the divine. "For," writes St. Augustine,

> the Truth would not say, Go, baptize all nations in the name of the Father and of the Son and of the Holy Spirit, unless Thou wast a Trinity. ...Nor would the divine voice have said, Hear, O Israel, the Lord thy God is one God, unless Thou wert so a Trinity as to be one Lord God.[21]

"Let us make man in our image and likeness," says the Genesis creation narrative, using plural language that trinitarian Christians have often seen as intratrinitarian.[22] "My Father and I are one," says the Johannine Jesus.[23]

How are these and many other relevant statements to be harmonized? Two relatively simple solutions, generally resisted since then by the vast majority of Christians, occurred quite early. Monarchianism—focused

---

20 See, for example, E. Feser, "Has Trinitarianism Been Shown to Be Coherent?" *Faith and Philosophy* 14, no. 1 (January 1997): 87–97. Compare Timothy W. Bartel, "The Plight of the Relative Trinitarian," *Religious Studies* 24, no. 2 (June 1988): 129–155. Attacking the coherency of trinitarian doctrine has, of course, been a staple of Muslim polemics for many centuries. A notable example has been published, with translation and commentary, as *Anti-Christian Polemic in Early Islam: Abu 'Isa al-Warraq's "Against the Trinity,"* trans. David Thomas (Cambridge: Cambridge University Press, 1992). At the time of my first draft of this paper, my then-colleague David Paulsen shared with me an interesting unpublished paper by Stephen T. Davis, entitled "Modes without Modalism," that seeks to sketch a view of the Trinity that is both faithful to mainstream Christian tradition and logically defensible.

21 Augustine, *On the Trinity*, NPNF 3:227. Augustine, of course, is citing Christ's instruction at Matt. 28:19, and the *shema* of Deut. 6:4.

22 Gen. 1:26.

23 John 10:30.

on the deity of the Father, usually granting that the Son was divine in a secondary sense (e.g., through adoption at the time of his baptism). Modalism — sometimes called Patripassianism in Western Christianity, but also known as modalistic monarchianism and (after Sabellius, a third-century Libyan priest and Christian theologian) Sabellianism — held that Father, Son, and Holy Spirit were simply manifestations, appearances, of the one God. The great fourth century heretical threat of Arianism might be viewed as a form of monarchianism, but its separation of Father from Son and Holy Spirit was so sharp that it can also be regarded as an incipient tritheism.

Mainstream teaching tried to navigate a middle way. In a sermon delivered between 379 and 381 AD, St. Gregory Nazianzus warned his fellow Christians that

> When I speak of God you must be illumined at once by one flash of light and by three....We would keep equally far from the confession of Sabellius and from the divisions of Arius, which evils are diametrically opposed yet equal in their wickedness. For what need is there heretically to fuse God together, or to cut Him up into inequality?[24]

Although passages that can surely be interpreted in a trinitarian fashion are easily located in first century writers like St. Clement of Rome, the full-blown doctrine of the Trinity cannot be found in Clement or in any of his contemporaries. In the early second century, the *Shepherd of Hermas* (which Irenaeus, Clement of Alexandria, and Origen all seem to have regarded as canonical) insisted that there is one and only one God, but manifestly did not quite know what to do with the Son and the Spirit. The church fathers of the second through the fourth centuries invented esoteric terms like *trinitas* and *homoousios*, and exploited difficult technical vocabulary such as *ousia* and *hypostasis*, as they confronted denials of the deity of Christ and the personality of the Holy Spirit. Most no doubt believed that they were simply teasing out the doctrine implicit in the biblical data, but it is unmistakably clear from our perch in the twenty-first century that their exegesis was conditioned (as exegesis always is) by the cultural milieu in which they worked. In the words of contemporary Protestant theologian Lynne Faber Lorenzen, "the original doctrine of the Trinity was indebted to the philosophical vocabulary and thought of its time and so was authentic

---

24 Gregory Nazianzus, Oration 39, NPNF ser. 2, 7:355–356.

to its context."[25] By "the original doctrine of the Trinity," she intends the concept spelled out in the fourth century at the great ecumenical council of Nicea (325 AD) and — after more than a half-century of controversy involving Arianism and Semi-Arianism — at the follow-up council of Constantinople (381 AD).

As William La Due observes,

> Nicaea did not settle the christological controversy by any means. As a matter of fact, for thirty years after the council, the term *homoóusios* was hardly used. Actually, Cyril of Jerusalem (ca. 315–86) was always uneasy about employing the Nicene terminology. Athanasius does not mention *homoóusios* in his work, *On the Incarnation*, written prior to 325, and it was not until his writings after 350 or so that he became an outspoken proponent of the Nicene formula. One of the causes of the problem over *homoóusios* was that the representatives at the council added no explanation as to the manner in which the term was to be understood.[26]

Some of the fathers rejected Nicea out of conservatism, because they felt that the new terminology went beyond the mandate of scripture. (The late Raymond Brown once noted that, by the time of Nicea, functional understanding of Christ and his role, in the manner of the Bible, had lost ground before an ontological one.[27] Some were presumably less pleased with that trend than others.) And indeed, along with the Bible, Platonism and Greek philosophy generally were to prove a major resource for early formulators of trinitarianism. A principal source for St. Augustine's *On the Trinity*, for instance, besides scripture, was Aristotle's *Categories*.[28] Thus, Augustine speaks of

> God as good without quality, as great without quantity, as the Creator who lacks nothing, who rules but from no position, and who contains all things without an external form, as being whole everywhere without limitation of space, as eternal

---

25　Lynne Faber Lorenzen, *The College Student's Introduction to the Trinity* (Collegeville: Liturgical Press, 1999), 3. The term *homoousios*, incidentally, appears to have been coined by Origen, one of the "Christian Platonists of Alexandria."

26　See William J. La Due, *The Trinity Guide to the Trinity* (Harrisburg: Trinity Press International, 2003), 43–44.

27　Raymond Brown, *An Introduction to New Testament Christology* (Mahwah, NJ: Paulist Press, 1994), 171.

28　The ancient Greek philosopher and scientist Aristotle (384–322 BC) was, of course, one of the greatest intellectual figures of Western history.

without time, as making mutable things without any change in Himself, and as a Being without passion.[29]

Augustine hereby rules out eight of Aristotle's ten categories, arguing that the divine being transcends them — leaving only substance and relation as applicable in discussions of the Trinity.

Resistance to philosophical and quasi-philosophical language persisted, however. Despite the fact that the documents produced by the Council of Constantinople avoided the term *homoousios*, preferring to use a vocabulary derived from scripture, Constantinople too left some uneasy.[30]

Nonetheless, the doctrine that emerged from these councils very quickly won wide acceptance across Christendom — an acceptance that it has maintained over the centuries — and it seems directly to contradict Joseph Smith's teaching of a plurality of Gods. "Whoever will be saved," says the Athanasian Creed, *quicunque vult salvus esse*, must

> worship one God in Trinity. ...The Father is God: the Son is God: and the Holy Spirit is God. And yet they are not three Gods: but one God.

Whoever fails to keep this doctrine "whole and inviolate," the Creed warns, "shall without doubt perish for eternity."[31]

Three centuries later, the Creed of the Eleventh Council of Toledo (AD 675) repeats that

> They are not three gods, he is one God....All three persons together are one God.[32]

In a sermon given at the Council of Constantinople, Gregory Nazianzus advised his hearers as follows:

---

29 Augustine, *On the Trinity*, 285.

30 Significantly, the term is also seldom used by St. Hilary of Poitiers (ca. 315–367) in his work *On the Trinity*.

31 Symbolum Quicunque ("The Athanasian Creed"), 1–3, 15–16. The original Latin text of the document is conveniently accessible, along with an English translation (which I have followed rather loosely), in *The Creeds of Christendom*, ed. Philip Schaff and David Schaff (Grand Rapids: Baker Book House, 1983), 2:66–67.

32 Cited by Cornelius Plantinga, Jr., "Social Trinity and Tritheism," in *Trinity, Incarnation, and Atonement: Philosophical and Theological Essays*, ed. Ronald J. Feenstra and Cornelius Plantinga, Jr. (Notre Dame: Notre Dame University Press, 1989), 21. Plantinga's entire essay occupies pages 21–47, and is a superb statement of the social model of the Trinity that will be discussed at some length later in this paper.

> Let us...bid farewell to all contentious shiftings and balancings of the truth on either side, neither, like the Sabellians, assailing the Trinity in the interest of the unity and so destroying the distinction by a wicked confusion; nor like the Arians, assailing the Unity in the interest of the Trinity, and by an impious distinction overthrowing the Oneness....But we walking along the royal road which is the seat of virtues...believe in the Father, the Son and the Holy Ghost, of one Substance [*ousia*] and glory; in Whom baptism has its perfection...acknowledging the Unity in the Essence [*ousia*] and in the undivided worship, and the Trinity in the *Hypostases* or Persons (which term some prefer).[33]

Nicea and Constantinople did not, however, end trinitarian reflection, nor — since the creeds they produced were comparable in some ways to negotiated treaties or joint communiqués, papering over substantial differences[34] — did they silence trinitarian controversy. Although the creedal language itself has rarely been disputed, what one pair of Protestant historians characterize as "the struggle of the fathers to say enough about the Trinity, but not too much," has continued through periods of greater or lesser intensity to the present day.[35]

Eastern theology has tended to concentrate on the "threeness" or trinity of God, or, perhaps more accurately, on the Father as unoriginated God and then, subsequently, on the Son and the Holy Spirit as God derivatively. Thus, for example, Father Thomas John Hopko insists that

> the Word and Spirit of God are revealed and known to be *persons* in Their own right, *acting* subjects who are other than who the Father is, essential to God's being, to be sure, yet not defined in any way in which they lose the integrity of Their personal existence by being explained as parts, aspects, components, actions, instruments, or relations in and of God's innermost nature.[36]

---

33 Gregory Nazianzus, Oration 42 ("The Last Farewell"), NPNF ser. 2, 7:90.

34 Constantine, for instance, had wanted a creed that as many Christians as possible could accept.

35 The quoted phrase is from Roger E. Olson and Christopher A. Hall, *The Trinity* (Grand Rapids: Eerdmans, 2002), 25.

36 Thomas John Hopko, "God and the World: An Eastern Orthodox Response to Process Theology" (unpublished doctoral dissertation, Fordham University, 1982), 206, cited in Lorenzen, *The College Student's Introduction to the Trinity*, 91 (emphasis as found).

Classical Trinitarianism, East and West

In the classical teaching of the Eastern Church, trinitarianism is a central doctrine that integrates — even implicitly summarizes — soteriology and Christology, and implies an understanding of salvation as transfiguration or transformation.[37] Further, the transfiguration of Jesus' humanity by Christ's divinity prefigures the destiny of the redeemed: "God became man," as the widespread formula of the ancient Church had it, "so that man could become God." We are created in the image of the Father, which gives us the hope of *theosis*, the Son bridges the gap between the human and the divine so that we can move in the direction of *theosis*, and the Holy Spirit is present within believers in order, by transforming them, to effect *theosis*. Each of the three divine persons, and thus their very "threeness," is necessary for our ultimate salvation. Yet, although each plays a particular role, they do not act separately but in perfect union.[38] "This Trinity is united," writes Lynne Lorenzen, "in its loving purpose of creating and saving the world."[39]

St. Gregory of Nyssa expressed it this way, in the latter fourth century:

> As it is impossible to mount to the Father unless our thoughts are exalted thither through the Son, so it is impossible also to say that Jesus is Lord except by the Holy Spirit. Therefore Father, Son and Holy Spirit are to be known only in a perfect Trinity, in closest consequence and union with each other, before all creation, before all ages, before any thing whatever of which we can form an idea.[40]

---

37 Such thinking becomes visible early—for example, in the second-century teachings of St. Irenaeus of Lyons. The broad resemblance between Latter-day Saint ideas of human destiny and the Irenaean view, as the latter is sketched, for example, in John H. Hick, *Death and Eternal Life* (San Francisco: Harper and Row, 1976), would be a worthy topic for further examination.

38 See Lorenzen, *The College Student's Introduction to the Trinity*, 3–4, 60, 93–94, 106, 108. Strikingly, the formula "God became human so that human beings should be deified" appears in Jürgen Moltmann, *The Spirit of Life: A Universal Affirmation*, trans. Margaret Kohl (Minneapolis: Fortress, 1992), 291–292.

39 Lorenzen, *The College Student's Introduction to the Trinity*, 108. In the Book of Moses, part of the canonical Latter-day Saint book The Pearl of Great Price, God tells Moses that "This is my work and my glory—to bring to pass the immortality and eternal life of man" (Moses 1:39).

40 Gregory of Nyssa, *On the Holy Spirit*, NPNF ser. 2, 5:319. Significantly, Cyril Richardson, *The Doctrine of the Trinity* (Nashville: Abingdon, 1968), 135, 140, objects to Gregory's description of the distinct roles of Father, Son, and Holy Spirit in salvation and, not coincidentally, rejects trinitarianism outright.

In fact, the very establishment of classical trinitarianism was driven by concerns about redemption. Athanasius's insistence, against Arius, on the full deity of the Son was motivated wholly or in large part by his conviction that only a fully divine Son could fully deify believers.[41] Had Christ not been *homoousios* with the Father, of the same essence or nature, there could be no hope that we could ever be "partakers of the divine nature."[42] "Sin," on this understanding, "is not participating in the process of salvation and thus refusing to enter into relationship with God."[43]

Many of the most prominent Western theologians, by contrast, have focused intensely on God's "oneness" or unicity, which has "resulted in an abiding Western tendency toward modalism."[44] St. Augustine, his thought rooted in something like the One of Plotinian Neoplatonism, is an excellent representative of this tendency. Augustine's psychological model of the Trinity, in which he offers memory, understanding, and will—the *vestigia Trinitatis*—as an analogue to the relationship between the three divine persons, has exerted enormous influence on subsequent thinkers. Yet, as Colin Gunton has observed—and although his thought certainly includes genuine Christology and pneumatology— Augustine can say relatively little about the individual divine persons, "who, because they lack distinguishable identity, tend to disappear into the all-embracing oneness of God."[45] Jürgen Moltmann argues that Augustine's psychological model inescapably implies modalism and reduces the Holy Spirit effectively to a "glue" between the Father and the

---

41   Lorenzen, *The College Student's Introduction to the Trinity*, 11–13, 21. For an examination of the centrality of *theosis* in the thought of St. Athanasius, see Keith E. Norman, *Deification: The Content of Athanasian Soteriology* (Provo, UT: FARMS, 2000). The relationship of divinity and humanity within the man Jesus was a topic of vast controversy in the early Christian centuries. Although relevant to the discussion here, it is simply beyond the scope of this essay.

42   2 Pet. 1:4 (King James Version). Of course, many ancient theologians correctly insisted, Jesus had to be fully human, too. If not, his life and suffering would have no relevance for us.

43   Lorenzen, *The College Student's Introduction to the Trinity*, 97.

44   La Due, *The Trinity Guide to the Trinity*, 143. Beside those mentioned in the text, Eberhard Jüngel and Robert Jenson will serve as examples of contemporary theologians who likewise stress the oneness of God, possibly to the detriment of the divine multiplicity. McGrath, *Understanding the Trinity*, 130–131, seems to me to teeter on the brink of modalism.

45   Colin Gunton, *The Promise of Trinitarian Theology* (Edinburgh: T. and T. Clark, 1991), 42. In fairness, I note that La Due, *Trinity Guide to the Trinity*, 53, insists that the divine persons are individuals even in Augustine. Plantinga, "Social Trinity and Tritheism," 33, doubts that Augustine's position is ultimately coherent.

Son, depersonalized, a mere "it."[46] Memory, understanding, and will are not in any sense "persons," and it is difficult to see how any psychological relation between them is really much like interpersonal relationships.

In the medieval period, the Benedictine monk, abbot, philosopher, and theologian St. Anselm of Canterbury (d. 1109) taught that "everything in God is identical except where opposed relations (as in Father, Son, and Holy Spirit) stand in the way of identity."[47] (Anselm's proposition was eventually given authoritative status at the Council of Florence in the fifteenth century.) St. Thomas Aquinas emphasized the divine unity (*de Deo uno*), and only secondarily attempted to make a place for the multiplicity of divine persons (*de Deo trino*). There seems little vigor to the three persons of the Trinity in Thomas's notion of them as subsistent relations within one divine essence. In modern times, Karl Barth — "who stands out as perhaps the most important contributor to the theology of the Trinity in the mid-twentieth century"[48] — rejected use of the term *person* for the members of the Trinity, fearing lest Christians construe it to suggest that three distinct personalities exist within the one God.[49] "We are," he said, "speaking not of three divine 'I's, but thrice of the one divine 'I'."[50] He preferred to speak of a "mode of being" rather than of a "person."[51] In Barth's thinking, God is actually one; the divine threeness seems to derive from our limited ability to perceive or conceive him otherwise. Consequently, he has sometimes been accused of implicit modalism.[52]

On the Roman Catholic side, the eminent Jesuit theologian Karl Rahner (who admitted that most believers find the Trinity virtually unintelligible) similarly favored the formula "mode of being" over the more traditional "person" — or alternatively, preferred to speak of "three distinct manners of subsisting" — in order to ward off any sense that Father, Son, and Holy Spirit each possess "a distinct center of

---

46 Jürgen Moltmann, *The Trinity and the Kingdom of God: The Doctrine of God*, trans. Margaret Kohl (San Francisco: Harper and Row, 1981); Jürgen Moltmann, *The Spirit of Life: A Universal Affirmation*, trans. Margaret Kohl (Minneapolis: Fortress Press, 1992).

47 As summarized by Fortman, *The Triune God: A Historical Study of the Doctrine of the Trinity* (Grand Rapids: Baker, 1972), 227.

48 La Due, *The Trinity Guide to the Trinity*, 125.

49 Karl Barth, *Church Dogmatics I.1: The Doctrine of the Word of God*, (New York: Scribner, 1955) Chapter II, Part I.

50 Ibid., 403.

51 Ibid., 415.

52 As noted by Olson and Hall, *The Trinity*, 97. Plantinga, "Social Trinity and Tritheism," 33, levels the accusation.

consciousness and will," and thus, in turn, to avoid even the slightest hint of tritheism.[53] "There are not," Rahner insisted,

> three consciousnesses in God; rather, one consciousness subsists in a threefold way. There is only one real consciousness in God, which is shared by Father, Son, and Spirit, by each in his own proper way."[54]

Trinity and Salvation

How have Western theories of the Trinity affected Western soteriology? A crucial distinction to keep in mind when discussing this topic is that between the "immanent Trinity" — God in relation to himself, in his inner life — and the triune God as he relates to the world external to himself, the so-called "economic Trinity."[55] While Eastern theology has always been oriented essentially to the economy of salvation, Western trinitarian theology has concentrated on God's immanent inner relatedness, his transcendent independence, with little relevance to Christian life and praxis.

Even orthodox Trinitarians acknowledge that "at times trinitarian theology has taken flights of speculative fancy and lost any solid connection with salvation and Christian worship, devotion, and discipleship."[56] It is largely for this reason that Renaissance humanist thinkers like Erasmus of Rotterdam, and reformers like Martin Bucer, Menno Simons, and, later, Count von Zinzendorf, grew impatient with what they saw as the hairsplitting irrelevance of medieval scholasticism, and focused, instead, on "following Christ," or, in the case of Philip Melanchthon, on the more practical "economic Trinity" at the expense of the "immanent Trinity." In his masterpiece *Der christliche Glaube*, the founder of modern Protestant theology, Friedrich Schleiermacher (1768–1834), struggled with how to present the doctrine of the Trinity because he did not feel that it could be deduced from the statements of Jesus and the apostles. Ultimately, he presented it at the end of his book, so that readers would be less likely to assume that faith in it was necessary to Christian belief and redemption. Earlier, Immanuel Kant

---

53   Karl Rahner, *The Trinity*, trans. Joseph Donceel (New York: Herder and Herder, 1970), 103–115.

54   Rahner, *The Trinity*, 107.

55   It undoubtedly seems odd to most theologically uninitiated modern readers to use the word *economic* in this fashion. The term refers to the "economy" of salvation, and reflects the original Greek sense of *oikonomia* as the management of a household.

56   Thus Olson and Hall, *The Trinity*, 3.

had remarked that the number of persons in the Deity was irrelevant, since the question had no practical implications for everyday life.[57]

Kant was correct in an important sense, but wrong in another. Views of the Trinity and of the nature of God have perfectly enormous theological consequences for every major aspect of salvation, for concepts of divine omnipotence and transcendence, and for notions of predestination. And, as many contemporary thinkers now argue, trinitarian theology influences views of ecclesiastical structure, social relationships, and ideal human behavior.[58]

Lynne Lorenzen regards St. Augustine's concentration on the oneness of God—founded upon a concern that Eastern theologies were perhaps coming too close to tritheism—as his primary contribution to trinitarian reflection. Still, she remarks,

> His emphasis on the oneness as the divine simplicity shows us what happens when the doctrine of the Trinity is separated from the concepts of christology and salvation, and thus fails in its original function. It becomes abstract and appears to be a riddle that requires explanation rather than a shorthand description of an entire theology.
>
> This happens because Augustine develops a very different understanding of salvation in which "becoming like God" is a description of sin at its worst, and salvation is described as being elected by God. This happens because God in the East is persuasively related to the world while for Augustine God in relation to the world is all-powerful in such a way that God's grace is irresistible.[59]

The thinking of the mature Augustine conceives humanity as an incorrigible wreck from which some, and only some, will be saved by the sovereign election of God. It is God who

> elects those predestined for salvation. The second person of the Trinity contributes his death as a sacrifice for sin, which makes election possible. However, since the election occurred before the foundation of the world, before the incarnation in Jesus, and before the fall of Adam and Eve, the relationship or dependence of salvation upon the event of the incarnation is

---

57   Cited by Jürgen Moltmann, in *The Trinity and the Kingdom of God*, 6.

58   This will be further discussed below.

59   Lorenzen, *The College Student's Introduction to the Trinity*, 94.

questionable. It seems in fact that the salvation of humanity is dependent solely upon the election of God apart from God's life as Trinity.[60]

The irresistible grace furnished by the Son is external to us. The Holy Spirit's function is not sanctification, but to bind Father and Son together. Augustine's theology, in other words, is largely if not entirely focused upon the inner-trinitarian life of the "immanent Trinity." Thus, Lorenzen argues, "Augustine is operating with a received doctrine of the Trinity that does not fit with his understanding of salvation, Christ, or God."[61]

Nearly a millennium later, in his *De Deo Trino*, St. Thomas Aquinas paid little attention to the divine saving mission.

> Aquinas denied that God has any real relation to the created universe. Creation has a real relation to God, but God has no real relation to creatures.[62]

Against this background, Lorenzen concludes, many "Western Christians have focused theology and faith on the person of Jesus to the exclusion of any other theological categories" — including the Father and the Holy Spirit.[63] As William La Due writes,

> For Christians, fixing our eyes and hearts on Jesus is relatively easy. It happens almost daily for many. His generous life and engaging personality spontaneously attract our attention and generate an abiding loyalty in believers. The mystery of the Trinity, however, does not arouse the same kind of unrehearsed attraction and allegiance. From early on we were told that the Trinity is a mystery, and indeed, the loftiest and most impenetrable of mysteries. We were not expected to understand it, but simply to believe it.[64]

For believers who concentrate entirely on the accessible person of Jesus, says Lorenzen, "the doctrine of the Trinity does not work at all." Instead, it becomes "an abstract dogma that is no longer required to tell the story of salvation."[65]

---

60   Ibid., 30.
61   Ibid., 95.
62   La Due, *The Trinity Guide to the Trinity*, 117.
63   Lorenzen, *The College Student's Introduction to the Trinity*, 1.
64   La Due, *The Trinity Guide to the Trinity*, xi.
65   Lorenzen, *The College Student's Introduction to the Trinity*, 1, 41; compare 95–96.

Lorenzen also faults Martin Luther on the grounds that his teaching on the Trinity seems to offer no role for the Holy Spirit in human salvation and requires at most only a dyad of Father and Son. "Clearly," she writes, "the Trinity functions not as the integrating element for [Luther's] theology, but on the periphery."[66]

John Calvin agrees with Luther in locating the actual reality of salvation in the world to come. Calvin expects no human participation in sanctification prior to death, and no non-human sanctification at all, and salvation is wholly determined outside this world:

> By an eternal and immutable counsel, God has once for all determined, both whom he would admit to salvation and whom he would condemn to destruction.[67]

What Lorenzen says of three twentieth century Protestant theologians seems, therefore, applicable to their great reforming forerunner as well:

> Jenson, Jüngel, and Barth in an effort to remove theology from the context of the world have limited the salvific action of God in the world to Jesus and then only to the elect. God in Christ no longer permeates the world and the Spirit no longer transfigures the world into the kingdom of God by means of the work of the faithful. Instead, God makes a sovereign decision to forgive rather than punish, and this is revealed in Jesus who is the only instance of the presence of God in the world. And since salvation occurs in God and not in the world the role of the Holy Spirit is not to transfigure anything in this world, but to witness to the fact that Jesus is Lord.[68]

Karl Rahner was concerned that too strong a focus on the inner life of God and on the divine unity of being or divine simplicity misleads Christian believers into missing the strong link between trinitarian doctrine and soteriology. He sought to make trinitarianism practical. Such concern undergirds his famous formula "The 'economic' Trinity is the 'immanent' Trinity and the 'immanent' Trinity is the 'economic' Trinity," often dubbed "Rahner's Rule."[69] However, as we have seen, Rahner's thought, despite his concern for practicality, tended in a modalistic direction. Jürgen Moltmann laments that both Barth's and

---

66   Ibid., 32.

67   John Calvin, *The Institutes of the Christian Religion*, III.xxi.7. See, on Luther and Calvin, Lorenzen, *The College Student's Introduction to the Trinity*, 30–35, 95.

68   Lorenzen, *The College Student's Introduction to the Trinity*, 47.

69   The Rule is to be found at Rahner, *The Trinity*, 22.

Rahner's focus on the unity and simplicity of the divine consciousness hindered them from achieving their own goals, which were to keep the doctrine of the Trinity grounded, respectively, in the Word of God and in the process and experience of salvation.[70]

Catherine Mowry LaCugna reviewed what she called "The Emergence and Defeat of the Doctrine of the Trinity," surveying the history of trinitarianism from its origins through the eras of Constantine and St. Augustine down to St. Thomas Aquinas in the thirteenth century West and St. Gregory Palamas in the fourteenth century East. As she saw it, this is a tale of the decreasing practical relevance of the doctrine with it becoming mired ever deeper in abstraction and speculation, fed by an unhealthy obsession with Greek ideas of impassibility and divine perfection. The doctrine becomes essentially irrelevant to Christian prayer, worship, and discipleship.[71]

"Even more conservative Christians," remark Roger Olson and Christopher Hall,

> often wonder whether Augustine and other church fathers and theologians have gone too far in asserting the importance of the doctrine of the Trinity. Can it really be so intrinsically connected with the gospel of salvation that denying it ...results in loss of salvation or at least loss of status as a Christian? ...How can it be so important if it is not explicitly stated in scripture?[72]

And what of the notion of *theosis*? That very ancient Christian idea survives—if not fully, still more than merely nominally—in the Christian East. Yet Western theologians have repeatedly criticized Eastern Christian thought as either Pelagian or Semi-Pelagian, referring to an ancient Christian theological school (named after the fourth-fifth-century British monk Pelagius, commonly though perhaps unfairly known as a heretic) which held that human nature has not been so tainted by original sin as to be incapable of choosing good or evil without special divine aid.[73] Increasingly, in the Western understanding, it was felt that the image of God had been so overcome by sin as to have been completely

---

70 See Jürgen Moltmann, *The Crucified God*, trans. R. A. Wilson and John Bowden (New York: Harper and Row, 1974); Moltmann, *The Trinity and the Kingdom of God*.

71 Catherine Mowry LaCugna, *God for Us: The Trinity and Christian Life* (San Francisco: HarperSanFrancisco, 1993), 21–205.

72 Olson and Hall, *The Trinity*, 1.

73 See the brief comment of Lorenzen, *The College Student's Introduction to the Trinity*, 2.

lost. This different understanding had immense consequences. As Lynne Lorenzen remarks,

> Once the image is lost and the grace of God becomes external to us theosis becomes impossible. What then develops is a doctrine of salvation that is objective. It happens to humanity without humanity's free assent or cooperation. The internal connection between God and humanity in human nature is no longer possible, nor is the direct experience of God by humans in a mystical experience possible.
>
> The effects of salvation in the West are mediated by the assurance of faith rather than directly experienced as in the East.[74]

Latter-day Saints indisputably reject the solution to the trinitarian problem associated with standard readings of Nicea. But their rejection of mainstream Nicene orthodoxy does not necessarily place them in opposition to the project it represents. Nor, as has become more and more evident, does it leave them isolated and alone.

Social Trinitarianism

One relatively recent account, often known as "social trinitarianism," seems, indeed, to resemble the common Latter-day Saint understanding of the divine unity in several salient aspects. Social trinitarianism has not been wholly unknown in the West, historically speaking. Some, for instance, have even thought they recognized intimations of it in the Cappadocian fathers of the later fourth century, and particularly in Gregory of Nazianzus.[75] Earlier, the third-century Roman presbyter Novatian had complained that modalism obscured the fact that Father and Son are two persons just as plainly as were the mortal humans Paul and Apollos.[76] A better example is surely Richard of St. Victor in the twelfth century, who took the threeness of the Father, Son, and Holy Spirit as his point of departure, and then attempted to account for their

---

74 Lorenzen, *The College Student's Introduction to the Trinity*, 35.

75 However, Olson and Hall, *The Trinity*, 37, are probably right to follow Phillip Cary in claiming that the Cappadocians compared the Trinity to a society of three human beings for the very purpose of showing that the comparison should not be taken too far.

76 Novatian, *Concerning the Trinity*, Chapter 27. Novatian, it is true, is typically classed as a "heretic." But this label stems from his rigorist stance during the Decian persecution, not from his doctrinal opinions, which were wholly orthodox for his time.

oneness. For Richard, it was necessary that there be a plurality in God, with a second person in some real sense the equal of the first, in order for there to be love. And God *is* love.[77] Unfortunately (probably in response to the teaching of Richard's younger contemporary, Joachim of Fiore, which went far beyond Richard's social analogy to something truly very near tritheism), the Fourth Lateran Council in 1215 affirmed the absolute simplicity and immutability of the one divine substance, declaring that Father, Son, and Holy Spirit are nothing more than distinct relations within that substance. They are to be distinguished only by their differing origins. All three are identical with the divine nature, but not with each other, for the Father is ungenerated, while the Son is eternally generated or begotten by the Father and—the notorious *filioque*—the Spirit eternally proceeds from both the Father and the Son. Oneness was now primary. Threeness was secondary—and difficult to maintain.

Today, however, theologians such as Leonardo Boff, Jürgen Moltmann, John O'Donnell, Catherine Mowry LaCugna, Wolfhart Pannenberg, Joseph Bracken, and John Zizioulas again seek to demonstrate that the doctrine of the Trinity is essential for Christian living, and intimately related to human salvation, and do so — to one degree or another — by means of at least a loosely social model of the Trinity.[78]

A principal concept employed by social Trinitarians is that of *perichoresis*. *Perichoresis* is the Greek term popularized by St. John of Damascus (d. AD 750) to refer to the mutual indwelling of the divine persons, their "coinherence" or "interpenetration." Gerald O'Collins describes it well as it occurs in the writing of St. Thomas Aquinas:

> Thomas along with other medieval theologians endorsed the radical, loving interconnectedness (*circumincessio*) of the three divine persons, something better expressed in Greek as their *perichoresis*, or reciprocal presence and interpenetration. Their innermost life is infinitely close relationship with one another in the utter reciprocity of love.[79]

---

77 1 John 4:8.

78 See Leonardo Boff, *Trinity and Society*, trans. Paul Burns (Maryknoll, NY: Orbis, 1988); John O'Donnell, *The Mystery of the Triune God* (Mahwah, NJ: Paulist Press, 1989); LaCugna, *God for Us*; John D. Zizioulas, *Being as Communion: Studies in Personhood and the Church* (Crestwood, NY: St. Vladimir's Press, 1985). Walter Cardinal Kasper, too, seeks to relate his trinitarianism primarily to salvation, though it is less clear that he does so within a social trinitarian framework. See Walter Kasper, *The God of Jesus Christ*, trans. Matthew J. O'Donnell (New York: Crossroad, 1986).

79 Gerald O'Collins, *The Tripersonal God* (New York: Paulist Press, 1999), 147.

Clearly, the concept can be and has been employed in varied forms of trinitarian thought. But it will prove crucial for the social model.

Modern social trinitarianism might reasonably be said to have begun with the British theologian Leonard Hodgson.[80] In the Eastern manner, Hodgson begins with the three persons, and then attempts to show how these three are one. "The doctrine of the Trinity," he writes,

> is . . an inference to the nature of God drawn from what we believe to be the empirical evidence given by God in His revelation of Himself in the history of this world.

"He refuses," Lynne Lorenzen observes of Hodgson, "to subordinate this revelation to the philosophical idea of oneness, i.e., undifferentiated simplicity."[81] Moreover, in Hodgson's theology, the Trinity returns to service as a practical formula for Christian life, as a guide to prayer and devotion:

> We shall speak to the Spirit as to the Lord who moves and inspires us and unites us to the Son; we shall speak to the Son as to our Redeemer who has taken us to share in His Sonship, in union with whom we are united to His Father and may address Him as our Father.[82]

This passage has obvious soteriological implications. Yet Hodgson seems not to have exploited them. Lorenzen laments that, although it aims to be a pattern for Christian community on earth, Hodgson's social trinitarianism fails to function, as the doctrine of the Trinity does in the East, to integrate Christology, soteriology, and the concept of God. It is still not a core doctrine, but remains a problem to be solved.[83]

The German theologian Jürgen Moltmann has been much more explicit about the implications of a social model of the Trinity for earthly human relationships. Again, in the Eastern style, he commences with the threeness of God, since this is the way the Trinity is portrayed in the story of Jesus and in the biblical texts. Then the divine unity must be explained, and this is to be done by means of the concept of *perichoresis*. In his view, inner-trinitarian *perichoresis* corresponds to the ideal experience within the Christian community, when it is united by and in the Holy Spirit:

---

80   Leonard Hodgson, *The Doctrine of the Trinity* (New York: Charles Scribner's Sons, 1944).

81   Lorenzen, *The College Student's Introduction to the Trinity*, 50.

82   Hodgson, *The Doctrine of the Trinity*, 179–180.

83   Lorenzen, *The College Student's Introduction to the Trinity*, 55–56.

> The more open-mindedly people live with one another, for one another and in one another in the fellowship of the Spirit, the more they will become one with the Son and the Father, and one in the Son and the Father.[84]

In his book *The Crucified God*, Moltmann has sought to go beyond the impassible God of classical theism, and to render the thought of God more appropriate to the genocidal world that arose in the twentieth century. God, he feels, must die with and on behalf of the innocent. And, Moltmann says, God did so on the cross. But not only on the cross. Because, in Moltmann's view, God is a genuine community of three distinct persons who feel love for one another, they are also capable of experiencing pain and sorrow when one of them suffers. Viewed in this way, the redemptive suffering of the Son becomes an inner-trinitarian ordeal, undertaken out of unfathomable love for humankind.[85]

The contemporary Brazilian liberation theologian Leonardo Boff, too, seeks to make practical use of social trinitarianism, but in a much more overtly political way than Hodgson and Moltmann have done. Like them, Boff describes the perichoretic unity of Father, Son, and Holy Spirit not as sameness of substance but as a complete unity of love and perfect communion. Each divine person, he says,

> is itself, not the other, but so open to the other and in the other that they form one entity, i.e., they are God. …Such an exchange of love obtains between the three Persons: life flows so completely between them, the communion between them is so infinite, with each bestowing on the others all that can be bestowed, that they form a union. The three possess one will, one understanding, one love.[86]

---

84 Moltmann, *The Trinity and the Kingdom of God*, 158. Moltmann believes that many of the structural problems and abuses of Christian ecclesiastical history are connected with a faulty view of the Trinity, and that a more adequate trinitarian theology can assist in ecclesiastical reform. Compare Leonardo Boff, discussed below. A relevant study that I have not yet seen at time of writing is Thomas Robert Thompson, *Imitatio Trinitatis: The Trinity as Social Model in the Theologies of Jürgen Moltmann and Leonardo Boff* (unpublished Ph.D. dissertation, 1996). Catherine LaCugna also leans in this direction.

85 For Latter-day Saint reflections on a related topic, see Daniel C. Peterson, "On the Motif of the Weeping God in Moses 7," in *Revelation, Reason, and Faith: Essays in Honor of Truman G. Madsen*, ed. Donald W. Parry, Daniel C. Peterson, and Stephen D. Ricks (Provo, UT: FARMS, 2002), 285–317.

86 Boff, *Trinity and Society*, 32, 84.

The union within the Trinity, in turn, serves as a paradigm of what human community can and ought to be, and, in Boff's case, inspires his own theology of liberation in the context of Latin America.

> The community of Father, Son and Holy Spirit becomes the prototype of the human community dreamed of by those who wish to improve society and build it in such a way as to make it into the image and likeness of the Trinity.[87]

Theology, for Boff, is no merely theoretical exercise. It should motivate us to build a society that reflects and embodies the perichoretic unity of Father, Son, and Holy Spirit. Specifically, he believes that hierarchical models of the Trinity have legitimized and fostered repressive, hierarchical human societies, and he calls for social egalitarianism patterned after the co-equal Trinity, as he conceives it. His reading of inner-trinitarian relations as a pattern for earthly human life is also shared by the feminist theologian Elizabeth A. Johnson, who sees the persons of the Trinity united in mutuality, friendship, and maternal caring. "Their unsurpassed communion of love," she contends, "stands as the ideal model of mutuality for all people in the world."[88]

> She emphasizes that the Trinity can best be viewed as a communion in relationship that invites all of us into its circle. The incomprehensible threefold *koinonia* [Greek: "communion" or "fellowship"] opens out to create a community of sisters and brothers. This vision had largely been lost for a thousand years or more in favor of the image of a solitary God.[89]

Yet another thinker who seems to have developed a social model for understanding the Trinity is the Jesuit process theologian Joseph Bracken.[90] Once again, he begins with the threeness of God and thereafter

---

87 Ibid., 7.

88 As summarized by La Due, *The Trinity Guide to the Trinity*, 172. I have not yet looked at Johnson's book *She Who Is* (New York: Crossroad, 1992).

89 Again, as summarized by La Due, *The Trinity Guide to the Trinity*, 173, this time from Elizabeth A. Johnson, "Trinity: To Let the Symbol Sing Again," *Theology Today* 54 (October 1997): 299–311.

90 The discussion of his thought that follows is based upon Joseph A. Bracken, *The Triune Symbol: Persons, Process, and Community* (New York: University Press of America, 1985). Father Bracken and I spent two months together in a 1990 seminar sponsored by the National Endowment for the Humanities, led by Huston Smith at the Pacific School of Religion in Berkeley, California. After a party on the last night of our seminar, he washed the dishes while I dried them. Father Bracken was amused at the

proceeds to explain the divine unicity. For Bracken, the concept of a *person* is to be distinguished from that of an *individual*. Whereas an individual is separate from other individuals, valuing autonomy and self-sufficiency above relatedness, a person is always related to a community. He thus agrees with the Orthodox Bishop Kallistos Timothy Ware that "to be a person is by definition to be internally related to other persons as persons of the Trinity are eternally, internally related to each other."[91] In Bracken's view, "Father, Son and Holy Spirit constitute a divine community."[92] Because of the strength of the interpersonal ties between its members, however, that community is not tritheistic. Bracken disputes the usual modern, Western definition of community as "a network of relationships between separate individuals who are first and foremost themselves and only in the second place associated with one another," a definition presuming that "only the individual entities ultimately exist." He faults St. Thomas Aquinas for accepting an Aristotelian attitude that views the individual as primary, and, hence, focuses excessively on the oneness of God.[93]

Persons and community cannot, Bracken says, be abstracted from one another, or understood in isolation. Since they are correlative concepts, the community too — and not merely the individual preferred by "classical" Western thinkers — has ontological status. In the specific instance of the trinitarian community, he writes,

> even though each divine person has his own mind and will, they are of one mind and will in everything they say and do,

---

thought of a Jesuit process theologian and a Mormon Islamicist working side by side at such a task. I expect that he would be even more amused by my use of him, now, to set out my thoughts on "Mormonism and the Trinity." I would not have expected it myself.

91   Olson and Hall, *The Trinity*, 90, summarizing an argument advanced by Bishop Kallistos. Such reasoning, which I find persuasive, has led theologians such as Leonard Hodgson, Leonardo Boff, and John Zizioulas to argue that God must necessarily be multiply personal, lest he be dependent for his "personality" upon the existence of the world. See the discussion at Olson and Hall, *The Trinity*, 105, 107, 113. La Due, *The Trinity Guide to the Trinity*, 107, 179, rightly notes that the concept of "person" has shifted substantially over the past several centuries. The Oxford social trinitarian David Brown usefully applies Stephen Lukes's distinction between French *individualisme* and German *Individualität* (as the words came to be used in the early nineteenth century) to the trinitarian persons, affirming the latter (which is akin to Bracken's "person") while denying the former. See David Brown, "Trinitarian Personhood and Individuality," in *Trinity, Incarnation, and Atonement*, 48–78.

92   Bracken, *The Triune Symbol*, 87.

93   Ibid., 16.

both with respect to one another and in their relationship with human beings and the whole of creation.[94]

So unified are Father, Son, and Holy Spirit, on Bracken's view, that "they hold everything in common except the fact of their individual personhood, their relatedness to one another precisely as Father, Son and Holy Spirit."[95]

One of the most forthright and cogent recent advocates of what he terms "a strong or social theory of the Trinity" is Cornelius Plantinga, Jr., of Calvin Theological Seminary. "By strong or social trinitarianism," he writes,

> I mean a theory that meets at least the following three conditions: (1) The theory must have Father, Son, and Spirit as distinct centers of knowledge, will, love, and action. Since each of these capacities requires consciousness, it follows that, on this sort of theory, Father, Son, and Spirit would be viewed as distinct centers of consciousness or, in short, as *persons* in some full sense of that term. (2) Any accompanying sub-theory of divine simplicity must be modest enough to be consistent with condition (1), that is, with the real distinctness of Trinitarian persons....(3) Father, Son, and Spirit must be regarded as tightly enough related to each other so as to render plausible the judgment that they constitute a particular social unit. In such social monotheism, it will be appropriate to use the designator *God* to refer to the whole Trinity, where the Trinity is understood to be one thing, even if it is a complex thing consisting of persons, essences, and relations.[96]

Plantinga contends that

> The Holy Trinity is a divine, transcendent society or community of three fully personal and fully divine entities: the Father, the Son, and the Holy Spirit or Paraclete. These three are wonderfully unified by their common divinity, that is, by the possession by each of the whole generic divine essence — including, for instance, the properties of everlastingness and of sublimely great knowledge, love, and glory. The persons are also unified by their joint redemptive purpose, revelation, and work...

---

94 Ibid., 26.
95 Ibid., 30.
96 Plantinga, "Social Trinity and Tritheism," 22.

Each member is a person, a distinct person, but scarcely an *individual* or *separate* or *independent* person. For in the divine life there is no isolation, no insulation, no secretiveness, no fear of being transparent to another. Hence there may be penetrating, inside knowledge of the other as other, but as co-other, loved other, fellow. Father, Son, and Spirit are "members of one another" to a superlative and exemplary degree.[97]

Criticisms of Social Trinitarianism

Notwithstanding the protests of its advocates, critics of social trinitarianism have, of course, been quick to denounce the model as tritheistic.[98] Many have also feared that it opens the gate to a Christian pantheon not sufficiently unlike the squabbling gods of Olympus.[99] Roger Olson and Christopher Hall, for example, declare that

The will and activity of God is…one.…All analogies drawn from human life ultimately break down when applied to trinitarian relationships. For example, Jane and John might share a common human nature but choose as individual persons to exercise their wills in opposition to one another. Their individuality as persons surely leaves the autonomous exercise of their wills as a genuine possibility. Not so with God. Although God's being is characterized by the hypostatic distinctions of Father, Son, and Spirit, all three persons are one in their will and activity. They are not autonomous persons in the modern nuance of "individual," each with its own separate "ego" and "center" of consciousness. Rather, they have always and will always purpose and operate with one will and action. They are one God, not three.[100]

---

97   Ibid., 27, 28, emphasis in original. The phrase "members of one another" is taken from Rom. 12:5.

98   The charge of "tritheism" is even gently hinted at by the rather mild Roger E. Olson, *The Story of Christian Theology: Twenty Centuries of Tradition and Reform* (Downers Grove, IL: InterVarsity, 1999), 194.

99   Sensationalizing critics of Latter-day Saint beliefs often draw comparisons with the pantheons of ancient Greece and Rome, evidently hoping that their naïve audiences will assume that the mutual backstabbing, adulteries, and general foibles of the Olympians are present, likewise, in the Mormon conception of heaven. This is, of course, simply false.

100   Olson and Hall, *The Trinity*, 36.

Alister McGrath expresses a similar view, albeit laced with disdain. Mocking "the way in which a lot of Christians think about the Trinity," McGrath says that,

> In their thinking, Jesus is basically one member of the divine committee, the one who is sent down to earth to report on things and put things right with the creation....[N]owhere in Scripture is God modeled on a committee. The idea of an old man in the sky is bad enough, but the idea of a committee somewhere in the sky is even worse. What, we wonder, might be on their agendas? How often would the chairman have to cast his vote to break a tie between the other two? The whole idea is ludicrous.[101]

However, a devout believer in social trinitarianism might respond that, although the individuality of the Father, Son, and Holy Ghost "surely leaves the autonomous exercise of their wills as a genuine possibility," in fact the holiness, righteousness, intelligence, wisdom, love, and harmony of the three divine persons are so utterly complete that no such discord will ever occur. Not because it is logically impossible, but because they are perfect. It is a matter of faith. "It goes without saying," remarks William La Due of Walter Cardinal Kasper's concept of the Trinity, "that there is an immeasurably greater interrelationality among the three divine subjects than there is in human interpersonal relations."[102] That should, in fact, go without saying in any serious discussion of social trinitarianism.

Cornelius Plantinga considers questions raised by critics of the social model on the theme of whether, if there really are three independent divine beings, one might withdraw and establish a rival kingdom, or, even, destroy the others. "The answer to these questions," he writes,

> is plainly negative. To see why this must be so, one has only to compare them with questions about any divine person's ability to harm, alienate, or destroy *himself*. No fully divine person could do that...No more could any of the social trinity persons leave the others derelict, or compete for intergalactic dominion, or commit intratrinitarian atrocities. For just as it is a part of the generic divine nature to be everlasting,

---

101 McGrath, *Understanding the Trinity*, 120. McGrath would presumably disdain Latter-day Saint doctrine as teaching not only "the idea of a committee in the sky" but "the idea of an old man in the sky." We are theologically unfashionable.

102 La Due, *The Trinity Guide to the Trinity*, 107.

omnipotent, faithful, loving, and the like, so it is also part of the personal nature of each Trinitarian person to be bound to the other two in permanent love and loyalty. Loving respect for the others is a personal essential characteristic of each member of the Trinity.[103]

Olson and Hall continue, saying that

what we mean by "social" on a human level breaks down when speaking of the divine persons. Human social relationships, for instance, are characterized by separate individuals or social groups interacting with other individuals or groups. These interactions can demonstrate marked agreement and harmony. At other times, tensions and disagreements rise to the surface. Such is not the case within the Trinity itself. Here there is no possibility of disagreement or conflict, because all three are one in will and activity.[104]

But this is precisely what a social trinitarian might affirm.

Cyril Richardson, objecting to the social doctrine of the Trinity advanced by Leonard Hodgson, declared that,

if there are three centers of consciousness in God, there are three Gods....It is simply impossible to say that God is really one in some ultimate sense, and still retain the idea of distinct centers of consciousness, which stand over against each other.[105]

Likewise, Phillip Cary asserts that

God is *not* three persons in the modern sense of the word—for three distinct divine persons, with three distinct minds, wills and centers of consciousness, would surely be three Gods.[106]

However, although, so far as I am aware, they shy away from the expressly tritheistic language that both Cary and Richardson employ for shock value, at least some social trinitarians are willing to accept precisely that consequence. As we have seen, Cornelius Plantinga certainly is. The contemporary German theologian Wolfhart Pannenberg likewise

---

103 Plantinga, "Social Trinity and Tritheism," 36, emphasis in original.
104 Olson and Hall, *The Trinity*, 37.
105 Richardson, *The Doctrine of the Trinity*, 94.
106 Phillip Cary, "Historical Perspectives on Trinitarian Doctrine," *Religious and Theological Studies Fellowship Bulletin* (November–December 1995): 5.

unabashedly discusses the three persons of the Trinity as three separate, dynamic centers of action and consciousness.[107]

Subordinationism

And it seems proper that he should. The most obvious reading of a New Testament passage like Mark 14:36, in which Jesus asks that the cup of his pending crucifixion be taken from him, surely seems to point to a numerical distinction in wills between the Father and the Son, made one by the Son's full submission: "Yet not what I will, but what thou wilt." When Jesus cries out from the cross, "My God, my God, why hast thou forsaken me?" the most natural understanding seems to be that one center of consciousness is begging an answer from another.[108]

Obviously, if one accepts the postbiblical notion that a divine nature and a human nature, mutually distinct, somehow coexisted in Jesus of Nazareth, a quite different understanding of such passages, one that does not, for example, support a distinction of wills and a subordination of the Son to the Father, is possible. Yet belief in true subordination of Son to Father seems to have been widespread in the first three centuries of Christianity. In the New Testament, as is often recognized, the Father is God *par excellence,* while Jesus seems to be secondarily divine.[109] "The Father is greater than I," says Jesus.[110] "There is little doubt," as Cornelius Plantinga observes, "that John presents at least a functional hierarchy, with the Father ultimately in control."[111] Paul refers to "the God and Father of our Lord Jesus Christ."[112] "There is," Paul says, "no god but one....For us there is one God, the Father, ...and there is one Lord, Jesus Christ."[113] The Father knows the time of the Second Advent, but the Son does not.[114] Even after the universal resurrection and the culmination of all things, according to St. Paul, "the Son himself will also be made subordinate to God."[115]

---

107 Wolfhart Pannenberg, *Systematic Theology,* trans. Geoffrey W. Bromiley (Grand Rapids: Eerdmans, 1991), 1:317–27.

108 Mark 15:34.

109 See Plantinga, "Social Trinity and Tritheism," 25–26, also the various references given at La Due, *The Trinity Guide to the Trinity,* 19–24, 38–40, 96, 160. These are only representative, and could be multiplied.

110 John 14:28.

111 Plantinga, "Social Trinity and Tritheism," 26.

112 Rom. 15:6.

113 1 Cor. 8:4, 6. Paul is, of course, echoing the famous *shema* of Deut. 6:4.

114 Matt. 24:36.

115 1 Cor. 15:28.

A distinction between "the Most High" and Yahweh seems to occur in the Hebrew Bible.[116] Strikingly, the New Testament identifies Jesus as "the Son of the Most High."[117] That distinction persists into Christian times, with certain documents such as the fourth-century *Clementine Recognitions* and Eusebius's fourth-century *Proof of the Gospel* evidently identifying Jesus Christ with Jehovah, "whom," as Eusebius says, "we call Lord in the second degree after the God of the Universe."[118] The mid-second-century St. Justin Martyr wrote in his *Dialogue with Trypho* that Jesus was "another God and Lord subject to the Maker of all things; who is also called an Angel...distinct from Him who made all things, — numerically, I mean, not (distinct) in will."[119] In his *First Apology,* St. Justin described the Son as being "in the second place, and the prophetic Spirit in the third."[120] The great early-third-century theologian St. Hippolytus of Rome taught that God the Father is "the Lord and God and Ruler of all, and even of Christ Himself."[121] St. Irenaeus of Lyon taught that "the Father is the only God and Lord, who alone is God and ruler of all."[122] Origen of Alexandria described Jesus as a "second God," while Eusebius called him a "secondary Being."[123] Novatian, for his part, described the Holy Spirit as "less than Christ."[124] "We say," wrote Origen, "that the Son and the Holy Spirit excel all created beings to a degree which admits of no comparison, and are themselves excelled by the Father to the same or

---

116   For example, in the Septuagint and Qumran versions of Deut. 32:8–9. Compare the similar understanding reflected in *Clementine Recognitions,* 2:42 and Eusebius, *The Proof of the Gospel,* 4:7. See, on this, Margaret Barker, *The Great Angel: A Study of Israel's Second God* (Louisville: Westminster John Knox Press, 1992), 5–6. Such a distinction is also arguably present in Ps. 91:9, properly read. (See the argument of Barker, *The Great Angel,* 198–99.)

117   See, for example, Luke 1:32.

118   *Clementine Recognitions,* 2:42; Eusebius, *The Proof of the Gospel,* 4:7.

119   Justin Martyr, *Dialogue with Trypho,* 56 (ANF 1:223). Admittedly, Justin's tendency to speak of the Son as an "angel" was not well received among later fathers. On this, see O'Collins, *The Tripersonal God,* 90.

120   Justin Martyr, *First Apology,* 13 (ANF 1:167).

121   Hippolytus, *Scholia on Daniel,* 7:13 (ANF 5:189).

122   Irenaeus, *Against Heresies,* 3:9:1 (ANF 1:422).

123   Origen, *Against Celsus* 5.39, 6.61, 7.57 (ANF 4:561, 601, 634); Eusebius, *The Proof of the Gospel* 1.5 (or 1.26?).

124   Novatian, *Concerning the Trinity* 16 (ANF 5:625).

even greater degree."[125] St. Irenaeus of Lyon wrote that the Father exceeds the Son in terms of knowledge.[126]

"Until Athanasius began writing," remarks R. P. C. Hansen, "every single theologian, East and West, had postulated some form of Subordinationism. It could, about the year 300, have been described as a fixed part of catholic theology."[127] "During the first three centuries of the Christian era," agrees William La Due, "practically all the approaches to the clarification of the mystery of the Trinity were tinged with some degree of either subordinationism or modalism."[128] On the eve of the Council of Nicea in AD 325, the most numerous faction at the council — "the great conservative 'middle party,'" as J. N. D. Kelly terms them — were subordinationists who believed in three divine persons, "separate in rank and glory but united in harmony of will."[129]

Enter Mormonism

Where does Mormonism fit with all of this?

"Three personages composing the great presiding council of the universe have revealed themselves unto man," wrote James E. Talmage in 1890. And yet he proceeded to teach that "the mind of any one member of the Trinity is the mind of the others; seeing as each of them does with the eye of perfection, they see and understand alike."[130]

The Father, Son, and Holy Spirit are "in perfect unity and harmony with each other," according to the semi-official 1992 *Encyclopedia of Mormonism.*

> Although the three members of the Godhead are distinct personages, their Godhead is "one" in that all three are united

---

125   Origen, *Commentary in Joannem* 13.25. It must be noted, incidentally, that, from a Latter-day Saint viewpoint, Origen's estimate of the gulf between the Father, on the one hand, and the Son and the Spirit on the other, appears vastly overdone.

126   Irenaeus, *Against Heresies*, 2.28.8 (ANF 1:402).

127   Richard Hanson, "The Achievement of Orthodoxy in the Fourth Century AD," in *The Making of Orthodoxy: Essays in Honour of Henry Chadwick*, ed. Rowan Williams (New York: Cambridge University Press, 1989), 153. So, too, Norbert Brox, *Kirchengeschichte des Altertums* (Düsseldorf: Patmos, 1983), 171, 175.

128   La Due, *The Trinity Guide to the Trinity*, 41. Illustrations might be multiplied indefinitely. See, for instance, La Due's discussion of Tertullian on pages 35–36, and of Origen on pages 38–39.

129   J. N. D. Kelly, *Early Christian Doctrines* (London: Adam & Charles Black, 1960), 247–248.

130   Talmage, *The Articles of Faith*, 39–40.

in their thoughts, actions, and purpose, with each having a fulness of knowledge, truth, and power.[131]

Perhaps because they are unmenaced by surrounding polytheisms and also because they have emerged from and historically reacted against a religious culture in which mainstream trinitarianism has been the norm, Latter-day Saints are less fearful than other social trinitarians of affirming a belief in "Gods" in the plural. But they are squarely within a form of what might be termed liberal social trinitarianism. What Kenneth Paul Wesche says of the Father, Son, and Holy Spirit in Eastern trinitarianism could easily have been said by a Latter-day Saint:

> These are not three separate actors, each one scheming against the other to effect his own agenda as one finds in the Olympian pantheon, nor is there one common operation performed independently by each of the Three as in the case, for example, of several human orators, or farmers, or shoemakers who each perform the same activity, but independently of others; there is but one natural operation which all three persons perform, each in his own way, but in natural union with the others. There is accordingly identity of purpose, will and knowledge; the Son knows what the Father is doing because his action is the Father's action and it is the very action perfected by the Holy Spirit.[132]

With the exception of his rejection of the plural term *Gods*, Latter-day Saints would feel perfectly comfortable affirming, with Bishop Kallistos Timothy Ware, that

> Father, Son and Spirit …have only one will and not three… None of the three ever acts separately, apart from the other two. They are not three Gods, but one God.[133]

Latter-day Saints confidently hold that their view of the Trinity is fully concordant with the biblical data. They would agree with Cornelius

---

131 Paul E. Dahl, "Godhead," in *Encyclopedia of Mormonism*, ed. Daniel H. Ludlow (New York: Macmillan, 1992), 2:552.

132 Kenneth Paul Wesche, "The Triadological Shaping of Latin and Greek Christology, Part II: The Greek Tradition," *Pro Ecclesia* 2, no. 1, 88, as cited in Olson and Hall, *The Trinity*, 39. Brief conspectuses of the some of the specific, distinct, but harmonious roles played by Father, Son, and Holy Spirit in Latter-day Saint belief occur, among many other passages that might be named, in 2 Ne. 31:10–12 and Moro. 9:25–26, 10:4, in the Book of Mormon.

133 Timothy Ware (Bishop Kallistos), *The Orthodox Way* (Yonkers, NY: St Vladimir's Seminary, 1995), 30.

Plantinga's declaration that "A person who extrapolated theologically from Hebrews, Paul, and John would naturally develop a social theory of the Trinity."[134] And they believe that such a view is logically preferable to mainstream trinitarianism. In this, they have support from the outside: After rigorous analysis, Oxford's Timothy Bartel declares that the only logically tenable account of the Godhead is one in which "each member of the Trinity is absolutely distinct from the other two: the Trinity consists of three distinct individuals, each of whom is fully divine."[135]

Surprisingly, the Latter-day Saint approach may not even be incompatible with the text of the Nicene Creed.[136] In the third-fourth century *Clementine Homilies*, the apostle Peter is represented as teaching that

> The bodies of men have immortal souls, which have been clothed with the breath of God; and having come forth from God, they are of the same substance.[137]

While the pseudo-Clementine literature is dubiously orthodox, the language of this passage raises intriguing questions. It is extraordinarily difficult to pin down the precise meaning of the very controversial term *homoousios*, so central to trinitarian doctrine after the Nicene consensus.[138] (The term's ambiguity may, indeed, have been central to its practical utility in a creedal agreement between various theological factions.) Prior to the fourth century, phrases such as "of one substance" and "of the same substance" seem, at least in the minds even of some of those who approved the creed, to have indicated a generic similarity, meaning something like "the kind of substance or stuff common to several individuals of a class." The point may have been simply that Jesus, like the Father, is divine — a concept that Latter-day Saints fully endorse.[139] It can, in fact, be argued that the chief objection to the term

---

134   Plantinga, "Social Trinity and Tritheism," 27.

135   Bartel, "The Plight of the Relative Trinitarian," 151.

136   This would be of, at best, mild interest to Latter-day Saints, who do not grant the authority of the classical creeds. As La Due, *The Trinity Guide to the Trinity*, 58, 59, indicates, the first four ecumenical councils have become canons of trinitarian orthodoxy alongside the New Testament itself for much of Christendom.

137   *Clementine Homilies* 16 (ANF 8:316).

138   See, for example, Christopher Stead's discussions in his *Divine Substance* (Oxford: Clarendon Press, 1977), 242–266, and his *Philosophy in Christian Antiquity* (Cambridge: Cambridge University Press, 1994), 160–172, as also Lorenzen, *The College Student's Introduction to the Trinity*, 14–20, and Olson and Hall, *The Trinity*, 22, 34.

139   Kelly, *Early Christian Doctrines*, 234–235. The quoted definition occurs on page 234.

homoiousios, with its fatal iota, was its potential usefulness to advocates of subordinationism. Creedal formulas were devised not so much to specify what God is, but to rule out what he isn't. Those eager to protect the full deity of Christ were not necessarily intending to proscribe what we now know as social trinitarianism.

Trinity and Salvation

Somewhat analogously to the Eastern tradition, the transformative power of the Holy Spirit, which results in a fundamental reordering of the human heart, is a recurrent theme in the Book of Mormon.[140] In response to a powerful sermon delivered by their prophetic king Benjamin, the Nephites of the late second century BC enter into formal covenant to live righteously, and declare that, "because of the Spirit of the Lord Omnipotent, which has wrought a mighty change in us, or in our hearts, ...we have no more disposition to do evil, but to do good continually."[141] Alma 17–27 recounts the remarkable transformation of the people of Ammon from a violent and bloodthirsty paganism to a Christian covenant, according to which they forever abandon warfare and because of which many of them suffer martyrdom.

Alma the Younger, actively apostate son of the high priest under Mosiah, last of the Nephite monarchs, is converted through a spectacular angelophany. When he emerges from a lengthy coma and is finally able to speak, he tells those around him that he has been "born of the Spirit." And so, he says, must all be who will be saved:

> And the Lord said unto me: Marvel not that all mankind, yea, men and women, all nations, kindreds, tongues and people, must be born again; yea, born of God, changed from their carnal and fallen state, to a state of righteousness, being redeemed of God, becoming his sons and daughters;
>
> And thus they become new creatures; and unless they do this, they can in nowise inherit the kingdom of God.
>
> I say unto you, unless this be the case, they must be cast off; and this I know, because I was like to be cast off.[142]

---

140   In addition to the passages alluded to in the text, see Mosiah 5:7, Alma 5:12–13, Hel. 15:7, and Ether 12:14.

141   Mosiah 5:2; compare Alma 19:33.

142   Mosiah 27:24–27.

A decade or two later, his father is dead and Alma himself is the high priest over the Nephites. In one of his greatest sermons, he poses a question to his audience that unmistakably emerges from his own miraculous transformation:

> I ask of you, my brethren of the church, have ye spiritually been born of God? Have ye received his image in your countenances? Have ye experienced this mighty change in your hearts?[143]

Righteousness, in the Book of Mormon and in Mormonism generally, is not merely forgiveness of sins, though it surely includes divine forgiveness. Nor is it merely imputed, extrinsic to the believer. It is genuine alignment with God in heart and in action. Yet this alignment is not effected by human effort alone. It is made possible by the redemptive atonement of Christ, and comes through a synergy of faithful human discipleship and the transformative sanctification of the Holy Spirit. Through inspiration, faithful believers will, to the extent of their transformation, say and do what the Lord himself would say and do.[144]

Thus, the Book of Mormon prophet Nephi promises his readers that

> If ye shall follow the Son, with full purpose of heart, acting no hypocrisy and no deception before God, but with real intent, repenting of your sins, witnessing unto the Father that ye are willing to take upon you the name of Christ, by baptism...behold, then shall ye receive the Holy Ghost; yea, then cometh the baptism of fire and of the Holy Ghost; and then can ye speak with the tongue of angels....And now, how could ye speak with the tongue of angels, save it were by the Holy Ghost? Angels speak by the power of the Holy Ghost, wherefore, they speak the words of Christ.[145]

---

143 Alma 5:14; compare 5:26.

144 In extraordinary cases, and within limits, Latter-day Saint scripture affirms that Godlike power has been granted to mortal men. In the Book of Mormon, for instance, one of the prophets receives such power by direct divine bestowal, "for thou shalt not ask that which is contrary to my will" (Hel. 10:4–11; quotation from 10:5). This story echoes the earlier biblical story of Elijah, who looms large in Mormon scripture and thought.

145 2 Ne. 31:13, 32:2–3. An amusing illustration of this principle, that angels speak the words of Christ, occurs toward the end of the Revelation of John. Twice—the second passage is clearer in this regard than the first—John, encountering a being who speaks in the first person as if he were himself God or the Son, quite understandably falls down to worship. Both times, the speaker, who is in fact an angel, sharply tells him not to do

Similarly, in a revelation given through Joseph Smith at Hiram, Ohio, in November 1831, the faithful bearers of the priesthood of the Church are assured that

> whatsoever they shall speak when moved upon by the Holy Ghost shall be scripture, shall be the will of the Lord, shall be the mind of the Lord, shall be the word of the Lord, shall be the voice of the Lord, and the power of God unto salvation.[146]

This transformation will ultimately occur not merely in individuals, but in human society as a whole and in the earth itself: "May the kingdom of God go forth," Joseph Smith prayed, "that the kingdom of heaven may come."[147] In that day, according to the Articles of Faith of the Church, "the earth will be renewed and receive its paradisiacal glory."[148] Latter-day Saints are millennialists, engaged in building the earthly Kingdom of God that will prepare the way for the return of Christ

Like Leonardo Boff and other social trinitarians, Latter-day Saints see in the fellowship of the Trinity a model for what human society ought to be. "And the Lord called his people Zion," one uniquely Mormon canonical text explains, in connection with a community led by the ancient patriarch Enoch, "because they were of one heart and one mind, and dwelt in righteousness."[149] In the first discourse of the risen Lord to his American saints in the Book of Mormon, an exhortation to avoid "disputations," "contention," and mutual "anger," is enclosed within two explicit declarations of the oneness of Father, Son, and Holy Spirit, and accompanied by a brief discussion of the varied but wholly united action of the three members of the Trinity.[150] "I say unto you, be one," commands a January 1831 revelation given to Joseph Smith in Fayette, New York, "and if ye are not one ye are not mine."[151] Unlike Boff's vision, however, but like the subordinationist Trinity seemingly favored in the first Christian centuries, the society for which Latter-day

---

so, for the speaker is simply relaying the divine words in the capacity of a messenger. See Rev. 19:10, 22:7–9.

146 D&C 68:4. Strikingly, both the prayer alluded to below (D&C 65) and the dedicatory prayer given in 1836 for the temple at Kirtland, Ohio (D&C 109) form part of the Latter-day Saint canon. Both are believed by Latter-day Saints to have been given by revelation. In these inspired prayers, it seems, the very words of the person praying were given by God and, then, offered back to God.

147 D&C 65:6.

148 Articles of Faith 10, in the Pearl of Great Price.

149 Moses 7:18. "And," the text continues, "there was no poor among them."

150 3 Ne. 11:27–38.

151 D&C 38:27.

Saints have historically striven — the Kingdom of God, Zion — is an unmistakably hierarchical one, as is the currently existing Church of Jesus Christ of Latter-day Saints. (Latter-day Saints can accept Joseph Bracken's description of the one God as "a structured society.")[152] It is perhaps worth noting in this context that the original name chosen for what is now Utah and much of the "Great Basin Kingdom" by the Mormon pioneers was *Deseret*, a word from the Book of Mormon signifying the honey bee,[153] and that the Utah state seal and state flag still feature a beehive as their central image. This arises not out of any supposed ambition to establish a theocratic fascism, as certain critics charge, but from a commitment to build a society of complete harmony and unity of purpose, obedient to the will of God.

In the Latter-day Saint view, furthermore, the perfect unity and harmony of the Trinity is not merely an ideal toward which earthly believers may strive. Joseph Bracken's explanation that "one major reason for the incarnation of the Son of God...was the need for a concrete model of human personhood, someone specifically to embody what the Father has in mind for all of us," resonates with Mormon understandings, particularly in view of his insistence that Christ's personhood is constituted at least in part by his intimate, perichoretic, relationship with the Father.[154] Through the atonement of Jesus Christ and the sanctifying influence of the Holy Spirit, such a relationship is also a fully realizable goal for the righteous of humankind in the life to come. Very much analogous to theosis in the Eastern tradition, this is deification — or, as Latter-day Saints tend to call it, exaltation.[155] The resurrected Jesus, speaking to his American disciples in the Book of Mormon, promises them that "ye shall be even as I am, and I am even as the Father; and the Father and I are one."[156]

An analogous theme appears in various social trinitarian writers, as well. In the thought of Leonardo Boff, for example, "All beings are invited to share in the sonship of the Son. ...The perichoretic life of God expands ever outward."[157]

---

152   Bracken, *The Triune Symbol*, 44.

153   See Ether 2:3.

154   Bracken, *The Triune Symbol*, 89.

155   A Dominican Catholic priest discusses parallels between Eastern theosis and the Latter-day Saint concept of exaltation in Jordan Vajda, *"Partakers of the Divine Nature": A Comparative Analysis of Patristic and Mormon Doctrines of Divinization* (Provo, UT: FARMS, 2002).

156   3 Ne. 28:10.

157   As summarized by La Due, *The Trinity Guide to the Trinity*, 166.

Boff writes that one can take two directions in describing the purpose of the Incarnation. One emphasizes the goal of healing human sinfulness and infirmity, while the other fixes on the creation of companions in love for the glory of God. Creation, according to this second approach, grew out of the wish of the divine figures to include others in their life of communion. This latter view, which was taught by the Franciscan John Duns Scotus (ca. 1266–1308), is preferred by Boff and many others because it is not based on the hypothesis of the sinful deficiencies of humankind, which contends that without human sin the Incarnation would seem to lack a purpose.[158]

Latter-day Saints see both functions in the atoning sacrifice of Christ. It is not an either/or. Humans are fallen, but they have the potential for exaltation, according to the Mormon understanding, because they are children of a divine Father. In his remarks to the pagan Athenians on Mars Hill, the apostle Paul approvingly quoted one of their poets to the effect that humans are of the *genos* — the "genus" or "kin" (another cognate) or "family" — of God.[159] As I have already noted, the *Clementine Homilies* declare human souls to be "of the same substance" with God. "But," the text goes on to say (in an argument strikingly similar to that advanced by Jesus himself at John 10:34–36),

> they are not gods. But if they are gods, then in this way the souls of all men, both those who have died, and those who are alive, and those who shall come into being, are gods. But if in a spirit of controversy you maintain that these also are gods, what great matter is it, then, for Christ to be called God? for He has only what all have.[160]

A revelation received by Joseph Smith in February 1832 describes those who are received into the highest degree of heaven:

> They are they into whose hands the Father has given all things —

---

158 Ibid., 166–67; cf. 165, 185.

159 Acts 17:28. On this passage and attendant issues, see Daniel C. Peterson, "'Ye are Gods': Psalm 82 and John 10 as Witnesses to the Divine Nature of Humankind," in Stephen D. Ricks, Donald W. Parry, and Andrew H. Hedges, eds., *The Disciple as Scholar: Essays on Scripture and the Ancient World in Honor of Richard Lloyd Anderson* (Provo, UT: FARMS, 2000), 471–594.

160 *Clementine Homilies* 16 (ANF 8:316).

They are they who are priests and kings, who have received of his fulness, and of his glory....

Wherefore, as it is written, they are gods, even the sons of God—

Wherefore, all things are theirs, whether life or death, or things present, or things to come, all are theirs and they are Christ's, and Christ is God's.[161]

A subsequent revelation teaches:

And they shall pass by the angels, and the gods, which are set there, to their exaltation and glory in all things...

Then shall they be gods, because they have no end; therefore shall they be from everlasting to everlasting, because they continue; then shall they be above all, because all things are subject unto them. Then shall they be gods, because they have all power, and the angels are subject unto them.[162]

In instruction offered at Ramus, Illinois, in April 1843, and now part of the Latter-day Saint canon, Joseph Smith taught that

When the Savior shall appear we shall see him as he is. We shall see that he is a man like ourselves.

And that same sociality which exists among us here will exist among us there, only it will be coupled with eternal glory, which glory we do not now enjoy.[163]

The juxtaposition here of highly anthropomorphic views of both God the Son and the heaven to which the Saints aspire is key to understanding the Latter-day Saint concept of salvation which, not unlike that of the Eastern Church, has often been dismissed as Pelagian.[164] Faithful Saints

---

161 D&C 76:55–56, 58–59.

162 D&C 132:19–20.

163 D&C 130:1–2.

164 Most anti-Mormon writing is too unsophisticated to avail itself of such terms as *Pelagianism*, but the charge is nonetheless fairly frequent. (Anti-Mormonism has produced an enormous "literature.") Anthony Hoekema, *The Four Major Cults: Christian Science, Jehovah's Witnesses, Mormonism, Seventh-Day Adventism* (Grand Rapids: Eerdmans, 1970), 52, for instance, pronounces Latter-day Saints "completely Pelagian with respect to the doctrine of original sin." The agnostic Sterling M. McMurrin, in his *The Theological Foundations of the Mormon Religion* (Salt Lake City: University of Utah, 1965), 74, makes the same identification, though without hostile intent. Bernhard

are offered entrance into the community of divine beings which is, in a very important sense, the one true God.

Brigham Young, speaking in the Tabernacle at Salt Lake City in 1859, declared that Mormonism is "designed to restore us to the presence of the Gods. Gods exist, and we had better strive to be prepared to be one with them."[165] "When will we become entirely independent?" he asked on another occasion. "Never, though we are as independent in our spheres as the Gods of eternity are in theirs."[166] Latter-day Saint monotheism will not be compromised by the eventual deification of any number of the saved, as that deification will occur only as they enter into essentially the same fellowship with the Father, Son, and Holy Spirit that the Trinity already enjoy among themselves—a fellowship that constitutes the Trinity "one God."[167]

Divine Oneness, Biblically Defined

As it turns out, there is indeed one passage in the New Testament where the nature of the divine unity is specified.[168] And, significantly, that same kind of unity is pronounced available, by no lesser figure than Jesus himself, to faithful believers. Knowing that his time on earth is short, Jesus prays to the Father for his disciples "that they may be one, as we are one."[169] And he has in mind not only the inner circle of the apostles:

> But it is not for these alone that I pray, but for those also who through their words put their faith in me; may they all be one:

Lange and Colleen McDannell, *Heaven: A History* (New Haven: Yale University Press, 2001), describe the Mormon view of heaven as one of the most concrete in Christian history.

165 Brigham Young, "Providences of God—Privileges and Duties of the Saints—Spiritual Operations and Manifestations—The Spirit World, &c," *Journal of Discourses* 7:238.

166 Brigham Young, "Blessings of The Saints—Covetousness, &c," *Journal of Discourses* 8:190.

167 It should be clearly understood, however, that the Trinity will not expand to become a Quaternity, or some such thing. In the hierarchical manner that characterizes Mormon thought in so many areas, members of the Trinity will continue to preside and the exalted righteous will continue to be subject to them. Presiding quorums in The Church of Jesus Christ of Latter-day Saints—e.g., bishoprics, stake presidencies, and the First Presidency that leads the Church as a whole—typically contain three members. This is yet another illustration of the way in which the Mormon understanding of heavenly society informs Latter-day Saint community life on earth.

168 Cardinal Kasper, too, sees the vital importance of this passage. See Kasper, *The God of Jesus Christ*, 303.

169 John 17:11.

as thou, Father, art in me, and I in thee, so also may they be in us, that the world may believe that thou didst send me. The glory which thou gavest me I have given to them, that they may be one, as we are one; I in them and thou in me, may they be perfectly one.[170]

There can be no question of modalism here, of a single person appearing under a multitude, now, of different masks. Nor does it seem plausible, for even the most perfectly united Christian community that might be conceived, to describe the relationship between believers as analogous to that between memory, understanding, and will, or to characterize members of such a community as "modes of being" or as subsistent relations within one essence rather than as individual centers of consciousness. This prayer of the Lord seems inescapably to imply a social model of the Trinity, bound together in absolute harmony by mutual indwelling or *perichoresis*. Moreover, Christ expressly asks that the faithful enjoy the same mutual indwelling ("they in us ...I in them and thou in me") that is enjoyed by the Father and the Son. And if perfect perichoretic union with the Father and the Son is not *theosis* or deification, it is difficult to imagine what it might be instead.

Final Reflections

While some Latter-day Saints, myself included, may be tempted to see in social trinitarianism a "coming around" of other Christians to our point of view, it may be more fruitful to see in it a potential bridge for more sympathetic mutual understanding.

Critics of The Church of Jesus Christ of Latter-day Saints have exaggerated and exploited the gap between mainstream Christendom and Mormonism on the issue of trinitarianism, but Latter-day Saints have commonly been their naïvely willing partners, overstating the separateness of the three divine persons of the Godhead. In doing so, Latter-day Saints have also unwittingly but artificially divided their understanding of the Trinity from their understanding of salvation, thus impoverishing both—a mistake that, in various forms, has occurred previously in the history of Christian doctrine. For Mormonism, its doctrine of the unity of the three divine persons can and should serve to ground its teaching on the ultimate destiny of the redeemed, as well as to justify its social and ecclesiastical vision and to inspire believers to ever richer cooperation, kindness, and mutual care. In other words,

---

170   John 17:20–23.

for Latter-day Saints, their understanding of the Trinity or the Godhead should be recognized as directly relevant to daily discipleship and praxis: "This is eternal life: to know thee who alone art truly God, and Jesus Christ whom thou hast sent."[171]

Particularly hostile critics tend to view Latter-day Saints as polytheists. This is simply wrong. It is no more accurate than is the common Latter-day Saint misreading of orthodox trinitarianism as modalism.

Phillip Cary lists seven propositions essential to trinitarian theology. Of these, the first three "confess the name of the triune God":

1. The Father is God.
2. The Son is God.
3. The Holy Spirit is God

The next three propositions "indicate that these are not just three names for the same thing":

4. The Father is not the Son.
5. The Son is not the Spirit.
6. The Holy Spirit is not the Father.

With his seventh and final proposition, Cary supplies the "clincher, which," he says, "gives the doctrine its distinctive logic":

7. There is only one God.

Two of Cary's own observations about these seven propositions are relevant here. First, he contends that they demonstrate that trinitarianism can be summarized without employing "abstract or unbiblical language." Second, he remarks,

> These seven propositions are sufficient to formulate the doctrine of the Trinity—to give the bare bones of what the doctrine says and lay out its basic logical structure. The logical peculiarities of the doctrine arise from the interaction of these seven propositions.[172]

Every one of these propositions, and all of them simultaneously, can be and are affirmed by The Church of Jesus Christ of Latter-day Saints.[173]

---

171 John 17:3.

172 Phillip Cary, "The Logic of Trinitarian Doctrine [Part I]," 2, as cited at Olson and Hall, *The Trinity*, 46.

173 Another way of making much the same point is to note that Latter-day Saints can agree with every one of the propositions deduced by the late-nineteenth-century

Cornelius Plantinga defends social trinitarianism as an acceptable form of monotheism "in," as he says, "appropriately enough, three ways." First, if the term *God* is used to refer uniquely or particularly to the Father, with the Son and Holy Spirit as derivatively divine—as, in fact, the New Testament typically uses it—social trinitarianism is certainly monotheistic. Second, if *God* is used to name the "divine essence"—"Godhead," "Godhood," or "Godness" (*divinitas, deitas,* or, in Greek, *theotes*)—as a set of attributes possessed by each divine person, social trinitarianism is, again, monotheistic. (And acceptably so: The notion of one "divine essence" is standard in many ancient and medieval discussions of the Trinity, particular in the Latin West.) Third, if *God* is employed to designate the Trinity as a whole—which it often is, even by standard Trinitarians—social trinitarianism remains securely monotheistic.[174]

The doctrine of The Church of Jesus Christ of Latter-day Saints satisfies all three of Cornelius Plantinga's conditions for monotheism.

I do not doubt that both critics and members of The Church of Jesus Christ of Latter-day Saints will be surprised to hear it, but Mormons are trinitarian Christians. The history of trinitarian doctrine is a long and complex one. But if there is room in trinitarian Christianity for the social model, there seems likewise to be room for the Latter-day Saints. The fundamental Mormon divergence from mainstream Christianity, doctrinally speaking, lies not in their beliefs regarding the nature of the divine unity, but in their rejection of an ontological chasm between divinity and humanity.[175]

Gregory Nazianzus remarks of Athanasius that, confronted with disturbing terminological differences between Eastern thinkers and "the Italians,"

> He conferred in his gentle and sympathetic way with both parties, and after he had carefully weighed the meaning of their expressions, and found that they had the same sense, and were nowise different in doctrine, by permitting each party to use its own terms, he bound them together in unity of action.[176]

Bishop of Exeter from his exhaustive and detailed survey of the relevant biblical data. See Edward Henry Bickersteth, *The Trinity* (Grand Rapids: Kregel, 1959).

174 Plantinga, "Social Trinity and Tritheism," 31–32.

175 Which is, of course, a subject for another paper—or book.

176 Gregory Nazianzus, *On the Great Athanasius*, NPNF ser. 2, 7:279.

Latter-day Saints and other Christians will continue to disagree on many things. But, if I'm correct, the doctrine of the Trinity need not loom quite so large among them.

Daniel C. Peterson *(Ph.D., University of California at Los Angeles) is a professor of Islamic studies and Arabic at Brigham Young University and is the founder of the University's Middle Eastern Texts Initiative, for which he served as editor-in-chief until mid-August 2013. He has published and spoken extensively on both Islamic and Mormon subjects. Formerly chairman of the board of the Foundation for Ancient Research and Mormon Studies (FARMS) and an officer, editor, and author for its successor organization, the Neal A. Maxwell Institute for Religious Scholarship, his professional work as an Arabist focuses on the Qur'an and on Islamic philosophical theology. He is the author, among other things, of a biography entitled* Muhammad: Prophet of God *(Eerdmans, 2007).*

Nephi's Obsession, or,
How to Talk with Nephi about God

Ralph C. Hancock

Review of Joseph M. Spencer, *1 Nephi: A Brief Theological Introduction* (Provo, UT: The Neal A. Maxwell Institute for Religious Scholarship, 2020). 146 pages. $9.99 (paperback).

Abstract: *Joseph Spencer's intimate familiarity with the Book of Mormon text, based upon years of close textual study and informed by a well-developed theological sensibility, is in full evidence in this lead-off volume in Neal A. Maxwell Institute's new series of books on the various books of the Book of Mormon. Leaving to prophets and apostles the responsibility for "declaring official doctrine," this new series approaches the book with the tools of the "scholarly practice" of theology. In Spencer's case at least, his practice is understood to be (1) informed by an emphasis on grace that is skeptical of claims of personal righteousness and (2) very much engaged with contemporary moral and social issues grounded in a fundamental concern for "equality." Accordingly, Spencer's reading is much more interested in "what God is doing in history with what we call the Abrahamic covenant" than with the more popular (non-scholarly) concerns of "everyday faithful living;" it is also more interested in Nephi's "realistic" and "mature" regret over his youthful over-boldness than in his confident statements of righteous faith. In the end, Spencer's extremely careful but theologically tendentious reading alerts us very skillfully to certain features of Nephi's imperfect humanity but reveals a consistent preoccupation with any possible faults in the prophet that might be extracted from an ingenious reading of the text. Finally, concerning women in the Book of Mormon, Spencer again expertly raises provocative questions about barely heard female voices but is too eager to frame these questions from the standpoint of the "modern sensibility" of "sexual egalitarianism."*

Joseph Spencer's academic qualifications for batting lead-off in the Neal A. Maxwell Institute's important new series of books on the various books of the Book of Mormon are notable. Professor Spencer, who has taught in BYU's ancient scripture department since 2015, is author of two previous books closely examining the Book of Mormon text[1] as well as scores of articles, chapters, and reviews on these and related topics. He is co-editor of the Book of Mormon Series (in which the present title appears) as well as editor of the Maxwell Institute's *Journal of Book of Mormon Studies*. (Let us note as well that Joseph Spencer holds a PhD in philosophy and has also published extensively in that demanding field of scholarship.) As he demonstrates in the present work, Spencer has devoted years of close and faithful study to the Book of Mormon and has much to offer the reader who is willing to join him in a fresh and searching engagement with an ancient and inspired text.

Interpretive Grace

Professor Spencer emphasizes that his approach to 1 Nephi is *theological*. "My first purpose in the following pages is ... to show how much we miss in 1 Nephi — how much we miss that's of a theological nature" (3). In this he echoes the series introduction: "This series focuses particularly on theology — the scholarly practice of exploring a scriptural text's implications and its lens on God's work in the world" (viii). It seems that the meaning of this "scholarly practice" is best understood (again from the series introduction) "as opposed to [that is, as distinct from] authoritative doctrine," that is, "as, literally, *reasoned* 'God talk'" (viii). This series, we read, intends to engage "each scriptural book's theology on its own terms" (viii) without imposing any "single approach to theology or scriptural interpretation" (ix). Thus, the Maxwell Institute's editorial approach enacts a rather abrupt division of labor between "prophets and apostles [in] their unique role of declaring official doctrines" (viii) and the theologian's scholarly practice of reasoned engagement with the scriptural text. From this point of view, it seems, it would be surprising if prophets reasoned or if a theologian's reasonings reckoned with prophetic authority.[2] The series introduction concludes quite decorously

---

1. Joseph M. Spencer, *An Other Testament: On Typology* (Salem, OR: Salt Press, 2012); Joseph M. Spencer, *The Vision of All: Twenty-Five Lectures on Isaiah in Nephi's Record* (Salt Lake City: Greg Kofford Books, 2016).

2. We should note that Spencer's "theological" interpretation seems to take as given the historicity of the Book of Mormon as an ancient record; he certainly treats Nephi as the author of the text under examination. This view of Book of

with a dedication to Elder Maxwell's "apostolic conviction that there is always more to learn from the Book of Mormon and much to be gained from our faithful search for Christ in its pages" (ix), as distinct, to be sure, from the official declaration of definitive doctrines.

If a "theological" approach is not to be confused with one that takes its bearings by "authoritative doctrine," then what kind of "God-talk" will serve as Spencer's interpretive touchstone? "And this might be the truest sign of prophecy," Spencer writes, "that it comes through those God exalts *despite* their human nature" (5, emphasis added). This insight or sensibility sets the tone of Spencer's theology and thus of his interpretation of 1 Nephi. To remember that prophets are, like us, "earthen vessels" (6; quoting 2 Corinthians 4:7), is to look at scripture as "an astonishing textual embodiment of *grace*" (5, emphasis added). With this in mind, the author will minimize any evidence of Nephi's own virtue or righteousness and highlight or, rather, seek out evidence — even the most subtle and indirect — of the prophet's all-too-human nature. And this interpretive choice, we will see, aligns nicely with Spencer's interest in the "questions [that] are most pressing right now, two decades into the twenty-first century" (4). (Direct attention to these contemporary questions occupies the second half of this book.) As we keep in mind both our dependence on grace and the contemporary issues that swirl around us, Spencer promises (in a characteristically self-effacing resort to the first person plural) to "show how much we miss in 1 Nephi — how much we miss that's of a theological nature" (3).

Textual Structure and Covenantal History

Along with this theological emphasis on grace/earthen vessels, Spencer's interpretive method relies heavily on his very searching investigations of the overarching structure of Nephi's writings (with due attention, of course, to the original chaptering). The theological purpose of the book can only come to light after we "ask how 1 Nephi is organized" (12). There is reason to believe that this organization is very careful and deliberate,

---

Mormon historicity is unmistakably affirmed in the Maxwell Institute's excellent *Maxwell Institute Study Edition* of the Book of Mormon. See editor Grant Hardy's "General Notes," which make a very strong case for real historicity on many grounds — linguistic, intra-textual, geographical (old world and new), reliable witnesses, etc. See Grant Hardy, ed. *The Book of Mormon: Another Testament of Jesus Christ, Maxwell Institute Study Edition* (Provo, UT: Neal A. Maxwell Institute for Religious Scholarship, Religious Studies Center at Brigham Young University/ Salt Lake City: Deseret Book, 2018).

since the account we are reading was written decades after the events recounted. Spencer proposes that the main theme or underlying concern of 1 Nephi is the "intertribal conflict between Nephites and Lamanites" (12). Attention to this concern leads Spencer to "connect Nephi's vision to Isaiah and Isaiah to Nephi's vision" (21), and this attention culminates in the major thesis of his interpretation: "For the most part, then, Isaiah's prophecies aren't for Nephi about everyday faithful living. They're about the long-term destiny of Israel" (22). Spencer is willing to indulge more naïve readers who look at 1 Nephi as "a collection of illustrative stories, vignettes modeling faith amid adversity" (22), as "just another means to the end of feeling the Spirit and receiving direction for our lives" (23), but he is clear that "Nephi asks us to read his work primarily in a different way" (22). In particular, while "we're certainly free to read 1 Nephi 8 as an allegory for our individual struggles to prove faithful" (30), Spencer strikingly suggests, mainly on the basis of "the sudden shift in the dream-scape, specifically when Laman and Lemuel refuse the tree," (29) that "the numberless concourses are the children of Laman and Lemuel — perhaps especially in the last days" (29), and thus that "the dream is primarily about Lehi's two oldest sons" (29). "Nephi's vision is about getting the children of Laman and Lemuel into God's presence" (32).

Spencer is thus much more interested in "what God is doing in history with what we call the Abrahamic covenant" (35) than with the more commonplace concerns of "everyday faithful living" (22). Concretely, this means seeing the Book of Mormon as "the iron rod that leads latter-day Lamanites — and Gentiles with them — along the gospel path" (36). From this perspective, the apostasy is less a matter of "early Christians jettison[ing] specific ordinances" than it is of forgetting "the covenants of the Lord, which he hath made unto the House of Israel" (35; 1 Nephi 13:23), as these have to do with the destiny of "latter-day Lamanites" (36). This is the meaning of Nephi's "likening" to Isaiah: "The two stories, Nephi's and Isaiah's, are one, although occurring among different branches of Israel" (41).

"We should share Nephi's obsession with the history of the Abrahamic covenant. Perhaps we should even share his obsession with Isaiah" (43). Why Spencer's focus on this "obsession?" And just what follows from it? Although he recognizes — as any passably attentive reader of Nephi must — that "Christ is the hero of the covenantal story Nephi has to tell" (61), that "to know Christ is to know the covenant, for Nephi" (62), Spencer seems determined to emphasize what we might call the historical and communalist features of Christ and the covenant.

This historical-covenantal "obsession" inevitably tends to the neglect of the plain meaning of the gospel for every faithful individual as this is explained by Nephi himself in his wonderful concluding statement of the "doctrine of Christ" in 2 Nephi 31. Is it not in Jesus Christ and his doctrine of faith, repentance, baptism, the gift of the Holy Ghost, and enduring to the end, that the Lord universalizes his covenant for all people? Why then would a student of Nephi's prophecies wish to set the "historical" and "covenantal" meaning of Nephi's teaching against the doctrine of Christ as it applies to each of us individually?[3]

---

3. If we were to brave just for a moment the Maxwell Institute's firm distinction between authoritative doctrine and the academic practice of theological interpretation, we might take note of President Russell M. Nelson's striking willingness to confuse the gathering of Israel with concerns related to personal righteousness:

> My dear young brothers and sisters, these surely *are* the latter days, and the Lord is hastening His work to gather Israel. That gathering is the most important thing taking place on earth today. Nothing else compares in magnitude, nothing else compares in importance, nothing else compares in majesty. And if you choose to, if you want to, you can be a big part of it. You can be a big part of something big, something grand, something majestic!

> When we speak of the *gathering*, we are simply saying this fundamental truth: every one of our Heavenly Father's children, on both sides of the veil, deserves to hear the message of the restored gospel of Jesus Christ. They decide for themselves if they want to know more. ...

> My question tonight to every one of you between the ages of 12 and 18 is this: Would you like to be a big part of *the greatest* challenge, *the greatest* cause, and *the greatest* work on earth today? ...

> Every child of our Heavenly Father deserves the opportunity to *choose* to follow Jesus Christ, to accept and receive His gospel with all of its blessings — yes, all the blessings that God promised to the lineage of Abraham, Isaac, and Jacob, who, as you know, is also known as Israel.

> My dear extraordinary youth, you were sent to earth at this precise time, the most crucial time in the history of the world, to help gather Israel. There is *nothing* happening on this earth right now that is more important than that. There is *nothing* of greater consequence. Absolutely *nothing*.

> This gathering should mean *everything* to you. This *is* the mission for which you were sent to earth. (Russell M. Nelson, "Hope of Israel," Worldwide Youth Devotional, June 3, 2018, https://www.churchofjesuschrist.org/study/new-era/2018/08-se/hope-of-israel.)

To inquire further into the reasoning behind Spencer's obsession with covenantal-collective history *as opposed to* the gospel as addressed to individuals would lead

Against "Individualism"

The answer to this question seems to emerge later in Spencer's book,[4] in the context of a discussion of Nephi's killing of Laban:

> Nephi learned through his encounter with the Spirit that God's purposes are bigger than our own. *The communal and the covenantal are to be privileged above our individual – and often selfish – concerns.* We're proud of our *modern individualism,* but Nephi's story suggests there's something important beyond our cloistered concerns. We're not to be hermits, demonstrating our *individual righteousness* to God and others in our withdrawal from the world. We're meant to live together in love, jointly keeping the commandments and making wherever we live a land of promise. (80, emphasis added)

This remarkable confessional statement provides the key, I think, to understanding Spencer's obsessions. He has already told us that a certain understanding of "grace" provides his theological touchstone, that is, that human beings are exalted, not so much through excellent personal qualities or the ongoing work of perfecting individual human nature, but "despite their human nature" (5). From this point of view, any preoccupation with "individual righteousness" can be classified with the "selfish" concerns of "modern individualism." Such spiritualized selfishness, from Spencer's point of view, constitutes a "withdrawal from the world," where "the world" is interpreted, not, say, as the allurement of a Great and Spacious Building, but as the commitment "to live together in love, *jointly* keeping the commandments and making wherever we live a land of promise" (80, emphasis added). Spencer's historical-covenantal

---

us to examine Spencer's impressive earlier writings on the Book of Mormon, and especially his *On Typology* (see, in the volume under review, endnotes 1.2, 2.1, and 4.1). The substantive question of Israel's covenant is bound up for Spencer with the textual-structural question of the divisions of Nephi's text. Surprisingly (at least to me), Spencer (following a 1986 article by Frederick W. Axelgard; see endnote 1.2) advocates not Nephi's own division between 1 Nephi and 2 Nephi, but a division between 2 Nephi 5 and 6. This division serves an argument that emphasizes Isaiah's prophecies and Nephi's "likening" of them over Nephi's concluding doctrinal chapters, and especially the remarkable "doctrine of Christ" set forth in 2 Nephi 31 in which Nephi is uniquely instructed *by the Father and the Son.* In Spencer's structural scheme, this powerful and luminous chapter can only figure as a kind of epilogue to the main treatment of Israel- and Lamanite-directed prophecy.

4. Part II, "The Theological Questions of 1 Nephi," chapter 4 (the first chapter in this Part), "Laban's Death" (66–81).

focus is thus rigorously associated with his theology of grace. And this theology of grace, despite the concession to "commandments" (qualified by *jointly*), implies a de-emphasis, at least, on personal righteousness, which would entail "our withdrawal from the world," and a distinct collective-historical turn towards "making wherever we live a land of promise" by "living together in love."

Spencer's highlighting of Nephi's preoccupation with the historical and collective Abrahamic covenant as it applies particularly to the descendants of the Lamanites is an important contribution to our understanding of Nephi's prophetic voice. Perhaps the central question the author puts to the reader is whether the collective-historical interpretation of grace — *as opposed to* the faithful individual's quest for salvation, enduring to the end while "relying wholly upon the merits of him who is mighty to save" (2 Nephi 31:19), according to the doctrine of Christ — best serves the cause of Israel's redemption.

As noted above, the other main fruit of Spencer's theology of grace-based interpretation is his emphasis on Nephi's quite flawed humanity, especially in his relations with his less righteous — or, shall we say, less-than-cooperative — brothers, Laman and Lemuel. Now, anyone who has read 2 Nephi 4 has heard Nephi himself confessing and grieving over his own imperfect humanity, and the context of this confession certainly suggests that Nephi's vexations have to do with his relations with his now thoroughly alienated brethren. Certainly Spencer is right, as Noel Reynolds showed long ago,[5] that Nephi's authorial perspective has much to do with the "intertribal conflict between Nephites and Lamanites" (12). The subtitle of 1 Nephi refers, after all, to the prophet's "reign and ministry." But Spencer wants to suggest further that a close reading of Nephi's text reveals his intention to apologize for his mistreatment of Laman and Lemuel:

> We're apt to feel that Nephi is unfair to his understandably baffled brothers and that maybe they were right to see Nephi as self-righteous and judgmental. If so, shouldn't we worry that Nephi lacks common feeling, that he was spiritually gifted but socially clueless? And could someone like that really be a reliable guide to living a rich spiritual life in community with others? (67) … Among these more human figures, Nephi looks almost pathologically faithful. (83)

---

5. Noel B. Reynolds, "The Political Dimension in Nephi's Small Plates," *BYU Studies* 27, no. 4 (1987):1–24. Cited by Spencer, endnote 5.3.

This criticism of Nephi[6] perfectly fits the mold of Spencer's interpretive scheme: Nephi went wrong in that he prioritized "judgmental" *personal* righteousness over the grace-enabled understanding that makes possible a *communal* spiritual life, "a rich spiritual life in community with others" (67). Spencer grants that Nephi is "neither dismissive nor mean" to his brothers, but he does blame Nephi for being "paternalistic" (95). From this point of view, the narrative of 1 Nephi appears "as an aspect of national propaganda," a propaganda that the rest of the story in the Book of Mormon suggests "worked too well" (85).

To be sure, Spencer's purpose is ultimately to vindicate Nephi insofar as the prophet eventually realized the error of his ways, and it is from the perspective of this mature recognition and communal spirituality that the books of Nephi were written. The point of bringing to light and emphasizing Nephi's "foibles" is "to make clear that we follow the prophets precisely because of what *God* does through them, not because of what or who they are *on their own*" (96, emphasis in original). For Spencer, Nephi's resolute statement of his readiness to obey the Lord's commandments in what is surely one of the most quoted passages in the Book of Mormon (1 Nephi 3:7, "I will go and do ... ") is an example of the prophet's youthful self-righteousness, later corrected or adjusted by his more "realistic" and "mature" statement that the Lord nourishes and strengthens those who keep the commandments and provides "means whereby they can accomplish the thing which he has commanded them" (1 Nephi 17:3).

I must say I am underwhelmed by the supposed contrast between these statements. More generally, I would say that Nephi's humanity is evident enough throughout his account (nowhere more than in 2 Nephi 4, to be sure), and needs no deepening through the attribution of immature and anti-social self-righteousness. There is no reason to contend, in response to Spencer's preoccupation with "humanizing" Nephi, that the prophet never made a misstep he regretted. But Spencer is perhaps a little overconfident of his capacity to judge the youthful Nephi. Is it a fault to be humorless and overly serious when coming out of a conversation with the Father and the Son into a squabble with faithless brothers who refuse to believe their own father and his claims to visions? And how much slack should Nephi have given Laman and Lemuel, who were known to have schemed and even attempted on multiple occasions to murder Nephi or his father, ultimately being restrained only by divine interventions? The fact that Nephi dwells so little on these facts in his writing seems indeed to point to his decades

---

6. My point is not that Spencer simply agrees with such criticism of Nephi, but he certainly takes his bearing by it and expands upon it.

of distance from the events being reported — but not quite to the kind of change of heart Spencer perceives. Nephi has certainly put the events of 1 Nephi into a much larger perspective by the time of his writing, but perhaps not a perspective that questions his earlier righteousness in quite the way or to the degree that Spencer aims to show.

The Theological Questions of Modern Morality

We will touch more lightly on the rest of the second half of Spencer's *1 Nephi*, "Part II, The Theological Questions of 1 Nephi." Interestingly, these theological questions arise not from the great questions of the theological tradition (the Godhead, salvation, atonement, etc.), which, to be sure, have been addressed to some degree in Part I as they emerge from the text, but from the characteristic preoccupations of contemporary social progressives, or let us say of younger Latter-day Saints influenced by a contemporary, progressive moral-political framework. Thus, the question of personal morality — pushed aside or demoted in Spencer's account of Nephi and his brethren, as it relates to the "doctrine of Christ," in favor of the collective-covenantal perspective — now returns in force, but from a contemporary moral perspective not drawn from but superimposed upon scripture. From this perspective, Spencer imagines his reader asking, or invites his reader to ask, whether, since "prophets aren't infallible ... could [Nephi] get something so seriously wrong that he leads us astray?" (67).

The first such "theological question" Spencer engages, in Chapter 4, is the classic one of Laban's death. His discussion of this hard case is careful and rewarding. Much to his credit, the author invites his readers to adopt a critical attitude concerning "strictly rational ethical demands" in "an increasingly secularized world" (70). He here seems to identify *rational* rather narrowly, I would say, with a liberal-secular view of "public reason," in which reason is defined *a priori* as excluding any religious or otherwise soulful considerations. In any case, Spencer shows himself ready to allow the Lord to "smash the rational and ethical idols we're tempted to place before the God of faith and obedience" (71).

But Spencer dismisses rather abruptly one sort of the argument that might be considered "rational" — namely, one that would justify Nephi's action as "excusable homicide under the public law of the time" (69), quite confident that the argument from legality to morality is of little worth, that "ethical questions generally eclipse legal questions for good reason" (70). I can see Spencer's point, but is there not good reason to regard positive laws as practical instantiations and indispensable determinations of ethical norms? Surely the legal deserves to be taken into account as an essential domain of the ethical.

In keeping with his overall approach, Spencer seems somewhat over-eager to interpret Nephi's killing of Laban as another example of his maturation from self-righteous youth to mature, covenant-focused prophet. That is, he is eager to distinguish motives that might well be considered as two aspects of one righteous motive: Nephi's interest in being a righteous person — a desire "tainted with a competitive spirit" (78) — *as opposed to* his obedience to divine commands understood as instrumental to "God's covenantal promises to whole peoples" (78). When he cannot quite prove this distinction from the text, Spencer resorts to leading questions: "Was [Nephi] interested in keeping commandments, or did he treat the commandments primarily as something to force himself into his role as ruler and teacher? … Is he depressed, aware that he has perhaps overreached? Or is he as confident as ever? We don't know" (76). No, in fact, we do not. And we have no reason to assume such overreach unless we insist *a priori* on dividing personal righteousness from covenantal promises.

Spencer's reading finally supports a faithful approach to the text in that he is ready to accept Nephi's action as commanded — or rather *constrained* — by the Spirit. (Spencer is convinced this distinction is important.) Indeed, he pushes back against those who adopt a "self-congratulating intellectual superiority" and are thus scandalized by the story of Laban's slaying. It's "hard to be critical without being hypocritical" (80), he wisely notices. But, characteristically, he reaches out to Nephi's critics and, braving his own warnings about hypocrisy, judges that "there are motes in Nephi's eyes, to be sure — maybe even beams" (80). Nephi is redeemed, from this point of view, by the fact that Nephi's own story, when read closely enough, shows that "he seems to hope we'll see those motes, or even those beams" (80).

Joseph Spencer's extremely careful reading certainly alerts us very skillfully to certain features of Nephi's imperfect humanity. But it seems to me that the author's own theological priorities — a certain understanding of grace motivates his determination to drive a wedge between personal righteousness and salvation and the collective-covenantal — consistently lead him to overstate Nephi's faults.

Women and Feminism

There is much that is valuable and, I think, quite original in Spencer's chapter 6 ("The Women") on women and sexuality. He rightly draws our attention to Jacob 3:6, which seems to tie the Lord's eventual mercy toward the Lamanites to what Spencer calls their "relative gender parity" (103). Once again, the author seems more confident than the textual evidence supports that the story of Nephites and Lamanites over ten centuries can be significantly structured around Lamanite superiority in terms of sexual morality and the treatment of women. It must be granted to Spencer's thesis that there is a striking and disturbing resonance between Jacob's condemnation of Nephite sexual practices very early in the story and Moroni's shocking revelations at the very end (Moroni 9:9-10). It must be noted, still, that the Lamanites are hardly models of morality,[7] and Moroni's late judgment against the Nephites takes the form of an equivalence with the Lamanites: "this great abomination of the Lamanites ... doth not exceed that of our people" (Moroni 9:9). Spencer is certainly right, in any case, to draw our attention to the sexual violence at the heart of Moroni's accusation of his own people.

Spencer also provides a very richly suggestive comparison between the "conflict between the sexes" (113) in the persons of Sariah and Lehi, on one hand, and the second-generation conflict between Nephi and Laman, in which the question of women's suffering is wholly subordinated to "rivalry between Israelite men ... in their own fights for dominance and inheritance" (113). But are we sure we want to reduce Nephi's struggle with his brethren to a fight for dominance or inheritance? More generally, the very expressions by which Spencer frames the Nephite/Lamanite comparison on sex and gender points once again to a certain excess or arbitrary tendency in Spencer's rhetorical framing of scriptural teachings and theological problems. What the prophet Jacob frames as monogamous chastity (as opposed to polygamy, concubinage, and whoredoms), Spencer expresses in keeping with the contemporary preoccupation with "gender parity" (103). Thus a very natural and surely legitimate concern for the mostly silent struggles of womankind is fitted to a distinctly contemporary ideological frame. Nephi's readers are urged to look for "a promise of sexual egalitarianism" and examples of "women willing to resist oppression" (113–14). This "oppression" seems to include any circumstances in which a woman's commitment to her "social role" (106, 115) might seem to trump her individual self-expression. It must be said that Spencer decidedly wavers here in his own critique of "modern individualism." In fact he plainly judges all earlier societies as "oppressive cultures" from the standpoint of our

---

7. See Moroni 9:8: "they [the Lamanites] feed the women upon the flesh of their husbands, and the children upon the flesh of their fathers."

apparently unimpeachable modern sensibilities. This is the standpoint from which "the Nephites' 'imperfections'" (114) — including, to be sure, Nephi's own — are scrutinized. If some belief or habit or social role tends to "make us cringe today" (114), this seems to provide a sufficient basis for moral judgment. At least, for Spencer, Nephi deserves credit for his "struggle against those attitudes" (114) that we have at last overcome in the name of the "modern sensibility" of "sexual egalitarianism."

To be sure, Professor Spencer acknowledges that even we (that is, we modern egalitarians) are all still struggling, since "we're as enmeshed in oppressive cultures as the prophets of the past" (115). But in this very acknowledgement, the author seems to convict living prophets as much as the rest of us; the implication is that the prophets were and are as enmeshed as we are, and that only modern moralists can begin to escape the oppression inherited from less enlightened times in that moment of awakening in which our individual consciousness is liberated from our "social roles," and thus from complicity in the oppression that modern prophets don't yet clearly see. The prophets are included in the convicted "we," and the author situates himself among those awakening from "oppression."

Invoking once again the convicting first person plural, Spencer confesses that "we're almost certainly blind to our own prejudices" (115).

I suppose we can agree on that.

Ralph C. Hancock *(PhD Harvard) is Professor of Political Science at Brigham Young University, where he teaches the tradition of political philosophy as well as contemporary political theory. He has taught three times as Visiting Professor at the University of Rennes, France, and was a Visiting Scholar at Liberty Fund in Indianapolis. He is the author of* Calvin and the Foundations of Modern Politics *(Saint Augustine's Press, 2011; Cornell University Press, 1989) as well as* The Responsibility of Reason: Theory and Practice in a Liberal-Democratic Age *(Rowman & Littlefield, 2011). He is also the editor of* America, the West, and Liberal Education *(Rowman & Littlefield, 1999) and, with Gary Lambert, of* The Legacy of the French Revolution *(Rowman & Littlefield, 1996) and translator of numerous books and articles from the French, including Pierre Manent's* Natural Law and Human Rights *(Notre Dame University Press, 2020). He has published many academic articles as well as articles in the press and online on the intersection of faith, reason and politics. Professor Hancock is a Consulting Editor of* Perspectives on Political Science *and a member of the editorial board of* Square Two, *an online journal of*

"Faithful Scholarship by Members of the Restored Church of Jesus Christ of Latter Saints on Contemporary Issues." He is also co-founder of Fathom the Good, which provides a history and humanities curriculum for home schools and independent schools grounded in the Western tradition of political philosophy.

An Intelligent, Thoughtful Work on One of the Richest Portions of the Book of Mormon

Jeff Lindsay

Review of Terryl Givens, *2nd Nephi: A Brief Theological Introduction* (Provo, UT: The Neal A. Maxwell Institute for Religious Scholarship, 2020). 124 pages. $9.95 (paperback).

Abstract: *Terryl Givens's well-written and enjoyable book does much to equip readers of the Book of Mormon with new tools to appreciate the riches of a text often viewed as the most difficult part of the Book of Mormon. Givens helps us recognize Nephi's sorrow over Jerusalem and his passionate hope and joy centered in the Messiah, Jesus Christ. He helps us understand the weightier matters that Nephi focuses on to encourage us to accept the covenants of the Lord and to be part of Zion. Readers will better respect 2 Nephi as a vital part of the Restoration with content critically important for our day.*

Terryl Givens's recent book *2nd Nephi: A Brief Theological Introduction*,[1] part of the Neal A. Maxwell Institute's series on the books of the Book of Mormon, exceeded my expectations. Givens, of course, is a popular, skilled, and intelligent writer who has done much to expand readers' appreciation of the scriptures. In spite of that, I approached this book wondering just how much he could do with the constraint of writing about 2 Nephi, a book many less experienced students of the scriptures feel is dull and difficult to understand, in part because of its emphasis on Isaiah and the paucity of action within its pages, rather unlike 1 Nephi with its dramatic tales of fleeing Jerusalem, obtaining the

---

1. Terryl Givens, *2nd Nephi: A Brief Theological Introduction* (Provo, UT: Neal A. Maxwell Institute, 2020).

brass plates, journeying across the Arabian Peninsula, and sailing to the New World. Givens surprised me by revealing both the poignancy and the spiritual depth in 2 Nephi with fresh perspectives. While *2nd Nephi: A Brief Theological Introduction* is a short work of 124 pages, it is packed with meaning and is a book I am pleased to recommend.

A useful introduction considers just how deeply Nephi must have been affected by Lehi's prophetic confirmation that Jerusalem had been destroyed and considers Nephi's possible motivation for starting a second volume in his writings. Givens then begins with a discussion of "The New (and Very Old) Covenant" in chapter 1, reminding us of the background to the grand plan of salvation and the covenant relationship that God invites us to enter into in order to return to Him. Some of this basic knowledge, including a knowledge of the premortal existence, was among the "plain and precious things" (1 Nephi 13:28) Nephi foresaw would be lost in our day but would be restored to those who would hear. Givens then briefly surveys covenant theology from the perspective of modern Protestantism and compares that to covenant theology in the Book of Mormon and shows some of the helpful additions brought by the perspective of the Book of Mormon.

Given notes that the Book of Mormon greatly emphasizes the theme of covenants, using the word far more (174 times) than the New Testament (30 times), and sees the covenant-oriented Book of Mormon as a text that would resonate with growing interest in covenant theology among many Christians in Joseph's day (22).

Givens discusses the Book of Mormon's unique combination of New Testament themes and a belief in Christ among Hebrews living the Law of Moses, followed by a "New World John the Baptist figure (Samuel the Lamanite, a descendant of Lehi)" (23) declaring the imminent birth of Christ, followed by the dramatic account of the visit of the Resurrected Lord to the New World, where the Savior then established His Church and commissioned twelve disciples. "It is as if the Book of Mormon rewrites the Old and New Testament records into a holistic gospel narrative in which Christ is the fulcrum rather than the culmination of Christian history, with both sides of the historic divide equally Christocentric" (23). That struck me as a beautiful way to summarize what the Book of Mormon does.

Givens emphasizes Nephi's passionate faith in Christ, rejoicing in His future Atonement and victory over death even as he kept the law of Moses long before the coming of the Lord. Givens also notes an important feature of the Book of Mormon is not just its focus on the House of Israel *per se* as the beneficiary of the Lord's covenants, but its additional focus on the Gentiles who can join Israel by adoption, a concept that is not a New Testament innovation but one that was known in Nephi's day. The universality of the covenants and blessings of the Gospel is an important contribution of the Book of Mormon (25–26).

In 2 Nephi, Givens sees a subtle but important shift in speaking of the future Savior as Christ rather than as the Messiah as in 1 Nephi. That semantic shift is accompanied by a shift in Nephi's spiritual field of vision as he moves from a focus on the local land of promise of the tiny Nephite people to a broad scope embracing "Jew and Gentile, literal Israel and spiritual Israel alike" (27) and even a shift that moves from a localized land of promise to the more universalized concept of Zion. Through his attention to such subtleties, Givens helps bring us closer to the meat of 2 Nephi and the intent of Nephi and his brother Jacob. This discussion of shifting perspectives in 2 Nephi makes an elegant segue to the second chapter, "They Are Not Cast Off."

A passage on the title page of the Book of Mormon speaks to the remnant of the House of Israel and tells them that one purpose of the book is "that they may know the covenants of the Lord, that they are not cast off forever." The latter phrase always struck me as odd. Why speak of not being cast off forever? Givens helped me better appreciate this. Four times in 1 Nephi we are warned that the wicked will be "cast off,"[2] and in 1 Nephi 17:47, Nephi fears that his wicked brethren might be "cast off forever." But 2 Nephi introduces another subtle shift. Instead of again raising the threat of being cast off, Jacob hopefully points to the possibility for just the opposite:

> And now, my beloved brethren, seeing that our merciful God has given us so great knowledge concerning these things, let us remember him, and lay aside our sins, and not hang down our heads, for we are **not cast off**; nevertheless, we have been driven out of the land of our inheritance; but we have been led to a better land, for the Lord has made the sea our path, and we are upon an isle of the sea. (2 Nephi 10:20)

Though not cast off, much has been lost because of the wickedness of others. Not only have they been driven from their initial land of inheritance and led away from Jerusalem, but Jerusalem itself, the holy city, has been destroyed. Givens helps us understand just how terrible the news of Jerusalem's destruction would be for Nephi's people, though it

---

2. See 1 Nephi 8:36, 10:21, 15:33, 17:47.

had been prophesied. But in spite of such trauma, God's mercy remains extended and they are not cast off.

Givens sees significance in Nephi's response to their second exodus after being driven from the land of Nephi toward another new territory in the wilderness (2 Nephi 5:5–7). After this loss of their first New World land of inheritance, which followed abandonment of their original land of inheritance in the Old World, Nephi builds a temple as if it were a marker for their new land of promise, however temporary, and moves forward. The land of promise can be fluid as the Lord leads His people, as with Nephi and Abraham, in a "pattern of guided exile" (37). Givens then applies this concept to the experience of the early Latter-day Saints and their repeated migrations. He also sees the shift in the focus from a particular geographical land of promise for the Saints to our more universal concept of Zion. In our day, I would also add that we have had and will likely yet experience a series of guided retreats from the world in various ways on the path to build Zion and a Zion people, wherever we may live.

The next chapter also draws upon a phrase from the title page of the Book of Mormon, and an important theme of Nephi's writings: "To the Convincing of Jew and Gentile that Jesus is the Christ." Givens reminds us of the unrelenting emphasis on Christ in Nephi's writings, as in the whole Book of Mormon. He addresses the obvious question about how a little band of Hebrews in 600 BC would know of Jesus Christ, citing often overlooked New Testament passages such as Hebrews 4:6, where Paul says the Gospel was first preached to the children of Israel (see also Acts 3:28 and 1 Peter 1:10–11), and he quotes Daniel Boyarin:[3] "[V]ersions of this narrative, the Son of Man story (the story that is later named Christology), were widespread among the Jews before the advent of Jesus; Jesus entered into a role that existed prior to his birth, and this is why so many Jews were prepared to accept him as the Christ, as the Messiah, Son of Man" (52). Givens also cites Shirley Lucass,[4] who "argues that far more than a vague 'pre-messianism' was present" (52) among early Jews.

Nephi is absolutely clear that based on the writings of other prophets and continuing revelation in his day, he and his people knew of the coming of Jesus Christ and of His Gospel centuries before Christ was born. Indeed, Givens observes that Nephi is able to bear personal witness of Christ and His redemption (2 Nephi 1:15), as does his brother Jacob in 2 Nephi 9–11, and that the Book of Mormon urges us to seek

---

3. Daniel Boyarin, *The Jewish Gospels* (New York: New Press, 2012), 72-73.

4. Shirley Lucass, *The Concept of Messiah in the Scriptures of Judaism and Christianity* (London: Bloomsbury, 2011), 13-14.

personal revelation on our own to know of the reality of Christ and the truthfulness of His Gospel.

Givens sees these prophetic, personal witnesses of Christ as

> a motif of incalculable significance in the Book of Mormon. If this sacred record were no more than inspired fiction, then the testimonies of its mythical figures would be no more than a literary charade. The power and efficacy of the book and the testimonies it conveys are mutually dependent. (53)

It is refreshing to see a respected scholar so keenly aware of the power of the Book of Mormon in our increasingly secular age.

Speaking of the painful distance that many Christians feel between "the vanished moments of [Christ's] living, breathing, bodily reality" (54) and the modern world with its scattered relics reminding us of ancient Jerusalem and His ministry, Givens writes:

> Into this immense historical vacuum strewn only with dusty fragments and well-worn stony paths, the Book of Mormon bursts with a remarkable, audacious claim: Jesus was not a once-in-eternity incarnation of the Divine, flashing like a shooting star into the long night of history. His Palestinian birth and ministry were not the beginning and end of his human interaction, and the Old World and its people are not the only setting in which he loved and healed. The Book of Mormon multiplies the field of Christ's operation and its perseverance across place and time. (54–55)

Givens nicely elucidates 2 Nephi's persistent focus on the future Messiah, Jesus Christ.

In the fourth and perhaps most ambitious chapter, "More Plain and Precious Things," Givens explores five doctrinal issues raised in 2 Nephi: (1) the fall as a fortunate occurrence, (2) the principle of opposition, (3) teachings on atonement, (4) the centrality of agency, and (5) the doctrine of Christ.

His treatment of the fall might be especially interesting for many readers who may not appreciate just how divergent the Book of Mormon view on the fall is from many other Christian views in our era. Givens considers statements by Jonathan Edwards and others, but could also have included views from Eastern Orthodox writers and many others. Givens recognizes how revolutionary it was to view the fall as necessary for human progress and ultimately joy, a teaching found in 2 Nephi 2:25

("Adam fell that men might be, and men are that they might have joy") and in the Book of Moses.[5]

Givens ably tackles the five topics of this chapter and adds a number of insights on such issues as the importance of choice with consequences for free agency to be meaningful (75–77) and the way Christ's Atonement allows us to be free, such that we can eternally persist in our choice for joy and righteousness through Christ (81). Some points in this chapter are rather philosophical and at times did not seem as clear as I would have liked, perhaps due to my inexperience in philosophy and theology. Nevertheless, readers should come away with enhanced appreciation for the richly satisfying intellectual content in 2 Nephi.

In this volume (as with many books) there are some things I would have liked to see included, but that list could quickly become unreasonably long, given the numerous treasures in Nephi's books. Nevertheless, prior scholars have had much to say about Nephi's writings that could have been profitably noted or incorporated into this volume, including exploration of the way Nephi used large chiasmic structures as part of his organization, the proposed reasons his writings were split into two books, his use of particular motifs, his many ancient poetical tools such as those in the unique gem of 2 Nephi 4 ("Nephi's Psalm"), his extensive allusions to the Exodus, etc. But for the scope Givens covers, he has done remarkably well and has given readers a generally approachable and thoughtful book that will add new reasons for respecting the Book of Mormon and new windows into the richness of Nephi's second book. It is a beautifully written, interesting, and thoughtful book worth studying carefully while also offering enjoyable and accessible content that may make for a pleasant initial quick read when time is short.

Congratulations to Terryl Givens for this contribution!

Jeffrey Dean Lindsay *recently returned to the United States after almost nine years in Shanghai, China. Jeff has been providing online materials defending the LDS faith for over twenty years, primarily at JeffLindsay. com. His Mormanity blog (http://mormanity.blogspot.com) has been in operation since 2004. He is currently a Vice President for The Interpreter Foundation and co-editor of* Interpreter: A Journal of Latter-day Saint Faith and Scholarship.

---

5. Moses 5:11, where Eve says, "Were it not for our transgression we never should have had seed, and never should have known good and evil, and the joy of our redemption, and the eternal life which God giveth unto all the obedient."

Jeff has a PhD in chemical engineering from BYU and is a US patent agent. He is currently Senior Advisor for ipCapital Group, assisting clients in creating intellectual property and innovation. He was recently the Head of R&D and IP for a US consumer product company, Lume Deodorant, and from 2011 to 2019 was the Head of Intellectual Property for Asia Pulp and Paper in Shanghai, China, one of the world's largest forest product companies. Formerly, he was associate professor at the Institute of Paper Science and Technology at Georgia Tech, then went into R&D at Kimberly-Clark Corporation, eventually becoming Corporate Patent Strategist and Senior Research Fellow. Every year since 2015, Jeff has been recognized as one of the world's top IP strategists by Intellectual Asset Magazine *in their global IAM Strategy 300 listing based on peer input. He is also lead author of* Conquering Innovation Fatigue *(John Wiley & Sons, 2009). He is active in the chemical engineering community and was recently named a Fellow of the American Institute of Chemical Engineers. Jeff served a mission in the German-speaking Switzerland Zurich Mission. He and his wife Kendra are the parents of four boys and have eleven grandchildren.*

FORMED IN AND CALLED FROM THE WOMB

Dana M. Pike

Abstract: *Drawing on his deep knowledge of biblical Hebrew, Dana Pike gives us a close reading of Jeremiah 1:5, the most important Old Testament verse relating to the Latter-day Saint understanding of premortal existence of human spirits and the foreordination of prophets to their appointed callings. He shows that the plain sense of this verse cannot be easily dismissed: first, and consistent with Latter-day Saint understanding, God knew Jeremiah before he was conceived and that afterward, in a second phase that transpired in the womb, he was, "according to the Israelite perspective preserved in the Bible," appointed to become a prophet.*

See Dana M. Pike, "Formed in and Called from the Womb," in *"To Seek the Law of the Lord": Essays in Honor of John W. Welch,* ed. Paul Y. Hoskisson and Daniel C. Peterson (Orem, UT: The Interpreter Foundation, 2017), 317–32. Further information at https://interpreterfoundation.org/books/to-seek-the-law-of-the-lord-essays-in-honor-of-john-w-welch-2/.]

Jeremiah's call narrative or vocation report includes a clear example of pre-birth divine election:

> (1:4) "Now the word of the LORD came to me saying,
>
> (1:5a) 'Before I formed you in the womb [*babbeṭen*] I knew you,

(5b) and before you were born [came forth from the womb/ *mērehem*] I consecrated you;

(5c) I appointed you a prophet to the nations'" (Jer. 1:4–5; NRSV).[1]

However, there is ambiguity about the meaning of the phrase "from the womb" and there are persistent questions about the relationship between Jeremiah 1:5a—"Before I formed you in the womb I knew you"—and 1:5b+c, "before you were born [came forth from the womb/ *mērehem*] I consecrated you; I appointed you a prophet to the nations." Therefore, this paper engages other biblical texts mentioning in-womb election to determine if the Bible itself provides a clearer indication of the meaning of divine election "from the womb" and how Jeremiah 1:5a and 1:5b+c ought to be understood in relation to each other.[2]

I argue that *in its biblical context* this passage claims YHWH "knew" Jeremiah before Jeremiah was conceived, and that he was later chosen to be a prophet by YHWH *in the womb*, distinguishing between pre-conception "knowing" (although exactly what that entails is not clear from the passage itself) and post-conception but pre-birth "consecrating" and "appointing."[3] However, such an approach is at least

---

I consider it an honor to participate in this volume celebrating Jack Welch's career and accomplishments. With energy and vision, Jack has contributed greatly to Latter-day Saint scholarship. And he has been active and gracious in encouraging and supporting others engaged in the same pursuit. The first version of this paper was presented several years ago in a "Latter-day Saints and the Bible" session at a national Society of Biblical Literature (SBL) meeting (as part of a larger study of mine on Jeremiah 1:5). Jack was instrumental in creating this SBL section, which continues to live on.

1   All English translations of biblical passages are taken from the New Revised Standard Version (NRSV) unless otherwise noted. I note in passing that there is a difference of scholarly opinion on whether Jeremiah 1:5 is poetry or not. Leslie C. Allen, *Jeremiah* (OTL commentary series; Louisville, KY: Westminster John Knox, 2008), 24, considers it prose ("I judge only vv. 14b–19 [in chapter 1] to be poetry"), as do others. Contrast the comments of Jack R. Lundbom, *Jeremiah 1–20* (Anchor Bible; NY: Doubleday, 1999), 227, who thinks verse 5 is poetry.

2   For a review of the concept of divine election and a survey of biblical and extra-biblical examples, see Dana M. Pike, "Before Jeremiah Was: Divine Election in the Ancient Near East," in *A Witness for the Restoration: Essays in Honor of Robert J. Matthews*, ed. Kent P. Jackson and Andrew C. Skinner (Provo, UT: Religious Studies Center, Brigham Young University, 2007), 33–59.

3   Because of its focus on a topic in the Hebrew Bible, in this paper I have chosen the commonly used form "YHWH" to represent the divine name of Israel's God, which occurs in Hebrew as *yhwh*, which is also represented by the hybrid anglicized form "Jehovah" and the substitute designation "the LORD." For further discussion of this name and these forms, see Dana M. Pike, "The Name and Titles of God in the Old

implicitly rejected by many commentators who understand Jeremiah 1:5 to indicate that the sum total of YHWH's knowing, consecrating, and appointing of Jeremiah all took place either before conception *or* after conception, depending on the authors and their perspectives.

Hebrew Nouns translated "Womb"

Two Hebrew nouns, *beṭen* and *reḥem*, are often rendered "womb" in English translations of the Bible.[4] The term *beṭen*, designates "innards, belly." A passage in which *beṭen* refers to the general abdominal area — in a man — is Judges 3:21: "then Ehud…took the sword from his right thigh, and thrust it into Eglon's belly [*beṭen*]" (see also, Job 32:19; Ezek. 3:3). This noun is also used figuratively, as in Jonah 2:2 (Hebrew Bible [HB] v. 3), "I called to the LORD out of my distress,…out of the belly [*beṭen*] of Sheol I cried" (see also, Job 38:29). An example of a passage in which the noun *beṭen* denotes a female womb is Genesis 25:24: "When her [Rebekah's] time to give birth was at hand, there were twins in her womb [*beṭen*]" (see also, Gen. 38:27; Eccles. 11:5).

The other Hebrew noun, *reḥem*, is *only* used in reference to females, as opposed to *beṭen*, which, as illustrated above, can refer to the innards of a male or a female. Thus, *reḥem* is routinely translated "womb."[5] The noun *reḥem* occurs in such passages as Genesis 29:31, "when the LORD saw that Leah was unloved, he opened her womb [*reḥem*]; but Rachel was barren," and Exodus 13:2, "Consecrate to me [YHWH] all the firstborn; whatever is the first to open the womb [*reḥem*] among the Israelites, of human beings and animals, is mine." Job 38:8 contains an example of the figurative use of *reḥem*, with the sea bursting forth "from the womb" when YHWH created the earth.

Testament," *Religious Educator* 11, no. 1 (2010): 17–31, especially 19–21; and Dana M. Pike, "Biblical Hebrew Words You Already Know, and Why They are Important," *Religious Educator* 7, no. 3 (2006): 97–114, especially 106–09.

4   For a fuller discussion and further citations of these terms, see Esther Fuchs, "Breasts and Womb," in *Encyclopedia of the Bible and Its Reception Online*, ed. Christine Helmer, et al. Vol. 4 (New York: Walter de Gruyter), 453–56 (http://www.degruyter.com/view/EBR/MainLemma_10196?pi=0&moduleId=common-word-wheel&dbJumpTo=breasts.) See also, T. Kronholm, "*reḥem*," in *Theological Dictionary of the Old Testament*, rev. ed., ed. G. Johannes Botterweck, Helmer Ringgren, and Heinz-Josef Fabry, trans. by David E. Green (Grand Rapids, MI: Eerdmans, 2004), 13:454–59.

5   As indicated in most Hebrew lexica, the relationship between the noun *reḥem* and the verbal root *rḥm*, usually translated "to have mercy, to love," is not entirely clear. The latter is generally considered to be denominative.

Several biblical passages contain *beṭen* and *reḥem* in parallel, including Jeremiah 1:5 (quoted above), Job 31:15 (quoted below), and Psalms 22:10 (KJV; HB v. 11): "I was cast upon thee from the womb [*reḥem*]: thou art my God from my mother's belly [*beṭen*]."[6] Other terms that refer generally to a person's inner torso and sometimes occur in parallel with *reḥem* or *beṭen* are *kilyōt* and *mēʿîm*.

Three important points of biblical theology are evident in connection with the use of *beṭen* and *reḥem*. First, God creates people in the womb. For example, Psalms 139:13 reads, "For it was you [YHWH] who formed my inward parts [*kilyōt*]; you knit me together in my mother's womb [*beṭen*]." And Job rhetorically asks: "Did not he [God] who made me in the womb [*beṭen*] make them? And did not one fashion us in the womb [*reḥem*]?" (Job 31:15; see also, Isa. 44:2, 24).[7] Second, God "opens" or "closes" the womb of a woman, allowing her to conceive or not. For example, 1 Samuel 1:5 reads: "the LORD had closed her [Hannah's] womb" (see also, Gen. 29:31, quoted above, and Gen. 30:2). And third, arguably utilizing midwife imagery, it is God who brings people forth from the womb, causing them to live. For example, "Why did you [God] bring me forth from the womb?" (Job 10:18; see also Ps. 22:9 [HB v. 10]; 71:6). Thus, a woman's womb is the place of God's creation, of first human life.[8] The language of these biblical womb- and birth-related reports has led Leslie Allen to correctly observe, "There is nothing special about the language of fetal development; the attribution to a divine creative shaping is a glorious commonplace."[9]

---

6   Modern translations often attempt to avoid the repetition of womb/womb or womb/belly. Thus, the NRSV translates this verse, "On you I was cast from my birth [literally, "from the womb," *reḥem*], and from the womb [*beṭen*] of my mother you have been my God."

7   Just as YHWH gave life in the womb, so he could terminate it there: "because he [YHWH] did not kill me in the womb; so my mother would have been my grave" (Jer. 20:17; see also Job 10:18–19).

8   As Gwynn Kessler, *Conceiving Israel, The Fetus in Rabbinic Narratives* (Philadelphia: University of Pennsylvania, 2009), 112, has observed, "except for God's involvement in biblical pregnancies, the Bible lacks any explicit theory of precisely how pregnancy occurs. Of course, sexual intercourse is often—but not always—alluded to or mentioned in bringing about pregnancy, but the Hebrew Bible never explicitly acknowledges the substances involved in bringing about pregnancy." However, at least some awareness of these substances is indicated in passages such as Gen. 38:6–9 and Lev. 12:2.

9   Leslie C. Allen, *Jeremiah*, 25. Additionally, see the language of Isa. 46:3, which depicts YHWH as a pregnant mother: "Listen to me, O house of Jacob,...who have been borne by me from your birth [*minnî-beṭen*], carried from the womb [*minnî-reḥem*]."

The prepositions and verbs used with *beṭen* and *reḥem* in these and related passages play an important role in the discussion that follows. This general overview of these two nouns provides a basis to now examine biblical passages that contain the phrase "from the womb" and to then deal with divine election claims containing *reḥem* and/or *beṭen*.

The Phrase "from the womb"

Of the biblical passages containing *babbeṭen* or *bāreḥem*, "in the womb," only Jeremiah 1:5 involves divine election, utilizing as it does both *babbeṭen* and *mēreḥem*. Election passages that mention the womb typically employ the forms *mēreḥem* and especially *mibbeṭen*, "*from* the womb."[10] (In the Hebrew Bible, the final letter, *n*, in the preposition *min*, "from," often assimilates to the following consonant, which is then doubled [*mibbeṭen*] or causes compensatory lengthening of the vowel [*mēreḥem*].) However, there is an inherent challenge in how to understand the intended meaning of the phrase "from the womb" in certain passages.

The translation of some texts containing *mēreḥem* and *mibbeṭen* is straightforward. For example, Job 1:21 and Jeremiah 20:18 are routinely understood as meaning "from within the womb." This is because of the action involved:

> Job 1:21: "He said, 'Naked I came from my mother's womb [*mibbeṭen*]'."[11]

> Jeremiah 20:18: "Why did I come forth from the womb [*mēreḥem*] to see toil and sorrow, and spend my days in shame?" (see also Ps. 22:10 [HB v. 9]; Job 3:11).

Here, "borne by me from (within) the womb" would be a better rendition, since it is paralleled by "carried from (within) the womb."

10   To be clear, these forms also occur in passages that have nothing to do with election, such as Judg. 3:22 and Jer. 20:18. See below. In the main, the Hebrew proposition *min*, "from," is used in the Bible with spatial (locational and directional), temporal, originating, and partitive senses. For discussion with examples, see Bruce K. Waltke and M. O'Connor, *An Introduction to Biblical Hebrew Syntax* (Winona Lake, IN: Eisenbrauns, 1990), 11.2.11.

11   Interestingly, the next phrase in this verse, "and naked shall I return there," figuratively references the earth as a type of womb. Job came forth from his human mother's womb and at death would "return" to the figurative womb of mother earth (cf. Gen. 3:19; this commingling of a female womb and the earth also occurs in Ps. 139:13–15). There is little or nothing to support trying to read more into this literary figure than that. Compare the imagery of the earth as the womb from which the sea "burst out" in the creation context in Job 38:8, cited above.

The individual in each of these passages was in the womb, and came forth from the womb.

However, as Lundbom Freedman (and others) have claimed: "in theological contexts *mibbeṭen* has two meanings, 'from within the womb' (Job 1:21; Ps. 22:10 [9]) or 'from birth' (Judg. 13:5; Ps. 58:4 [3]; 71:6)."[12] Although this claim is generally accepted concerning *mibbeṭen*, I do not agree with all of Freedman's examples. The challenge, of course, is knowing when *mibbeṭen* is intended to convey the sense of "from (within) the womb" and when it means "from birth," and if this distinction even matters (I think it does).

One passage cited by Freedman and others to demonstrate that *mibbeṭen* can have the sense of "from birth" is Psalms 71:6:

"Upon you [YHWH] I have leaned from my birth [*mibbeṭen*; "from the womb"];

it was you who took me from my mother's womb [*mimmĕ'ēy 'immî*]."

The current translation practice is to render *mibbeṭen* in Psalms 71:6 as "from birth" (e.g., NRSV, NIV, NET), rather than more literally as "from the womb" (KJV). The point of these poetic lines is to figuratively represent someone's trust in YHWH ever since they have been alive. However, this verse does not appear to be making a statement on whether pre-birth fetuses or post-birth infants have agency and choose to trust YHWH. Nor does it appear possible to tell from this verse, theologically speaking, whether or not the biblical author really intended to convey the possibility of trust "from (within) the womb."[13]

Similarly, another passage in which *mibbeṭen* is often understood to mean "from birth," is Psalms 58:3 (HB v. 4): "The wicked go astray from the womb [*mēreḥem*]; they err from their birth [*mibbeṭen*], speaking lies" (cf. Isa. 48:8, in which the "house of Jacob" is called "a transgressor from the womb" [KJV; *mibbeṭen*]). Presumptions that fetuses are not wicked and that they do not speak falsehood "from (within) the womb" can be claimed as support for the now common rendering of *mibbeṭen* (and

---

12   Lundbom Freedman, "*beṭen*," in *Theological Dictionary of the Old Testament*, rev. ed., ed. G. Johannes Botterweck and Helmer Ringgren, trans. by John T. Willis (Grand Rapids, MI: Eerdmans, 1977), 2:97.

13   Nor is this paper the place to thoroughly analyze the theological meaning of this or the verses that are cited next. However, given the biblical depiction of life beginning in the womb and the wording of Ps. 71:6, I see no biblical requirement to interpret *mibbeṭen* in 71:6a as "from birth" as opposed to "from (within) the womb."

mērehem) in this verse as "from birth."[14] (Although newborns do not speak either!) Whether the "incorrigibility of the wicked" decried in this verse is more a literary figure or a theological given is open to debate.[15] However, the parallel use of *mērehem* and *mibbeṭen* does nothing to help resolve the specific value and theological meaning of these expressions.

The challenge of interpreting the intent of these phrases raises questions about the timing of YHWH's election of individuals "from the womb." Realizing that *mibbeṭen* and *mērehem* can, depending on the passage (and on the translator), convey the sense of "from (within) the womb" or "from birth," I will now review the election passages that contain *mibbeṭen* and *mērehem*, and analyze them to determine which of these two meanings seems most appropriate.

Election Passages with "from the womb"

Some biblical passages convey a form of divine foreknowledge and election, but do not include *mērehem* or *mibbeṭen* ("from the womb"), such as Genesis 25:23: "And the LORD said to her [Rebekah], 'Two nations are in your womb [*bĕbeṭen*], and two peoples born of you shall be divided; the one shall be stronger than the other, the elder shall serve the younger'."

Other passages, such as Isaiah 44:2 and 49:5, indicate that YHWH formed his chosen "servant" *mibbeṭen*, "from the womb," which is usually now translated "*in* the womb" (e.g., NRSV, NET), since, as mentioned above, YHWH creates people *within* their mothers' wombs, not just when they are coming forth at birth. The KJV translates Isaiah 44:2 and 49:5 literally, "formed you from the womb," but this is awkward compared to the rendition of formed "in the womb."[16] However, the emphasis in Isaiah 44:2 and 49:5 is not on *where* the servant was chosen,

---

14 See similarly, Mitchell Dahood, *Psalms II: 51–100* (Anchor Bible 17; Garden City, NY: Doubleday, 1968), 56, 59 ("wayward from birth"); and Frank-Lothar Hossfeld, *Psalms 2: A Commentary on Psalms 51–100* (Hermeneia 19b; Minneapolis: Fortress, 2005), 78, 81 ("liars go astray from their birth").

15 See Dahood, *Psalms II: 51–100*, 59, for the quotation. Although the topic of wickedness from the womb / from birth is not the focus of this paper, several other passages of scripture may be related to this concept, including the description of Cain as a "murderer from the beginning" (Ether 8:15). Perhaps somewhat related are the descriptions of Satan as a "liar from the beginning" (D&C 93:25) and as a "murderer from the beginning" (John 8:44). Of course, the phrase "from the beginning" occurs in a variety of scripture passages with "beginning" having a variety of reference points. I thank an unnamed reviewer for mentioning these passages.

16 Isa. 44:24 similarly mentions YHWH creating his "servant" in the womb (*mibbeṭen*; cf. 44:21), but election is not emphasized in that verse.

only that YHWH created him (physically) *mibbeṭen*, so these passages add little to this discussion.

More to the point, Judges 13:3–5 recounts that, "the angel of the LORD appeared to the woman [Samson's mother] and said to her…'you shall conceive and bear a son. No razor is to come on his head, for the boy shall be a nazirite to God from birth [*min-habbeṭen*]. It is he who shall begin to deliver Israel from the hand of the Philistines'." As it often does, the NRSV renders, in this case *min-habbeṭen*, "from the womb," as "from birth." However, the NRSV of Judges 16:17 presents the adult Samson's reference to his divine election with a different rendition of the phrase in question: "So he [Samson] told her [Delilah] his whole secret, and said to her, '…I have been a nazirite to God from my mother's womb [*mibbeṭen*]'." This apparent inconsistency in translation highlights the question concerning the intent of these passages. Was Samson a nazirite "from (within) the womb" or only "from birth," i.e., when his mother delivered him?

The well-known election passage in Isaiah 49:1 reads, "The LORD called me [Israel personified] before I was born [*mibbeṭen*, "from the womb"]; while I was in my mother's womb [*mimmĕʿēy ʾimmî*; "from the innards of my mother"] he named me." By including the word "before" in its rendition, the NRSV of 49:1 conveys the sense that election took place before birth, while YHWH's servant was still *in* the womb, but the Hebrew text does not include the word "before."[17] However, the NET rendition entirely avoids in-womb election in this verse: "The LORD summoned me from birth [*mibbeṭen*]; he commissioned me when my mother brought me [*mimmĕʿēy ʾimmî*] into the world."

The variance in these two modern translations of Isaiah 49:1 and the inconsistency between the NRSV renditions of Judges 13:5 and 16:17 highlight the ambiguous nature of the phrase *mibbeṭen*, "from the womb." This situation raises questions about theological and other personal influences on translations and complicates the effort to confidently determine whether the Bible presents YHWH as choosing or electing people while they are alive "in the womb" or just from/at birth. Not surprisingly, the biblical form and ambiguity continues into the Greek New Testament, as found in Paul's claim in Galatians 1:15: "But

---

17 The Hebrew form *bĕṭerem*, "before," does not occur in the verse, as it does in Jer. 1:5. The NRSV includes "before" here to clarify the sense of "in the womb" rather than "from birth." The older KJV faithfully renders the Hebrew, but it does not provide an indication of how "from the womb" is understood: "The LORD hath called me from the womb [*mibbeṭen*]; from the bowels of my mother [*mimmĕʿēy ʾimmî*] hath he made mention of my name."

when God, who had set me apart before I was born [*ek koilias mētros mou*; "from my mother's womb"]..." (NRSV, again adding "before" to indicate in-womb election). Alternatively, the NET renders the phrase in question as: "set me apart from birth," thus avoiding in-womb election by their translation.

Thus, due to the nature of the Hebrew form *mibbeṭen*, Judges 13:5; 16:17; and Isaiah 49:1, in and of themselves, do not decisively clarify the timing of YHWH's election, whether in the womb or when the child was actually delivered and thus became fully human, although I think the former option is more likely. However, the position that at least some Israelites accepted in-womb divine election is definitely supported by Jeremiah 1:5 (discussed below) and it finds contextualization in similar claims in certain non-Israelite election texts. Oft-cited examples include king Pi/Piye, who conquered much of Egypt ca. 730 BC and established the 25th Egyptian dynasty, and of whom it was claimed: "It is [the god] Amun Re who is speaking...to his beloved son, king Pi, 'I said of you when you were still in your mother's body, that you would be ruler of Egypt, for I already knew you in the seed, when you were still in the egg, that you would become Lord'."[18] And Neo-Babylonian king Nabonidus (556–539 BC) claimed he was one "whose fate [the gods] Sin and Ningal (while yet) in the womb of his mother had destined for dominion."[19]

Returning to Jeremiah 1:5

As reviewed above, the Hebrew Bible is consistent in representing that YHWH creates people "in the womb," but there are differing positions, expressed through different renditions of *mēreḥem* and *mibbeṭen*, on whether YHWH elects or chooses people while they exist *in* the womb, or merely at their birth. However, this latter ambiguity is eliminated in Jeremiah 1:5:

> (1:5a) 'Before [*bĕṭerem*] I formed you in the womb [*babbeṭen*] I knew you,

> (5b) and before [*bĕṭerem*] you were born [came forth from the womb/*mēreḥem*] I consecrated you;

---

18   *Near Eastern Religious Texts Relating to the Old Testament*, ed. Walter Beyerlin, trans. Hellmut Brunner (Philadelphia: Westminster, 1978), 29.

19   Shalom M. Paul, "Deutero-Isaiah and Cuneiform Royal Inscriptions," *Journal of the American Oriental Society* 88, no. 1 (1968): 185. For several additional ancient Near Eastern examples of election, both in the womb and in a king's youth, see Pike, "Before Jeremiah Was: Divine Election in the Ancient Near East," 42–49.

(5c) I appointed you a prophet to the nations."

Jeremiah 1:5b contains the phrase *mēreḥem*, but the Hebrew word *běṭerem* explicitly indicates that Jeremiah was "consecrated" or sanctified before birth: "before [*běṭerem*] you came forth from the womb [*mēreḥem*]." This supports, or at least allows for, the plausibility of understanding the intent of in-womb election in Judges 13:5; 16:17; and Isaiah 49:1 (as well as Gal. 1:15). The fact that *mibbeṭen* is used in those verses instead of *mēreḥem* seems to have no bearing on the interpretation of "from the womb." However, given the ambiguity of the sense intended by *mibbeṭen* in these other passages, and given that we have no biblical discussion of the concept, it is difficult to know for sure whether or not all Israelites at all times shared a broad-based, common view of the concept of in-womb election (as explicitly evidenced by Jer. 1:5).

Although it is not the primary purpose of this paper to analyze all the components of Jeremiah 1:5, a few comments are in order on the words "knew" (5a), "consecrated" (5b), and "appointed" (5c). The Hebrew lexical root *yd'*, "to know," conveys a variety of related meanings in Hebrew, including to have awareness and understanding of something or someone (e.g., Judg. 13:21; Job 37:16), to know someone sexually through intercourse (Gen. 4:1; Num. 31:17), and to be aware of and care for someone (e.g., Gen. 18:19; 2 Sam. 7:20). I agree with commentators who view the sense of *yd'* in Jeremiah 1:5 as similar to its use in Amos 3:2, where YHWH says to Israelites, "You only have I known of all the families of the earth; therefore I will punish you for all your iniquities." Divine election and covenant were the combined basis for YHWH's unique knowing of collective Israel. We should likewise understand this meaning of *yd'* in Jeremiah 1:5: YHWH was not *just* aware of or acquainted with Jeremiah, but "knew" him in a relationship and chose him before he was conceived.[20]

The words "consecrated" (5b) and "appointed" (5c) further emphasize Jeremiah's status in his prophetic role. "Consecrated" or "sanctified" (KJV) translates the Hebrew verbal form *hiqdiš*, to set people or things apart from common or profane use, to dedicate them to God and his use. "Appointed" or "ordained" (KJV) translates the Hebrew lexical root *ntn*, "to give," which by extension here means to place upon or to create

---

20 As Jack R. Lundbom, *Jeremiah 1–20*, 231, has observed, "There has been a tendency to interpret the present usage [in Jer. 1:5] of *yd'* so as to make it synonymous with *bḥr*, "to choose," i.e., 'I knew you' = 'I chose you'." And as William L. Holladay, *Jeremiah 1* (Hermeneia; Minneapolis: Fortress, 1986), 33, has claimed, "'Know' here [in Jer. 1:5] then implies both intimacy and covenantal bond."

an opportunity for someone. Essentially, this passage declares that once YHWH "knew" or chose Jeremiah, he then gave him a prophetic assignment in which he was dedicated or set apart to represent YHWH.[21]

The second question I am exploring in this paper is, how does Jeremiah's election in the womb (1:5b+c) relate to the concept in 1:5a, that YHWH "knew" Jeremiah *before* he was "formed in the womb"? Variations on two possible options have been proposed for understanding the relationship between Jeremiah 1:5a and 5b+c. One approach has been to view 5a and 5b+c as essentially saying the same thing. Some scholars suggest that YHWH knew and called Jeremiah before Jeremiah was born and stop there, blurring into one pre-birth package any time differential between pre-conception and in-utereo. For example, in commenting on Jeremiah 1:5 the *New Bible Commentary* simply claims, "The Lord...knew and appointed him [Jeremiah] before he was born."[22] "Appointed," of course, is something YHWH did when Jeremiah was in the womb (1:5b+c). But 1:5a claims YHWH "knew" Jeremiah before he was even conceived.

Interestingly, a variation on this approach occurs when some Latter-day Saints blur the distinction of time and place in Jeremiah 1:5a and 5b+c, but in a different way. Latter-day Saints accept as doctrine the premortal existence of all humans as spirit children of God the Father. They further believe these premortal spirit beings were chosen or foreordained during their premortal existence to opportunities and responsibilities in this mortal life.[23]

Latter-day Saints regularly use Jeremiah 1:5 to support this doctrine. For example, Ellis Rasmussen claimed that, "this passage is one of the few clear revelations about foreordination in the scriptures. It tells of Jeremiah's being sanctified for special service and ordained to be a prophet in his premortal life — ...for it happened before his body was

---

21 As mentioned above, I am not dealing with the issue of agency in this study.

22 Gordon McConville, "Jeremiah," in *New Bible Commentary*, 21st Century ed. ed. Gordon J. Wenham, et al. (Downers Grove, IL: IVP Academic, 1994), 674. Similarly, Allen, *Jeremiah*, 25, provides an assessment of Jeremiah's call—"divine planning that antedated his conception and birth....Long ago a decision had been made, to set Jeremiah aside to belong to God"—that contains no delineation of time, either preconception or in-womb.

23 See "The Family: A Proclamation to the World—The First Presidency and Council of the Twelve Apostles of The Church of Jesus Christ of Latter-day Saints," *Ensign*, Nov. 1995, 102; and Gayle O. Brown, "Premortal Life," in *Encyclopedia of Mormonism*, ed. Daniel H. Ludlow, 4 vols. (New York: Macmillan, 1992), 1123–25.

even formed."[24] In actuality, Jeremiah 1:5 says Jeremiah was "sanctified" (KJV) or "consecrated" while he was *in the womb*, not before he was conceived. In this case, I presume a Latter-day Saint belief in premortal election coupled with a desire to support and emphasize the doctrine of premortality has prompted Rasmussen, and other Latter-day Saints who have similarly commented on this verse, to simply ignore the second, in-utero phase mentioned in 1:5b+c, which itself aligns closely with other biblical passages, mentioned above, that contain claims of in-womb election.[25] But the outcome is the same; the two stages represented in Jeremiah 1:5 — pre-conception and in-womb — are essentially and erroneously blurred into one. I know of no Latter-day Saint Church authority who has claimed that the phrase "from (within) the womb" is a biblical idiom or metaphor that really means *before conception*. And there is currently no evidence, scriptural or otherwise, to substantiate such a claim.[26]

Despite the claims of some Latter-day Saint and non-Latter-day Saint commentators, and given the regularity of the portrayal of the concepts that YHWH creates people in the womb and chooses people *mērehem* and *mibbeṭen*, "from (within) the womb," it is difficult to assume, based on the received canon of the Hebrew Bible, that ancient Israelites understood Jeremiah 1:5a and 5b+c as synonymous. A *biblically-based* rendition of this verse requires two separate activities at two chronologically distinct stages of Jeremiah's existence: (1) YHWH "knew" Jeremiah *before* he created Jeremiah in the womb (1:5a),[27] and (2) YHWH "consecrated" and "appointed" Jeremiah when he was *in* the womb (1:5b+c).

---

24 Ellis T. Rasmussen, *A Latter-day Saint Commentary on the Old Testament* (Salt Lake City: Deseret, 1993), 541.

25 See also Monte S. Nyman, *The Words of Jeremiah* (Salt Lake City: Bookcraft, 1982), 16, who states, "this verse substantiates the doctrines of premortal life and foreordination of the prophets," but mentions nothing about Jeremiah being consecrated and appointed in his mother's womb; and Kerry Muhlestein, *The Essential Old Testament Companion* (American Fork, UT: Covenant, 2013), 427, who notes that Jer. 1 teaches us about being known to and ordained by God "before the world was created," but again, Jer. 1:5 says he was "ordained" (KJV) or "appointed" "from (within) the womb."

26 Furthermore, while it might seem preferable to some Latter-day Saints to postulate that election "from (within) the womb" is merely a biblical metaphor or figure of speech for true premortal election, this can only remain speculation; there is nothing substantive in the Bible or elsewhere that supports such an assumption. I have tried in this study to work with the text of the Bible as we have received it.

27 And, from a Latter-day Saint view, this premortal phase could and did include divine appointing or foreordination.

Thus, treating the content of Jeremiah 1:5a and 5b+c as representing two separate phases of Jeremiah's existence and as two separate, but related, actions on YHWH's part is the other major interpretive option of dealing with these two portions of Jeremiah 1:5. Recognizing this biblical distinction may strike Latter-day Saints as odd, but it does allow for clearly asserting a premortal component to Jeremiah's existence, rather than merely seeing everything pre-birth as one fuzzily undefined phase. And it seems to make better sense of other biblical passages that place election in the womb.

Some non-Latter-day Saint scholars do note a difference in 1:5 between the pre-conception and in-utero stages. But they say nothing substantial about it, presumably because they do not accept the concept of premortality. They thus treat these claims, especially that YHWH "knew" Jeremiah before Jeremiah was conceived, as creative hyperbole.[28]

Of course, understanding the distinction between these two phases — preconception and in-womb — as explicitly mentioned in Jeremiah 1:5 raises the question of what is intended by it. Although we cannot be sure, since there is nothing else like this in the Hebrew Bible, my presumption as a Latter-day Saint is that there are two distinct phases of existence mentioned in Jeremiah 1:5, and that the consecrating and appointing associated with the second, in-womb phase (1:5b+c) may be understood in its biblical context as a reaffirmation and even an extension of the "knowing" that occurred previously during the pre-conception phase (1:5a), now that Jeremiah was an "observable" life-form in his mother's womb. (If the actions in the two phases are completely different and distinct, we cannot currently explain the difference[29]). This claim is viable since biblical "knowing" can convey a sense of relationship, and even choosing and covenanting with someone (see Amos 3:2, mentioned above).

In reality, we do not know what the biblically depicted in-womb consecrating and appointing was thought by Israelites to involve, nor do we know for sure why multiple biblical passages place such appointing *in* the womb, as opposed to before conception or after birth. It is no wonder that some commentators have bundled the preconception and

---

28 See for example, Lundbom, *Jeremiah 1–20*, 135, 230–31, 236; and Robert P. Carroll, *From Chaos to Covenant: Uses of Prophecy in the Book of Jeremiah* (London: SCM, 1981), 45.

29 In-womb divine appointing is not a doctrinal issue discussed by Latter-day Saints. Furthermore, the biblical evidence is sufficiently meager that we do not know if (some/all) Israelites believed that in-womb election was the norm for all people, or only for certain representatives of YHWH.

in-womb actions mentioned in Jeremiah 1:5 into just one phase of activity. However, *if* in-womb appointing is merely a biblical metaphor for premortal choosing, as some Latter-day Saints might assume, then why the distinction in Jeremiah 1:5 between preconception knowing and in-the-womb consecrating and appointing? The Bible presents in-womb divine election as a reality, but does little to aid our understanding of this phenomenon.[30]

Conclusion

Jeremiah 1:5 remains a theologically significant verse. We cannot easily dismiss the two separate phases or stages of Jeremiah's existence and calling represented in Jeremiah 1:5 as a poorly preserved biblical text, as an idiom, or by simply ignoring them. Beyond what Jeremiah 1:5a conveys with the declaration that YHWH "knew" Jeremiah before he was conceived, the biblical text declares that YHWH created Jeremiah in the womb, and that *after* Jeremiah was conceived — *after* he became a viable and recognizable human life-form in his mother's womb — he was, *according to the Israelite perspective preserved in the Bible*, "appointed" to become a prophet of YHWH. I think there is no avoiding this plain sense of the verse, although what the theological implications are is open to question. Thus, Jeremiah 1:5, in its biblical context, is best understood as attesting to *two* pre-birth phases of Jeremiah's existence. It also witnesses to an Israelite understanding of two phases of pre-birth election, that which occurred before conception and additionally that which occurred post-conception but in the womb. Although this raises questions we cannot currently answer, such queries in no way annul

---

30   A very helpful, unnamed reviewer brought to my attention the original reading of the text of what became D&C 84:28 and wondered about a possible connection between its content and the topic of this paper: "until John whom God raised up being fillid with the holy ghost from his Mothers womb, for he was baptised while he was yet in his mothers womb and was ordained by the Angel of God at the time he was eight days old unto this power." I note this passage here, but leave the matter to qualified Church historians to assess it. "Revelation, 22–23 September 1832 [D&C 84]," The Joseph Smith Papers, http://www.josephsmithpapers.org/paper-summary/revelation-22-23-september-1832-dc-84/1. Note 17 at that page states, "In preparation for the publication of this revelation in the 1835 edition of the Doctrine and Covenants, JS crossed out 'the womb' in the Revelation Book 2 manuscript and inserted "his Childhood." All published versions read 'baptized while he was yet in his childhood.' (Revelation Book 2, p. 23; [originally printed as] D&C 4:4, 1835 ed.)."

the biblical depiction, nor diminish the Latter-day Saint perspective on Jeremiah's premortal existence.[31]

Dana M. Pike *is professor of Ancient Scripture and Ancient Near Eastern Studies at Brigham Young University, and is currently serving as Associate Dean of Religious Education. He earned his PhD at the University of Pennsylvania in Hebrew Bible and Ancient Near Eastern Studies.*

---

31   I thank my student employee Courtney Dotson for assisting with the research for this paper.

"We Are a Remnant of the Seed of Joseph": Moroni's Interpretive Use of Joseph's Coat and the Martial *nēs*-Imagery of Isaiah 11:11–12

Matthew L. Bowen

Abstract: *Genesis 30:23–24 offers a double etiology for* Joseph *in terms of "taking away"/"gathering" ('āsap) and "adding" (yāsap). In addition to its later narratological use of the foregoing, the Joseph cycle (Genesis 37–50) evidences a third dimension of onomastic wordplay involving Joseph's* kĕtōnet passîm, *an uncertain phrase traditionally translated "coat of many colours" (from LXX), but perhaps better translated, "coat of manifold pieces." Moroni₁, quoting from a longer version of the Joseph story from the brass plates, refers to "Joseph, whose coat was rent by his brethren into many pieces" (Alma 46:23). As a military and spiritual leader, Moroni₁ twice uses Joseph's torn coat and the remnant doctrine from Jacob's prophecy regarding Joseph's coat as a model for his covenant use of his own coat to "gather" (cf. 'āsap) and rally faithful Nephites as "a remnant of the seed of Joseph" (Alma 46:12–28, 31; 62:4–6). In putting that coat on a "pole" or "standard" (Hebrew nēs — i.e., "ensign") to "gather" a "remnant of the seed of Joseph" appears to make use of the Isaianic nēs-imagery of Isaiah 11:11–12 (and elsewhere), where the Joseph-connected verbs yāsap and 'āsap serve as key terms. Moroni's written-upon "standard" or "ensign" for "gathering" the "remnant of the seed of Joseph" constituted an important prophetic antetype for how Mormon and his son, Moroni₂, perceived the function of their written record in the latter-days (see, e.g., 3 Nephi 5:23–26; Ether 13:1–13).*

The biography of Joseph the biblical patriarch surfaces in intriguing ways throughout the Book of Mormon, attesting its importance among the Nephites throughout their entire existence. For example, at the beginning of Nephite history, Nephi uses Joseph's name and biography as a literary means of framing his own familial role and his brothers' abusive treatment of him (e.g., "and they hated him *yet the more* [*wayyôsipû ʿôd*]" [Genesis 37:5, 8] ≅ "their anger did increase [*yāsap*] against me" [2 Nephi 5:2]).[1] At the very end of Nephite civilization, in his abridged book of Ether, Moroni₂ (son of Mormon) makes Joseph's name, his bringing his father down into Egypt, and his consequent preservation of his father "a type" for the preservation of "a remnant of the seed of Joseph," the building "again" (cf. *yôsîp*) of "the Jerusalem of old," the building of a "New Jerusalem," which would be "a holy city unto the Lord like unto the Jerusalem of old" and the promise that both "shall no more be confounded" (Ether 13:1–13).[2] Moroni returns to this promise at the very conclusion of the Book of Mormon (see Moroni 10:31).[3]

John Tvedtnes has keenly observed that the use of the "remnant" (*šěʾērît*) idiom in Ether 13:7 very closely matches the function of the idiom in Genesis 45:7 in the Joseph cycle ("And God sent me before you to preserve you a posterity [*šěʾērît*, literally, remnant] in the earth, and to save your lives by a great deliverance").[4] In other words, Joseph's removal to Egypt provided a typological preservation of the "remnant" of Israel, not merely the preserving of a "posterity" (as rendered in KJV). Tvedtnes writes, "The Genesis passage is particularly interesting because of its subtle yet telling contextual affinity to the way the Book of Mormon typically uses the expression 'remnant of Joseph.' In both cases the expression appears in contexts that imply or directly convey the idea of

---

1. On Nephi's autobiographic use of Joseph's name and permutation of the biblical wordplay on Joseph's name, see Matthew L. Bowen, "'Their Anger Did Increase Against Me': Nephi's Autobiographical Permutation of a Biblical Wordplay on the Name Joseph," *Interpreter: A Journal of Mormon Scripture* 23 (2017): 115-36. On Nephi's use of other details of Joseph's biography, see further Alan Goff, *A Hermeneutic of Sacred Texts: Historicism, Revisionism, Positivism, and the Bible and Book of Mormon* (MA thesis, Brigham Young University, 1989), 104-32. Citations of Book of Mormon passages in this study will generally reflect Royal Skousen, ed., *The Book of Mormon: The Earliest Text* (New Haven, CT: Yale, 2009).

2. On the onomastic wordplay involving the name Joseph evident in Ether 13:1-13, see Matthew L. Bowen, "'They Shall No More Be Confounded': Moroni's Wordplay on Joseph in Ether 13:1-13 and Moroni 10:31," *Interpreter: A Journal of Latter-day Saint Faith and Scholarship* 30 (2018): 91-104.

3. In both Ether 13:1-13 and Moroni 10:13, Moroni taps the language of 1 Nephi 14:2 and 1 Nephi 15:10 and the wordplay on Joseph found there (see Bowen, "No More Be Confounded").

4. John A. Tvedtnes, "The Remnant of Joseph," *Insights* 20, no. 8 (2000): 2.

being sent to another land in order to be *preserved*."[5] In view of Tvedtnes's observation, we also recall the iterative use of the Hebraistic *yôsîp* — "do again" — idiom in Zenos's allegory to describe the "preservation" of the natural fruit.[6] Although Jacob 5 does not use the word "remnant," "the conjunction of Moroni$_2$'s Joseph/*yôsîp* wordplay with his allusion to a "preserving" a "posterity"/"remnant" (*šĕʾērît*) from Genesis 45:7 in Ether 13 becomes all the more striking.

Tvedtnes further notes that the preservation of a "remnant" idiom (Hebrew *šĕʾērît/šĕʾār*) conveys a similar notion of preservation in Alma 46 (see especially vv. 23–27).[7] In the following article I propose that another significant use of Joseph's biography that, like Ether 13, manifests a consciousness of the Genesis wordplay on Joseph occurs in Mormon's account of the lengthy war between the Nephites led by Moroni$_1$ (the namesake of Mormon's son, Moroni$_2$) and the Lamanites led by Amalickiah and later Ammoron his brother. In that account, Mormon preserves a covenant speech by Moroni$_1$ in which the latter uses the patriarch Joseph's "rent" coat as an antetype for his own "rent" coat, of his people's "rent" garments, and (citing the patriarch Jacob's lost prophetic words) of the preservation of "a remnant of the seed of Joseph" — a remnant of which the Nephites and Lamanites constituted a part. In later years, Mormon recognized that Joseph's coat having been "rent by his brethren" and Moroni$_1$'s prophecy regarding his people's garments being "rent by our brethren" (Alma 46:23) came to ironic fulfillment when he saw his own people being "rent" by their "brethren" (see, e.g., Mormon 6).[8]

Moreover, I attempt to show that, in addition to the important biblical wordplay on Joseph's name in terms of the verbs *ʾāsap* ("gather," "bring

---

5. Ibid.

6. See the discussion in Matthew L. Bowen and Loren Blake Spendlove, "'Thou Art the Fruit of My Loins': The Interrelated Symbolism and Meanings of the Names Joseph and Ephraim in Ancient Scripture" *Interpreter: A Journal of Mormon Scripture* 28 (2018): 294–96. See also Matthew L. Bowen, "'I Have Done According to My Will': Reading Jacob 5 as a Temple Text" in *The Temple: Ancient and Restored: Proceedings of the Interpreter Matthew B. Brown Memorial Conference,* ed. Stephen D. Ricks and Donald W. Parry (Salt Lake City: Eborn Books and Interpreter Foundation, 2016), 247–48.

7. Tvedtnes, "The Remnant of Joseph," 2.

8. Cf. especially Mormon 6:16, where Mormon describes his soul as being "rent with anguish," quoting Nephi, whose "soul" was "rent with anguish because of [his brethren]," 1 Nephi 17:47).

in," "receive," "withdraw," "take away")[9] and *yāsap* ("add," "continue to do", "do again, more"),[10] a third type of wordplay involving the rare and opaque Hebrew word *passîm* links Joseph to his unique coat, the "remnant" of which becomes a metonym[11] for his posterity. Traditionally, *passîm* has been interpreted "many colors" (in "coat of many colors") but perhaps suggesting "a garment reaching to the wrists or ankles"[12] (on the basis of Aramaic *pas* "palm of the hand or sole of the foot," cf. the Septuagint [hereafter LXX] reading *chitōn karpōtos* = Vulgate *talari tunica* [2 Samuel 13:18-19])[13] or, on the basis of Aramaic *pas*, "part, share, lot" — i.e., "piece"[14] — and Phoenician *ps*, "tablet, piece" rather "a garment made of pieces of material sewn together."[15]

On this paronomastic[16] basis, the "remnant" of Joseph's coat becomes a natural metonymy for the "remnant of the seed of Joseph"[17] or the "remnant of Joseph."[18] Moreover, when Moroni$_1$ fastens his own "rent" and overwritten coat on a "pole" — later called a "standard" (i.e., an "ensign") — he taps into the emotive *nēs*-imagery of Isaiah 11:11-12. The latter text describes the Lord's use of a *nēs*, "ensign" or "standard," as a means of assembling or "gathering" the "*remnant* of his people." Moroni, in fact, uses a "standard" or ensign to "gather" a "remnant of the seed of Joseph" for the existential preservation of the Nephite nation. Mormon recognized that this written-upon "standard" or "ensign" (Alma 46:12-28) constituted something of an antetype of his own abridged record which would be used as a kind of ensign to gather "a remnant of the seed of Joseph" (3 Nephi 5:21-26).

---

9. Ludwig Koehler and Walter Baumgartner, *The Hebrew and Aramaic Lexicon of the Old Testament* (Leiden, NDL: Brill, 2001), 74. Hereafter cited as *HALOT*.

10. *HALOT*, 418.

11. A metonym is "a word, name, or expression used as a substitute for something else with which it is closely associated. For example, Washington is a metonym for the federal government of the US." *Lexico*, s.v. "Metonym," https://www.lexico.com/en/definition/metonym.

12. *HALOT*, 946.

13. Ibid.

14. Ibid., 1958.

15. Victor P. Hamilton, *The Book of Genesis: Chapters 18–50* (Grand Rapids, MI: Eerdmans, 1995), 408. Cf. *HALOT*, 946.

16. Richard A. Lanham defines paronomasia as "punning; playing on the sounds and meanings of words." Richard A. Lanham, *A Handlist of Rhetorical Terms*, 2nd ed. (Berkley: University of California Press, 1991), 110.

17. Alma 46:23, 27; 3 Nephi 5:23; 10:17; Ether 13:6–7, 10.

18. Amos 5:15; Alma 46:24.

Joseph's *Kĕtōnet Passîm*

Understanding the name *Joseph* as a symbol of divine "gathering" and iterative or resumptive divine action begins in the Genesis pericope that describes the births of Jacob's sons (Genesis 29–30). That pericope offers a double etiology for the name Joseph in a chiastic structure:

> A And she conceived, and bare *a son* [*bēn*];
>> B and said, God hath <u>taken away</u> [*'āsap*, gathered up] my reproach:
>>> C and *she* called his name <u>Joseph</u> [*yôsēp*];
>> B' and said, The Lord <u>shall add</u> [*yōsēp*; or, "may Yahweh add"] to me
> A' another *son* [*bēn*; i.e., Benjamin].
>
> (Genesis 30:23–24; emphasis in all scriptural citations is added).

The central (C) element with the name Joseph divides the somewhat antonymic, dual etymologies in B and B'. The "another son" in A' anticipates Benjamin, the last of Jacob's sons.[19]

Elements of both etiologies find expression throughout the Joseph Cycle (Genesis 37–50). Wordplay on Joseph in terms of *'āsap* recurs in the following passages:

- Genesis 42:17–18: "And he *put them all together* [*gathered them, wayye'ĕsōp 'ōtām*] into ward three days. And *Joseph* [*yōsēp*] said unto them the third day, This do, and live; for I fear God."
- Genesis 49:29: "and [Jacob] said unto them [i.e., Joseph and his brothers], I am *to be gathered* [*ne'ĕsāp*] unto my people."
- Genesis 49:33–50:1: "[Jacob] *gathered up* [*wayye'ĕsōp*] his feet into the bed … *and was gathered* [*wayyē'āsep*] unto his people [i.e., in the spirit world]. And *Joseph* [*yôsēp*] fell upon his father's face, and wept upon him, and kissed him."

These *'āsap* wordplays anticipate Moses's "gathering" of the elders of Israel in Exodus (see further Exodus 3:16; 4:29; cf. Isaiah 49:5).

In terms of the second etiology, wordplay on *yāsap* first resumes early in the Joseph cycle twice in Genesis 37:5, 8: "and they hated him <u>yet the more</u> [*wayyôsipû 'ôd*]"). The next recurrence in Genesis 44:23 (when Joseph

---

19. See Matthew L. Bowen, "Onomastic Wordplay on *Joseph* and *Benjamin* and *Gezera Shawa* in the Book of Mormon," *Interpreter: A Journal of Mormon Scripture* 18 (2016): 255–73.

says: "Except your youngest brother [i.e., Benjamin] come down with you, *ye shall* see my face *no more* [*lōʾ tōsipûn*]") recalls the second etiology for Joseph's name in Genesis 30:24 and its anticipation of Benjamin.

Moreover, the Joseph Cycle evidences a third dimension of wordplay on Joseph — a paronomasia involving *yôsēp* and *passîm* (consonantally, *ywsp* and *psym*). Moshe Garsiel writes, "The word here translated 'striped' [*passîm*, KJV "of many colours"], also constitutes a pun of some novelty upon 'Joseph' (*ywsp* - יוסף) of which it is nearly an anagram."[20] Although Garsiel's "anagram" relies entirely on the orthographic similarity between *ywsp* and *psym* rather than on any evident root relationship between the two words, the words nevertheless have three of four consonants in common in their written forms. In terms of their pronunciation, *yôsēp* and *passîm* share enough alliterative sound similarity to reasonably and cautiously posit a deliberate wordplay. Add to that the sheer rarity of the term *psym* (attested only five times and only in the Joseph and Tamar$_2$ stories)[21] seems to suggest its paronomastic relatability to *ywsp* constituted a primary consideration in its narrative inclusion by the ancient author/narrator.

This putative wordplay on Joseph in terms of *passîm* stands at the head of the paronomasia used throughout the Joseph cycle and leads into the subsequent wordplay on *yôsēp* in terms of *yāsap*:

> Now Israel loved <u>*Joseph*</u> [*yôsēp*] more than all his children, because he was the son of his old age: and he made him *a coat* [*kĕtōnet*] of <u>*many colours*</u> [*passîm*]. And when his brethren saw that their father loved him more than all his brethren, they hated him, and could not speak peaceably unto him. And Joseph dreamed a dream, and he told it his brethren: *and they hated him <u>yet the more</u>* [*wayyôsipû ʿôd*]. And he said unto them, Hear, I pray you, this dream which I have dreamed: For, behold, we were binding sheaves in the field, and, lo, my sheaf arose, and also stood upright; and, behold, your sheaves stood round about, and made obeisance to my sheaf. And his brethren said to him, Shalt thou indeed reign over us? or shalt thou indeed have dominion over us? And they hated him <u>*yet the more*</u> [*wayyôsipû ʿôd*] for his dreams, and for his words. (Genesis 37:3–8)

20. Moshe Garsiel, *Biblical Names: A Literary Study of Midrashic Derivations and Puns*, trans. Dr. Phyllis Hackett (Ramat Gan, ISR: Bar-Ilan University Press, 1991), 173.

21. Genesis 37:3, 23, 32; 2 Samuel 13:18–19.

Here the ambiguous and virtually untranslatable word *passîm*, forming a paronomastic pun on *yôsēp*, makes the coat a symbol of Jacob's "preferential love for Joseph"[22] and for the latter's favored status, which becomes the source of the brothers' "adding" (*wayyôsipû ʿôd*) to hate Joseph. KJV's English language rendering of *passîm* as "of many colours" owes its precise phraseology to John Wycliffe, who rendered the Latin Vulgate's *tunicam polymitam* (i.e., a "tunic woven with multicolored threads") as "cote of many colours." William Tyndale was content to retain this phrase in his translation from the Hebrew, and later translations followed suit. The Vulgate owes its rendition to LXX, which in turn renders Hebrew *passîm* with the Greek adjective *poikilos*, which can mean "many-colored" or "variegated." LXX thus constitutes the source of our traditional reading, "coat of many colors." However, the adjective *poikilos* also "pert[ains] to existence in various kinds or modes" and thus can also mean "diversified, manifold."[23] In other words, another — and perhaps better — translation for *kĕtōnet passîm* might be: *coat of diverse pieces* or a *coat of manifold pieces*.

The idea that Joseph's *kĕtōnet passîm* was in fact a garment originally composed of "diverse" or "manifold" parts sewn or stitched together — finds interesting and perhaps significant support in Moroni's statement "Joseph, whose coat was rent by his brethren into *many* pieces" (Alma 46:23). While Ephraim A. Speiser favored "an ornamented tunic,"[24] the idea of a "wrap-around garment, the overlapping layers of which seem like 'tablets', cf. Pun[ic]) פס [= tablet],"[25] finds philological support at least as strong as the former. A derivation from Akkadian

---

22. Garsiel, *Biblical Names*, 173.

23. Frederick William Danker, ed., *A Greek-English Lexicon of the New Testament and Other Early Christian Literature*, 3rd ed. (BDAG) (University of Chicago Press, 2000), 842.

24. Ephraim A. Speiser, *Genesis: Introduction, Translation, and Notes* (New York: Doubleday, 1964), 287, 289–90. See also Robert Alter, *The Hebrew Bible: A Translation with Commentary, Volume 1: The Five Books of Moses* (New York: Norton, 2019), 139. Alter earlier wrote, "The only clue about the nature of the garment is offered by the one other mention of it in the Bible, in the story of the rape of Tamar (2 Samuel 13), in which, incidentally, there is a whole network of pointed allusions to the Joseph story. There we are told that the *ketonet pasim* was worn by virgin princesses. It is thus a unisex garment and a product of ancient *haute couture*." (Robert Alter, *Genesis: Translation and Commentary* [New York: Norton, 1996], 209.)

25. *HALOT*, 946.

pasāmu/pussumu (verb to "veil", adjective "veiled") seems unlikely,[26] and Ugaritic *psm* offers no help, since its meaning remains uncertain.[27]

The subsequent twofold repetition of the idiom *wayyôsipû 'ôd* builds on the *yôsēp/passîm* wordplay and reemphasizes the connection between the name Joseph and his coat even as it hints at Joseph's imminent suffering at his brothers' hands. Later in the pericope, the *yôsēp/passîm* resurfaces when the brothers act on their "added" or redoubled hatred: "And it came to pass, when *Joseph* [*yôsēp*] was come unto his brethren, that they stript Joseph [*yôsēp*] out of his coat, his *coat* [*kĕtōnet*] *of many colours* [*passîm*] that was on him. And they took him, and cast him into a pit: and the pit was empty, there was no water in it" (Genesis 37:23–24). The removal of the coat symbolizes Joseph's forced loss of status and in a real sense the loss of his former identity. As Joseph was sold into slavery into a foreign country, Josephites of later generations, including Lehi and Nephi and their family, would have appreciated this particular moment in light of their own experiences and circumstances: going into exile into foreign countries. Near the end of his life, Jacob described the Nephites in autobiographic terms and in terms of the fraternal hatred in the Joseph story[28] as "a lonesome and a solemn people, wanderers cast out from Jerusalem, born in tribulation in a wilderness, and *hated of our brethren*, which caused wars and contentions; wherefore we did mourn out our days" (Jacob 7:26).[29]

---

26. Jeremy Black, Andrew George, and Nicholas Postgate, eds., *A Concise Dictionary of Akkadian*, 2nd corrected printing (Wiesbaden, DEU: Harrassowitz Verlag, 2000), 268, 279.

27. Gregorio del Olmo Lete and Joaquín Sanmartín, *A Dictionary of the Ugaritic Language in the Alphabetic Tradition*, 3rd rev. ed., ed. and trans. Wilfred G. E. Watson (Leiden, NDL: Brill, 2015), 2:675.

28. There may be a further echo of the fraternal enmity between the patriarch Jacob and Esau in the Jacob cycle as there is in 2 Nephi 4–5: "And Esau hated Jacob because of the blessing wherewith his father blessed him: and Esau said in his heart, The days of mourning for my father are at hand; then will I slay my brother Jacob" (Genesis 27:41). The Book of Mormon prophet/priest Jacob's son Enos unquestionably sees the Nephite-Lamanite relationship in terms of Jacob and Esau. See John A. Tvedtnes, "Jacob and Enos: Wrestling before God," *Insights* 21, no. 5 (2001): 2–3; Matthew L. Bowen "'And There Wrestled a Man with Him' (Genesis 32:24): Enos's Adaptations of the Onomastic Wordplay of Genesis," *Interpreter: A Journal of Mormon Scripture* 10 (2014): 151–60.

29. Even after long generations in the New World, the Nephites still viewed themselves in this light. As Alma stated to the apostate Nephites of Ammonihah, "And they are made known unto us in plain terms, that we may understand, that we cannot err; and this because of our being *wanderers in a strange land*" (Alma 13:23).

The final instance of wordplay on *yôsēp* and *passîm* occurs with the brothers' deceptive presentation of Joseph's coat to his father as ostensible evidence of the former's death:

> And they took *Joseph's coat* [*kětōnet yôsēp*], and killed a kid of the goats, and dipped the coat in the blood; and they sent *the coat of many colours* [*kětōnet happassîm*], and they brought it to their father; and said, This have we found: know now whether it be thy son's coat or no. And he knew it, and said, *It is my son's coat* [*kětōnet běnî*] an evil beast hath devoured him; *Joseph is without doubt rent in pieces* [*ṭārōp ṭōrap yôsēp*]. And Jacob rent [*wayyiqra'*] *his clothes*, and put sackcloth upon his loins, and mourned for his son many days. (Genesis 37:31–33)

The parallel syntax in at the beginning of v. 31 ("And they took *Joseph's coat* [*kětōnet yôsēp*]") and v. 32 ("and they sent *the coat of many colours* [*kětōnet happassîm*]") strengthens the case for a deliberate paronomastic connection between the name Joseph and the description of his coat. Joseph's coat as a metonymy of Joseph himself is further established by the exclamations *kětōnet běnî* and *ṭārōp ṭōrap yôsēp*. Thus Joseph's father "rending" his clothes seemingly amounts to more than an act of mourning: he reenacts what he believes to have befallen his son.

The "Coat" and the "Remnant" of Joseph

At first glance, Moroni's tearing of his coat appears to constitute something of an ad hoc means of rallying his people:

> And it came to pass that when he had poured out his soul to God, he gave all the land which was south of the land Desolation — yea, and in fine, all the land, both on the north and on the south — a chosen land, and the land of liberty. And he saith: Surely God shall not suffer that we who are despised because *we take upon us the name of Christ* shall be trodden down and destroyed until we bring it upon us by

Around this same time Ammon exclaimed: "Yea, blessed is the name of my God, who has been mindful of this people, who are a branch of the tree of Israel, and has been lost from its body in a strange land; yea, I say, blessed be the name of my God, who has been mindful of us, *wanderers in a strange land*" (Alma 26:36). These statements also echo the Gershom etiologies from Exodus: "And [Zipporah] bare him a son, and he called his name Gershom [*gēršōm*]: for he said, I have been *a stranger* [*gēr*] in *a strange* [*nokriyyâ*] land" (Exodus 2:22); "And her two sons; of which the name of the one was Gershom [*gēršōm*]; for he said, I have been *an alien* [*gēr*] in a strange [*nokriyyâ*] land" (Exodus 18:3).

our own transgressions. And when Moroni had said these words, he went forth among the people, *waving the rent of his garment in the air, that all might see the writing which he had wrote upon the rent,* and crying with a loud voice, saying: Behold, whosoever will maintain this title upon the land, let them come forth in the strength of the Lord, and enter into a covenant that they will maintain their rights, and their religion, that the Lord God may bless them. And it came to pass that when Moroni had proclaimed these words, behold, *the people came running together with their armors girded about their loins, rending their garments in token, or as a covenant, that they would not forsake the Lord their God. Or, in other words, if they should transgress the commandments of God — or fall into transgression — and be ashamed to take upon them the name of Christ, the Lord should rend them, even as they had rent their garments.* Now this was the covenant which they made; and they cast their garments at the feet of Moroni, saying: *We covenant with our God that we shall be destroyed, even as our brethren in the land northward, if we shall fall into transgression. Yea, he may cast us at the feet of our enemies, even as we have cast our garments at thy feet, to be trodden under foot, if we shall fall into transgression.* (Alma 46:17–22)

However, Moroni's words and actions quickly emerge as much more than a mere attempt to rally the troops. Moroni's "g[i]v[ing]" the land "a chosen land and the land of liberty" recalls at least three distinct scenes from earlier Nephite history. In a speech to his sons before his death, Lehi had declared the land would "be a land of liberty" to all those whom the Lord would bring and would "serve him according to the commandments which he hath given" (2 Nephi 1:7). It also recalls a later speech by Jacob after Lehi's death and the separation of the Lamanites from the Nephites in which Jacob states, "And this land shall be a land of liberty unto the Gentiles [Hebrew *gôyîm* = 'nations'], and there shall be no kings upon the land who shall raise up unto the Gentiles [nations]" (2 Nephi 10:11). These sermons were important in light of the "others" — i.e., the non-Israelites — whom Lehi and his descendants must have encountered in the New World[30] but also because of the "remnant of the seed of Joseph" who would exist among the "gentiles" in the latter-day.

Some time ago Mark J. Morrise noted the simile curses Moroni uses in Alma 46:21–22 with the people symbolically "rending their garments"[31] in token of what would happen to them if they failed to keep the covenant which they had made. In the text that follows, Moroni₁ makes the story of Joseph's coat a kind of "historical prologue"[32] to the simile-curse covenant under which his people subsequently bind themselves. Moroni declares to his soldiers and followers that they "are a remnant of the seed of Joseph" and proceeds to tell a part of that story that has been lost from the extant canonical version of the Joseph story (Genesis 37–50):

> Moroni said unto them: Behold, *we are a remnant of the seed of Jacob.* Yea, we are *a remnant of the seed of Joseph, whose coat was rent by his brethren into many pieces.* Yea, and now behold, let us remember to keep the commandments of God, or our garments shall be rent by our brethren, and we be cast into prison, or be sold, or be slain. Yea, let us preserve our liberty as a *remnant of Joseph.*[33] Yea, let us remember the words of Jacob, before his death. For behold, he saw that a part of *the remnant of the coat of Joseph* [kĕtōnet yôsēp, Genesis 37:31] was preserved and had not decayed. And he saith: Even as *this remnant of garment of my son's* hath been preserved, so shall *a remnant of the seed of my son be preserved* by the hand of God and be taken unto himself, while *the remainder of the seed of Joseph shall perish, even as the remnant of his garment.* Now behold, this giveth my soul sorrow. Nevertheless, my soul hath joy in my son because of *that part of his seed which shall be taken unto God.* Now behold, this was the language

---

30. John Gee and Matthew Roper, "'I Did Liken All Scriptures unto Us': Early Nephite Understandings of Isaiah and Implications for 'Others' in the Land," in *Fullness of the Gospel: Foundational Teachings of the Book of Mormon*, ed. Camille Fronk Olson, Brian M. Hauglid, Patty Smith, and Thomas A. Wayment (Salt Lake City: Deseret Book; Provo, UT: Religious Studies Center, Brigham Young University, 2003), 51–65.

31. Mark J. Morrise, "Simile Curses in the Ancient Near East, Old Testament, and Book of Mormon," *Journal of Book of Mormon Studies* 2, no. 1 (January 1993): 134.

32. Ibid.

33. The only other scriptural attestation of the collocation "remnant of Joseph" occurs in Amos 5:15: "Hate the evil, and love the good, and establish judgment in the gate: it may be that the Lord God of hosts will be gracious unto *the remnant of Joseph* [šĕʾērît yôsēp]." Cf. "house of Joseph" (bêt yôsēp) in Amos 5:6.

of Jacob. And now, who knoweth but what *the remnant of the seed of Joseph* which shall perish as his garment are those who have dissented from us? (Alma 46:23–27)

Understanding Joseph's coat and its "rents" or rent pieces as having a tribal or gentilic reference finds an excellent analogue in the rending of the cloak in 1 Kings 11:29–31 and the prophet Ahijah's rending of Jeroboam's new garment: "And it came to pass at that time when Jeroboam went out of Jerusalem, that the prophet Ahijah the Shilonite found him in the way; and he [ambiguous, but probably Jeroboam] had clad himself with a new garment; and they two were alone in the field: And Ahijah caught the new garment that was on him, *and rent [wayyiqrāʿehā] it* in twelve *pieces [qĕrāʿîm,* literally twelve "rents"[34]]: And he said to Jeroboam, Take thee ten *pieces [qĕrāʿîm]:* for thus saith the Lord, the God of Israel, Behold, *I will rend [hinĕnî qōrēaʿ] the kingdom out of the hand of Solomon, and will give ten tribes to thee.*"

Consistent with his understanding of the symbolism of the Joseph story as a whole and Jacob's prophecy in particular, Moroni₁ offers a description of the "tearing" or "rending" of Joseph's coat, which he implicitly understands as a metaphor of what will happen to the body of Joseph's descendants: "Joseph, whose coat was *rent [niqraʿ]* by his brethren into many *pieces [qĕrāʿîm]*" (Alma 46:23). Moroni₁ knew all too well that the Nephites of his time risked being "torn by our brethren" in a manner similar to Joseph's *kĕtōnet passîm* because of covenant infidelity. The Nephites of Moroni₁'s time were then a part of the "remnant of Joseph" or the "remainder of the seed of Joseph" that had yet to "perish" — which may mean to experience "exile" in the sense of losing the knowledge of one's historical identity, as the Lamanites and the Nephites who survive among them do later.[35] For Mormon, compiling the record hundreds of years later, Moroni₁'s emotive image of descendants of Joseph being "torn" by their "brethren" had become prophecy fulfilled before his own eyes.[36]

---

34. Cf. John A. Tvedtnes, "Hebraisms in the Book of Mormon: A Preliminary Survey," *BYU Studies* 11, no. 1 (1970): 50. See also Book of Mormon Central, "Why Did Moroni Quote the Patriarch Joseph about a Piece of Joseph's Coat?", https://knowhy.bookofmormoncentral.org/content/why-did-moroni-quote-the-patriarch-jacob-about-a-piece-of-joseph%E2%80%99s-coat.

35. See, e.g., 1 Nephi 13:30; Alma 45:13–14; Moroni 1:1–3; 9:24 (cf. also Moroni 9:17).

36. See, e.g., Mormon 2:15: "I saw thousands of them hewn down in open rebellion against their God and heaped up as dung upon the face of the land"

In Moroni's words, "our garments shall be rent by our brethren, and we be cast into prison, or sold or be slain," there seems to be a tacit recognition that Joseph the patriarch had *unjustly* suffered the consequences of covenant violation that his descendants would *justly* suffer if they failed to faithfully keep to the covenant that they had made with God — i.e., as Joseph had remained faithful. Joseph's biography and the story of his coat thus becomes part of the "simile curse" in the covenant: to be "rent by ... brethren," "cast into prison," or be "sold," if not "slain" (Alma 46:23).

A verb translated "preserve" occurs four times in Alma 46:24 as part of Moroni$_1$'s use of the preservation of "a remnant of Joseph" and the "remnant of the coat of Joseph" as a simile for the preservation of the Nephites' liberty as part of the "remnant of Joseph." A verb translated "preserve" occurs twenty times[37] throughout the allegory in Jacob 5, expressive of the Lord of the vineyard's intent to preserve the fruit and trees in his vineyard. There is an interesting and potentially significant connection to be drawn here between Moroni's intent to "preserve" the Nephites and their liberty as part of the preserved "remnant of Joseph" (symbolized by the metaphor of the "remnant of the coat of Joseph" and the Lord of the vineyard's intent to "preserve" the "good fruit"; cf. Nephi < Eg. *nfr* = "good"[38]), oft-stated in the allegory in terms of

(Mormon 2:15); Mormon 4:11: "And it is impossible for the tongue to describe — or for man to write a perfect description of the horrible scene of the blood and carnage which was among the people, both of the Nephites and of the Lamanites. And every heart was hardened, so that they delighted in the shedding of blood continually."

37. Jacob 5:8, 11 (2 x), 13, 20, 23, 33, 36–37, 46, 53–54 (3 x), 60 (3 x), 74–75 (3 x), 77.

38. On Nephi as an Egyptian name derived from the lexeme *nfr*, see John Gee, "A Note on the Name *Nephi*," *Journal of Book of Mormon Studies* 1, no. 1 (July 1992): 189–91; Gee, "Four Suggestions on the Origin of the Name Nephi," in *Pressing Forward with the Book of Mormon: The FARMS Updates of the 1990s*, ed. John W. Welch and Melvin J. Thorne (Provo, UT: FARMS, 1999), 1–5. On the wordplay on Nephi evident in numerous Book of Mormon passages, see Matthew L. Bowen, "Internal Textual Evidence for the Egyptian Origin of Nephi's Name," *Insights* 21, no. 11 (2001): 2; Bowen, "'O Ye Fair Ones': An Additional Note on the Meaning of the Name Nephi," *Insights* 23, no. 6 (2003): 2; Bowen, "Nephi's Good Inclusio," *Interpreter: A Journal of Mormon Scripture* 17 (2016): 181–95; Bowen, "'O Ye Fair Ones' — Revisited," *Interpreter: A Journal of Mormon Scripture* 20 (2016): 315–44. See most recently, Matthew L. Bowen, "Laman and Nephi as Key-Words: An Etymological, Narratological, and Rhetorical Approach to Understanding Lamanites and Nephites as Religious, Political, and Cultural

the *yôsîp*-idiom[39] ("to do [something] again"). In two verses, these ideas closely converge: The Lord of the vineyard asks his servant: "What shall we do unto the tree *that I may* preserve *again* good fruit thereof unto mine own self?" (Jacob 5:33). Later he declares: "And because that *I have preserved* the natural branches and the roots thereof, and that *I have grafted in the natural branches again* into their mother tree and *have preserved* the roots of their mother tree, that perhaps, the trees of my vineyard *may* bring forth *again* good fruit, and *that I may* have joy *again* in the fruit of my vineyard, and perhaps that I may rejoice exceedingly that *I have preserved* the roots and the branches of the first fruit" (Jacob 5:60). The allegory concludes with the report that as a result of the efforts of the servants the Lord of the vineyard "had *preserved* unto himself that the trees *had* become *again* the natural fruit" (Jacob 5:74). The Lord of the vineyard subsequently declares, "and thou beholdest that I have done according to my will; *and I have preserved* the natural fruit, *that it is good* even like as it was in the beginning. And blessed art thou, for because that ye have been diligent in laboring with me in my vineyard, and have kept my commandments — and *it hath* brought unto me *again* the natural fruit, that my vineyard is no more corrupted and the bad is cast away — behold, ye shall have joy with me" (Jacob 5:74–75).

Moroni's use of the "remnant of the coat of Joseph" as a symbol of divine preservation and Zenos's allegory as related by Jacob share another significant link. Jacob frames Zenos's allegory in terms of Isaiah 11:11–12 and the gathering of Israel: "And in the day that *he shall set* his hand *again* [*yôsîp*] the second time to recover his people [quoting Isaiah 11:11] is the day — yea, even the last time — that the servants of the Lord shall go forth in his power to nourish and prune his vineyard; and after that the end soon cometh" (Jacob 6:2). Moroni uses his coat (as a parallel to the coat of Joseph) hoisted atop a "pole," "standard," or "ensign" — i.e., the Hebrew *nēs* that we meet in Isaiah 11:12 — as the means of "gathering" and "assembling" the "remnant" of Judah-Israel.

The "Gathering" Standard or "Ensign to the Nations": Moroni's Use of Isaiah 11:11–12

The etiological association between the name "Joseph" and "gathering" (*'āsap*) occurs in Mormon's account of Captain Moroni and the "title of liberty" in several subtle instances. The entire pericope revolves around

---

Descriptors," FairMormon Conference, Provo, UT, August 2019, https://www. fairmormon.org/conference/august-2019/laman-and-nephi-as-key-words.

39. The *yôsîp*-idiom potentially occurs in Jacob 5:29, 33, 58, 60–62, 68, 73–75.

the account of Joseph's coat. It begins with Mormon stating that members of the church rebelled against Helaman's authority: "And it came to pass that as many as would not hearken to the words of Helaman and his brethren *were gathered together against their brethren*." Although the Nephites at this period of time also included the Judahite descendants of Muloch (Mulek),[40] and were probably also descended in part from "others,"[41] the Nephites primarily identified themselves as descendants of Joseph in Egypt.[42] Mormon's use of "gather" begins to frame what follows as a Josephite versus Josephite conflict.

Kerry Hull has shown at length that Moroni's use of the "title of liberty" (or "standard of liberty," see below) fits well within a Mesoamerican context in which "war banners" enjoyed widespread use and that the title or standard functioned as such.[43] Nevertheless, just as Moroni₁ invokes a scriptural precedent in the covenant use of his rent coat, he also appears to have scriptural precedents in mind in his use of what is rendered in translation as a "pole" or "standard."

One of the most prominent motifs in the Book of Isaiah is the image of "ensign" (Isaiah 5:26; 11:10, 12; 18:3; 30:17; 31:9), "standard" (Isaiah 49:22; 59:19; 62:10), or "banner" (Isaiah 13:2) — all expressions of the Hebrew noun *nēs* in English translation. In addition to "ensign," "standard," or "banner," another way of rendering Hebrew *nēs* is "pole" as the KJV translators opted to translate it in the bronze serpent pericope of Numbers 21: "And the Lord said unto Moses, Make thee a fiery serpent, and *set it upon a pole* [*nēs*, i.e., a "standard"]: and it shall come to pass, that every one that is bitten, when he looketh upon it, shall live. And Moses made a serpent of brass, and *put it upon a pole* [*nēs*], and it came to pass, that if a serpent had bitten any man, when he beheld the serpent of brass, he lived" (Numbers 21:8–9).

The first instances of the *nēs*-theme in the Book of Isaiah all involve a *nēs* being lifted up to the *gôyim* ("nations"/"gentiles"):

- "And he will lift up *an ensign* [*nēs*] *to the nations* [*laggôyim*] from far, and will hiss unto them from the end of the earth: and, behold, they shall come with speed swiftly"

40. On the original spelling of Mulek as Muloch, see Royal Skousen, *Analysis of Textual Variants of the Book of Mormon, Part Three: Mosiah 17–Alma 20* (Provo, UT: FARMS, 2006), 1464–70.

41. Gee and Roper, "'Liken All Scriptures,'" 51–65.

42. See, e.g., 1 Nephi 5:14–16; 6:2; 2 Nephi 3:4; Alma 10:3.

43. Kerry Hull, "War Banners: A Mesoamerican Context for the Title of Liberty," *Journal of Book of Mormon Studies* 24 (2015): 84–118.

(Isaiah 5:26; this passage is usually understood to have reference to the destruction of Israel and Judah while the following have reference to Israel and Judah's gathering);

- "And in that day there shall be a root of Jesse, *which shall stand for an ensign* [*nēs*] *of the people; to it shall the Gentiles* [*gôyim*] *seek* ... " (Isaiah 11:10–11)

- "And it shall come to pass in that day, that the Lord shall *set* his hand *again* [*yôsîp*] the second time to recover the remnant of his people. ... And he shall set up *an ensign* [*nēs*] *for the nations* [*laggôyim*], and shall *assemble* [*wě'āsap*] *the outcasts of Israel, and gather together the dispersed of Judah* from the four corners of the earth."

The strongest evidence that Nephi considered these Isaiah *nēs*-passages related to the bronze serpent and the *nēs* upon which it was raised is his use of the expression "the nations" (Hebrew *gôyim*), which occurs in 2 Nephi 25:20: "And as the Lord God liveth that brought Israel up out of the land of Egypt and gave unto Moses power that he should *heal the nations* [Hebrew *haggôyim*] after that they had been bitten by the poisonous serpents, if they would cast their eyes unto *the serpent which he did raise up before them*" (2 Nephi 25:20). Nephi had quoted Isaiah 11:11 and 29:14 together in 2 Nephi 25:17 and would describe the fulfillment of these prophecies as fulfilling the promises made to Joseph in 2 Nephi 25:21. In 2 Nephi 25:20, however, the expression "the nations" clearly has reference to the tribes of Israel rather than simply non-Israelites. There exists at least one possible precedent for this use of *gôyim* in the Isaianic corpus itself: Isaiah 9:1 [MT 8:23] (2 Nephi 19:1) describes Galilee as "Galilee of the nations" (*gĕlîl haggôyim*).

The bronze serpent on the *nēs* ("pole") in Numbers 21 and the Isaianic *nēs*-theme provides the conceptual framework for Mormon's account of Moroni₁'s creation of the "pole" or "standard" (*nēs*) in response to Amalickiah and the Lamanite threat:

And it came to pass that *he rent his coat; and he took a piece thereof* and wrote upon it: In memory of our God, our religion and freedom, and our peace, our wives and our children. And *he fastened it upon the end of a pole* [Hebrew *nēs*] thereof. And he fastened on his head-plate and his breastplate and his shields and girded on his armor about his loins. And *he took the pole* [*nēs*] which had on the end thereof his rent coat, and he called it the title of liberty. And he bowed himself to the earth, and he prayed mightily unto his God for the blessings of liberty to rest upon his brethren so long as there should a band of Christians *remain* to possess the land. (Alma 46:12–13)

The idea that Joseph's *kĕtōnet passîm* was a kind of "wrap-around garment, the overlapping layers of which seem like 'tablets', cf. Pun[ic]) פס [= tablet]"[44] — or at least the idea of the stitched pieces as (writing) "tablets" — may have suggested to Moroni$_1$ the written-on banner function in which he used his coat. But Moroni$_1$ appears to have also received inspiration from Isaiah 11:10–12 and perhaps the other Isaiah *nēs*-texts (Isaiah 5:26, 49:22, etc.).

Mormon initially reports that Moroni$_1$ called this "pole" with its ad hoc banner "the title of liberty" (Alma 46:13). However, at least twice the language used to describe it shifts to the expression "standard of liberty." The first occurs as Moroni disseminates his initial "title of liberty" in the form of many duplicates: "And it came to pass also that he caused the title of liberty to be hoisted upon every tower which was in all the land, which was possessed by the Nephites. And thus Moroni planted *the standard of liberty* among the Nephites" (Alma 46:36). The second occurs in Alma 62:4–6 (see below).

Moroni$_1$'s "Gathering" of the "Remnant of the Seed of Joseph"

On one level, what follows Moroni's rendition of an otherwise unknown part of the biblical narrative[45] regarding Joseph's coat clearly represents an ad hoc interpretation and application of that story:

> And now, who knoweth but what *the remnant of the seed of Joseph* [*yôsēp*] *which shall perish as his garment are those who have dissented from us*; yea, and even *it shall be us if we do not stand fast in the faith of Christ.* And now it came to pass that when Moroni had said these words, he went forth, and also sent forth, in all the parts of the land where there were dissensions and *gathered together* [cf. Hebrew *wĕ'āsap*] all *the people* who were desirous to maintain their liberty, to stand against Amalickiah and those who had dissented, who were called Amalickiahites. (Alma 46:27–28)

---

44. *HALOT*, 946.

45. Mormon elsewhere indicates that this fuller narrative existed on the plates of brass: "Behold, our father Jacob also testified concerning a remnant of the seed of Joseph. And behold, are not we a remnant of the seed of Joseph? And these things which testify of us, are they not written upon the plates of brass which our father Lehi brought out of Jerusalem?" (3 Nephi 10:17).

On another level Mormon's inclusion of Moroni₁'s statement looks forward on the end of Nephite civilization when the Nephite remnant of Joseph did *not* stand fast in the faith of Christ and became the part of Joseph's garment that perished in that story. At this point Mormon notes that Moroni₁ attempted to "gather together" all those who wished to be counted among the faithful "remnant of the seed of Joseph" vis-à-vis the dissenting unfaithful. The emphasis on "gathering together" here echoes the name Joseph and the initial literary etiologizing of that name in terms of the verb *'āsap* ("take away," "gather"). Mormon also emphasizes that those willing to "gather" bound themselves together by a covenant: "Moroni thought it was expedient that he should take his armies, which had *gathered* themselves *together* and armed themselves and entered into a covenant to keep the peace. And it came to pass that he took his army and marched out with his tents into the wilderness to cut off the course of Amalickiah in the wilderness" (Alma 46:31).

Moroni₁'s Second "Gathering" of "a Remnant of the Seed of Joseph" to the "Standard of Liberty"

Moroni proliferates the "gathering" by replicating the "title of liberty" and causing it "to be hoisted upon every tower" (Alma 46:36). Mormon then alters the appellation "title of liberty" in a way that links it firmly to the *nēs*-texts of Isaiah: "And thus Moroni *planted the standard of liberty* among the Nephites" (Alma 46:36). Years later, near the end of the war, Mormon reports that Moroni continued to pursue a policy of replicating the "standard of liberty" — again, using a deliberate wording change from "title of liberty" — and thus continued to promote the "gathering" of a remnant of the seed of Joseph:

Alma 62:4–6	Isaiah 5:26 and 11:11–12 (2 Nephi 21:11–12)
	And he will *lift up an ensign* to the nations from far, and will hiss unto them from the end of the earth: and, behold, they shall come with speed swiftly. (Isaiah 5:26)
And he did raise the standard of liberty in whatsoever place he did enter, *and gained* [*wayyiqen*] whatsoever force he could in all his march towards the land of Gideon. And it came to pass that *thousands did flock unto his standard* [i.e., of the "remnant of the seed of Joseph"] and did take up their swords in the defence of their freedom, that they might not come into bondage. And thus when Moroni had *gathered together* whatsoever men he could in all his march, he came to the land of Gideon.	And it shall come to pass in that day, that the Lord shall <u>set</u> his hand <u>again</u> [*yôsîp*] the second time *to recover* [*liqnôt*, literally "to gain," or "[re-]acquire"] *the remnant of his people* ... And he shall set up [*wĕnāśāʾ, raise up*, lift up] *an ensign* [*nēs*, standard, as in Isaiah 49:22] for the nations [cf. "a standard unto my people," 2 Nephi 29:2], <u>*and shall assemble*</u> [*wĕʾāsap, and shall gather in*] *the outcasts of Israel, and* <u>*gather together*</u> the dispersed of Judah from the four corners of the earth. (Isaiah 11:11–12 (2 Nephi 21:11–12)

In detailing Moroni₁'s use of the "standard of liberty," Mormon seems aware of the similarities or parallels between Moroni₁'s actions and Isaiah's description of the Lord's use of the ensign or standard (Hebrew *nēs*) in Isaiah 5:26 and 11:11–12. Moroni's "rais[ing] the standard" corresponds to the Lord "lift[ing] the ensign" or "set[ting] up an ensign." Moroni's using the *nēs* to "gain" (*wayyiqen*, "and [he] gained") his force, composed of "a remnant of the seed of Joseph," corresponds to the Lord using the *nēs* to "recover" — *liqnôt*, literally "to gain" or "acquire" the "remnant of his people." The response to Moroni's "raising" a *nēs* was that "thousands did flock to unto his standard," matching the (non-Israelite) martial response to the Lord's lifted-up "ensign" in Isaiah 5:26: "they shall come with speed swiftly" (i.e., the martial response of Israel's enemies). The result of Moroni's *nēs* activity here in Alma 62, as earlier in Alma 46, was that Moroni successfully "gathered together" a faithful "remnant of the seed of Joseph" just as the Lord would one day "set his hand again [*yôsîp*]" and "assemble" [*wĕʾāsap*] and "gather together" the "remnant of his people" — i.e., "the outcasts of Israel" and the "dispersed of Judah."

"A Remnant of the Seed of Joseph" Preserved: The Legacy of Joseph's Coat and Moroni's use of Isaiah 11:11–12

Mormon recognized that Moroni₁'s use of the brass plates account of Joseph's coat had implications not only for the Lehites of the latter's time but also prophetic implications for the Lehites of later generations. As far as we know, Moroni was first to use the collocation "remnant of the seed of Jacob" (see below),[46] and he derives the collocation "a remnant of the seed of Joseph" from Alma 46:23 ("we are a remnant of the seed of Jacob. Yea, we are a remnant of the seed of Joseph, whose coat was rent by his brethren into many pieces"; cf. Alma 46:27).

The "preservation" of Joseph's "remnant" constitutes one of the most important prophetic implications of the story of Joseph's coat: "Even as this remnant of garment of my son's hath been preserved, *so shall a remnant of the seed of my son be preserved by the hand of God* and be taken unto himself, while the remainder of the seed of Joseph shall perish, even as the remnant of his garment" (Alma 46:24).[47]

Mormon's use of the collocations "a remnant of the seed of Jacob" and "a remnant of the seed of Joseph" harks back to Moroni₁'s recounting of the narrative of Joseph's coat and the "title"/"standard of liberty." Here, too, the echoes of Isaiah 11:11–12 are strong:

> Surely he hath blessed the house of Jacob and hath been merciful unto *the seed of Joseph* [*yôsēp*]. And insomuch as the children of Lehi have kept his commandments, he hath blessed them and prospered them according to his word. Yea, and surely *shall he again* [cf. Hebrew *yôsîp*] bring *a remnant of the seed of Joseph* [*yôsēp*] to the knowledge of the Lord their God. And as surely as the Lord liveth *will he gather in* [cf. Hebrew *wĕʾāsap/yēʾāsēp*][48] from the four quarters of the earth *all the*

---

46. In addition to Moroni's use of it in Alma 46:23, this collocation recurs in Mormon's writings in 3 Nephi 5:24, Mormon 5:24, and Mormon 7:10.

47. Cf. Genesis 45:5.

48. If the verb that Mormon has in view here is *ʾāsap/yēʾāsēp* (rather than *qibbēṣ/yĕqābbēṣ*, the paronomastic sound play on *Joseph* is even richer. In either case, the wordplay appears to exploit Joseph's name in terms of the first of the biblical etiologies offered for it (see the *ʾāsap* etiology).

remnant of the seed of Jacob, which are scattered abroad upon all the face of the earth. And as he hath covenanted with all the house of Jacob, even so shall the covenant wherewith he hath covenanted with the house of Jacob be fulfilled in his own due time, unto the restoring all the house of Jacob unto the knowledge of the covenant that he hath covenanted with them. And then shall they know their Redeemer, which is Jesus Christ, the Son of God; and then *shall they be gathered in* [cf. Hebrew *yē'āsēpû(n)*] from the four quarters of the earth unto their own lands, from whence they have been dispersed. Yea, as the Lord liveth, so shall it be. Amen. (3 Nephi 5:21–26)

Indeed, footnote *a* to 3 Nephi 5:23 in the 1981 and 2013 Latter-day Saint editions of the Book of Mormon direct the reader back to Moroni's use of the phrase "a remnant of the seed of Joseph." In Alma 46:23, Mormon's linking of "the children of Lehi" to that remnant here suggests that his view of the "remnant of the seed of Joseph" already extends beyond his own people, the Nephites, and includes the Lamanites. Moreover, Mormon echoes the gathering language of Isaiah 11:11–12, where the prophet describes the "ensign" or "standard" (*nēs*) as signal to gather.

Mormon explicitly returns to the brass plates account of Joseph's coat as part of his narrative bridge from the cataclysmic events of 3 Nephi 8–10 to the ministry of the resurrected Christ to the Nephites and Lamanites in 3 Nephi 11–26. He states: "Behold, our father Jacob also testified concerning *a remnant of the seed of Joseph*. And behold, are not we *a remnant of the seed of Joseph*? And these things which testifies of us, are they not written upon the plates of brass which our father Lehi brought out of Jerusalem?" (3 Nephi 10:27). Mormon's placement of this statement at this point in his narrative is significant, especially in view of Jesus's recorded description of the Lamanites and Nephites who survived the cataclysmic events of 3 Nephi 8–10 as "remnant of the house of Joseph" (3 Nephi 15:12), but also in view of the tragic state of the Nephites and Lamanites when Mormon is writing and compiling his account (see, e.g., Mormon 5:8–20). Up to a point, Mormon had held out hope that the Nephites, "would *again* [cf. Hebrew *yôsîpû*] become a righteous people" (Mormon 2:12). Instead they became the perishing part of Joseph's seed, as symbolized by the perishing part of Joseph's coat while the Lamanites (and dissenting Nephites) would be preserved so "that they shall *again* [cf. Hebrew *yôsîpû*] be brought to the true knowledge, which is the knowledge of their Redeemer ... and be numbered among his sheep" (Helaman 15:13; see also Helaman 15:11, 15–16).

Conclusion

The paronomasia between Joseph's torn *kĕtōnet passîm* and the name *yôsēp*, together with Jacob's prophecy regarding the preservation of "a part of the remnant of the coat of Joseph"[49] as a type of "remnant of the seed of Joseph," appears to have suggested to Moroni₁ his covenant use of a torn part ("rent") of his own coat as symbol of his people as that "remnant." Isaiah's prophecy of the Lord "<u>set</u>[ting] his hand <u>*again*</u> [*yôsîp*] to recover the remnant of his people" using martial imagery including that of a battle "ensign"/"standard" (*nēs*) to "assemble [*wĕʾāsap*]" or "gather" that remnant provided a scriptural paradigm for Moroni hoisting his rent coat on a "standard" in a Nephite martial context.

Moreover, Mormon recognized in Moroni₁'s use of the "standard" or "ensign" to "gather"[50] a "remnant of the seed of Joseph" a type or foreshadowing of the Latter-day gathering of the descendants of Joseph. Moroni₁ uses a *nēs* as a covenant means of gathering and thus preserving a "remnant of the of seed of Joseph" (Alma 46:23, 27), most of which would ironically perish centuries later at the hands of the Lamanites, who also constituted a "remnant of the seed of Joseph."[51] Mormon, who had named his beloved son after this military leader (whom he clearly admired)[52] and who had watched his nation perish during his own time, would not have missed this irony. At his death, Mormon left it to his son Moroni₂ to complete the written record that would itself become the figurative, written "standard"[53] or "ensign" to gather the Lamanite "remnant of the seed of Joseph" in the Lord's "own due time."[54] As Isaiah and Mormon knew, the Lord would "*set* his hand *again* [*yôsîp*] the second time" to gather the "remnant of his people" Israel (Isaiah 11:11–12; 2 Nephi 25:17; 29:1) and that "surely *shall he again* [cf. *yôsîp*] bring a remnant of the seed of *Joseph* to the knowledge of the Lord their God" (3 Nephi 5:23).

---

49. Alma 46:24.

50. Alma 46:28, 31; 62:6.

51. 3 Nephi 5:23; 10:17.

52. See especially Alma 48:16–18: "And this was the faith of Moroni. And his heart did glory in it — not in the shedding of blood, but in doing good, in preserving his people, yea, in keeping the commandments of God, yea, and resisting iniquity. Yea, verily, verily I say unto you: *if all men had been and were and ever would be like unto Moroni, behold, the very powers of hell would have been shaken forever. Yea, the devil would never have no power over the hearts of the children of men.* Behold, he was a man like unto Ammon the son of Mosiah, yea, and even the other sons of Mosiah, yea, and also Alma and his sons, for *they were all men of God*."

53. Cf. D&C 45:9.

54. 2 Nephi 27:10 (cf. v. 21); 3 Nephi 5:25; 3 Nephi 20:29; Mormon 5:12.

[The author would like to thank Suzy Bowen, Jeff Lindsay, Allen Wyatt, Victor Worth, Don Norton, Tanya Spackman, and Daniel C. Peterson.]

Matthew L. Bowen *was raised in Orem, Utah, and graduated from Brigham Young University. He holds a PhD in Biblical Studies from the Catholic University of America in Washington, DC, and is currently an associate professor in religious education at Brigham Young University-Hawaii. He is also the author of* Name as Key-Word: Collected Essays on Onomastic Wordplay and The Temple in Mormon Scripture *(Salt Lake City: Interpreter Foundation and Eborn Books, 2018). He and his wife (the former Suzanne Blattberg) are the parents of three children: Zachariah, Nathan, and Adele.*

Chiastic Structuring of Large Texts: Second Nephi as a Case Study[1]

Noel B. Reynolds

Abstract: *In this important paper, Noel Reynolds extends his 1980 argument for the chiastic structure of 1 Nephi to demonstrate that 2 Nephi can be seen as a matching structure with a similar nature. Taken together, these findings demonstrate that chiasmus is not a phenomenon that confines itself to the details of words and phrases at the level of scriptural verses but can extend to much larger units of meaning, allowing the rhetorical beauty and emphasis of their overall messages to shine more brilliantly when they are considered as purposefully crafted wholes.*

[**Editor's Note:** Part of our book chapter reprint series, this article is reprinted here as a service to the LDS community. Original pagination and page numbers have necessarily changed, otherwise the reprint has the same content as the original.

See Noel B. Reynolds, "Chiastic Structuring of Large Texts: Second Nephi as a Case Study," in *"To Seek the Law of the Lord": Essays in Honor of John W. Welch,* ed. Paul Y. Hoskisson and Daniel C. Peterson (Orem, UT: The Interpreter Foundation, 2017), 333–50. Further information at https://interpreterfoundation.org/books/to-seek-the-law-of-the-lord-essays-in-honor-of-john-w-welch-2/.]

In 1967, John W. Welch was serving as a missionary in Germany and noticed a scholar's explanation of chiasmus as a rhetorical

---

1   This paper began as a slide presentation to the Society for Mormon Philosophy and Theology at Brigham Young University, Provo, Utah, 8 October 2015, entitled "All the Learning of My Father."

structure that recurs in various parts of the Bible. While the penchant for parallelism that characterized Old Testament writers was widely recognized by that time, the discovery that reverse parallelism was also commonly used by Old and New Testament writers was relatively recent and not yet widely accepted. Welch was no ordinary missionary in terms of his scholarly and scriptural preparation, and he immediately saw the possibility that Nephi and his successors may have been familiar with that rhetorical pattern and may have used it in the writings that we now know as the Book of Mormon. He went to work immediately and found numerous clear and impressive examples of chiastic structures in the Book of Mormon text. These discoveries fueled Welch's 1970 master's thesis and a long list of subsequent publications that presented additional discoveries and further refinements in his understanding of the phenomenon, addressed both to Book of Mormon readers and to biblical scholars generally.

Rhetorical criticism in biblical studies

About three centuries ago, a few European scholars — sometimes without any awareness of the parallel efforts of others — began to notice rhetorical structures featuring repetition and parallelism in the books of the Hebrew Bible. By the 19th century, a few had also begun to notice reverse parallelisms (chiasms) as well. Initially, it was short chiasms where the key terms were close together, as in poetry. But gradually chiasmus, like parallelism generally, was recognized as an organizational principle that could be used for larger texts — and even for entire books of prose. As a result of this growing body of rhetorical studies and reinterpretations of the books of the Old Testament, it is now widely recognized by biblical scholars that in the 8th and 7th centuries BCE Hebrew writers shared a highly developed set of rhetorical principles and techniques which distinguish their work dramatically from the ancient rhetorical traditions of Greece and Rome. These discoveries constitute a powerful step forward in our ability to understand Hebrew writing strategies and the messages their works promote.

My review of two recent books in this field presents a more comprehensive report on these developments.[2] In this paper, I will

---

2. For a brief introduction to the current state of understanding as represented in Hebrew rhetorical studies, see Noel B. Reynolds, "The Return of Rhetorical Analysis to Bible Studies," *Interpreter: A Journal of Mormon Scripture* 17 (2016): 91–98, http://www.mormoninterpreter.com/the-return-of-rhetorical-analysis-to-bible-studies/#more-7735. The two works selected for this review were Jack R. Lundbom,

rely principally on the discovery that when longer texts are organized chiastically, the ordered elements of that chiasm will consist of subordinate units of text that will themselves be delimited and organized according to some rhetorical principle — and will not necessarily be best understood through a listing of all the repeated words, phrases, or topics that may occur in a chiastic order. In fact, these subordinate units may contain their own subordinate units — thus illustrating the principle of subordinating levels of rhetorical structure in Hebrew writing that some analysts have found extending to as many as eight levels when they include grammatical and philological parallels.[3]

Strong confirmation for this insight about rhetorical levels comes from J. P. Fokkelman's study of narrative patterns in the Hebrew bible. While he sees the single story as "the first level at which a text may largely be understood as an entity in itself," he also sees it fitting into higher levels of narrative organization all the way up to the book or even macro-plots that include multiple books and being composed in turn of lower levels of text down to the sentence and even to words and sounds. Reflecting on the universality of this type of organization in the Bible, he concludes that "the Hebrew storytellers must have received excellent literary training, as time and again they demonstrate a strong preconception of form, and consummate mastery of it at all these levels."[4]

Roland Meynet emphasized the importance of looking for rhetorical organization of longer texts and specifically at the level of an entire book.

> In order to step up in the organization of the book, one can say that the most specific contribution of rhetorical analysis is the bringing to light of textual units composed of several pericopes, which I call sequences. Let me add that rhetorical analysis…does not seek to solely identify or extract a sequence or another from the book, but to see how the whole of the book is organized in sequences which cover the entirety of the text. The sequences are then organized in sections and the whole of the sections form the book.[5]

Biblical Rhetoric and Rhetorical Criticism (Sheffield: Sheffield Phoenix Press, 2013), and Roland Meynet, *Rhetorical Analysis: An Introduction to Biblical Rhetoric* (Sheffield: Sheffield Academic Press, 1998).

3. For the most detailed explanation of rhetorical levels, see Meynet, *Rhetorical Analysis,* 199–308. It should be mentioned that Meynet represents a formalistic extreme in his approach when compared to other rhetorical analysts.

4 J. P. Fokkelman, *Reading Biblical Narrative: An Introductory Guide* (Louisville, KY: Westminster John Knox Press, 1999), 161–62.

5 Meynet, *Rhetorical Analysis,* 171.

Rhetorical analysis does not expect to find the mathematical precision between parallel elements of long texts that is often demonstrated in short segments of poetry. Rather, the analyst looks for the ways that the author might reasonably have expected readers to see connections and parallels between the sequences or pericopes that constitute the larger text.

Nils Lund almost single-handedly launched the renewed interest in scholarly study of biblical chiasmus that grew so rapidly in the second half of the twentieth century. His 1942 publication of *Chiasmus in the New Testament* established beyond question the extensive role that this rhetorical form had played in the writing of both testaments of the Bible.[6] But it was left to the rhetorical criticism that emerged later to show how chiasmus fit in as one significant part of a much larger tool chest of Semitic rhetorical patterns that were developed in the 8th and 7th centuries and that were used extensively in most biblical writings from that period. The prominent leader of the form-criticism movement, James Muilenburg, took the occasion of his presidential address at the 1968 meeting of the Society for Biblical Literature to announce that the form-critical approach had reached its limits and to urge scholars to engage the new and broader approach of rhetorical criticism:

> What I am interested in, above all, is in understanding the nature of Hebrew literary composition, in exhibiting the structural patterns that are employed for the fashioning of a literary unit, whether in poetry or in prose, and in discerning the many and various devices by which the predications are formulated and ordered into a unified whole. Such an enterprise I should describe as rhetoric and the methodology as rhetorical criticism.[7]

Jack Lundbom led and chronicled the subsequent rise of rhetorical criticism among American biblical scholars, while Roland Meynet has performed a similar role for the parallel, though largely independent continental movement.[8]

The growing understanding of and appreciation for Hebrew rhetoric of the 7th century suggests strongly that we look at the writings of Nephi—born and educated in 7th century Jerusalem, and who opens his

---

6   Nils Wilhelm Lund, *Chiasmus in the New Testament: A Study in the Form and Function of Chiastic Structures* (Peabody, MA: Hendrickson Publishers, 1942).

7   James Muilenburg, "Form Criticism and Beyond," *Journal of Biblical Literature* 88, no. 1 (March 1969): 1–18, in particular, 8.

8   See note 2 above.

narrative telling us: "I was taught somewhat in all the learning of my father" (1 Ne. 1:1) — to see if the insights of rhetorical criticism might provide us with new insights. In this paper I will make a first attempt to apply the principles of Hebrew rhetoric to an interpretation of the Book of Second Nephi, which to this point has frustrated a number of interpretive efforts, my own included, and about which no consensus analysis has yet emerged.

There are a few general warnings that scholars of Hebrew rhetoric raise for those who want to develop these new skills. Commentators have noted that the rhetoric we have learned in the western tradition is *hypotactic* in that it is direct, open, and logical. Hebrew rhetoric, in contrast, is *paratactic* in that it tends to be indirect, making important points both through its structure and through words that may have their full meaning provided and adjusted gradually throughout the text.[9]

They also point out that different kinds of parallelism and repetition ground most rhetorical constructions. For example, the repetition of the same word or phrase at the beginning and end of a rhetorical unit forms an *inclusio*, which marks the boundaries for that unit.[10] Parallelism can take many forms and is often reversed, making the rhetorical unit chiastic. Further, parallelism can occur in the repetition of words, synonyms, concepts, grammar, or even opposites (antithetical parallels). One of the most important guidelines offered is the necessity of locating the boundaries of rhetorical units, boundaries which can be signaled in verbal or structural terms, such as the inclusio — which is the device most frequently used in many texts.[11] Finally, Hebrew rhetoric is notable for its extensive resort to multiple rhetorical levels in longer texts. All rhetorical units may be subdivided into second-level rhetorical units with their own structures. And these can be subdivided again and again — going down several levels — all of which can employ any of the usual rhetorical structures.

Rhetorical analysis of Second Nephi

All rhetorical writing is designed to persuade, and Nephi's writings are no exception. While most Old Testament writings have provided modern

---

9 See the discussion in Lundbom, *Biblical Rhetoric*, 73–74.

10 For a helpful explanation of *inclusio*, the history of this usage in studies of biblical rhetoric, and biblical examples of its use, see Lundbom, *Biblical Rhetoric*, 325–327.

11 In *Biblical Rhetoric*, 25–36, Lundbom provides general principles and common patterns by which texts can be delimited into sub-units. He provides an instructive example when he goes on in chapter 4 to apply these to his analysis of Jeremiah (37–59).

scholars with bottomless opportunities for speculation about their true purposes, Nephi seems anxious to make his motives perfectly clear. In First Nephi he assures his readers that "the fullness of mine intent is that I may persuade men to come unto the God of Abraham and the God of Isaac and the God of Jacob and be saved" (1 Ne. 6:4). And in Second Nephi he says the same thing in a different way: "For we labor diligently to write, to persuade our children and also our brethren to believe in Christ and to be reconciled to God" (2 Ne. 25:23).[12]

In 1980 I published a proposed rhetorical outline of First Nephi.[13] While that effort will now require significant revision in light of these new developments in Hebrew rhetoric, I will focus this paper on a proposed rhetorical outline of Second Nephi. Should this exploratory outline prove persuasive, suggesting that Second Nephi does seem to be informed by the principles of Hebrew rhetoric, it would then be appropriate to proceed with a comprehensive rhetorical analysis of the entire book at all levels. In this experimental paper, only the central chapter will be analyzed at all four levels.

I will be following the procedure outlined by Muilenburg in his 1968 launch of rhetorical criticism as a sub-field of biblical studies regarding the delimitation of literary units in the text: "The first concern of the rhetorical critic...is to define the limits or scope of the literary unit, to recognize precisely where and how it begins and where and how it ends." Further, "the literary unit is...an indissoluble whole, an artistic and creative unity, a unique formulation. The delimitation of the passage is essential if we are to learn how its major motif...is resolved."[14] He then goes on to explain the second major concern of the rhetorical critic — recognizing the structure of a composition and discerning "the configuration of its component parts." This will require a delineation of "the warp and woof out of which the literary fabric is woven" and identification of "the various rhetorical devices that are employed for marking," 1) "the sequence and movement of the pericope," and 2) "the shifts or breaks in the development of the writer's thought."[15]

Following Muilenburg's guidelines, then the first task is to establish the boundaries of the principle rhetorical units in Second Nephi. It may be surprising to some that there has actually been some controversy

---

12 Book of Mormon quotations are taken from the 2009 Yale edition: Royal Skousen, editor, *The Book of Mormon: The Earliest Text* (New Haven, Yale University Press, 2009).

13 Noel B. Reynolds, "Nephi's Outline," *BYU Studies* 20 no. 2 (1980): 1–18.

14 Muilenburg, "Form Criticism," 8–9.

15 Ibid., 10.

about the appropriate rhetorical dividing line between First and Second Nephi. I will not give here all my reasons for rejecting the 1994 proposal of Fred Axelgard that the real dividing line is between 2 Nephi chapters 5 and 6, even though his theory has been revived recently by Joseph Spencer.[16] Rather, I will assume herein that the obvious division made by Nephi was intended to guide his readers in a straightforward way to see that one major rhetorical structure had ended and that a new rhetorical structure was beginning, in spite of the fact that there is no break in the story between the last verses of First Nephi and the opening verses of Second Nephi. An important principle of rhetorical interpretation is that one must let the author organize the material as he sees fit, without attempting to force it into interpreters' preconceived rhetorical forms or making it convey messages preferred by the interpreters. There is no question that the division into two books as we have it in today's Book of Mormon was present in the original translation, and presumably was taken directly from the very plates engraved by Nephi himself. In my judgment, it would take an extraordinarily powerful argument to undermine that presumption—far more powerful than what has been offered. I take, therefore, the entire Book of Second Nephi as the top level of rhetorical organization to be considered, and proceed to divide it into sub-units according to cues provided in the text. The hypothesis guiding these divisions is that Nephi, having been educated in 7th-century Jerusalem, may have incorporated the principles of Hebrew rhetoric in vogue in that time and place into his own writing.

The following analysis finds thirteen level-two text units identified principally by inclusios. Furthermore, these units appear to be organized chiastically at this level. Table 1 lists the boundary markers or reasons for seeing each of these thirteen units as separate principal sub-units of the text. Table 2 will then list the key language or other characteristics of each pair of units in the proposed thirteen-element chiasm that structures Second Nephi. It will be seen that this chiasm focuses the entire text on the gospel promise of salvation through Jesus Christ in this life and in the next.

Commentary on this structure

Even in this exploratory analysis a few observations are suggested. First, it may be noticed that the first four elements identified (A–D),

---

16   See Frederick W. Axelgard, "1 And 2 Nephi: An Inspiring Whole," *BYU Studies* 26, no. 4 (1986): 53–65, and Joseph M. Spencer, *An Other Testament: On Typology*, (Provo, UT: The Neal A. Maxwell Institute for Religious Scholarship, 2016), 34–35.

Table 1

Label	Text	Rhetorical boundary markers
A	2 Nephi 1:1–1:30	"out of the land of Jerusalem"
B	2 Nephi 1:31–2:4	Zoram and Jacob "blessed"
C	2 Nephi 2:5–30	"know good" / "have chosen the good part"
D	2 Nephi 3:1–4:12	Lehi "speaks"—to Joseph / all his household
E	2 Nephi 4:13–5:34	Laman & Lemuel angry /wars and contentions
F	2 Nephi 6–11:1	words/things "Jacob spake"
G	2 Nephi 11:2–8	"the words of Isaiah"
F*	2 Nephi 12–24	Lord's house established/Zion founded
E*	2 Nephi 25:1–6	"Isaiah spake/hath spoken"
D*	2 Nephi 25:7–31:1	"mine own prophecy/my prophesying"
C*	2 Nephi 31:2–21	"the doctrine of Christ"
B*	2 Nephi 32:1–8a	"ponder in your hearts"
A*	2 Nephi 32:8b–33:15	Nephi "must speak/commanded to seal" words

*Note that these phrases are all thematic somewhere in Nephi's writings.

when compared to the final four (D*–A*), remind us of the division of First Nephi between Lehi's account (chapters 1–9), so labeled by Nephi, and Nephi's own account (chapters 10–22). The first four feature Lehi's testimony, preaching, teachings, and prophecies. The last four focus on

Table 2

A	Lehi's final testimony and call *to his family* to repentance
B	<u>The Spirit</u>—Jacob redeemed—in the service of God.
C	Lehi's detailed explanation of *the way* of salvation based on "the things which [he] had read."
D	Lehi's last blessings (prophecies) *to his people.*
E	Historical interlude—the founding of "the people of Nephi"—"my soul delighteth/grieveth."
F	Jacob's teachings witness of Christ.
G	Nephi's witness of Christ
F*	Isaiah's prophecies witness of Christ
E*	Historical interlude—the education of "my people"—"my soul delighteth/delighteth."
D*	Final restatement of Nephi's prophecies—*to all people.*
C*	Nephi's detailed explanation of *the way or doctrine* of Christ based on what he learned from the Father and the Son directly.
B*	<u>The Spirit</u>—the Holy Ghost will show you what to do.
A*	Nephi's final testimony and call *to all people* to repentance.

the testimony, preaching, teachings, and prophecies of Nephi. Second, while the First Book of Nephi focused on ways in which the Lord delivered Lehi, Nephi, and their people from their enemies and the trials of their journeys, leading them to a promised land in this world, the Second Book of Nephi focuses on the Lord's ability—through the atonement of Christ—to deliver the faithful from the devil and lead them to eternal life in the next world. Third, the chiastic organization of Second Nephi reveals how the first half of the book focuses on specific accounts of specific people — usually Lehi and his family — and on the teachings, blessings, and prophecies directed to them. But the second half takes those same teachings and prophecies in turn and universalizes them by applying them to "all people." The story of Lehi and his people becomes a surrogate for the Lord's plan of deliverance for all peoples, in the same way that chosen Israel is an exemplar for all nations of how they can be blessed by Israel's god, or punished — according to their willingness to repent and take up his covenants and endure to the end.

Finally, the language and organization of Nephi's writing explicitly invokes the biblical motif of the Two Ways. While it was thought for some time by scholars that this motif was mostly a development of early Christians derived from the Savior's reference to himself as "the way," it is now widely understood that its significant usage in the Dead Sea Scrolls and its appearance in Old Testament writings such as Deuteronomy and Jeremiah and even more obviously in the wisdom literature demonstrates its firm origins in the Jewish traditions. Both Lehi in his exposition of the plan of salvation, and Nephi in his detailed presentation of the gospel or doctrine of Christ, as taught to him by the Father and the Son, deliberately speak of these as God's ways for man. Further, Lehi develops the contrast between this and the devil's way, as he develops his teaching on the necessity of opposition in all things and his account of human beginnings. As suggested above, First Nephi details how God fulfilled his covenant with Lehi and Nephi (like Abraham) by protecting their growing posterity and leading them to a promised land. And Second Nephi turns the journey motif into an account of the gospel as a path or way leading to eternal life.[17] Just as the miraculous director was given to Lehi to point the way for his party to travel toward the promised land, so Nephi will explain that as one progresses on the path that leads to eternal life, "the Holy Ghost...will shew unto you all things what ye should do" (2 Ne. 32:5).

Analyzing lower rhetorical levels

If the division of Second Nephi into thirteen sub-units that are organized chiastically is correct, we might expect some or all of these to exhibit additional subordinate levels of rhetorical organization. To test this hypothesis further, I will focus in this paper on the seventh or central element G from the first analysis. Again, to the extent this proves successful, Second Nephi would seem to invite similar analyses for the

---

17 See, Noel B. Reynolds, "This is the Way," *Religious Educator* 14, no. 3 (2013): 71–83. https://rsc.byu.edu/archived/re-14-no-3-2013/way.

other twelve level-two text units. Table 3 outlines the central unit G of the level-2 chiasm as an eight-element chiasm at level 3. Tables 4a–4d will provide a rhetorical analysis of each of those eight elements at level 4. The entire text of G is included in the analysis and in these tables.

In Tables 4a–4d, the complete text of the four pairs of chiastic elements from Table 3 will be analyzed as pairs to examine their internal rhetorical structures and the various ways in which their parallel characters can be described at rhetorical level 4.

The eight-element chiasm of G is framed by two parallel triplets — A and A*. But as with Hebrew poetry generally, the second element provides added or intensified meaning by adding phrases or changing some of the words. The first lines (a/a) of each triplet are virtually identical, providing this central text unit G with an easily recognizable inclusio, which frequently signals that the material within the inclusio may be

Table 3. 2 Nephi 11:2–8

1	A	And now I Nephi write more of the words of Isaiah,
2	B	Wherefore I will send their words forth unto my children to prove unto them that my words are true. (a proof by citing three witnesses)
3	C	Behold, my soul delighteth in proving unto my people the truth of the coming of Christ
4	D	And also my soul delighteth in the covenants of the Lord which he hath made to our fathers
5	D*	yea, my soul delighteth in…the great and eternal plan of deliverance from death.
6	C*	And my soul delighteth in proving unto my people that save Christ should come all men must perish.
7	B*	For if there be no Christ there be no God. And if there be no God we are not, for there could have been no creation. But there is a God and he is Christ, and he cometh in the fullness of his own time. (a proof by logical reasoning)
8	A*	And now I write some of the words of Isaiah,

Table 4a

1	A	a	And now I Nephi write more of the words of Isaiah,
		b	for my soul delighteth in his words.
		c	For I will liken his words unto my people.
8	A*	a	And now I write some of the words of Isaiah,
		b	that whoso of my people which shall see these words may lift up their hearts and rejoice for all men.
		c	Now these are the words, and ye may liken them unto you and unto all men.

structured as another chiasm — as G indeed turns out to be. But line b in the second triplet (A*) adds meaning as Nephi's personal delight in Isaiah's words becomes the rejoicing of his people *for all men*. And in lines c/c just as Nephi could "liken" Isaiah's words unto his people in A, so his readers are invited in A* to liken these words unto themselves "and *unto all men*." In this way, the first pair of parallel elements in G introduces us to the universalizing theme of the second half of Second Nephi.

The second pair of parallel elements (B/B*) presents a more complicated text and might escape notice were not the following two pairs (C/C* and D/D*) so obvious — driving us to look more carefully for B/B*. As analyzed above, B presents us with two very different but closely linked rhetorical structures. The first and last lines of the first structure are nearly identical, forming an inclusio, and setting the first structure off from the second — the difference between a and a* being that *them* (the words of Isaiah) in a becomes *their words* (the words of Isaiah *and* Jacob) in a*. But inside the inclusio, we find not another chiasm, but instead a form known by biblical rhetoricians as alternating parallels. Lines b and b* are obviously similar, as each reports that a different prophet — Isaiah and Jacob respectively — has seen the Redeemer. Lines c and c* each contain Nephi's personal witness that he also has seen the Redeemer.

The second rhetorical structure contained in B turns out to be a short chiasm that steps aside from the historical facts Nephi has just reported

Table 4b

2	B	a	And I will send them [his words] forth unto all my children,
		b	for he (Isaiah) verily saw my Redeemer,
		c	even as I have seen him.
3		b*	And my brother Jacob also hath seen him
		c*	as I have seen him.
		a*	Wherefore I will send their words forth unto my children
		aa	to prove unto them that my words are true.
		bb	Wherefore by the words of three, God hath said,
		cc*	I will establish my word.
		bb*	Nevertheless God sendeth more witnesses,
		aa*	and he proveth all his words.
7	B*	a	For if there be no Christ
		b	there be no God;
		c	and if there be no God we are not,
		c*	or there could have been no creation.
		b*	But there is a God,
		a*	and he is Christ,

Ballast line: and he cometh in the fullness of his own time.

to explain why those facts amount to a proof to Nephi's children that his witness of the Redeemer is true. God has given the standard that the word of three witnesses is proof of his word—possibly alluding to Deuteronomy (4:26 and 17:6)—and Nephi has provided three eye witnesses. And God has sent and will send more witnesses. The theme of proving the prophecies of Christ before he comes is what binds B and B* together as parallel elements in this level-4 chiasm.

B* picks up the "proof" theme—but in a new way—offering a logical proof from theological reasoning. While this brief passage composed of seven very short clauses may not satisfy a modern reader's learned preference for syllogisms, it is clearly framed rhetorically as a chiasm composed principally of antithetically parallel elements. Line a* positively contradicts the negative hypothesis raised in a, and b* positively negates the negative conclusion proffered in b. The central lines c/c* state and restate the counterfactual conclusion to be drawn from a and b that neither we nor creation itself could exist without God—a fundamental premise that was likely accepted universally in 7th century Israelite and quite possibly in all middle-eastern cultures.

The final independent clause in B* is not part of its chiastic structure. It does extend the teaching about Christ with Nephi's affirmation that he will come "in the fullness of his own time"—the important additional

Table 4c

4	C	a	Behold, my soul delighteth in proving unto my people
		b	the truth of the coming of Christ,
		c	for for this end hath the law of Moses been given.
		b*	And all things which have been given of God from the beginning of the world unto man
		c*	are the typifying of him (Christ).
6	C*	a	And my soul delighteth in proving unto my people
		b	that save Christ should come
		c	all men must perish.

information drawn from the visions received by Nephi, Lehi, Jacob, and Isaiah, that has not yet been articulated in the series of proofs. By completing or rounding out what has been said in the rhetorical form, this line fills the role that biblical rhetorician Jack Lundbom recognizes as a "ballast line" — as he and others find these frequently bringing balance at the conclusion of small rhetorical structures in biblical writing.[18]

The repetition of the opening line (a) in C and C* supplemented by the common content of b in each is more than sufficient to establish the parallelism of these two short elements in the level-3 chiasm — even though the two have rather different internal rhetorical structures at level 4. C begins with a normal triplet reiterating Nephi's sense that his writing will prove the truth of the prophesied coming of Christ for his people, in a and b, but adding in c the further connection between the law of Moses and the coming of Christ. Nephi has already informed us that the Nephites "did observe to keep the judgments and the statutes and the commandments of the Lord, in all things according to the law of Moses" (2 Ne. 5:10). And now he explains their understanding that the law of Moses was given to remind Israel of the future coming of Christ in c. The next sentence goes on to restate and expand b and c in b* and c* respectively, producing another example of alternate parallelism. C* begins with the same statement as C, but develops into a simple triplet with the added conclusion in c that without Christ's coming "all must perish."

With D and D* we have finally arrived at the rhetorical center of Second Nephi. Here, two triplets face each other in the chiastic structure of G. Their equivalence in a parallel structure is provided once again by starting each triplet with the same principal clause: "my soul delighteth." To the extent this pair of triplets constitutes a turning point for all of Second Nephi, and simultaneously for its central text unit G, we are led once again to the comparison between First and Second Nephi. The first triplet (D) expresses Nephi's delight in the covenants the Lord made with "our fathers," which we should understand to include specifically Abraham, Moses and all Israel at Sinai, and Lehi most recently. The second turns our focus to the atonement of Christ, which Lehi, Nephi, and Jacob, now understand as the mechanism through which the Lord has established his gospel as part of "the great and eternal plan of deliverance from death" and as the fuller understanding of the ancient

---

18 Lundbom borrows the concept of ballast lines from Muilenburg and George Adam Smith and illustrates the form these took in Isaiah in *Biblical Rhetoric*, 133–135.

Table 4d

5	D	a	And also my soul delighteth
		b	in the covenants of the Lord
		c	which he hath made to our fathers.
	D*	a	Yea, my soul delighteth
		b	in his grace and his justice and power and mercy,
		c	in the great and eternal plan of deliverance from death.

covenants as demonstrated in the forward-looking significance of the Law of Moses as just discussed.

Conclusions

The experiment conducted in this paper has been the application of the principles of Hebrew rhetoric—as that has come to be understood by biblical scholars over the last half century—to the Book of Second Nephi, self-described as personally written by Nephi, who was educated in Jerusalem at the end of the 7th century BCE, a time and place where these principles are now thought by scholars to have been *de rigeur*. The experiment did not refute the hypothesis, but instead did produce a plausible division of the book into 13 sub-units that readily organize themselves chiastically as a whole. The experiment also took the central rhetorical sub-unit G and explored its internal rhetorical structure down two more levels. That analysis has produced a plausible chiastic structure in which every word of the passage fits comfortably into yet another lower level of rhetorical structures. In addition, 2 Nephi 11:2–8 turns out to feature the principal theses of Nephi's writings at the same time that it explains the inclusion and placement of the long excerpts from Lehi, Jacob, and Isaiah, even though it is a passage that has rarely been featured in Book of Mormon analyses. These results are sufficiently positive and justify moving the project forward to the much larger task of providing rhetorical analyses for the twelve remaining major textual subdivisions of the book.

Also, contrary to my 1980 assessment, Second Nephi is not a random collection of teachings and prophecies that did not fit into First Nephi's structure.[19] Rather, the book promises to be best seen as a matching structure which required its own book. Both structurally and thematically, the two books appear to be designed as a pair—each with its own message and emphases. While First Nephi provides Nephi's proofs based on Lehi's travels to the promised land that "the tender mercies of the Lord is over all them whom he hath chosen because of their faith to make them mighty, even unto the power of deliverance" (1 Ne. 1:20), Second Nephi elevates the traditional meaning of the Abrahamic/Lehite promises for this life into a focus on the atonement and gospel of Christ which provide the way of deliverance to eternal life. And so God's prophecies and covenants with Israel turn out to be surrogates for the eternal promises he offers to all his children—in all times and in all places (2 Ne. 30:2).

Noel Reynolds *(PhD, Harvard University) is an emeritus professor of political science at Brigham Young University, where he taught a broad range of courses in legal and political philosophy, American Heritage, and the Book of Mormon. His research and publications are based in these fields and several others, including authorship studies, Mormon history, Christian history and theology, and the Dead Sea Scrolls.*

---

19   Reynolds, "Nephi's Outline," 16.

Jacob — The Prophet of Social Justice

Stephen O. Smoot

Review of Deidre Nicole Green, *Jacob: A Brief Theological Introduction* (Provo, UT: The Neal A. Maxwell Institute for Religious Scholarship, 2020). 148 pages. $9.99 (paperback).

Abstract: *Deidre Nicole Green, a postdoctoral research fellow at the Neal A. Maxwell Institute for Religious Scholarship, offers an analysis of the theology of the book of Jacob with her new contribution to the Institute's brief theological introduction series to the Book of Mormon. Green focuses on the theology of social justice in Jacob's teachings, centering much of her book on how the Nephite prophet framed issues of atonement and salvation on both personal and societal levels. Her volume offers some intriguing new readings of otherwise familiar Book of Mormon passages.*

Deidre Nicole Green is a postdoctoral research fellow at the Neal A. Maxwell Institute for Religious Scholarship and is the author of the institute's volume on the book of Jacob in its series of brief theological introductions to the Book of Mormon.[1] Green brings with her a PhD in Religion from Claremont Graduate University, a Master of Arts in Religion from Yale Divinity School, and a Bachelor of Arts in Philosophy from Brigham Young University. Besides these impressive credentials, as a specialist on the Danish philosopher Søren Kierkegaard — one of the

---

1. Deidre Nicole Green, *Jacob: A Brief Theological Introduction* (Provo, UT: The Neal A. Maxwell Institute for Religious Scholarship, 2020). Citations of this volume will be in the body of this review. As of this writing, the Maxwell Institute has published five out of its twelve planned volumes in the series. See https://mi.byu.edu/publications/.

most influential and important Christian philosophers of the modern age — Green is well equipped to provide theological analysis.[2]

Although it is a relatively short book in the Book of Mormon, the book of Jacob is nevertheless theologically dense. Not only does it feature Jacob's important temple sermon (Jacob 2–3) but also Zenos's allegory of the olive tree (Jacob 5) and the confrontation with Sherem (Jacob 7). The prophet providing us this content was the "firstborn in the days of [Lehi's] tribulation in the wilderness" (2 Nephi 2:1). As Green observes in her introductory remarks, this makes Jacob a "unique voice in the Book of Mormon" who offers a "rare and distinct perspective" on account of his vulnerable upbringing. "Jacob concerns himself largely with issues of social justice," she writes, "demonstrating that religious life and social life should not be separated into distinct spheres. Jacob's personal experience of suffering, his compassion for those on the margins of society, his concern for equality, and his commitment to forming a faithful and just community inform his testimony of Jesus Christ in a way that highlights many of the salient issues of the twenty-first century" (2).

After her introduction (2–5), Green structures her theological analysis of the book of Jacob as follows: a brief biography of Jacob (8–15), a look at Jacob's theodicy and theology of holy suffering (18–28), Jacob's teachings on building a sacred society (30–57), the temple sermon (60–93), the allegory of the olive tree (96–107), and final thoughts and conclusion (110–121). The theological stream Green identifies running through the book of Jacob is summarized in her conclusion: "[Jacob] invites all people to view the death of Christ and, I believe, to view every aspect of reality through the lens of reconciliation that it affords. In this way, we are reminded of God's infinite and ever available love. … This love shows us the way through to flourishing and fruitfulness, reminding us that all objectives worth seeking ultimately rely upon faithful communities who strive to reach back in love toward the divine for their attainment" (120). As would befit a social justice prophet like Jacob, Green emphasizes that the "communal and faithful" love of God "requires us to see all human beings as equals, a vision that is facilitated by viewing one another through the lens of the death of Christ: we are all equally in need of reconciliation to God and all equally loved by both God and Christ, a truth attested by Christ's willingness to suffer and make the atonement equally available to all" (120).

---

2. Green's biography and examples of her work can be found at "Deidre Nicole Green," Scholars, Maxwell Institute, https://mi.byu.edu/scholars/deidre-nicole-green/.

There was much that I appreciated about Green's analysis of the book of Jacob. I was particularly interested in her reading of the allegory of the olive tree as more than just pertaining to the scattering and gathering of Israel. While this is certainly the primary intent of the allegory, Jacob 5 can also, as Green shows, be fruitfully read as touching on the atonement of Jesus Christ and the reconciliation of humanity with God. "Jacob senses deeply his responsibility to teach that the atonement is universally accessible, necessary, and efficacious and that it not only restores individuals and societies torn apart by trauma and sin to wholeness but also seals relationships with the divine and with others" (99–100). Green's Christological and soteriological reading of Zenos's allegory was a new, invigorating way of approaching the text I had never before considered and found most welcome. Indeed, although it should have been more obvious, it had never before occurred to me that the eschatological restoration of Israel and the infinite atonement of Israel's Messiah are two theological matters that are deeply intertwined. As such, reading them together simultaneously in Jacob 5 strikes me as entirely appropriate. As Green writes,

> This allegory is most often understood in terms of the scattering and gathering of Israel as an integral part of divine covenant. It can also be read in more expansive terms, with the restored vineyard representing the integration, reconciliation, and wholeness possible only through the atonement of Jesus Christ for both individuals and societies who have been fragmented and disintegrated through traumatic experience or sin. This reading amplifies the breadth and profundity of God's love for humanity. (100)

True to the theme of the book, Green couches this soteriology in the context of social justice. "Just as Jacob has shown us that all suffering and sin are inherently social, so too is the work of redemption. In Jacob 5 we read an elaboration of how it is that communities are healed and reconciled, and we avail ourselves of a greater appreciation and understanding concerning the fact that atonement operates on every level of existence, reconciling individuals to themselves, to God, and with their communities" (100–101). While I found her analysis insightful overall, I was disappointed that Green does not appear to draw from or otherwise alert her readers to the significant 1994 volume *The Allegory of the Olive Tree: The Olive, the Bible, and Jacob 5.*[3] Not only is this landmark publication on Jacob 5 essential reading on Zenos's allegory, but it also extends theological insights into this chapter that would have nicely complimented Green's own reading.[4]

I was likewise underwhelmed somewhat by Green's reading of the temple sermon in Jacob 2–3. Green correctly identifies the three cardinal sins in Nephite society of his time that Jacob singles out and condemns (namely: classism, sexual immorality, and racial prejudice) and articulates some important theological points that can be drawn from the temple sermon in addressing these systemic problems that sadly still haunt us today (60–93). However, Green's examination and the points she draws out from Jacob's sermon, while helpful, could have been strengthened with some historicized perspective such as is offered by Brant A. Gardner. As Gardner explores at length, Jacob's conceptual linkage (and subsequent condemnation) of seeking riches and unauthorized polygamy becomes more intelligible when his sermon is placed in an ancient Mesoamerican and biblical background.[5] Gardner's historicized reading, I feel, offers a more grounded context for making sense of a number of the features in Jacob's condemnation of unauthorized, exploitative polygamy. This includes why Jacob singled out David and Solomon (Jacob 2:24) as unrighteous polygamists worthy of condemnation but not Abraham and his own ancestral namesake (cf. Genesis 16:1–3; 29:21–30; 30:1–4, 9), and also why Jacob allows for plural marriages to be contracted under specific circumstances

---

3. Stephen D. Ricks, *The Allegory of the Olive Tree: The Olive, the Bible, and Jacob 5*, ed. John W. Welch (Salt Lake City: Deseret Book; Provo, UT: FARMS, 1994). Green does not appear to cite this volume in her reading of Jacob 5 and does not list it in her recommendations for further reading (122-23).

4. I'm thinking in particular of the offerings in Truman G. Madsen, "The Olive Press: A Symbol of Christ," in *The Allegory of the Olive Tree*, 1-10, and Paul Y. Hoskisson, "The Allegory of the Olive Tree in Jacob," in *The Allegory of the Olive Tree*, 70-103, both of which give readings of Jacob 5 that are consonant with Green's.

5. Brant A. Gardner, *Second Witness: Analytical and Contextual Commentary on the Book of Mormon* (Salt Lake City: Greg Kofford Books, 2007), 2:483-99; Gardner, *Traditions of the Fathers: The Book of Mormon as History* (Salt Lake City: Greg Kofford Books, 2015), 197-204. For accessible summary treatments of Gardner's points, see "What Does the Book of Mormon Say About Polygamy?" KnoWhys, Book of Mormon Central, March 28, 2016, https://knowhy.bookofmormoncentral. org/knowhy/what-does-the-book-of-mormon-say-about-polygamy; "Why Does the Book of Mormon Warn Against Seeking after Riches?" KnoWhys, Book of Mormon Central, May 30, 2019, https://knowhy.bookofmormoncentral.org/ knowhy/why-does-the-book-of-mormon-warn-against-seeking-after-riches.

(Jacob 2:30).[6] The issue for Jacob is not that plural marriage is *inherently* sinful or exploitative, only that it *can be* if improperly practiced.

Green is right that the problem was that the form of polygamy being practiced by the Nephites in Jacob's day was turning women into sexual commodities that robbed them of their agency (80–85). But she could have taken her reading further by exploring, as Gardner does, how the specific historical and social circumstances of the early Nephite colony in the New World affected the content of Jacob's temple sermon.[7] As a text deriving from the ancient world (both the ancient biblical world and ancient America), at least *some* effort should be made on the part of the exegete to situate the Book of Mormon's theological teachings in their ancient context before bringing other potentially useful modern interpretive paradigms into the discussion. This is not to say that Green's reading of Jacob 2:23–35 is necessarily wrong, only that I felt it could have been stronger.

Other interesting insights Green provides in her study include her view of Sherem as a sort of ironic, unintended witness for Christ (49–57). "Jacob's treatment of Sherem is unique in the Book of Mormon because, rather than silencing him, Jacob gives Sherem the opportunity to repent and to influence the Nephites for good by testifying of Christ and the atonement. It is Jacob's humility and love for his neighbor that makes it possible for Sherem to be an instrument of God" (49). As with her treatment of Jacob 5, this is a noteworthy way to look at Jacob 7 I had not heretofore considered. Sure enough, the ironic outcome at Jacob 7:17–21 would seem to reinforce Green's intriguing reading of the showdown

---

6. Latter-day Saints since at least the mid-nineteenth century have read Jacob 2:30 as an exemption to what is otherwise Jacob's unflinching condemnation of polygamy. The comments by Orson Pratt, "Polygamy," *Journal of Discourses* (London: Latter-day Saints' Book Depot, 1859), 6:350-51, serve as one illustrative example of how historically Latter-day Saints have (justifiably) read this verse.

7. Green's observation that "every instance of polygamy in the Book of Mormon serves as a negative example" (82), while true, would likewise have benefitted from some historical context. See for instance Taylor Halverson, "Deuteronomy 17:14-20 as Criteria for Book of Mormon Kingship," *Interpreter: A Journal of Latter-day Saint Faith and Scholarship* 24 (2017): 1-10, https://journal.interpreterfoundation.org/deuteronomy-1714-20-as-criteria-for-book-of-mormon-kingship/. Green also overlooks the likelihood that the righteous Amulek was a polygamist. See "Why is Amulek's Household Significant?" KnoWhys, Book of Mormon Central, June 8, 2016, https://knowhy.bookofmormoncentral.org/knowhy/why-is-amuleks-household-significant.

between Jacob and Sherem that doesn't strike me as being too clever for its own good (as some other recent treatments of Jacob 7 have been[8]).

Whatever diverging views I may have with Green on this or that point throughout her volume,[9] I ultimately appreciate her sensitivity to the Book of Mormon's emphasis on equality, which Green underscores as "a fundamental ethos" of the record. "Calling out pride, greed, and violations of the law of chastity, Jacob's unrelenting critique of Nephite society also decries attitudes and practices that oppress based on differences in wealth, skin color, and gender" (32). In Green's recasting, Jacob is the prophet of social justice *par excellence* who, mindful of his own vulnerable and marginalized origins as Lehi's "firstborn in the wilderness" who "suffered afflictions and much sorrow" (2 Nephi 2:2–3), boldly proclaims that love and equity towards all men and women is *"required* of followers of Christ" (32, emphasis in original). As with his brother Nephi who declared that "all are alike unto God" (2 Nephi 26:33), Jacob joins the chorus of ancient and modern prophets who stress that being truly reconciled through Christ can only come when the children of

---

8. I am thinking of, for instance, Jana Riess, "'There Came a Man': Sherem, Scapegoating, and the Inversion of Prophetic Tradition," in *Christ and Antichrist: Reading Jacob 7*, ed. Adam S. Miller and Joseph M. Spencer (Provo, UT: Neal A. Maxwell Institute for Religious Scholarship, 2018), 1-17, which, upon recent rereading, struck me as an undeniably sophisticated reading of the text that is more fanciful than actually insightful. For additional engagement with Riess's effort, see Kevin Christensen, "Light and Perspective: Essays from the Mormon Theology Seminar on 1 Nephi 1 and Jacob 7," *Interpreter: A Journal of Latter-day Saint Faith and Scholarship* 31 (2019): 25-70, https://journal.interpreterfoundation. org/light-and-perspective-essays-from-the-mormon-theology-seminar-on-1-nephi-1-and-jacob-7/; Duane Boyce, "Text as Afterthought: Jana Riess's Treatment of the Jacob-Sherem Episode," *Interpreter: A Journal of Latter-day Saint Faith and Scholarship* 33 (2019): 123-40, https://journal.interpreterfoundation.org/ text-as-afterthought-jana-riesss-treatment-of-the-jacob-sherem-episode/.

9. If I had one main critique of Green's book, it would be her apparent reluctance to acknowledge or reference valuable work on the book of Jacob that has preceded her. To cite another example, as with her failure to acknowledge or otherwise engage the important FARMS volume *The Allegory of the Olive Tree* when discussing Jacob 5, I was also disappointed that Green did not offer even a brief comment or note on John W. Welch's important legal analysis of the confrontation between Sherem and Jacob in Jacob 7. John W. Welch, "The Case of Sherem," in *The Legal Cases in the Book of Mormon* (Provo, UT: Brigham Young University Press and the Neal A. Maxwell Institute for Religious Scholarship, 2008), 107-38. Welch's reading of Jacob 7 through the lens of ancient law is not mere academic navel-gazing. His legal analysis offers some important theological insights into the text, including a point discussed by Green: the significance of Sherem's confession.

God work together "to build bridges of understanding rather than create walls of segregation."[10] Green's brief theological introduction to Jacob's teachings helpfully explores ways that readers of the Book of Mormon can appreciate and work toward this prophetically-mandated ideal.

Stephen O. Smoot *is a doctoral student in Semitic and Egyptian Languages and Literature at the Catholic University of America. He previously earned a Master's degree in Near and Middle Eastern Civilizations from the University of Toronto and Bachelor's degrees in Ancient Near Eastern Studies and German Studies from Brigham Young University.*

---

10. Russell M. Nelson, "President Nelson Shares Social Post about Racism and Calls for Respect for Human Dignity," Church Newsroom, The Church of Jesus Christ of Latter-day Saints, June 1, 2020, https://newsroom.churchofjesuschrist.org/article/president-nelson-shares-social-post-encouraging-understanding-and-civility.

Itty Bitty Books with Big Lessons: Enos, Jarom, Omni

Jasmin Gimenez Rappleye

Review of Sharon J. Harris, *Enos, Jarom, Omni: A Brief Theological Introduction* (Provo, UT: The Neal A. Maxwell Institute for Religious Scholarship, 2020). 144 pages. $9.95 (paperback).

Abstract: *Sharon Harris, a professor of English at Brigham Young University, offers an analysis of the theology of the "small books" of Enos, Jarom, and Omni in this next installment of* The Book of Mormon: Brief Theological Introductions *by the Neal A. Maxwell Institute for Religious Scholarship. Harris argues that the theology of these small books focuses on the covenant with the Nephites and Lamanites, the importance of genealogy, and the role kenosis plays in several of these Book of Mormon prophets. Harris presents both new and familiar readings of these compact books, providing a fair contribution to their study.*

Sharon J. Harris is an assistant professor of English at Brigham Young University and is the author of the volume on Enos through Omni, in the series *The Book of Mormon: Brief Theological Introductions* by the Neal A. Maxwell Institute for Religious Scholarship.[1] Harris earned her PhD in English from Fordham University in 2018 and also has degrees from the University of Chicago and Brigham Young University. She is a newcomer to Book of Mormon studies, specializing primarily in early modern English, but provides a fresh perspective and is an effective communicator.[2] Her prose cogently conveys innovative ideas to a general

---

1. Sharon J. Harris, *Enos, Jarom, Omni: A Brief Theological Introduction* (Provo, UT: The Neal A. Maxwell Institute for Religious Scholarship, 2020).

2. Harris's contributions to Book of Mormon studies up to this point consist of a chapter in a volume of collected essays from the Mormon Theological Seminar in 2017. Harris has also researched the history of Latter-day Saint singles

audience. She balances introducing readers to the characters and story while also drawing out lessons, principles, themes, and theological underpinnings of each Book of Mormon author.

While many authors of this series may have wrestled with condensing a vast work into a short theological treatise, Harris faced the challenge of expanding upon very few words to tease out a theological framework for these small books. She faced an additional challenge of formulating a unified theological thrust when her section of the Book of Mormon contained more distinct authors and voices than all the other books combined. Harris surmounted these challenges fairly well, making this volume a welcome contribution to the small body of scholarship dedicated to Enos–Omni.[3]

Harris divides her book into a series of short chapters. In addition to an introductory chapter, she devotes one chapter each to Enos, Jarom,

---

wards and has published on the intersection of the Restoration with sound. See Sharon J. Harris, "Reauthoring Our Covenant Obligation to Scripture and Family," in *Christ and Anti-Christ: Reading Jacob 7*, Adam S. Miller and Joseph M. Spencer, eds. (Provo, UT: The Neal A. Maxwell Institute for Religious Scholarship, 2017), 111–24; Sharon J. Harris and Peter McMurray, "Sounding Mormonism," *Mormon Studies Review* 5, no. 1 (2018): 33–45, https://scholarsarchive.byu.edu/msr2/vol5/iss1/23/; Sharon Harris, "LDS Singles and Their Wards," presented at One Body: The State of Mormon Singledom (symposium, May 16, 2015), https://soundcloud.com/mormonsingledom/sharon-harris-lds-singles-and.

3. Only a few handfuls of articles and books are written on Enos–Omni, compared to the many dozens written on 1 Nephi, for example. Much more work is needed on these small books, and any addition to this corpus of work is welcome. Some of notable contributions to the study of these books include Claudia L. Bushman, "Big Lessons from Little Books," in *Big Lessons from Little Books: 2 Nephi 4 — Words of Mormon*, Robert A. Rees and Eugene England, eds. (Salt Lake City: Signature Books, 2008), vii–xxii, https://archive.bookofmormoncentral.org/content/big-lessons-little-books; John S. Tanner, "Literary Reflections on Jacob and His Descendants," in *The Book of Mormon: Jacob Through Words of Mormon, To Learn With Joy*, Monte S. Nyman and Charles D. Tate Jr., eds. (Provo, UT: Religious Studies Center, Brigham Young University, 1990) 251–69, https://archive.bookofmormoncentral.org/content/literary-reflections-jacob-and-his-descendants; Brant A. Gardner, *Second Witness: Analytical and Contextual Commentary on the Book of Mormon*, vol. 3, Enos–Mosiah (Salt Lake City: Greg Kofford Books, 2007); "Why Do the Authors on the Small Plates Follow a Pattern?," Book of Mormon Central (April 8, 2016), https://knowhy.bookofmormoncentral.org/knowhy/why-do-the-authors-on-the-small-plates-follow-a-pattern. To see a more extensive bibliography on Enos through Omni, see "Come Follow Me 2020: Enos — Words of Mormon," Book of Mormon Central, https://bookofmormoncentral.org/come-follow-me/book-of-mormon/come-follow-me-2020-enos-words-of-mormon.

and Omni. I start my review of Harris's contribution to this series by looking at the Introduction, and then at each successive chapter, in turn.

Introduction

In her Introduction, Harris acknowledges challenges to studying and enjoying the small books, yet expresses optimism in the fruits of laboring in this section of the Book of Mormon. At the outset, she presents what she sees as the overarching theological themes of the small books: covenant and inheritance. She defines the macro Book of Mormon covenant as "God's promise to gather the descendants of Lehi and Sariah's family again. God will do so by making sure the surviving remnant of this line of the house of Israel receives the record of their ancestors, the Book of Mormon" (3–4).

As part of the terms of this covenant, Nephite prophets bear the responsibility of inheriting and perpetuating the records that must survive to the latter days. With the stewardship over the plates comes a consciousness and inheritance of generations as well. Nephite prophets hearken back to and reflect traits of their fathers and ancestors before them, who also bore the responsibility of transmitting the Nephite record in fulfillment of God's covenant.

Harris asserts the importance of the small books at both the introduction and conclusion of this volume by drawing on the dictation order of the Book of Mormon. She argues that since the small books were the final words translated in the Book of Mormon, they serve as a deliberate and weighty conclusion to the Book of Mormon. Since Mormon designed the small books to be the final refrain of the Book of Mormon, readers should take them very seriously. Harris additionally seems to argue that the effect of this reconfiguration is that readers are first presented with a story of a prosperous and destroyed civilization before being presented with a prequel or origin story in the small plates.

While I certainly agree that readers should take the small books seriously on their own terms, Harris could have been more tempered in her conclusion that the small plates were Mormon's intended conclusion to the Book of Mormon. Mormon explained that the Spirit prompted him to append this unabridged collection to his *magnum opus* for an unknown purpose (Words of Mormon 1:6–7).[4] At the very least,

---

4. Mormon professed no foreknowledge that Martin Harris would lose the equivalent counterpart to this narrative in Mormon's abridgement. Nephi, the creator of this record, also professes no foreknowledge of this 1828 event but indicates a prompting to create another record nonetheless (1 Nephi 9:5). See

Mormon seemed to intend for his readers to experience a complete narrative arc from Lehi's departure from Jerusalem to the destruction of the Nephites (Mormon's abridgement), before reaching an appendix of primary source documents (the small plates).

In addition, if the small plates were intended as the capstone message of the Book of Mormon, the concluding words the readers would encounter would not be those of Omni (or as Harris submits, Amaleki dramatically calling into the abyss for his lost brother, pp. 107–108), but rather those of Words of Mormon. Mormon's *subscriptio* at the end of the small plates is the final voice of this section and explains the redaction and provenance of the small plates.[5] Regardless of Mormon's intention and literary design, reading the small plates *after* Mormon's abridgement is sure to open new insights and avenues for inquiry.

Enos

In her chapter on Enos, Harris focuses primarily on *kenosis,* or a spiritual self-emptying. She begins her chapter by first introducing the reader to the protagonist Enos, and presenting three immediate lessons a reader can learn from Enos's impassioned repentance (19):

1. Forgiveness can come early in a spiritual journey. Forgiveness is not necessarily the same thing as remission of sins (Enos 1:5, 8).

---

also Don Bradley, *The Lost 116 Pages* (Salt Lake City: Greg Kofford Books, 2019), 107–109.

5. William J. Hamblin, "Metal Plates and the Book of Mormon," in *Pressing Forward with the Book of Mormon: The FARMS Updates of the 1990s,* John W. Welch and Melvin J. Thorne, eds. (Provo, UT: FARMS, 1999), 20–22, https://archive.bookofmormoncentral.org/node/238; "Why is 'Words of Mormon' at the End of the Small Plates?," Book of Mormon Central (April 14, 2016), https://knowhy.bookofmormoncentral.org/knowhy/why-is-words-of-mormon-at-the-end-of-the-small-plates. It can be challenging for readers to feel a sense of conclusion with Words of Mormon, since the lost 116-page manuscript has made it ambiguous to know where exactly Words of Mormon ends. See Jack M. Lyon and Kent R. Minson, "When Pages Collide: Dissecting the Words of Mormon," *BYU Studies Quarterly* 51, no. 4 (2012): 120–36, https://byustudies.byu.edu/content/when-pages-collide-dissecting-words-mormon; Brant A. Gardner, "When Hypotheses Collide: Responding to Lyon and Minson's 'When Pages Collide'," *Interpreter: A Journal of Mormon Scripture* 5 (2013): 105–19, https://journal.interpreterfoundation.org/when-hypotheses-collide-responding-to-lyon-and-minsons-when-pages-collide/; "What if Martin Harris Didn't Lose all of the 116 Pages?," Book of Mormon Central (June 26, 2017), https://knowhy.bookofmormoncentral.org/knowhy/what-if-martin-harris-didnt-lose-all-of-the-116-pages; Bradley, *The Lost 116 Pages,* 276–78.

2. Being forgiven and entering into a covenant is followed by lots and lots of work. Enos did "go to" and preached to the Lamanites to try to restore them to the covenant (Enos 1:8, 19).

3. We can be forgiven and enter into beautiful covenants, but our temptations and blind-spots may not go away (Enos 1:20).

While the small books in general may be oft neglected by Latter-day Saints, the book of Enos is probably the best-known and beloved of the set. Harris cogently articulates what about the Enos story is so captivating to many readers:

> Enos is a spiritual Everyman who experiences the miracle of being known, heard, and forgiven by the Savior of the world. And in his struggles to understand and draw near to God, his prayer becomes woven into God's covenant, poised to reach countless people beyond Enos's personal sphere of influence. (20)

This story is both intimate in meaning and corporate in scope. Enos's personal forgiveness is what sparks his petition for the Lamanites, which becomes part of the reiterated covenant. It is a story of forgiveness of an individual soul, which catalyzes ultimate redemption for an entire civilization.

The greatest focus of this chapter comes in discussing Enos's "self-emptying" for the welfare of the Lamanites. When Enos received forgiveness for his sins, he poured out his whole soul for the welfare of the Lamanites. Harris categorizes this selfless consecration as a form of kenosis, expanding on the traditional Christological definition. Kenosis comes from the Greek word κενόω, "to empty." In New Testament theology, kenosis primarily refers to a facet of Christology, derived from Philippians 2:5–11, which describes Christ's condescension into mortality. Kenosis conveys how Jesus Christ, a fully divine being, nonetheless "emptied" himself of certain divine qualities to become like man. This extreme condescension ultimately enabled Christ to become exalted above all.[6] This has led to vigorous debate in Christian history as to the exact nature and extent of this "emptying." Because Philippians 2:5 invites readers to emulate Jesus Christ in this way, Harris seems to extend the concept of *kenosis* to any "emptying of power that increases power" (28).

---

6. Colin Brown, "Empty," in *The New International Dictionary of New Testament Theology*, Colin Brown, ed. (Grand Rapids, MI: Zondervan, 1975), 1:546–49; Albrecht Oepke, "κενός, κενόω, κενόδοξος, κενοδοξία," in *Theological Dictionary of the New Testament*, Herhard Kittel, ed. (Grand Rapids, MI: Eerdmans, 1965), 3:661–62.

Harris points out a potential wordplay in English with the word "whole" (Enos 1:8–9). As part of the process of kenosis, Enos needed to empty out his *whole* soul for the welfare of others in order for his soul to become *whole* or well (29). While there are perhaps limitations with extending this English wordplay to the underlying ancient text on the plates,[7] readers can appreciate the devotional application of selfless giving as the key to our own welfare. It would have been helpful for Harris to defend her interpretation of this passage a little more robustly. The doublet of "whole" in Enos 1:8–9 likely has less to do with an underlying, ancient wordplay but is possibly a product of the Book of Mormon translator's interaction with the King James Bible during the translation process, since the phrase "thy faith hath made thee whole" may be an intertextual allusion unique to the King James Bible.[8]

The result of Enos's metaphorical "self-emptying" is noteworthy. Harris suggests that Enos's faith became unshaken in connection with hearing of the future Nephite destruction and his newfound love for the Lamanites. As he emptied himself, he found new charity for others — the Lamanites, whom he then considered family in referring to them as "my brethren." "Enos's experience suggests that the same people we view as antithetical to our ideals could ultimately play a key role in our salvation" (37).[9] Yet even when Enos experienced transformative conversion and a newfound love for the Lamanites, he was derisive of the Lamanites'

---

7. The word כֹל *col* ("whole, all") in Hebrew, does not contain the same double meaning of being "well," "sound," "uninjured." The word תמים *tamim* can include meanings of "uninjured," "free of blemish," and "perfect," but does not necessarily contain the double meaning of "all, entire." See Ludwig Koehler and Walter Baumgartner, *The Hebrew and Aramaic Lexicon of the Old Testament* (Leiden, NLD: Brill, 1994), 473–75, 1748–50. I cannot comment on possible Egyptian parallels.

8. Depending on the translation model one subscribes to, the translator could be Joseph Smith or an unidentified, divine translator with Joseph Smith acting more as transmitter than translator. For occurrences of "thy faith hath made thee whole," see Mark 5:34, Mark 10:52, Matthew 9:22, and Luke 17:19. The underlying Greek text for the adjective "whole" is the verb σώζω, meaning "to save, keep," "to preserve," and in this case "to heal." Thus, the English construct of subject-verb-object-adverb in "thy faith hath made thee whole" is not present in the underlying Greek text, which more literally translates as subject-verb-object in "your faith has healed you."

9. "Salvation" in this context is not being used to refer to Enos's personal salvation of the soul but rather the salvation of the Nephite legacy. The preservation of the Nephite record, and subsequent conversion of future Lamanites, would be the means of saving the Nephites as a people.

savage behavior (Enos 1:20). In addition, Harris speculates that Enos may have fallen into notions of self-importance (46–47), drawing on Enos's use of colophons.[10] Harris observes,

> Maybe this is why Enos's account is so compelling: in a soup of his own noble and selfish desires, God's will and God's compromises, and the consequences of others' agency, he models the lifelong wrestle to understand and keep covenants. Why bring up Enos's weaknesses? What does it help? At a minimum it shows at least two things: first, people are complicated, and second, God can handle it. (47)

While this exploration of Enos's supposed weaknesses is speculative, Book of Mormon characters are indeed often more complex than a superficial reading indicates. Moreover, God can effect great miracles using complicated and imperfect people. I hope this lesson inspires readers to critically engage the book of Enos for more robust readings.

Jarom

The chapter on Jarom contains Harris's strongest and weakest theological material. Jarom is the shortest book in the Book of Mormon with only 733 words. Thus, responsibly teasing out any profound theological vision is challenging. I believe Harris succeeded in parsing out meaningful theological gems in Jarom, with the possible exception of her note on "filthiness."

---

10. Harris is misguided to use colophons as evidence for Enos's emulating Nephi, as colophons are a well-attested, ancient literary standard and certainly not unique to Nephi. Harris writes, "If Enos felt a kinship with Nephi's tendencies, it is no surprise that he adopted Nephi's signature narrative address. Five times he writes, 'I, Enos,' echoing 'I, Nephi' (Enos 1:1, 6, 11, 17, 19)" (47). For literature on ancient colophons and their attestation in the Book of Mormon, see John A. Tvedtnes, "Colophons in the Book of Mormon," in *Reexploring the Book of Mormon: A Decade of New Research*, John W. Welch, ed. (Salt Lake City and Provo, UT: Deseret Book and FARMS, 1992), 13–17, https://archive.bookofmormoncentral.org/node/150; Thomas W. Mackay, "Mormon as Editor: A Study of Colophons, Headers, and Source Indicators," *Journal of Book of Mormon Studies* 2, no. 2 (1993): 90–109, https://scholarsarchive.byu.edu/cgi/viewcontent.cgi?article=1048&context=jbms; "Why Does Nephi Begin by Saying 'I, Nephi ...'?" Book of Mormon Central (October 16, 2018), https://knowhy.bookofmormoncentral.org/knowhy/why-does-nephi-begin-by-saying-i-nephi; "Why Did Book of Mormon Authors Use Colophons?," Book of Mormon Central (June 21, 2018), https://knowhy.bookofmormoncentral.org/knowhy/why-did-book-of-mormon-authors-use-colophons.

Filthiness

Harris argues that *filthiness* came to have racially derogatory connotations in the small plates, specifically toward the Lamanites (51–57). It is first used when describing the river in Nephi's vision of the Tree of Life (1 Nephi 12:16), and she persuasively argues that the filthy river may allude to the fate of the Lamanites. From there, it is used in connection with Laman and Lemuel in 1 Nephi 15:27 when they debated the meaning of the vision. Jacob later condemned the Nephites for considering the Lamanites filthy when they were more righteous than the Nephites (Jacob 3:5). Enos also referred to the Lamanites as full of filthiness (Enos 1:20).

However, after establishing a possible lexical pattern with "filthiness," she perhaps overreaches by underscoring its absence in the book of Jarom. She suggests that since Jarom did not use the word "filthy" in describing the Lamanites, Jarom may have transcended the racial prejudice of his forebears. It is true that Jarom is the first author not to use the "filthy" epithet, but considering the book of Jarom has only 733 words, its absence should be more cautiously interpreted rather than argued as evidence of Jarom's progressive stance toward the Lamanites. Jarom, after all, still maintains the *status quo* by characterizing the Lamanites as the political and religious enemies of the Nephites (Jarom 1:6–7, 9).[11] Spending appreciable space expounding on 1 Nephi simply to argue for a datum of negative evidence in the book Jarom struck me as unfocused and tenuous.[12]

---

11. Harris suggests that Jarom 1:6 is a dispassionate statement about the Lamanite religious practices, more than an aspersion against their character. She exegetically grounds her argument with a brief analysis of Mesoamerican and ancient Israelite religious and military practices, for which she should be commended. However, I don't think loving "murder" can qualify as dispassionate since it describes an unequivocally malicious or unlawful practice. I find it unpersuasive to parse out an enlightened tolerance from Jarom based on so few words. Noah Webster, *American Dictionary of the English Language*, s.v. "Murder," http://webstersdictionary1828.com/Dictionary/murder.

12. Harris does not address the absence of the word "filthy" among the book of Omni's many authors. Her line of reasoning would suggest that Omni, Chemish, Abinadom, and Amaleki were also paragons of racial unity, yet that would seem an extreme assumption to make, given the paucity of data. While linking the ultimate fate of the Lamanites to the filthy fountain of water may have merit, proposing a generations-long lexical pattern based on a few data points and negative evidence is perhaps unwarranted.

The Middle of Days

The rest of this chapter provides keen analysis and helpful application to modern readers. Harris juxtaposes Enos's prophecy of ultimate Nephite destruction with the perpetual tension of their experience with the Lamanites. She points out how the Nephites' possible knowledge of their destruction could potentially affect their attitudes toward the Lamanites in the present.[13] Righteousness is essential for Nephite survival, but it could also be easy for the Nephites to look for Lamanite wickedness at every opportunity.

She invites readers to compare Jarom's day with our own. Jarom was situated in the middle of the Nephite story, just as Latter-day Saints today may be in the middle of a dispensation. However, our possible location in the middle of this grand timeline is not an indication of its importance or sense of urgency. Jarom shows readers how to thrive and excel even in the middle of times. The key to Nephite success during this period was to "look forward unto the Messiah, and believe in him to come as though he already was" (Jarom 1:11). By treating the present as the future, the Nephites lived their lives in the light of Jesus Christ:

> By now we've seen how the Nephites in Jarom's day take the prophecies of their ancestors seriously. These revelations are their guide to avoid destruction, so the leaders and teachers stay busy reminding the people that righteousness is essential. The Nephites also understand these small plates to be expressly for gathering the Lamanites in the latter days. They relate to Christ and his coming as though he has already come, placing themselves in an everlasting and ever-present state of redemption. We have also seen that if we, as members of the restored church in the twenty-first century, liken ourselves to the Nephites, we are likening to the group that was destroyed for its wickedness. Jarom's people exercised constant vigilance in keeping their covenants for fear of their own apocalyptic destruction. Like them, we, too, can look forward to the coming of the Savior, but we await his second coming and are alert to its signs including the signs of the end of times. (71)

---

13. Harris assumes the Nephites as a people have a knowledge of the prophecies concerning the ultimate fate of the Nephite and Lamanite civilizations. However, the text explicitly identifies only prophets and leaders such as Nephi as possessing such knowledge. It is unclear how much access the people as a whole had to these prophecies of destruction and annihilation.

One area of inquiry that could have strengthened this chapter is an analysis of Nephite cycles of prosperity in Jarom, since the documentation of Nephite wealth and military innovation takes a large portion of his record. I would have loved to see Harris discuss how Nephite prosperity factored into broader themes of the Lord's covenant with Book of Mormon peoples in the small books. Jarom seemed somewhat conflicted about Nephite prosperity, since it correlated to their hard hearts (Jarom 1:3), yet their military might led them to victory in the Lord (Jarom 1:7–9). It would be instructive to explore the role this period of history might play in the overarching message the Book of Mormon sends about wealth and riches.[14]

Overall, I found Harris's treatment of Jarom provoking and uplifting. She contributes new insights to this often-overlooked book in the Nephite text and leaves the reader with opportunity for personal introspection and self-improvement.

Omni

The book of Omni is simultaneously exciting and confusing because of its many authors and voices. Genealogy comes out prominently in this book, as the plates were passed down to sons and brothers in a long lineage. This chapter helpfully begins by introducing each author in the book of Omni with a short character profile. Harris then meanders to a note on how contention is used in Omni and other parts of the Book of Mormon. She observes that "contention" is rarely used to signify domestic malcontent but is rather used mostly in military or political contexts (84–88). In essence, contention "involves a severe breach between groups of people that includes lethal violence" (85). Yet Harris is careful to warn that the Book of Mormon still views individual and familial discord as a precursor to large-scale contention (Mosiah 4:14).

Harris points out that the fixation on genealogy in Omni seems at odds with Nephi's stated purpose for the small plates (1 Nephi 9:4). But she argues that the persistence of genealogical lines in Omni serves three purposes: 1) it connects families and scripture, 2) it keeps the prophetic tradition alive in the plates, and 3) it is emblematic of the importance of family and relationships in the small plates (90–91).

By commanding the record be kept by each generation, it ensures the plates' survival. By the time of King Benjamin, the mere presence of

---

14. "Why Does the Book of Mormon Warn Against Seeking after Riches?" Book of Mormon Central (May 30, 2019), https://knowhy.bookofmormoncentral. org/knowhy/why-does-the-book-of-mormon-warn-against-seeking-after-riches.

the plates certified their truth and integrity. Each entry is just one piece to the story, but in its entirety, it creates a strong genealogical line of the plates' provenance and legacy. By continuing to write, each author continued the prophetic tradition and extended the record through time and space to touch millions of minds and hearts today.

In concluding her thoughts on the book of Omni and all the "itty bitty books," she jumps to an insight in the book of Alma. The diligence of the authors of these small books to preserve and transfer the record is a lesson in keeping the plates bright (97–98). Alma 37:5 says that "if they are kept they must retain their brightness." Harris provides both historical explanation of this verse and personal application of its value. Here, Harris draws on John L. Sorenson to explain how the brightness of the plates may be a reference to their meticulous polishing by trained, ancient metallurgists. It may be a tedious and unglamorous chore to polish the plates, but fastidiously preserving the record ensured their survival and brought to pass great things.

The meticulous maintenance and preservation of the plates encourages readers to similarly keep their own records as both a monument to faith and a connection to history. The small plates connected generations of disciples in both lineal and lateral transitions. When a son was not an option, a recordkeeper often pivoted to a brother. In Enos's day, the Lamanites threatened to destroy the plates, even though the message of the gospel was destined for their people, so the audience shifted to the Lamanites' future descendants. While the primary audience of the Book of Mormon is the Lamanites, all who read become part of the story and community. Because the Book of Mormon connects people both lineally and laterally, Harris compares the resulting community not just to a chain, but to a chain mail, encompassing all God's children in the love and light of the gospel (100–103).

This chapter provides solid reflection on complicated lines of transmission and provides readers with practicable ways to transform their discipleship.

Impressions on Brief Theological Introductions

Harris's volume fits well with what has been published in this introductory series. I personally appreciate the consistency in length and scope and also that each volume thus far has been written in very accessible prose. I hope this series helps general Church readership open up new perspectives and insights on these scriptures from a theological lens.

The physical books themselves are well produced and aesthetically attractive. The orange monochrome woodcuts placed at the end of chapters give the books character and life. Bright manicules serve as asides or pseudo-footnotes to expound on tangential, interesting thoughts. One typographical error in this volume is on page 41, where there are two endnotes designated "9." The Neal A. Maxwell quote should be listed as endnote 10.

It would be instructive for the Maxwell Institute to have laid out some methodological expectations for the series. While each volume contains a short preface to the series, it may have been beneficial to lay out, for example, why they discouraged more thorough footnoting and crediting the work of previous scholars to the extent possible. For example, on pages 23–24, Harris draws a parallel between Enos and the biblical patriarch Jacob. She compares Enos's wrestle with Jacob's wrestle with the angel at Bethel. In addition she notes that Enos called his father a "just man," a possible reference to the Lord calling Noah a just man. These insights seem to be derivative from Matt Bowen's onomastic work on Enos, yet there is no citation or reference to Bowen to be found.[15] It is possible that the series intends to keep the endnotes deliberately light, but they make themselves vulnerable to accusations of plagiarism by not including clear documentation when drawing upon work of other scholars. At the very least, such accusations could be mitigated by more explicitly setting reader expectations about what they consider worthy of citation.

In addition, I think it would be helpful to include references when Harris uses niche definitions. Her usage of both *kenosis* (26–41) and *messianic* (67–76) seem to diverge from the most common understandings of these terms in Christian theology. Thus, references to where readers could learn more would be most welcome.

Conclusion

Readers of varied educational backgrounds and persuasions can find value and insight in this volume of *Brief Theological Introductions*. Harris balances the task of providing analysis while maintaining devotional

---

15. Matthew L. Bowen, "'And There Wrestled a Man with Him' (Genesis 32:24): Enos's Adaptations of the Onomastic Wordplay of Genesis," *Interpreter: A Journal of Mormon Scripture* 10 (2014): 151–60, https://journal.interpreterfoundation.org/and-there-wrestled-a-man-with-him-genesis-3224-enoss-adaptations-of-the-onomastic-wordplay-of-genesis/. To Harris's credit, she includes this paper in the Further Reading appendix at the back of the book but simply does not include a direct endnote citation.

appeal. She sometimes veers into more creative speculation, but such is almost unavoidable in these "itty bitty books."

Harris writes lucidly to a general audience, yet encourages probing analysis of the seemingly less-glamorous small books. Her devotion to the gospel of Jesus Christ comes through in this book, and I appreciated her willingness to contextualize at least some of her theological arguments within an ancient, historical setting (97–98), though more engagement with existing literature would have strengthened her work. I personally believe that any reading of the Book of Mormon is strongest when it is grounded in historical exegesis. I look forward to seeing Harris participate in Book of Mormon studies in the future, hopefully in a venue that allows her more thoroughly to engage with previous scholarship and exegetically contextualize her theological apologetic.

Sharon Harris attentively centers her reading of Enos–Omni on the Lord's covenant with his people. Indeed, this is a central theme throughout the entire Book of Mormon, which invites all God's children to partake in the gospel of Jesus Christ through reading these ancient records. On the last page of her treatise, Harris joins the Book of Mormon in inviting all readers to participate in the marvelous work of redemption:

> This is the invitation of the itty bitty books and the whole Book of Mormon: you are your brother and sister's keeper. Reading the book gives you access to the covenant. As God instructs Enos, go to — gather the rest of the world as well. (108)

Jasmin Gimenez Rappleye *is a content manager, web developer, and graphic designer for Book of Mormon Central. She graduated from Brigham Young University in 2015 with a bachelor's degree in Ancient Near Eastern Studies. Jasmin has presented at conferences for FairMormon, Book of Mormon Central, and The Interpreter Foundation. Her areas of academic interest include Latter-day Saint temple liturgy and the cultural contexts of the Book of Mormon.*

PROPER NAMES FROM THE SMALL PLATES: SOME NOTES ON THE PERSONAL NAMES ZORAM, JAROM, OMNI, AND MOSIAH

Stephen D. Ricks

Abstract: *With a selection of a few notable examples (Zoram, Jarom, Omni, and Mosiah) that have been analyzed by the ongoing Book of Mormon names project, Stephen Ricks argues that "proper names in the Book of Mormon are demonstrably ancient."*

[**Editor's Note:** Part of our book chapter reprint series, this article is reprinted here as a service to the LDS community. Original pagination and page numbers have necessarily changed, otherwise the reprint has the same content as the original.

See Stephen D. Ricks, "Proper Names from the Small Plates: Some Notes on the Personal Names Zoram, Jarom, Omni, and Mosiah," in *"To Seek the Law of the Lord": Essays in Honor of John W. Welch,* ed. Paul Y. Hoskisson and Daniel C. Peterson (Orem, UT: The Interpreter Foundation, 2017), 351–58. Further information at https://interpreterfoundation.org/books/to-seek-the-law-of-the-lord-essays-in-honor-of-john-w-welch-2/.]

John W. Welch (Jack) invited me to join the Foundation for Ancient Research and Mormon Studies (FARMS) early in the fall of 1981 when I was a brand-spanking-new faculty member at Brigham Young University (BYU), fresh from graduate studies at University of California, Berkeley, Graduate Theological Union (also in Berkeley, California), and the Hebrew University in Jerusalem. Among my pleasant recollections is gathering with other members of the foundation, including Paul Hoskisson and his wife Quina, eating popcorn, and stuffing envelopes to be sent out to members of the foundation. A part of the continuing legacy of the foundation is our current work on the Book of Mormon Names Project (which we also refer to as the Onomasticon Project). This project has been continuing for the past five years and will result in a published volume as well as an ongoing presence as a website (onoma.lib. byu.edu). The participants in the project—John Gee, Paul Y. Hoskisson, Robert F. Smith, and myself—are specialists in Hebrew, Semitic philology, Egyptian language and linguistics, and Assyriology. The four proper names presented here—Zoram, Jarom, Omni, and Mosiah—are each of ancient Hebrew origin, although they are not found in the Bible. The study of each name represents the meticulous care with which the Book of Mormon Names Project has been undertaken. The work is also a tribute to the interests and vision of Jack, the founder of FARMS.

The first serious study of the origins of Book of Mormon names was made by Janne M. Sjodahl, a Swedish convert to The Church of Jesus Christ of Latter-day Saints. Before becoming a Latter-day Saint, Sjodahl studied Biblical Hebrew and Greek at a Baptist seminary in London, England. After joining the Church, he served as a missionary in Palestine, where he learned Arabic. In the final years of his life, Sjodahl worked on a commentary on the Book of Mormon that made use of his knowledge of Arabic and biblical Hebrew in studying Book of Mormon personal names. His commentary was only partially complete at the time of his death in 1939. Sjodahl's son-in-law, Philip C. Reynolds, combined his manuscript with materials by his father, George Reynolds,[1] a member of the Quorum of the Seventy, and published it in a seven-volume *Commentary on the Book of Mormon* in 1955.[2]

In his numerous contributions on the Book of Mormon, the legendary Hugh Nibley significantly moved forward the study of Book of Mormon personal names, tracing many Book of Mormon names from Egyptian and Arabic roots.[3] John Tvedtnes, now an emeritus staff member at FARMS and the Neal A. Maxwell Institute for Religious Scholarship, has made numerous contributions to Hebrew names and Hebraisms in the Book of Mormon. He also wrote two entries, "Names of People: Book of Mormon" and "Hebraisms in the Book of Mormon,"

---

1   Bruce A. van Orden, "George Reynolds: Loyal Friend of the Book of Mormon," *Ensign* (August 1986).

2   George Reynolds and Janne M. Sjodahl, *Commentary on the Book of Mormon* 7 vols. (Salt Lake City: Deseret Book, 1955).

3   For example, Nibley discusses Book of Mormon names in *Since Cumorah* (Salt Lake City: Deseret Book, 1988) 168–72, 464; and Nibley, *Lehi in the Desert; The World of the Jaredites; There Were Jaredites* (Salt Lake City: Deseret Book, 1988), 25–42, 242–46.

to the multivolume *Encyclopedia of Hebrew Language and Linguistics*, published by Brill and edited by a consortium of Israeli, European, and North American scholars.[4] Robert F. Smith, a collaborator on the Book of Mormon Names Project, in both published and unpublished materials, has contributed significantly to an understanding of the ancient Near Eastern origins of Book of Mormon names.[5]

Zoram

Zoram is the name of the servant of Laban and friend of Nephi (1 Ne. 4:35, 37; 16:7; 2 Ne. 1:30; 5:6: Alma 54:23) and of later Nephite leaders and renegades (Alma 16:5, 7; 30:59; 31:1). This name may be composed of the element *ṣûr*, "rock" (as in "rock of our salvation," Ps. 95:1) and *'am*, "(divine) kinsman"; thus, "(my divine) kinsman is a rock." Another reasonable possibility is *ṣûr 'am*[6] "rock of the people."[7]

Jarom

Jarom was a Nephite scribe and historian, the son of Enos and grandson of the prophet Jacob, who continued the history of the Nephites from the end of Enos's ministry to the beginning of Omni's record (Jarom 1:1, 14; Omni 1:1). Jarom may well be a hypocoristic[8] form of Jaromel or

---

4   John A. Tvedtnes, "Names of People: Book of Mormon," in *Encyclopedia of Hebrew Language and Linguistics*, ed. Geoffrey Khan (Leiden: Brill, 2013), 2:787–88; and John A. Tvedtnes, "Hebraisms in the Book of Mormon," in *Encyclopedia of Hebrew Language and Linguistics*, 2:195–96.

5   Among his publications dealing with Book of Mormon language and names are "Book of Mormon Event Structure: The Ancient Near East," *Journal of Book of Mormon Studies* 5, no. 2 (1996): 98–147; "New Information about Mulek, Son of the King," in *Reexploring the Book of Mormon*, ed. John W. Welch (Salt Lake City: Deseret Book, 1992), 142–44; and "Old World Languages in the New World," in Welch, *Reexploring*, 29–31; "'It Came To Pass' in the Bible and the Book of Mormon," FARMS Preliminary Report SMI-80b (Provo, UT: FARMS, 1980/updated 1981, 1983); and "Table of Relative Values," in John W. Welch, "Weighing and Measuring in the Worlds of the Book of Mormon," *Journal of Book of Mormon Studies* 8 no. 2 (1999):46.

6   I wish to thank Paul Y Hoskisson, who first proposed the etymology *ṣûr 'am* "rock of the people."

7   The derivation of Zoram from the Hebrew *ṣûrām* "their rock," as in Deuteronomy 32:31 (a suggestion originally made by John A. Tvedtnes), is possible, even though the reference in Deuteronomy is to a foreign god and it would be an unusual PN. It is also possible to derive the proper name Zoram from *zōra' 'am*, a possible byform of *zera' 'am*, "seed, offspring, child of the people," although it would be difficult to explain phonetically.

8   A "hypocoristic" name is one in which the name of deity (here in this name, for example, the "el," "iah," meaning "God; the Lord") is suppressed or left out; thus the hypothetical Jaromel or Jaromiah becomes Jarom.

Jaromiah, "may, let [God/the Lord] be exalted," a jussive form (translated "may, let") of the Hebrew *rām*, "to rise; be lifted up, exalted."[9] In the printer's manuscript there is a variant form Joram that Royal Skousen, in his magisterial textual study of the Book of Mormon, sees as a scribal error,[10] although the *o*'s and *a*'s in the original manuscript are nearly indistinguishable. In any event, Joram would, like Jarom, be a name from the same root *rām* and with a virtually identical meaning, being equivalent to the Hebrew *yôrām* "Jehovah is exalted."[11]

Omni

Omni is the name of another Nephite historian and scribe, the son of Jarom and descendant of Jacob and Enos (Jarom 1:15; Omni 1:1). The personal name Omni is based on the Hebrew root *ʾ'MN, meaning "to be true, faithful," as well as "to confirm, support," and may be linked to the noun form *ʾōmen*, "faithfulness, trust."[12] The name Omni could be a hypocoristic form of *ʾomniyyāhû* or *ʾomnîēl*, "faithfulness of [the Lord/God,"] with the so-called "*ḥireq compaginis*,"[13] or, alternatively, "[the Lord/God is] (the object of) my trust,"[14] with *omnî* as an objective genitive[15] ("the object of my trust") or the substantive *ʾōmen* with a first common singular pronominal suffix, thus *ʾomnî*, "my faithfulness, trust."

Mosiah

The personal name Mosiah, representing the names of two prophet-kings (Omni 1:12, 14–20, 23; Mosiah 1:2, 10; 2:1; 28:1), may derive from the Hebrew for *môšîʿyāhû*, "the Lord delivers, saves."[16] The name can be parsed as the causative stem (hiphil) participle of the Hebrew root

---

9 The Hebrew *rām*, "to rise; be lifted up, exalted," was originally proposed by JoAnn Hackett.

10 Royal Skousen, *Analysis of Textual Variants of the Book of Mormon* (Provo, UT: FARMS, 2004–09), 2:1104; 6:3579.

11 I wish to thank John A. Tvedtnes for this suggestion.

12 I wish to thank Robert F. Smith for suggesting the link of Omni with *ʾomen*, "faithfulness, trust."

13 For a discussion of the *ḥireq compaginis* see *Gesenius' Hebrew Grammar* ed. E. Kautsch and A. E. Cowley (Oxford: Clarendon Press, 1970), 47.

14 This was first suggested by JoAnn Hackett.

15 For example, the "love of God" could be understood as an "objective genitive" as the love of individuals for God; as a "subjective genitive," "love of God" could be understood as God's love for individuals

16 This suggestion was first made by Robert F. Smith and JoAnn Hackett.

YSʿ, "to save, deliver,"[17] with the "theophoric"[18] element *yāhū*, "Jehovah, Lord."[19] Isaiah, *yešaʿyāhû*, "the Lord is deliverance, salvation," presents a compelling analogue. Alternatively, the name may have been the hiphil participle form "deliverer"—*môšîʿa*—which occurs at least 17 times with verbal or nominal force in the Old Testament, with the suppressed name of deity,[20] in Judges 3:9; and the participle with suffixes: Judges 3:15; 2 Samuel 22:42; Isaiah 49:26; Jeremiah 14:18; Psalm 7:11; 17:7; 18:42; 106:21.

Conclusion

Carl Mosser and Paul Owen, in a presentation made at the Evangelical Theological Society Far West Annual Meeting in 1997, made (for Evangelicals) these sobering observations:

> There are no books from an evangelical perspective that responsibly interact with contemporary LDS scholarly and apologetic writing. In a survey of twenty recent evangelical books criticizing Mormonism we found that none interact with this growing body of literature. Only a handful demonstrate any awareness of pertinent works. Many of the authors promote criticisms that have long been refuted; some are sensationalistic while others are simply ridiculous. A number of these books claim to be "the definitive" book on the matter. That they make no attempt to interact with contemporary LDS scholarship is a stain upon the authors' integrity and causes one to wonder about their credibility.[21]

In the intervening years there has been little if any change in this pattern of somnambulant Evangelical scholarship. But this lack of engagement with Latter-day Saint scholarship is not true merely of Evangelicals. A few weeks ago one of my colleagues discussed a

---

17   Ludwig Köhler and Walter Baumgartner, *Hebrew and Aramaic Lexicon of the Old Testament*, CD-Rom Edition (Leiden: Brill, 1994–2000).

18   A theophoric name is one containing the name of God (in Hebrew, an "-*ēl*" or "-*yāhû*") in it; thus, for example, in the personal name Isaiah, in Hebrew *yešaʿyāhû*, "the Lord is deliverance, salvation," the element *yāhû*, "Lord" is a theophoric.

19   I wish to thank Paul Y. Hoskisson, who first made this suggestion.

20   The same meaning of *môšîʿa* is given by John W. Welch, "What Was a 'Mosiah'?" in *Reexploring the Book of Mormon*, ed. John W. Welch (Salt Lake City: Deseret Book, 1992), 105–07, citing John Sawyer, "What was a Mosiʾa?" *Vetus Testamentum* 15 (1965): 475–86.

21   Carl Mosser and Paul Owen, "Mormon Apologetic Scholarship and Evangelical Neglect: Losing the Battle and Not Knowing It?" *Trinity Journal* 19 (Fall 1998): 183.

lengthy letter by a disaffected Mormon who enumerated the reasons for his withdrawal from activity in the Church. Remarkably, he simply listed his objections to Latter-day Saint doctrine without responding to, let alone citing, LDS scholarship that supports these claims. And LDS scholarship that directly or indirectly supports the scriptures, history, and faith claims of Latter-day Saints has been increasing. For instance, as I mentioned, John Tvedtnes has contributed two articles on Book of Mormon names to the multivolume *Encyclopedia of Hebrew Language and Linguistics* published by Brill.[22] Though the editors of this encyclopedia do not deal with the faith implications of the Book of Mormon, they do recognize the distinctly Hebrew/Semitic features of the book that deserve examination.

Above the box outside my office door is a plaque containing a trenchant observation made by Austin Farrer, who, in discussing C. S. Lewis as an ardent and articulate defender of Christianity, states: "Though argument does not create conviction, lack of it destroys belief. What seems to be proved may not be embraced; but what no one shows the ability to defend is quickly abandoned. Rational argument does not create belief, but it maintains a climate in which belief may flourish."[23] (This quotation was cited on several occasions by Neal A. Maxwell.) In the spirit of this quotation, I believe that proper names in the Book of Mormon are demonstrably ancient. Mosser and Owen, astutely writing about LDS Book of Mormon scholarship, observe that Latter-day Saints "believe the Book of Mormon to be an ancient text written by people of Jewish heritage. A number of studies which have been done attempt to reveal Hebraic literary techniques, linguistic features, cultural patterns and other markers which, it is argued, Joseph Smith would not have been capable of fabricating."[24] In a modest measure, we who have been working on the Book of Mormon Names Project believe that we are fulfilling the requirements for satisfying the aims and requirements of Book of Mormon scholarship in showing that the Book of Mormon is arguably an ancient document. With regard to critics of the Book of Mormon, the question may thus be shifted to "If the Book of Mormon is not an ancient document, why are there so many features in it—including proper names—that are so demonstrably ancient?" The results of the Book of Mormon Names Project, whose names discussed here are a small but

---

22   See note 4 above.

23   Austin Farrer, "The Christian Apologist," in *Light on C. S. Lewis*, ed. Jocelyn Gibb (New York: Harcourt, Brace, and World, 1965), 26.

24   Mosser and Owen, "Losing the Battle?" 204.

representative part, reflect and promote the vision of FARMS and are a tribute to the vision of its founder, Jack Welch.

Stephen D. Ricks *completed his BA in Ancient Greek and MA in the Classics at Brigham Young University, and then received his PhD in ancient Near Eastern religions from the University of California, Berkeley and the Graduate Theological Union. While completing his doctoral work he spent two years studying at the Hebrew University in Jerusalem. He is now professor of Hebrew and Cognate Learning at Brigham Young University where he has been a member of the faculty for nearly thirty-six years.*

"I Will Deliver Thy Sons": An Onomastic Approach to Three Iterations of an Oracle to Mosiah II (Mosiah 28:7; Alma 17:35, 19:23)

Matthew L. Bowen

ABSTRACT: *Three times in his narrative Mormon recounts the Lord's oracle (revelation) to Mosiah II regarding his sons undertaking a mission among the Lamanites (Mosiah 28:7, Alma 17:35, and Alma 19:23). In all three instances, the Lord's promises of deliverance revolve around the meaning of the name* Mosiah *("Yahweh is Deliverer" or "Yahweh is Savior"), emphasizing that the Lord (Hebrew* yhwh) *himself would act in his covenant role as* môšiaʿ *in delivering Mosiah's sons, and sparing Ammon in particular. In two of the iterations of the oracle, Mosiah 28:7 and Alma 19:23, we find additional wordplay on the name* Ammon *("faithful") in terms of "many shall believe" (Hebrew* yaʾămînû) *in the first instance and* ʾĕmûnâ *("faith," "faithfulness") in the latter. In Alma 19:23 the Lord also employs an additional wordplay on his own name, Yahweh (Jehovah), to emphasize his ability to bring to pass his promises to Mosiah regarding Ammon.*

Ammon and his brothers' decision to undertake an evangelizing mission among the Lamanites represents one of the axial moments in Lamanite-Nephite history as Mormon recounts it. The events of Alma 17–28 dramatically reshaped Lamanite-Nephite polity and interrelations for the remainder of that history. Thus, of similar seminal importance was the revelation or oracle that King Mosiah II received in which the Lord not only affirmed that Ammon and his brothers' proposed mission would result in a large number of Lamanite conversions but also promised that he himself would "deliver" them from the Lamanites (Mosiah 28:7). Mormon invokes or refers to this oracle on three distinct occasions: first, near the time of Ammon and his brothers' conversion (recounted in Mosiah 27:8-37); second, at the time Ammon first faces martial combat among the Lamanites early in his mission (see Alma 17:27-39); and third, when Ammon lay prone on the floor in an ecstatic vision next to Lamoni and his wife (see Alma 19:14-36):

Mosiah 28:6–7	Alma 17:35	Alma 19:23
And it came to pass that[1] king Mosiah went and inquired of the Lord if he should let his sons go up among *the Lamanites* to preach the word. And *the Lord said unto Mosiah:* Let them go up, for *many shall believe* on *their words.* And they shall have eternal life; and *I will deliver thy sons out of the hands of the Lamanites.*	Therefore *they did not fear Ammon*, for they supposed that one of their men could slay him according to their pleasure, for *they knew not that the Lord* had promised *Mosiah* that he would *deliver* his sons out of their hands, neither did they know anything concerning *the Lord*; therefore they delighted in the destruction of their brethren, and for this cause they stood to scatter the flocks of the king.	Now we see that *Ammon* could not be slain, for the Lord had said unto *Mosiah* his father: *I will spare him, and it shall be unto him* according to *thy faith* ['*ĕmûnātekā*]. Therefore *Mosiah* trusted him unto *the Lord*.

Each reiteration of the oracle emphasizes different aspects of the initial oracle and even modifies specific elements. In this brief study, I examine the three iterations of the oracle to Mosiah, discussing the salient commonalities and differences between them and their significance. It emerges that the language of the oracle revolves around the meaning (or perceived meaning) of the name *Mosiah* in all three instances and the name *Ammon* in the first and the third. In all three, the Lord emphasizes that he will act in his covenant role as *môšia'* ("deliverer," "savior") in "deliver[ing]" Mosiah's sons out danger among the Lamanites, and "spar[ing]" Ammon in particular. In Mosiah 28:7, additional wordplay on *Ammon* ("faithful") links his name with the foreseen success of the Lamanite mission ("many shall believe [have faith] on their words"), a mission largely accomplished through Ammon's "faithfulness" (cf. Alma 18:2, 10, 35). Alma 19:23 also predicates the fulfillment of the

---

1. All Book of Mormon citations follow Royal Skousen, ed., *The Book of Mormon: The Earliest Text* (New Haven, CT: Yale University Press, 2009), emphasis added.

Lord's promises regarding Mosiah's sons on the latter's own "faith" and faithfulness.

"Many Shall Believe"/"I Will Deliver Thy Sons" (Mosiah 28:7)

Following his account of the conversion of Alma and the sons of Mosiah (Mosiah 27:8–37), Mormon describes the desire of the sons of Mosiah to undertake a mission to "impart the word of God to their brethren the Lamanites, that perhaps they might bring them to the knowledge of the Lord their God" (Mosiah 28:1). He additionally describes their persistent requests for their father Mosiah's permission to undertake this mission: "And it came to pass that they did plead with their father many days that they might go up to the land of Nephi" (Mosiah 28:5). Their father eventually accedes to these pleas and asks the Lord to reveal his will on the matter: "And it came to pass that king Mosiah went and inquired of the Lord if he should let his sons go up among *the Lamanites* to preach the word. And *the Lord said unto Mosiah*: Let them go up, *for many shall believe* on their words; and they shall have eternal life. And *I will deliver thy sons out of the hands of the Lamanites*" (Mosiah 28:6–7).

The Lord's oracle in response to Mosiah's inquiry revolves around both of the names *Ammon* and *Mosiah*. Although, Mormon mentions the name Mosiah in verse 7, the Lord mentions neither name — at least directly — in the oracle. The meanings of both names constitute keys to the promises the Lord makes to Mosiah regarding Ammon and his sons and the success of their mission.

The Etymology and Meaning of the Name *Ammon*

Of the realistic etymological possibilities for the Book of Mormon name Ammon,[2] only two hold much promise. The Semitic gentilic name *ʿammôn* (with an initial *ʿayin* [ʿ]) putatively denotes something like "little uncle" or "little kinsman," which has reference to the nation of Ammon that bordered ancient Israel. This name has not, as far as I am aware, ever attested of an individual, at least not in the biblical corpus. In any case, this name and the related name *Ben-ammi* ("son of my kinsman") acquire distinctly pejorative connotations in Genesis 19 (see especially Genesis 19:38).

The second and more promising possibility is that Ammon constitutes a variation of the royal Hebrew biblical name *Amon* (*ʾāmôn*),

---

2. Paul Y. Hoskisson, *Book of Mormon Onomasticon*, s.v. "Ammon," https://onoma.lib.byu.edu/index.php/AMMON.

which denotes "faithful"[3] (cf. also Amnon [*'amnôn*], "faithful").[4] As such, Ammon would derive from the Hebrew verbal root *'mn*, which had the basic meaning "to be firm, trustworthy, safe"[5] and thus in its passive stem "to prove to be firm, reliable, faithful."[6] (Hugh Nibley's suggestion[7] that the name Ammon reflects the Egyptian theonym *'imn* [*Amun, Amen, Amon,* or *Ammon*] can probably be regarded as conjuncting with this suggestion, since, as Robert F. Smith notes, Egyptian Ammon "comes from the root *mn* or *'imn*, 'establish, make firm; be firm, remain; eternal.' … *'imn* also means 'right, west, westward.'"[8] Both of these Egyptian verbs are cognate with the Hebrew roots *'mn* and *ymn*. The Hebrew spelling of the Egyptian name *Amon* [*'āmôn*] is, moreover, identical to the spelling of the Hebrew name *Amon* [*'āmôn*], "faithful.")[9] The causative form of the Hebrew verb *'mn* means "to regard something as trustworthy, to believe in."[10] In other words, it is the exclusive verb in Hebrew for expressing the idea "to believe" or "to have faith."

We can detect a deliberate, allusive wordplay on the name Ammon in the Lord's response to Mosiah's inquiry regarding Ammon and his brothers' mission: "Let them go up, for *many shall believe* [Hebrew *ya'ămînû*] *on their words*; and they shall have eternal life." The wordplay on Ammon in terms of "[they] shall believe" — Hebrew *ya'ămînû* — powerfully hints at Ammon and his faith and faithfulness as a key instrument in the Lamanites (those who had dwindled in "unbelief") "believing" — that is, acquiring covenant "faith" and "faithfulness" (i.e., Hebrew *'ĕmûnâ*). Ammon will embody the faith and "faithfulness" (Alma 18:2, 10) that will also come to define his Lamanite converts (Alma 23:6; 27:26–27).

---

3. Martin Noth, *Die israelitischen Personennamen im Rahmen der gemeinsemitischen Namengebung* (Hildesheim: Georg Olms Veragsbuchhandlung, 1966), 228; see also Ludwig Koehler and Walter Baumgartner, *The Hebrew and Aramaic Lexicon of the Old Testament* (Leiden, NDL: Brill, 2001), 62. Hereafter cited as *HALOT*.

4. Noth, *Personennamen*, 32, 228; see also *HALOT*, 65.

5. *HALOT*, 63.

6. Ibid.

7. Hugh W. Nibley, *Lehi in the Desert; The World of the Jaredites; There Were Jaredites* (Salt Lake City: Deseret Book, 1988), 25; Nibley, *An Approach to the Book of Mormon*, 3rd ed. (Salt Lake City: Deseret Book, 1988), 286–87.

8. Robert F. Smith's comments are included in Hoskisson, s.v. "Ammon."

9. See, e.g., Jeremiah 46:25; Nahum 3:8.

10. *HALOT*, 64.

The Etymology and Meaning of Mosiah

The oracle of Mosiah 28:7 also obliquely mentions Mosiah, Ammon's father, by wordplay. The Lord expressed the promise, *"and I will deliver* [Hebrew *wĕhiṣṣaltî* or *wĕhôšaʿtî*][11] thy sons out of the hands of the Lamanites." In Hebrew, the Lord's promise, "and I will deliver" would most likely find expression in either of two conceptually related Hebrew verbs *nṣl* (*hiṣṣîl*) or *yšʿ* (*hôšîaʿ*; less likely a form of *mlṭ/plṭ*, but see below). The verbs *nṣl* and *yšʿ* are sometimes paired or used in close conjunction with each other (see, e.g., Jeremiah 15:20–21; 42:11; Psalms 7:1 [Masoretic Text 2, hereafter MT]; Psalm 31:2 [MT 3]; 33:16; 59:2 [MT 3]; 71:2; 1 Chronicles 11:14; 16:35; see also Isaiah 19:20). Jeremiah 15:20–21 provides a particularly salient example of this phenomenon, highlighting Yahweh's role as the divine *môšîaʿ* mentioned earlier by Jeremiah[12]: "And I will make thee unto this people a fenced brasen wall: and they shall fight against thee, but they shall not prevail against thee: for I am with thee *to save thee* [*lĕhôšîʿăkā*] *and to deliver thee* [*ûlĕhaṣṣîlekā*], saith the Lord. And *I will deliver thee* [*wĕhiṣṣaltîkā*] *out of the hand* of the wicked, and *I will redeem* [*ûpĕditîkā*] *thee out of the hand* of the terrible." Regarding the picture of divine deliverance created by Jeremiah's use of these verbs together in Jeremiah 15:20–21, J.A. Thompson observes:

> The promise of deliverance is expressed in three significant OT verbs of deliverance, namely *hôšîaʿ*, 'save,' *hiṣṣîl*, 'deliver,' and *pāḏâ*, 'redeem' or 'rescue.' They are found in such significant passages such as the Exodus story, although they have a more general application. The total picture of deliverance is many-sided and each verb provides a different emphasis. Thus *hôšîaʿ*, 'save,' and its related nouns lay stress on the bringing out of those under restraint into a broad place. The verb *hiṣṣîl*, 'deliver,' pictures the activity of one who snatches his prey from the grasp of a powerful possessor. By extension of the physical idea Israel thought of deliverance from death, the grave, sins, trouble, fear, etc. The verb *pāḏâ* was normally used in reference to liberation from the possession of by the giving up of a ransom. It is used of the Exodus, although by a metaphorical

---

11. See, e.g., Ezekiel 34:22; 36:29; 37:23.
12. Jeremiah 14:18.

use, it came to refer to acts of deliverance in daily life, including the rescue of Israel from sins and fear of the grave.[13]

The relatedness of the idioms *hiṣṣîl miyyad X*, "deliver out of the hand[s] of X," and *hôšîaʿ miyyad X*, "deliver/save out of the hand[s] of X" is further evident in such passages as Genesis 37:21 where Reuben rescues Joseph from being killed by his brothers: "And Reuben heard it, *and he delivered him* [*wayyaṣṣilēhû*] out of their hands [*miyyādām*]; and said, Let us not kill him." The Deuteronomistic editor of the Book of Judges describes the raising up of "judges" who "delivered" or "saved" Israel: "Nevertheless the Lord raised up judges, *which delivered them* [*wayyôšîʿûm*] out of the hand [*miyyad*] of those that spoiled them" (Judges 2:16); "And when the Lord raised them up judges, then the Lord was with the judge, *and delivered them* [*wĕhôšîʿām*] out of the hand [*miyyad*] of their enemies all the days of the judge" (Judges 2:18). Some of the heroic figures described in the book of Judges are described with the term *môšîaʿ* performing the action of *yšʿ*, to "save" or "deliver" (Judges 3:9, 15; cf. Judges 3:31).

These examples are important in the context of the oracle of Mosiah 28:7, since the name *Mosiah* is best explained as a derivation from the substantivized Hebrew participle מושיע (*môšîaʿ*, "deliverer, savior,"[14] literally "one who saves") and the theophoric element יהו (*yhw*, i.e., Yahweh or Jehovah), perhaps written defectively like משעיהו (*mōšîʿyāhû*), "Yahweh is Savior" or "The Lord is Savior."[15] King Benjamin, on the occasion of his son Mosiah's accession to the throne, invoked the title *môšîaʿ* both as a reference to Jesus Christ and as wordplay on the name of his son Mosiah, whom he had named for his father: "And moreover, I say unto you, that the time shall come when the knowledge of *a Savior* [Hebrew *môšîaʿ*] shall spread throughout every nation, kindred, tongue, and people" (Mosiah 3:20). Matthew 1:21 offers a similar, Semitic-based explanation for the naming of Jesus that works in both Greek and Semitic: "and thou shalt call his name *JESUS* [Greek *Iēsoun*, Aramaic/Hebrew *yēšûaʿ*]: *for he shall save* [Greek *sōsei*, Hebrew *yôšîaʿ*] his people from their sins." In the Hebrew Bible, Yahweh himself is designated as *môšîaʿ* in 1 Samuel 10:19; Isaiah 43:3, 11; 45:15, 21; 49:26; 60:16; 63:8; Jeremiah 14:18; Psalm 7:11; 17:7; 18:42 (2 Samuel 22:3); and Hosea 13:4.

---

13. J.A. Thompson, *The Book of Jeremiah*, New International Commentary on the Old Testament (Grand Rapids, MI: Eerdmans, 1980), 398-99.

14. *HALOT*, 562.

15. See, e.g., John W. Welch, "What Was a 'Mosiah'"? in *Reexploring the Book of Mormon*, ed. John W. Welch (Salt Lake City: Deseret Book, 1992), 105-007.

By promising "I will deliver thy sons out of the hands of the Lamanites," the Lord — Yahweh — effectively promised Mosiah that he would perform the role of *môšiaʿ* for his sons, as he had in times past (see, e.g., Mosiah 28:4). As Ammon himself stated it, the Lord "in his great mercy *hath brought us over* that everlasting gulf of death and misery, *even to the salvation* [Hebrew *yĕsûat*] of our souls" (Alma 26:20). Thus the Lord himself was speaking to the promise or hope embodied in Mosiah's own name: "Yahweh is Savior" or "Yahweh is Deliverer."

One of the most important biblical texts — and one of numerous Isaianic texts — that designates Yahweh as *môšiaʿ* held special meaning for the Nephites. It occurs twice on Nephi's small plates, including once in Jacob's foundational covenant speech:

Isaiah 49:24–26 (KJV)	1 Nephi 21:24–26	2 Nephi 6:16–18
Shall the prey be taken from the mighty, or the lawful captive delivered? But thus saith the Lord, Even the captives of the mighty shall be taken away, and the prey of the terrible shall be delivered: *for I will contend with him that contendeth with thee, and I will save* ['*ôšîaʿ*] *thy children* [or, sons]. And I will feed them that oppress thee with their own flesh; and they shall be drunken with their own blood, as with sweet wine: and all flesh shall know that *I the Lord* [*yhwh*] *am thy Saviour* [*môšîʿēk*] and thy Redeemer, the mighty one of Jacob.	*For* shall the prey be taken from the mighty or the lawful captive delivered? But thus saith the Lord: even the captive of the mighty shall be taken away, and the prey of the terrible shall be delivered. *For I will contend with him that contendeth with thee, and I will save* ['*ôšîaʿ*] *thy children.* And I will feed them that oppress thee with their own flesh. They shall be drunken with their own blood as with sweet wine. And all flesh shall know that I the Lord [*yhwh*] am thy Savior [*môšîʿēk*] and thy Redeemer, the Mighty One of Jacob.	*For* shall the prey be taken from the mighty or the lawful captive delivered? But thus saith the Lord: Even the captives of the mighty shall be taken away, and the prey of the terrible shall be delivered, *for the Mighty God shall deliver his covenant people. For thus saith the Lord: I will contend with them that contendeth with thee.* And I will feed them that oppress thee, with their own flesh. And they shall be drunken with their own blood as with sweet wine. And all flesh shall know *that I the Lord* [*yhwh*] *am thy Savior* [*môšîʿēk*] and thy Redeemer, the Mighty One of Jacob.

Jacob's speech makes it clear that the Lord's acting in his capacity as Divine Warrior and *môšiaʿ* ("deliverer," "savior";[16] cf. the less common

---

16. *HALOT*, 562.

maṣṣîl, "deliverer," "life-saver"[17]) to "deliver" the captives and "save" Israel's sons was a function of his covenant with Israel: "the mighty God shall deliver his covenant people." The latter phrase, not found in the Masoretic text of Isaiah 49 or elsewhere in the Hebrew Bible, describes Yahweh with the title "the Mighty God" (*'ēl gibbôr*) found in Isaiah 9:6 and 10:21 (2 Nephi 19:6; 20:21).[18] The adjective *gibbôr* ("manly, vigorous")[19] was often used substantively — i.e., as a virtual noun — to describe men as "warriors" and "hero[es]."[20] The epithet *'ēl gibbôr* designated Yahweh as a warrior God.

"The Lord Had Promised Mosiah That He Would Deliver His Sons"

Mormon endeavors to show that the Lamanites initially regarded Ammon as a manifestation of the Divine Warrior — i.e., as "the Great Spirit" (Alma 18:2-5, 11, 18-19; 19:25-27). Mormon's portrait of Ammon favorably compares and contrasts Ammon with the biblical portrait of David.[21] Like David versus Goliath, Ammon stands forth as a divinely empowered warrior: "And those men again stood to scatter their flocks; but Ammon said unto his brethren: Encircle the flocks round about that they flee not; and *I go and contend* with these men who do scatter our flocks. Therefore, they did as Ammon commanded them, and he went forth and *stood to contend* with those who stood by the waters of Sebus; and they were in number not a few" (Alma 17:33-34).

Mormon frames what follows in terms of covenant language: "Therefore *they did not fear Ammon*, for they supposed that one of their men could slay him according to their pleasure, for *they knew not that the Lord* [yhwh] had promised <u>Mosiah</u> [*mōšî'yāhû*] that <u>he would deliver his sons out of their hands, neither did they know anything concerning the Lord</u> [yhwh]; therefore they delighted in the destruction of their brethren, and for this cause they stood to scatter the flocks of the king" (Alma 17:35). Here Mormon revisits the wordplay on *Mosiah* ("Yahweh is Deliverer," "Yahweh is Savior") in terms of the Lord's earlier promise

---

17. *HALOT*, 717.

18. See also the Jeremiah's variation in Jeremiah 32:18: *hā'ēl haggādôl haggibbôr* = "the Great, the Mighty God" (KJV) or "O great and mighty God" (NRSV).

19. *HALOT*, 172.

20. Ibid.

21. Matthew L. Bowen, "Faithfulness of Ammon," *Religious Educator* 15, no. 2 (2014): 64-89.

to "deliver" Mosiah's sons "out of the hands of the Lamanites." The Lord's acting in the role of *môšiaʿ*, and performing the action of *hiṣṣîl* or *hôšiaʿ*, was a function of his ancient covenant with Israel and perhaps also a personal covenant with Mosiah himself.

Mormon describes the Lord's oracle as a "promise" which, within the same reality as reflected in Jacob 4:13, Ether 3:12, Hebrews 6:16–18, etc. (i.e., God is a "God of truth" who does not and *cannot* lie), amounted to an oath or an immutable promise. Moreover, a verb translated "know" occurs twice in this verse. In Hebrew, the verb *yādaʿ* ("know") had important covenant implications.[22] Mormon emphasizes the Lamanites' lack of covenant knowledge. They had no knowledge that Yahweh makes promises of divine deliverance and salvation and that he keeps such. Some Lamanites evidently held the concept that "it was the Great Spirit that had always attended the Nephites, who had ever delivered them out of their hands" (Alma 19:17), but did not know this deity as Yahweh. Moreover, they did not know the covenant roots of that concept as captured in Nephi's great thesis statement, "I, Nephi, will show unto you that the tender mercies of the Lord are over all those whom he hath chosen, because of their faith, to make them mighty even unto the power of deliverance" (1 Nephi 1:20).

The aftermath of Ammon's confrontation with the Lamanite plunderers emphasizes the surpassing "faithfulness" (*ʾĕmûnâ*) that qualified Ammon for being made "mighty ... unto the power of deliverance." The covenant dimension of Ammon's "faithfulness" works on two levels. First, Ammon's willingness to contend with the Lamanite plunderers reflected his personal faith in the Lord (Yahweh), faith that gave him courage to act in the face of very real danger. Second, Ammon demonstrated "faithfulness" to Lamoni, whose "servant" he became: "And when they had all testified to the things which they had seen and he had learned of *the faithfulness* [*ʾĕmûnat*] *of Ammon* in preserving his flocks and also of his great power in contending against those who sought to slay him, he was astonished exceedingly, and said: Surely, this is more than a man. Behold, is not this the Great Spirit who doth send such great punishments upon this people because of their murders?" (Alma 18:2). The collocation "the faithfulness of Ammon" constitutes a sublime paronomasia (wordplay) in Hebrew: *ʾĕmûnat ʾammôn/ ʾāmôn* [or *ʾĕmûnat ʿammôn*]. Beyond that, Mormon's statement that Ammon's "faithfulness" consisted in "preserving [the king's] flocks" and "contending against" those who sought to plunder

---

22. See, e.g., RoseAnn Benson and Stephen D. Ricks, "Treaties and Covenants: Ancient Near Eastern Legal Terminology in the Book of Mormon," *Journal of Book of Mormon Studies* 14, no. 1 (2005): 48–61, 128–29.

them has important implications for the Lord's own faithfulness. Just as Ammon had, as warrior, preserved Lamoni's flocks, the Lord would preserve Ammon and his brothers.

The wordplay on Ammon resumes in a dramatic way only verses later: "Now when king Lamoni heard that Ammon was preparing his horses and his chariots he was more astonished, because of *the faithfulness* [*ʾĕmûnat*] *of Ammon*, saying: *Surely there has not been any servant among all my servants* that has been *so faithful* [*neʾĕmān*] as this man; for even he doth remember all my commandments to execute them" (Alma 18:10). Lamoni's statement echoes words attributed to Ahimelech to Saul regarding David in the biblical story of David's accession to kingship in Israel: "And who is *so faithful* [*neʾĕmān*] *among all thy servants* as David" (1 Samuel 22:14).[23]

The verb *believe* (perhaps Hebrew *ʾmn*) is repeated about seventeen times, the passive form "faithful" (*neʾĕmān*) once, "faith"/"faithfulness" (Hebrew *ʾĕmûnâ*) six times, and "true," "trust," and "unbelief" once each in Alma 18–19. Mormon uses this extensive paronomasia to link Ammon and his faithfulness to the Lamanites' transition from a rudimentary level of faith ("we do not believe that a man has such great power" [Alma 18:3] and "Notwithstanding they believed in a Great Spirit, they supposed that whatsoever they did was right" [Alma 18:5]) to faith in the Nephite traditions concerning Christ ("I will believe all thy words" [Alma 18:23]; "I will believe all these things which thou hast spoken" [Alma 18:33]; and "the king believed all his words" [Alma 18:40]).

As a result of Ammon's "faithful" efforts and Lamoni's choice to "believe" Ammon's words, "the dark veil of unbelief was ... cast away from [Lamoni's] mind" (Alma 19:6). Lamoni himself has a vision in which he sees Jesus Christ and learns that "he shall redeem all mankind who believe on his name" (Alma 19:13). An additional wordplay on Lamoni (a name likely formed as a *nisba* or *nisbe*[24] of "Laman," thus "of Laman" or "Lamanite")[25] and "unbelief" emphasizes Lamoni's turn from "unbelief" (cf. Hebrew *lōʾ-ʾēmun*, Deuteronomy 32:20) as the broader turning point for Lamoni's people, and later many more Lamanites, from "unbelief."

---

23. See Bowen, "Faithfulness of Ammon," 66, 73-74, 83.

24. As a grammatical term, *nisba* or *nisbe* refers to an adjective formed from a noun (or proper name).

25. John Tvedtnes, "Hebrew Names in the Book of Mormon" (paper, Thirteenth World Congress of Jewish Studies, Jerusalem, August 2001), https://www.fairmormon.org/wp-content/uploads/2011/12/tvedtnes-HebrewNames.pdf.

Thus, Lamoni himself becomes a messenger of faith: "as many [of the Lamanites] as heard his words believed, and were converted unto the Lord" (Alma 19:31). The Lamanites in Lamoni's court, in their turn, become the instruments of conversion for many more Lamanites: "And it came to pass that *there was many that did believe* [cf. Hebrew *he'ĕmînû*] in their words. And as many as *did believe* were baptized. And they became a righteous people; and they did establish a church among them. And thus the work of the Lord did commence among the Lamanites. Thus the Lord did begin to pour out his Spirit upon them. And we see that his arm is extended to all people who will repent and *believe* [cf. *ya'ămînû*] on his name" (Alma 19:35-36).

Ammon thus accomplished his desire to "lead them *to believe* [cf. **lĕha'ămîn*] in my words" (Alma 17:29). The converted Lamanites would become "the people of Ammon," a people "*firm in the faith* of Christ, even unto the end" (Alma 27:26-27; see also especially Alma 23:5-6). More importantly, however, the Lord's oracle to Mosiah as recorded in Mosiah 28:17, "*many shall believe* [*ya'ămînû*] *on their words*; and they shall have eternal life" would soon stand fulfilled.

"I Will Spare Him and It Shall Be unto Him According to Thy Faith"

The final iteration of the Mosiah 28:7 oracle occurs as a part of Mormon's narration of the ecstatic theophanies that occurred in Lamoni's palace. As a participant in these theophanies, along with Lamoni, his wife, and other Lamanite courtesans, and lying prone on the floor of the palace, Ammon was then at his most vulnerable. Mormon then reports the mortal danger that approached Ammon: "Now, one of them, whose brother had been slain with the sword of Ammon, being exceedingly angry with Ammon, drew his sword and went forth that he might let it fall upon Ammon, to slay him; and as he lifted the sword to smite him, behold, he fell dead" (Alma 19:22).

Mormon then draws a conclusion from the immediate death of the Lamanite who attempted to kill Ammon, recalling the Lord's oracle to Mosiah II with its covenant promise: "Now we see that _Ammon_ could not be slain, for *the Lord had said unto _Mosiah_ his father: I will spare him, and it shall be unto him according to _thy faith_* [*'ĕmûnātekā*]. *Therefore _Mosiah_ _trusted_ him unto the Lord*" (Alma 19:23).

Here Mormon rephrases the promise "and I will deliver thy sons" from the initial oracle as "I will spare him, and it shall be unto him according to thy faith." The apparent change of verb — or translation of a verb — rendered "deliver" (Hebrew *hiṣṣîl* or *hôšiaʿ*) to "spare" is notable: "And thus did the Spirit of the Lord work upon them, for they were the very vilest of sinners. And *the Lord saw fit* in his infinite mercy *to spare them*; nevertheless they suffered much anguish of soul because of their iniquities, suffering much and fearing that they should be cast off forever" (Mosiah 28:4). Perhaps it is also worth noting that Alma and Ammon both describe their being "spared" in terms of the verb "snatch" (Mosiah 27:28–29; Alma 26:17, possibly forms of Hebrew *nṣl*).[26] In any case, the phrase "I will spare him" in Alma 19:23 still revolves around the meaning of the name *Mosiah*: "Yahweh is Savior" or "Yahweh is Deliverer." The language of this third rendition of the oracle focuses almost exclusively on Ammon himself and the Lord's specific promises regarding him.

Just as noteworthy, however, is the clear wordplay on Ammon's name that follows the Lord's initial promise: "and it shall be unto him according to *thy faith* [*ʾĕmûnātekā*]." The term for "faith" or (better) "faithfulness" in Hebrew is *ʾĕmûnâ*, a term very close to the name Ammon in sound and perhaps also in etymology from the root *ʾmn*, as noted above. In either case, an intentional paronomastic association seems clear. The promise "it shall be unto [Ammon] according to thy faith" also recalls another promise from the original oracle: "Let them go up, for *many shall believe on their words*" (Mosiah 28:7). In that initial rendition, the onomastic wordplay on Ammon and "many shall believe" (Hebrew *yaʾămînû*) hinted at — and emphasized — Ammon's leadership role[27] in accomplishing the mission on which the Lord was sending Mosiah's sons. This third rendition reflects a similar onomastic wordplay on Ammon in terms of *ʾmn*, this time in terms of the cognate noun *ʾĕmûnâ*, "faith," "faithfulness." In this rendition, the Lord conditions the outcome of Ammon's mission and his protection on his father Mosiah's faithfulness (which evidently excelled).

We should also note yet another onomastic wordplay in the third rendition of Mosiah's oracle. The phrase "*and it shall be unto him* [*wĕhāyâ-lô*]" — a hebraistic expression consisting of the verb *hāyâ*, "to be, become" or "to exist," and the preposition *l*, "to," with the masculine singular suffix *-ô*. Jeremiah's declaration, "his life *shall be unto him*

---

26. Cf. Mosiah 27:29, footnote d, in *The Book of Mormon* (The Church of Jesus Christ of Latter-day Saints, 1980).

27. See especially Alma 17:18: "Now Ammon being the chief among them, or rather he did administer unto them, and he departed from them, after having blessed them according to their several stations, having imparted the word of God unto them, or administered unto them before his departure; and thus they took their several journeys throughout the land."

[wĕhāyĕtâ-lô] for a prey" (Jeremiah 21:9) and Hosea's statement, "altars *shall be unto him* [hāyû-lô, or 'have been unto him'] to sin" (Hosea 8:11) are but two examples. The phrase "it shall be unto him" (wĕhāyâ + lô or its equivalent) functions in the oracle as an onomastic play on Yhwh ("the Lord" or Yahweh), a name which meant — or was understood to mean — something like "He creates the (divine) hosts"[28] or "He who causes to happen"[29] — i.e., "He causes to be" or "He brings to pass."[30]

Thus the wordplay in the rendition of the Mosiah's oracle Alma 19:23 recalls the onomastic wordplay on Yhwh in Exodus 3:14: "And God said unto Moses, I AM THAT I AM ['ehyeh 'ăšer 'ehyeh]: and he said, Thus shalt thou say unto the children of Israel, I AM ['ehyeh] hath sent me unto you."[31] The force of the wordplay on Yhwh in Mosiah's oracle is that the Lord — Yahweh — will bring to pass or cause to "be" exactly what he promised, as he always does.

Conclusion and the Legacy of Mosiah II's Parental Faith in the Lord

Mormon presents an oracle or revelation to Mosiah II regarding his sons undertaking a mission among the Lamanites in three separate iterations: Mosiah 28:7; Alma 17:35; and Alma 19:23. The oracle in each one of its iterations revolves around the meaning of the name *Mosiah* ("The Lord is Deliverer" or "The Lord is Savior"). Two of the iterations also revolve around the name *Ammon* and its meaning (or perceived meaning) in terms of "faithful."

Mormon demonstrates that this prophetic revelation comes to complete fulfillment and that "he had also *verified* his word unto [Ammon and the other sons of Mosiah] in every particular" (Alma 25:17) as the Lord himself acted in the covenant role of *môšiaʿ* ("Deliverer," "Savior") for Mosiah's sons, delivering them out of the hands of the Lamanites so they could preach the doctrine of Christ and the doctrines of salvation among the Lamanites. As a result of the Lord's help and Ammon's personal "faith" and "faithfulness" (see, e.g., Alma 18:2, 10, 19) many Lamanites "heard" and "believed" (Alma 19:31, 35) and became a people of surpassing faithfulness (see Alma 23:5–6), "the people of Ammon … *firm in the faith* of Christ, even unto the end."

---

28. Frank Moore Cross, *Canaanite Myth and Hebrew Epic* (Cambridge, MA: Harvard, 1973), 65.

29. Margaret Barker, *The Great Angel: A Study of Israel's Second God* (Louisville, KY: Westminster, 1992), 104.

30. See Matthew L. Bowen, "'Creator of the First Day': The Glossing of Lord of Sabaoth in D&C 95:7," *Interpreter: A Journal of Mormon Scripture* 22 (2016): 56.

31. Cf. Hosea 1:9.

In closing, surely worth noting is the legacy of Mosiah II's parental "faith" in addition to the "faithfulness" (*'ĕmûnâ* [*'ĕmûnat*]) of Ammon and the other sons of Mosiah in their missionary labors. As those who had been "saved" and "delivered" because of parental faith, Ammon and his brothers' faith eventually bore generational fruit in the faithfulness of the converted Lamanites' sons. Helaman records: "But behold, my little band of two thousand and sixty fought most desperately. Yea, they were *firm* before the Lamanites. … And as the remainder of our army were about to give way before the Lamanites, behold, these two thousand and sixty were *firm* and undaunted. Yea, and they did obey and observe to perform every word of command with exactness. Yea, and even *according to their faith* [*'ĕmûnātām*] it was done unto them. And I did remember the words which they said unto me that their mothers had taught them" (Alma 57:19-21). These faithful sons lived up to the faithfulness of their mothers and fathers (see Alma 23:5-6; 27:26-27). The *'ĕmûnâ* of these young men stemmed from that of their mothers.[32]

They were "spared" because of that "faith" and so became a reciprocal means of sparing the Nephites: "And now their preservation was astonishing to our whole army, yea, that they should *be spared*, while there was a thousand of our brethren who were slain. And we do justly ascribe it to the miraculous power of God *because of their exceeding faith* [cf. Hebrew *'ĕmûnātām*] in that which they had been taught to believe, that there was a just God, and whosoever did not doubt, that they should be preserved by his marvelous power" (Alma 57:26). The faith of the Ammonites and their sons mirrored that of Mosiah and his sons (Ammon, Aaron, Omner, and Himni). Those parents trusted essentially the same promise(s) that Mosiah trusted: "I will *spare* him, and *it shall be unto him according to thy faith*" (Alma 19:23); "I will deliver thy sons out of the hands of the Lamanites" (Mosiah 28:7).

The Lord had abundantly fulfilled his promise to Mosiah II regarding his sons' missionary efforts: "many shall believe on their words" (Mosiah 28:7). The legacy of Mosiah's faith and the faithfulness manifest in Ammon and his brothers' missionary labors could be summed up no more succinctly and appropriately than Helaman's conclusion to his letter to Moroni regarding the Ammonites' sons: "*their faith* [*'ĕmûnātām*] is

---

32. Matthew L. Bowen, "Laman and Nephi as Key-Words: An Etymological, Narratological, and Rhetorical Approach to Understanding Lamanites and Nephites as Religious, Political, and Cultural Descriptors" (presentation, FairMormon Conference, Provo, UT, August 2019), https://www.fairmormon.org/conference/august-2019/laman-and-nephi-as-key-words.

strong in the prophecies concerning that which is to come" (Alma 58:40) — i.e., faith in the Savior [*môšiaʿ*] of all, the Lord Jesus Christ.

[Author's Note: I would like to thank Pedro Olavarria, who has helped hone my thinking on the onomastic wordplay on Mosiah evident in Mosiah 28:7, an important aspect of this study. I would also like to thank Suzy Bowen, Allen Wyatt, Victor Worth, Jeff Lindsay, Don Norton, Tanya Spackman, and Daniel C. Peterson.]

Matthew L. Bowen *was raised in Orem, Utah, and graduated from Brigham Young University. He holds a PhD in Biblical Studies from the Catholic University of America in Washington, DC, and is currently an associate professor in religious education at Brigham Young University-Hawaii. He is also the author of* Name as Key-Word: Collected Essays on Onomastic Wordplay *and* The Temple in Mormon Scripture *(Salt Lake City: Interpreter Foundation and Eborn Books, 2018). He and his wife (the former Suzanne Blattberg) are the parents of three children: Zachariah, Nathan, and Adele.*

Joseph Smith's Translation Projects under a Microscope

Brant A. Gardner

Review of *Producing Ancient Scripture: Joseph Smith's Translation Projects in the Development of Mormon Christianity,* edited by Michael Hubbard MacKay, Mark Ashurst-McGee, and Brian M. Hauglid (Salt Lake City: University of Utah Press, 2020). 544 pages with index. Hardback, $70. Paperback $45, eBook $40.

Abstract: Producing Ancient Scripture *is a collection of sixteen detailed essays with an introduction by the editors. This is the first such collection that examines the greater range of Joseph Smith's translation projects. As such, it is uniquely positioned to begin more sophisticated answers about the relationship between Joseph Smith and both the concept of translation and the specific translation works he produced.*

I find this a particularly difficult book to review. It is a large work, and even the separate articles are large in content and complex in understanding. A review that simply describes the contents of the book does not really do it justice. An in-depth interaction with each article could easily be nearly half as large at the text itself.

The next problem is that this review is being written for the *Interpreter* journal, which is subtitled "A Journal of Latter-day Saint Faith and Scholarship." Publishing in this venue creates an expectation that I will review this book from the perspective of a believing Latter-day Saint, which I am doing. However, that also creates a superficial conflict with the nature of the articles in the book I'm reviewing. *Producing Ancient Scripture* is not devotional in nature; it is not necessarily faith-affirming. It is a work of scholarship, written by scholars for scholars, and made available for the rest of us to consult. By editorial choice, the articles do not examine the question of whether or not there was divine participation in Joseph's translations. Therefore, even though I review the book as a believer, I do not review it on the basis of its relationship to faith.

In *Producing Ancient Scripture,* the authors carve out the middle ground where the issue isn't belief but rather understanding. Terence J. Keegan discussed a similar issue with critical biblical scholarship. He notes that the "resulting tendency among recent scholars has been to emphasize the human activity involved in the production of Scripture while politely ignoring the question of precisely how they are of divine origin."[1] That wise scholarly approach informs this volume.

Joseph Smith's translation projects occurred within a known timeframe and have the benefit of multiple recoverable accounts that clarify (and infelicitously muddy, at times) the human side of the production of what members of The Church of Jesus Christ of Latter-day Saints consider sacred scripture.

I will try to cover the essential introduction to the articles in this volume, and then provide some insights I have gained from the articles.

Overview of the Contents

Introductions to collected articles necessarily provide a brief indication of what those articles will be and something of the perceived importance. This introduction does that, but it also attempts to set the stage for the vision of the book as a whole. Readers really should resist the temptation to jump into a particular article and instead begin with the introduction. It demonstrates the validity of a work where the whole is greater than the sum of the parts.

In general, the book is organized into chronological sections that move through aspects of the various translation projects.

Part I: Context and Commencement

"By the Gift and Power of God": Translation among the Gifts of the Spirit (Christopher James Blythe). This article places the early Mormon understanding of translation into the same sphere as other gifts of the spirit.

"Bringing Forth" the Book of Mormon: Translation as the Reconfiguration of Bodies in Space-Time (Jared Hickman). Where the previous article placed the concept of translation into the realm of gifts of the spirit, this article suggests that Joseph's use of the concept of translation was much more expansive. Readers intrigued by this article

---

1. Terence J. Keegan, *Interpreting the Bible: A Popular Introduction to Biblical Hermeneutics* (New York: Paulist Press, 1985), 12.

should also read Samuel Morris Brown's *Joseph Smith's Translation: The Words and Worlds of Early Mormonism*.[2] Hickman notes that some of the ideas in his article came from discussions with Brown, and Brown's book expands greatly upon them.

Performing the Translation: Character Transcripts and Joseph Smith's Earliest Translating Practices (Michael Hubbard MacKay). A perhaps forgotten or at least easily forgotten translation project was Joseph's interaction with the characters copied from the plates. This is an episode preliminary to the translation of the Book of Mormon and is given its due in this article.

Reconfiguring the Archive: Women and the Social Production of the Book of Mormon (Amy Easton-Flake and Rachel Cope). Aside from later deep-dives into translation issues (a personal interest of mine), this is my favorite article in the book. Easton-Flake and Cope rightfully emphasize the important role played by four women in the coming forth of the Book of Mormon: Lucy Mack Smith, Lucy Harris, Mary Musselman Whitmer, and Emma Hale Smith. This article should be read by all Latter-day Saints, even if they have no interest in the rest of the articles in the book.

Part II: Translating the Book of Mormon

Seeing the Voice of God: The Book of Mormon on Its Own Translation (Samuel Morris Brown). Brown's article interacts with concepts from both Blythe's and Hickman's articles. This is a look at the conceptual result of the translation rather than a method of production. Brown describes his approach as "metaphysics of translation" (138).

Joseph Smith, Helen Schucman, and the Experience of Producing a Spiritual Text: Comparing the Translating of the Book of Mormon and the Scribing of A Course in Miracles (Ann Taves). The idea of comparing Helen Schucman and Joseph Smith is obvious. Both produced long and complicated dictated texts without obvious recourse to outside prompts. It is an important and instructive comparison.

Nephi's Project: The Gold Plates as Book History (Richard Lyman Bushman). Bushman steps into the text to examine the Book of Mormon story as a record of the creation of a book. He looks at the implications of how the text says it was created. This is more a question of the text before translation for believers, but an artifact of translation in academic discussion.

Ancient History and Modern Commandments: The Book of Mormon in Comparison with Joseph Smith's Other Revelations (Grant Hardy).

---

2. Samuel Morris Brown, *Joseph Smith's Translation: The Words and Worlds of Early Mormonism* (New York: Oxford University Press, 2020).

Hardy examines the important question of how the nature of the Book of Mormon as a translated text compares to the dictated revelations, most of which were not considered to be translations, at least in the same sense as the Book of Mormon.

Part III: Translating the King James Bible

The Tarrying of the Beloved Disciple: The Textual Formation of the Account of John (David W. Grua and William V. Smith). This article moves to questions of biblical translation but deals with a text not typically examined as part of Joseph's translation projects — a letter from John as recorded in Doctrine and Covenants 7.

A Recovered Resource: The Use of Adam Clarke's Bible Commentary (Thomas A. Wayment and Haley Wilson-Lemmon). Wayment and Wilson-Lemmon examine evidence that, in some sections of the translation of the Bible, Joseph consulted Adam Clarke's Commentary and that Clarke's commentary influenced the way in which certain translations were written.

Lost Scripture and "the Interpolations of Men": Joseph Smith's Revelation on the Apocrypha (Gerrit Dirkmaat). The inclusiveness of this volume on Joseph's translating process is underscored by the inclusion of this interesting examination of a translation that wasn't done and the story behind it.

Translation, Revelation, and the Hermeneutics of Theological Innovation: Joseph Smith and the Record of John (Nicholas J. Frederick). Frederick examines the interrelationship between the received Gospel of John and development of Joseph's theological thought.

Part IV: Pure Language, the Book of Abraham, and the Kinderhook Plates

"Eternal Wisdom Engraven upon the Heavens": Joseph Smith's Pure Language Project (David Golding). Of all of Joseph's projects, the one that has received the least attention has been his pure language project. Nevertheless, it is an important foundation to much of his translating work.

"Translating an Alphabet to the Book of Abraham": Joseph Smith's Study of the Egyptian Language and His Translation of the Book of Abraham (Brian M. Hauglid). Joseph had translated the Book of Mormon from characters described as reformed Egyptian. In an era that was fascinated with and promoted multiple amateur ideas about language (and Egyptian in particular), the chance to study papyri with actual Egyptian characters led to another project not well-known to lay Mormons. Hauglid examines both the history and nature of the studies

of Egyptian and how those studies interacted with the development of the book of Abraham.

Approaching Egyptian Papyri through Biblical Language: Joseph Smith's Use of Hebrew in His Translation of the Book of Abraham (Matthew J. Grey). Grey notes that in popular thought, Hebrew was considered an original language and therefore must have been related to Egyptian. Joseph's opportunity to interact with the Egyptian papyri appears to have initiated his desire to learn Hebrew, which was taught through classes in Kirtland. Grey examines the ways in which Joseph's growing understanding of Hebrew language and culture influenced aspects of the book of Abraham.

"President Joseph Has Translated a Portion": Joseph Smith and the Mistranslation of the Kinderhook Plates (Don Bradley and Mark Ashurst-McGee). The history of Joseph's interaction with the Kinderhook plates is fascinating. For decades, faithful Saints believed that Joseph had translated them. Then, they were discovered to be forgeries, and the assumption had to be revisited. Bradley and Ashurst-McGee carefully lay out the history and then the evidence for the nature of the purported translation. They find that Joseph did provide a "translation" but one based on a secular style of translation rather than revelation.

Impressions of the Importance of the Book

Collections of papers inevitably produce uneven results, with some papers being stronger than others. That perspective could be applied to this collection as well but with the caveat that all papers cover their topics remarkably well, and the relative strength may ultimately rest in the personal interests of the reader. I can say without hesitation that many of the papers have so well defined their topic that they are now the standard references for that topic. For some topic areas, there may be little left to be said.

Since I have declared that I cannot do justice to the papers individually, I will give my impressions of where these papers steer future research. I will begin with Ann Taves's paper comparing Joseph Smith and Helen Schucman. First, it must be clarified that this paper aptly fits the parameters of the quotation from Terence Keegan that I cited early in this review. This is a paper making a comparison, not a judgment; there is no intent to suggest that one person is right and the other wrong. This is a paper making the comparison between two methods that similarly produced a text through the process of a smooth dictation.

The value of this comparison for the future of Joseph Smith translation studies is that Helen Schucman is more recent and modern, and interviews could ask questions we only wish we could ask Joseph. For me, the comparison lays the foundation for an important insight into Joseph as a translator. Schucman, while learned and articulate, could offer no explanation for how she scribed her book. Joseph is known to have been obscure in his descriptions, relying on the phrase "the gift and power of God," without any attempt to help modern scholars understand that definition. I find the important takeaway from the comparison to be that it is quite plausible that Joseph could not describe how he translated any more than Schucman could. For scholars of Joseph's translations, it means we really do have to resort to other avenues of investigation. It also strongly suggests that, comparable to Schucman, there is no apparent intent at subterfuge or dishonesty. Both Joseph and Schucman produced a text by means they considered beyond normal.

Beginning with that understanding, the rest of the evidence presented clearly examines Joseph Smith as an integral part of the translation process. As Keegan has noted, they are an examination of the humanity in the development of scripture.

Whatever explanations we finally accept for those translations, the articles in this book demonstrate that we cannot remove Joseph Smith the person from his resulting translations. Many articles provide clear evidence of proposed ways in which Joseph's mind participated in the translation process. Among those most important to the thesis would be the papers by MacKay, Hardy, Grua and Smith, Wayment, and Wilson-Lemmon, Frederick, Golding, Hauglid, and Grey. Even for believers, the evidence is strong that however we see the Divine's participation in the translation process, we must also understand the very human Joseph as an important participant in the process.

The comprehensiveness of the treatment of Joseph Smith's translation projects, the quality and depth of the specific papers, and the way in which many papers confirm or interact with the others in the book support the assertion that this is currently the most important single work examining the whole of Joseph Smith's translation projects. For many years to come, anyone attempting to discuss any of Joseph Smith's translation projects must refer to *Producing Ancient Scripture*.

Brant A. Gardner *(MA State University of New York Albany) is the author of* Second Witness: Analytical and Contextual Commentary on the Book of Mormon *and* The Gift and Power: Translating the Book of Mormon, *both published through Greg Kofford Books. He has contributed articles to* Estudios de Cultura Nahuatl *and* Symbol and Meaning Beyond the Closed Community. *He has presented papers at the FairMormon conference as well as at Sunstone.*

"A Prophet Like Moses" (Deuteronomy 18:15–18) in the Book of Mormon, the Bible, and the Dead Sea Scrolls

David R. Seely

Abstract: *David Seely provides a wide-ranging survey of interpretations of the prophecy in Deuteronomy 18:15–18 concerning "a prophet like unto Moses." He examines relevant passages in the Book of Mormon, the Bible, and the Dead Sea Scrolls and shows how the prophecy has been fulfilled by Jesus Christ and others, continuing with Joseph Smith's role in the Restoration and onward to the present day.*

[**Editor's Note:** Part of our book chapter reprint series, this article is reprinted here as a service to the LDS community. Original pagination and page numbers have necessarily changed, otherwise the reprint has the same content as the original, with very little minor editing.

See David R. Seely, ""A Prophet Like Moses" (Deuteronomy 18:15–18) in the Book of Mormon, the Bible, and the Dead Sea Scrolls," in *"To Seek the Law of the Lord": Essays in Honor of John W. Welch,* ed. Paul Y. Hoskisson and Daniel C. Peterson (Orem, UT: The Interpreter Foundation, 2017), 359–74. Further information at https://interpreterfoundation.org/books/to-seek-the-law-of-the-lord-essays-in-honor-of-john-w-welch-2/.]

There is a passage in Deuteronomy 18:15–18 that speaks of a future prophet like Moses. Biblical scholars argue whether this prophecy was meant to refer to the continuation of the institution in general fulfilled by a variety of future prophets or to a specific, future individual prophet. Early Christians interpreted this passage in Deuteronomy as being fulfilled by Christ (Acts 3:20–23). Likewise, the Book of Mormon also alludes to the prophecy twice, identifying the future prophet as Christ. The first time it is Nephi declaring "that this prophet of whom Moses spake was the Holy One of Israel" (1 Ne. 22:21). The second time it is Jesus during his visit to the Americas attesting "Behold, I am he of whom Moses spake, saying: A prophet shall the Lord your God raise up unto you of your brethren, like unto me" (3 Ne. 20:23). This paper surveys the variety of interpretations of the pronouncement in Deuteronomy 18 beginning with the Hebrew Bible and ending with the Christian interpretation in Acts, with a focus on the rich traditions preserved in the Dead Sea Scrolls in order to consider how the Book of Mormon and New Testament identification of the prophet as Christ fit into these traditions. In particular, the survey is looking for any interpretations that point to a single individual future prophet, and if other interpretations before the New Testament identify this prophet with the Messiah.

"A Prophet Like Moses" in the Bible

Chapters 16–18 in Deuteronomy describe four institutions in Israel: judges (16:18–17:13), the king (17:14–20), Levitical priests (18:1–8), and the prophet (18:18–22). Especially for the Deuteronomistic History, these definitions continue as important landmarks for these respective institutions.

The term "prophet" (Hebrew: *nabi'*) only occurs eight times in three passages in Deuteronomy: in chapter 13 where false prophets are condemned; in chapter 18 where the characteristics of the true prophet are described; and in chapter 34:10–12, the only passage that explicitly refers to Moses as a prophet (*nabi'*) in Deuteronomy or the Torah—besides the two passages in chapter 18 that imply Moses was a prophet. The text in 34:10–12 reads: "Never again did there arise in Israel a prophet like Moses—whom the LORD singled out face to face, for the various signs and portents that the Lord sent him to display in the land of Egypt, against Pharaoh and all his courtiers and his whole country, and for all the great might and awesome power that Moses displayed before all Israel."[1] The title of Moses as prophet is relatively rare in the Hebrew Bible and is only alluded to here and elsewhere in Hosea 12:14. However, throughout Deuteronomy and the rest of the Bible, Moses is

---

[1] Translations of the Hebrew Bible are from the New Jewish Publication Society (*NJPS*) and translations of the Apocrypha and the New Testament are from the New Revised Standard Version (*NRSV*) unless noted otherwise.

called by titles referencing prophets: "the servant of the Lord" (Deut. 34:5; Num. 12:7–8; Josh. 1:1) and "the man of God" (Deut. 33:1; Josh. 14:6; Ps. 90:1). Moses is considered functioning as a prophet—although not explicitly called as such.

Here we are interested in the passage in Deuteronomy 18:15–18 that talks about the Lord raising up a prophet "like Moses." In the two relevant passages, verses 15 and 18, the Lord speaking to Moses says:

> 15. The LORD your God will raise up for you a prophet from among your own people, like myself; him you shall heed.

> 18. I will raise up a prophet for them from among their own people, like yourself: I will put My words in his mouth and he will speak to them all that I command him.

Because the noun "prophet" (*nabi'*) is in the singular, at first glance it may seem that these passages are explicitly referring to a single future individual "like Moses." However, read in context it seems more likely that "prophet" is meant in a collective sense, referring to the future succession of prophets, just as the singular "king" in 17:14–20 refers to the institution of kingship and a succession of kings, and "the Levite" in 18:6 refers to the institution and succession of Levites. Thus, this passage seems to describe the continuation of the institution of prophecy—that prophets would be raised up to receive and deliver the words of the Lord as did Moses—rather than a single individual. Elsewhere in the Bible, many are called by the title of "prophet" and a passage such as Hosea 12:11–14 refers to a succession of prophets following Moses.

The standard scholarly interpretation of this passage is expressed by S.R. Driver:

> The "prophet" contemplated is not a single individual, belonging to a distant future, but *Moses' representative for the time being*, whose office it would be to supply Israel, whenever in its history occasion should arrive, with needful guidance and advice: in other words, that the reference is not to an individual prophet, but to a *prophetical order.*[2]

While there is no evidence in the Old Testament that the prophecy of a prophet like Moses specifically referred to a specific future messiah, some scholars argue that this passage is fulfilled by a specific prophet

---

2   S. R. Driver, *A Critical and Exegetical Commentary on Deuteronomy* (Edinburgh: T&T Clark, 1902), 229.

like Joshua—the successor to Moses.[3] Other scholars have noted that portrayal of Moses in Deuteronomy introduced a succession of prophets and influenced the portrayal of the prophets throughout the Deuteronomistic History (2 Kings 17:13). The figure of Samuel shows characteristics of a prophet like Moses,[4] and Römer notes, "Elijah is also constructed in comparison and contrast to Moses."[5] Thus, throughout the Deuteronomistic History the prophecy of a future prophet like Moses is fulfilled in a series of Moses-like prophets. Jeremiah also understood himself to be a prophet like Moses. The account of his call in Jeremiah 1 shows parallels with the call of Moses in Exodus 3. Jeremiah recorded, "The LORD put out his hand and touched my mouth, and the LORD said to me: Herewith I put My words into your mouth" (Jer. 1:9). This echoes Deuteronomy 18:18: "I will put My words in his mouth."[6]

Early Jewish and Christian Interpretations of Deuteronomy 18:15–18

Later interpreters, however, including Jews (1 Macc. 4:46; Philo, *De specialibus legibus* 1:64–65), Christians (John 1:21, 45; 6:14; 7:40; Acts 3:22; 7:37) and Muslims (who identify this prophet as Muhammad in the *Quran* 7:157) interpreted the singular reference to a prophet as a specific individual. In particular, some of these interpretations read this passage as referring to an eschatological figure who would come in the end-time preceding the messiah or messiahs.

In order to give some perspective to the passages related to the issue of "a prophet like Moses" let us look at a few representative examples of Jewish and Christian interpretations. In 1 Maccabees there are two passages that allude to a future prophet in language resembling Deuteronomy 18. 1 Maccabees 4:45–46 reads: "So they tore down

---

3   Hans M. Barstad, "The Understanding of the Prophets in Deuteronomy," *Scandinavian Journal of the Old Testament* 8, no. 2 (1994): 243.

4   Mark Leuchter, "Samuel: A Prophet Like Moses or a Priest Like Moses," in *Israelite Prophecy and the Deuteronomistic History: Portrait, Reality, and the Formation of a History*, Mignon R. Jacobs and Raymond F. Person Jr, eds. (Atlanta: Society of Biblical Literature, 2013), 147–68.

5   Thomas C. Römer, "Moses, Israel's First Prophet, and the Formation of the Deuteronomistic and Prophetic Libraries," in *Israelite Prophecy and the Deuteronomistic History*, 129–46, in particular 141.

6   William L. Holladay, "The Background of Jeremiah's Self Understanding: Moses, Samuel and Psalm 22," *Journal of Biblical Literature* (*JBL*) 83, no. 2 (1964): 153–64 and "Jeremiah and Moses: Further Observations", *JBL* 85, no. 1 (1966): 17–27. See also Römer, "Moses, Israel's First Prophet," 136–40 and Jack R. Lundbom, *Jeremiah: Prophet Like Moses* (Eugene, OR: Cascade Books, 2015).

the altar, and stored the stones in a convenient place on the temple hill until a prophet should come to tell what to do with them." And 1 Maccabees 14:41: "The Jews and their priests have resolved that Simon should be their leader and high priest forever, until a trustworthy prophet should arise." While these passages are somewhat vague they appear to refer to the coming of a future individual prophet although they do not necessarily refer to this prophet being like Moses.

Elsewhere, a passage in Philo does allude to the prophet like Moses talked about in Deuteronomy 18:15–18. After describing the nature of humans to seek after the future through divination and omens, as condemned in Deuteronomy 18:14, Philo says: "A prophet possessed by God will suddenly appear and give prophetic oracles" (*De specialibus legibus* 1:64–65).[7] This is one of the clearest passages that demonstrates the Jewish interpretation of a single future prophet.

Later, Christians apparently interpreted the passage in Deuteronomy 18 as the promise of a single messianic prophet at end time that they would identify with Jesus (John 1:21, 24, 45; 6:14; 7:40–41; Acts 3:22; 7:37). A passage from the Gospel of John demonstrates that in the first century there was the idea of a future prophet and a Messiah as is also attested in the Qumran texts. The passage reads: "When they heard these words, some in the crowd said, 'This is really the prophet.' Others said, 'This is the Messiah'" (John 7:40–41). And a passage in Acts 7:37 reads: "This is the Moses who said to the Israelites, 'God will raise up a prophet for you from your own people as he raised me up.'"

Consequently, much of the scholarship on the "prophet like Moses" has been generated by New Testament studies and much of this scholarship deals with the eschatological prophet in conjunction with the future messiah or messiahs.[8]

"A Prophet Like Moses" in the Dead Sea Scrolls

At least two texts from Qumran, both of which are considered sectarian texts, directly cite or allude to Deuteronomy 18 in regards to prophets, and both appear to interpret verses 18–20 as a reference to an eschatological prophet like Moses (1QS 9:9–11 and 4QTestimonia

---

7 *Philo VII*, trans. F. H. Colson, (Cambridge, MA: Harvard University Press, 1937), 137.

8 See for example Dale Allison, *The New Moses: A Matthean Typology* (Minneapolis: Fortress Press, 1993) and John Lierman, The New Testament Moses: *Christian Perceptions of Moses and Israel in the Setting of Jewish Religion* (Mohr Siebeck: Tübingen Germany, 2004).

[4Q175], lines 5–8). In addition there are many other passages that may or may not be related to the coming of a prophet "like Moses." Here we will look at these passages to address four questions: 1) What are the views of the Dead Sea Scrolls about the future prophet "like Moses." 2) What is the role that this prophet is to have? 3) Who are the possible candidates to fulfill this role? And, 4) How do the interpretations of this prophet in the Dead Sea Scrolls fit in with the history of the interpretation of this prophecy in Judaism and Christianity?

There is a great wealth of literature on this topic with many different interpretations of the data.[9] To facilitate our discussion we will focus our attention on the most important related texts.

The passage that is most often identified with the expectation of an eschatological prophet like Moses is found at the conclusion of the rules in the *Rule of the Community* (1QS) from Cave 1. The passage reads:

> They shall deviate from none of the teachings of the Law, whereby they would walk in their willful heart completely. They shall govern themselves using the original precepts by which the men of the *Yahad* began to be instructed, doing so until there come the Prophet and the Messiahs of Aaron and Israel. (1QS IX, 9–11)[10]

This passage presents the idea of a future prophet and two messiahs — all three seem to be eschatological figures — and all three may be considered messianic figures — that is anointed ones.[11] Let us take a moment to analyze exactly what the Rule of the Community says about the role of these three eschatological figures. The passage in 9:9–11 occurs in the text after the rules of the Community (*Yahad*) are given, and it says that the Community is to be governed by these rules until

---

9   See John J. Collins, *The Scepter and the Star: The Messiahs of the Dead Sea Scrolls and Other Ancient Literature* (New York: Doubleday, 1995); Alex P. Jassen. *Mediating the Divine: Prophecy and Revelation in the Dead Sea Scrolls and Second Temple Judaism* (Leiden: Brill, 2007); Michael A. Knibb, "Apocalyticism and Messianism" in *The Oxford Handbook of the Dead Sea Scrolls*, John J. Collins and Timothy H. Lim, eds. (Oxford: Oxford University Press, 2010), 403–32; and most recently see Jeffrey Stackert, *A Prophet Like Moses: Prophecy, Law, and Israelite Religion* (Oxford: Oxford University Press, 2014).

10   Translation from *The Dead Sea Scrolls Reader, Volume 1*, 2nd ed., Donald W. Parry and Emanuel Tov, eds.(Leiden: Brill, 2014), 27.

11   The passage about the prophet and the two messiahs in not found in the other copies of the *Rule of the Community* found at Qumran, which raises the issue of the dating of the manuscripts and the development or deletion of the idea of the coming of a prophet and two messiahs.

the coming of the three eschatological figures who will then apparently overturn the old rules and institute new ones. The reference to the "Prophet" (*nabi'*) appears to be an allusion to Deuteronomy 18:15. While it is not clear if the three figures together, or one or another of them, will fulfill this role in the Rule of the Community, it seems apparent in Testimonia (4Q175), which was written in the same hand as 1QS, that this legal role is the role of the future prophet "like Moses" referred to in Deuteronomy.

The sectarian texts from Qumran place great emphasis on eschatology. Several texts, such as the War Scroll (1QM) and the Pesharim, deal almost exclusively with the end of time. The prevailing view in the sectarian texts is that during the end time two messiahs will appear to lead the congregation.[12] From these passages it is possible to learn much about these messianic figures. On the other hand the prophet mentioned in the Rule of the Community IX, 9–11 who will serve as a forerunner to these messiahs is only specifically mentioned in the scrolls here and in Testimonia. From this we can deduce that there was less interest in the eschatological prophet than in the eschatological messiahs, and it is thus more difficult to understand the perceived role of this prophet and who he might be. From a close reading of the text we can summarize what we do know. First, it seems clear that the intention is of a single prophet; second, that this prophet is an eschatological prophet; and third, that his function in the Rule of the Community seems to be as lawgiver to replace the current set of rules with new ones; and fourth, both texts agree that the prophet will come before, perhaps as a forerunner, to the two messianic figures: the Messiah of Aaron and the Messiah of Israel. So who are these figures and what is the relationship between them? And, is the prophetic figure himself a messianic or "quasi-messianic" figure as some scholars have argued?

The role of the "prophet like Moses" is also specifically mentioned in Testimonia accompanied by the reference in Deuteronomy. Because it appears to be written in the same scribal hand as 1QS, Testimonia is considered to be from the same time period with a similar point of view. Testimonia is a short text composed of four units of citations of scripture, the first three providing a scriptural proof-text for each of

---

12 The Damascus Document (CD) talks of the coming of the messiah(s) with a singular noun: "And this is the exact interpretation of the rules by which [they shall be ruled until there arise the messiah] of Aaron and of Israel. And their iniquity will be atoned..." (CD XIV, 18–19). The singular noun "messiah" has led some to believe that CD anticipated a single priestly messiah. See the discussion in Michael A. Knibb, "Apocalyticism and Messianism," 421–22.

the three anticipated eschatological figures: the prophet, the king, and the priest or Levite — the same three offices described in Deuteronomy 16–18 and referred to in the Rule of the Community 9:11. The Prophet is described in the terms of Deuteronomy 5:28–29 and 18:18–19 — a prophet "like Moses."[13] The King is described in terms of Balaam's prophecy in Numbers 24:17: "A star rises from Jacob, A scepter arises from Israel."[14] And the Priest is described in terms of Deuteronomy 33:8–11 "And of Levi he said: Let your Thummim and Urim Be with Your faithful one." The fourth citation is a reference to Joshua and the foundation of Jericho.

The passage in Testimonia that describes the prophet quotes the passage in Deuteronomy 18:18–19 and reads:

> I will raise up a prophet for them from among their own kindred like you and I will put my words in his mouth, and he will speak to them all that I command him. If there is someone who does not heed my words which the prophet speaks in my name, I myself will call him to account. (4Q175, 5–8)[15]

Here the biblical idea that the Lord would simply call a succession of future prophets to replace Moses after he died appears to be changed. Testimonia shifts the calling of a prophet like unto Moses as a reference to a succession of prophets into a single eschatological figure and defines one of his tasks to be a mediator of law. If read in conjunction with the passage in the Rule of the Community an argument could be made that the prophet who is to precede the two messiahs is the one to be the lawgiver for the new laws.

The two messiahs — "anointed (ones) of Aaron and of Israel" — are mentioned elsewhere together in the Dead Sea Scrolls (CD 12:23; 14:19; 19:10–11; 20:1; 1QS 9:11) and scholars have argued that these two anointed ones — messiahs — are based on other similar models in

---

13 A scriptural discussion also combining Deut. 5:28–29 and 18:18 is found in 4QReworked Pentateuch (4Q158), but it does not discuss the future prophet. See the discussion in James C. Vanderkam, *The Dead Sea Scrolls and the Bible* (Grand Rapids, MI: Eerdmans, 2012), 39–43.

14 In the Damascus Document (7, MS A) the scepter in the oracle of Balaam is interpreted as the "Prince of the Congregation"—the Davidic messiah, and the star, instead of being interpreted as the priest by analogy to the messiahs of Aaron and Israel, is interpreted as "the Interpreter of the Law." See John J. Collins, *The Scepter and the Star: The Messiahs of the Dead Sea Scrolls and Other Ancient Literature* (New York: Doubleday, 1995), 63–64, 102.

15 Translation from James H. Charlesworth ed., *The Dead Sea Scrolls: Hebrew, Aramaic, and Greek Texts with English Translations, Volume 6B: Pesharim, Other Commentaries, and Related Documents* (Tübingen: Mohr Siebeck, 2002), 313.

scripture that include a spiritual and a political leader. Such pairs include Moses and Aaron, Aaron and Israel, Solomon and Zadok, the two "sons of oil" Jeshua and Zerubbabel, and later Bar Kochba and the High Priest Eleazar.[16]

Related to the prophet like Moses figure, a passage found in the Damascus Document identifies an important individual who will come as an eschatological teacher. This passage reads: "Until the rise of one who will teach righteousness (*yoreh hatsedek*) in the end of days" (CD VI, 10–11).[17] It is possible that this is a reference to the eschatological prophet. The image in Testimonia of the Lord putting words in the mouth of the prophet that he will speak in the Lord's name can easily be interpreted as one who "teaches righteousness." In addition a passage in Hosea 10:12 alludes to a future prophet, "until he comes and teaches righteousness" which may be the language from which CD 6:11 is drawn.[18]

Identification of the Prophet

Elsewhere in the Qumran texts the king and the priest are called by other titles. For example the king is called the "Prince of the Congregation" (CD 7:20; 4Q285.5.5; 6:2–10; 1QM 5, 1; 4QpIsa^a 2:14), and the priest is called the "interpreter of the Law" (CD 7:18; 4QFlor 1.i.11). Reflecting the emphasis in the Dead Sea Scrolls on the messianic figures over the future prophet much has been written about the significance and identification of the two messianic figures.[19] Let us look at some texts from Qumran that describe the prophet, and the possible candidates of this figure, to develop a list of similar epithets and characteristics of the future prophet like Moses to see if a possible identification of who this prophet was thought to be is possible. We will first examine two candidates that have been proposed for the "prophet like Moses" at Qumran: the Teacher of Righteousness and Elijah.

---

16 Lawrence H. Schiffman, *Reclaiming The Dead Sea Scrolls* (Philadelphia: Doubleday, 1995), 322.

17 Translation from James H. Charlesworth, ed., *The Dead Sea Scrolls: Hebrew, Aramaic, and Greek Texts with English Translations*, 23.

18 Collins, *The Scepter and the Star*, 113–14.

19 Collins, *The Scepter and the Star*; Michael A. Knibb, "Eschatology and Messianism in the Dead Sea Scrolls." In *Essays on the Book of Enoch and Other Early Jewish Texts and Traditions*. SVTP 22 (Leiden: Brill, 2009), 307–26. James C. VanderKam, "Messianism and Apocalypticism" in J. J. Collins, B. McGinn, and S. J. Stein, eds., *The Encyclopedia of Apocalypticism*. 3 vols. (New York: Continuum, 1998), vol. 1, 193–228.

From the beginning many scholars advanced the idea that the Teacher of Righteousness could be identified as a prophet, and specifically as the prophet "like Moses."[20] The main objection to this idea is that the Teacher of Righteousness is never specifically called a "prophet" (*nabi'*) in any of the texts. In fact he is specifically identified as a priest in *Pesher Habbakuk* (1QpHab 2:8–9) and the Pesher Psalms (4QpPsa 1–10.iii.15). Nevertheless, there is much evidence in the Qumran texts that suggest he may anciently have been considered a prophet and his ministry reflects many of the attributes of Moses: teacher, giver of the law, and interpreter of the law. In particular some believe that the Teacher of Righteousness was the author of the Temple Scroll, a work that may have been intended to serve as the law for the eschatological period as alluded to in the Rule of the Community.21 A study by George Brooke titled "Was the Teacher of Righteousness Considered to Be a Prophet?" provides a comprehensive survey of the evidence for whether the Teacher was considered a prophet at all and if so whether he was considered to be the prophet "like Moses."[22]

As evidence that the Teacher of Righteousness was portrayed with the qualities and functions attributed to biblical prophets we can identify passages in the Damascus Document and in the Pesharim. The passage found in the Damascus Document that identifies the eschatological teacher has also been interpreted as a reference to the Teacher of Righteousness. This passage reads: "Until the rise of one who will teach righteousness (*yoreh hatsedek*) in the end of days" (CD 6:10–11). From this description some have identified this eschatological teacher with the prophet "like Moses" and in particular with the Teacher of Righteousness. The Hebrew words for "teach" and "righteousness" *yoreh hatsedek* here are the same words used in the title Teacher of Righteousness *Moreh Hatsedek* and describes a figure who will, like Moses, and the Teacher of Righteousness before him, continue to teach righteousness. Of course the office of eschatological teacher may also be one assumed by the Teacher of Righteousness as a priest.

20 Michael O. Wise, "The Temple Scroll and the Teacher of Righteousness," in *Mogilany 1989: Papers on the Dead Seas Scrolls*, Vol. 2, Z. J. Kapera, ed. (Kraków: Enigma, 1991), 142.

21 Michael O. Wise, *A Critical Study of the Temple Scroll from Qumran Cave 11* (Chicago: The Oriental Institute of Chicago, 1990), 184.

22 George J. Brooke, "Was the Teacher of Righteousness Considered to be a Prophet?" in *Prophecy after the Prophets? The Contribution of the Dead Sea Scrolls to the Understanding of Biblical and Extra-Biblical Prophecy*, K. De Troyer, A. Lange, L. L. Schulte, eds. (Leuven: Peeters, 2009), 77–97.

Two examples from the Pesher Habakkuk (1QpHab) are similarly interpreted as references to the Teacher of Righteousness as the eschatological prophet, or teacher in that he is described as one who receives mysteries from God and as one who serves as a mediator — both characteristics of Moses. In Pesher Habakkuk 7:4 the Teacher of Righteousness is described: "Interpreted this concerns the Teacher of Righteousness, to whom God made known all the mysteries (*raz*) of the words of His servants the Prophets."[23] And in 8:1–3: "Interpreted, this concerns all those who observe the Law in the House of Judah, whom God will deliver from the House of Judgement because of their suffering and because of their faith in the Teacher of Righteousness."[24]

In regards to the question as to whether the Teacher of Righteousness was to be considered a prophet at all, if we were to assume there is autobiographical material about the Teacher of Righteousness in the Hodayot, there are many examples of the author portraying himself with prophetic attributes. As noted by Brooke: "This was not done explicitly by him claiming the title 'prophet,' but in terms of how he projected himself indirectly as a new Moses, as a new Jeremiah, as imitating the prophetic servant of the Isaianic servant songs, and even in his very act of writing hymnic poetry that could be understood prophetically."[25]

Even if the Teacher of Righteous was considered by the Community to be a prophet, it is strange that the term is never used about him. In terms of the identification of the Teacher of Righteousness as the eschatological prophet "like Moses," or even in his priestly office as the eschatological teacher, a further problem is that the texts were written and transmitted within the time period, either directly before, during, or after his lifetime and there is no indication that he was the forerunner of the two eschatological messiahs. It seems that if indeed the Teacher of Righteousness were to be identified with this eschatological figure there would have been some identification of this in connection with the two messiahs in the texts.[26] In addition, all of the text talk of him as a historical figure in the past and separately mention the eschatological prophet and/ or teacher in the future. In order to solve this problem some scholars have postulated the idea that the Teacher of Righteousness would rise

---

23   Geza Vermes, *The Dead Sea Scrolls in English*, 4th ed. (London: Penguin Books, 1995), 343.

24   Ibid, 344.

25   Brooke, "Was the Teacher Considered a Prophet?" 84–85.

26   Collins, *The Scepter and the Star*, 102–04.

from the dead and reappear but these theories have not gained universal acceptance.[27]

Brooke concludes that the question of whether the Teacher of Righteousness could be considered a prophet can be answered with a qualified "yes" or a qualified "no," but it is very unlikely that he was the eschatological prophet like Moses. In the end Brooke says, "The Teacher of Righteousness remains a somewhat shadowy figure."[28] Another scholar, James Bowley, similarly summarizes the evidence, "Though in some ways he can be compared to Moses, the authority of the Teacher is nowhere explicitly based on the claim that he was a *nabi'*. Rather, he is presented as the divinely inspired and ordained exegete of the prophetic word."[29] The consensus among scholars is that while the Teacher of Righteousness had many of the characteristics of a prophet, and may even have been considered by the Community as a prophet, he should not to be equated with the prophet "like Moses." Ironically, the fact that Moses is actually never explicitly called a prophet in Deuteronomy or in the Torah, the Teacher of Righteousness may be exactly a prophet "like Moses" in the sense that he, like Moses, functioned as a prophet, but was never actually called a prophet.

Another proposed identification of the prophet "like Moses" is the prophet Elijah. In the biblical passage at the end of Malachi the Lord exhorts Israel to "Be mindful of the Teaching of My servant Moses" and says, "Lo, I will send the prophet Elijah to you before the coming of the awesome, fearful day of the LORD," (Mal. 3:22–23; [English 4:4–5]). A passage in Ben Sira (48:10) refers to Malachi when it talks of the future coming of Elijah to calm the wrath of God in order to restore Israel: "At the appointed time, it is written, you [Elijah] are destined to calm the wrath of God before it breaks out in fury, to turn the hearts of parents to their children, and to restore the tribes of Jacob."

Thus, Jewish and Christian interpreters have identified Moses and Elijah as important persons that figure into the future. Perhaps echoing Malachi, Qumran texts also expect the return of Elijah and a Moses-like prophet among the sectarian (1QS, 4Q175, 11Q13) and the non-sectarian

---

27   Ibid..

28   Brooke, "Was the Teacher Considered a Prophet?" 97.

29   James E. Bowley, "Prophets and Prophecy at Qumran," in *The Dead Sea Scrolls after Fifty Years, Vol. 2*, Peter W. Flint and James C. VanderKam, eds. (Leiden: Brill, 1999), 354–78, in particular 371.

texts (4Q558, 4Q521).[30] And in 4Q558 Malachi 3:23 [4:5] is quoted directly referring to the return of Elijah.

So the most common specific identification of the eschatological prophet "like Moses" in all of these traditions is Elijah. This fits well with the fact that since Elijah did not die but was taken into heaven he would be able to return (2 Kings 2:11).

The New Testament tradition recognizes both Elijah and Moses, perhaps based on Malachi as well. In John 1:21 the people ask John the Baptist if he is either: "And they asked him, 'What then? Are you Elijah?' He said, 'I am not.' 'Are you the prophet?' He answered, 'No.'" Later rabbinic traditions (*b. Sanh* 118a; *b. 'Eruv* 43b) also relate the future coming of Elijah as related in Malachi.

Summary and Conclusions

In regards to the history of the interpretation of the prophet like Moses we can summarize: the biblical passage in Deuteronomy refers to the institution of prophecy in Israel and a future succession of prophets in including perhaps specific prophets who are portrayed with characteristics of Moses. Influenced perhaps by Malachi 3 [English 4], interpreters in the inter-testamental period began to read this passage as referring to a single future prophet, and identified the specific future prophet as Elijah — an interpretation that continues in Christianity and rabbinic Judaism.

As illustrated by the passages in the Rule of the Community and Testimonia the expectation of the Community at Qumran had the expectation of the coming of a future eschatological prophet "like Moses" as prophesied by Deuteronomy 18. This prophet would receive and deliver the word of the Lord, would establish the new laws, and would precede the coming of the two messiahs. The allusion to a prophet "like Moses" in verses 15–18 evokes all of the characteristics known of Moses through the biblical text: leader, lawgiver, teacher, worker of miracles, and one who received revelation and spoke with the Lord "face to face." The Damascus Document talks of an eschatological teacher who would teach "righteousness" before the end. It is not clear if this figure is to be equated with the prophet or not. In any case, whenever the texts of Qumran speak of the coming of a prophet "like Moses," it was to

---

30   Alex P. Jassen, *Mediating the Divine: Prophecy and Revelation in the Dead Sea Scrolls and Second Temple Judaism* (Leiden: Brill, 2007), 188. See also John C. Poirier, "The Endtime Return of Elijah and Moses at Qumran," *Dead Sea Discoveries* 10.2 (2003): 221–42.

be a figure who would be anointed, and would have power to bring the word of the Lord, to be a herald, and to precede the coming of the two messiahs. His power was not just that he would be a prophet, but that he would be a prophet "like Moses."

The New Testament followed by early Christian interpreters specifically identifies the prophet like Moses as the Messiah (Acts 3:17–26). So while the idea that the prophet like Moses was a specific future individual is attested in inter-testamental literature including the Dead Sea Scrolls, the identification of this prophet as the Messiah seems to be distinctive to Matthew and the New Testament. That this identification is also attested anciently in the Book of Mormon may be best explained by prophetic foresight.

While the Book of Mormon, like the New Testament, specifically identifies the future prophet like Moses as Christ, it also develops the idea that the institution of prophecy that continued in Israel included other future prophets like Moses. Similar to the Deuteronomistic History, the Book of Mormon records the continuation of the institution of prophecy in its history and in several cases specifically portrays prophets with characteristics of Moses. The prophets Lehi and Nephi, for example, like Moses spoke with the Lord, and delivered their family from destruction in Jerusalem and led them through the wilderness to the promised land. They became prophetic leaders and lawgivers to their people, and constantly reiterated the blessings and curses of the covenant, similar to those in Deuteronomy, associated with the promised land. The commandment repeated by prophets throughout the Book of Mormon: "And inasmuch as ye shall keep my commandments, ye shall prosper...And inasmuch as thy brethren shall rebel against thee, they shall be cut off from the presence of the Lord" (1 Ne. 2:20–21; cf. 1 Ne. 4:14) is reminiscent of the language and theology of Deuteronomy (cf. 28:15, 29 and 29:9). And Lehi, like Moses, blessed his posterity before his death (2 Ne. 1–4; Deut. 33).[31] Likewise, Abinadi confronted King Noah with the same language Moses faced Pharaoh. King Noah's response to

---

31   See Noel B. Reynolds, "Nephite Kingship Reconsidered," in *Mormons, Scripture, and the Ancient World*, ed. Davis Bitton (Provo, UT: FARMS, 1998), 172–77 for a list of 21 points of comparison between Nephi and Moses; "Lehi as Moses," *Journal of Book of Mormon Studies* 9, no. 2 (2000): 26–35; and "The Israelite Background of Moses Typology in the Book of Mormon," *BYU Studies Quarterly* 44, no. 2 (2005): 5–23. See also George S. Tate, "The Typology of the Exodus Pattern in the Book of Mormon," in *Literature of Belief: Sacred Scripture and Religious Experience*, Neal E. Lambert, ed. (Provo, UT: Religious Studies Center, Brigham Young University, 1981), 246–62 and S. Kent Brown, "The Exodus Pattern in the Book of Mormon," in *From Jerusalem to*

the prophet "Who is Abinadi?" (Mosiah 11:27) echoes Pharaoh's "Who is the LORD?" (Exod. 5:2), and Abinadi threatened the people with a series of plagues reminiscent of those performed by Moses and Aaron on the Egyptians including pestilence, hail, the east wind, and insects (Mosiah 12:3–7; Exod. 7–10). Additionaly, Abinadi, as a synopsis of the law of Moses, delivered the Ten Commandments to Noah's priests.[32]

Finally, Latter-day Saint tradition continues to describe their prophets as prophets "like Moses." Joseph Smith was said to have received revelations "even as Moses" (D&C 28:2) and to lead his people like Moses (D&C 103:16). Brigham Young is referred to by the saints as the Mormon Moses or the American Moses who delivered them from bondage and led them into the wilderness to the Promised Land.[33] For Latter-day Saints the prophecy of Deuteronomy 18 that the Lord will raise up a prophet like Moses has been fulfilled in the past by Christ and others and continues to be fulfilled through the Restoration to the present day.

David R. Seely *is professor of Ancient Scripture at Brigham Young University. He received his undergraduate and Masters degree at BYU in ancient Greek and Classics and his PhD from the University of Michigan in Near Eastern studies. Together with Professor Moshe Weinfeld, he published the Barkhi Nafshi hymns from Qumran in the Oxford series* Discoveries in the Judean Desert *and he co-authored with William Hamblin the book* Solomon's Temple in Myth and History, *and with Richard Holzapfel and Dana Pike* Jehovah and the World of the Old Testament. *In addition, he co-edited with John W. Welch and Jo Ann H. Seely the volume* Glimpses of Lehi's Jerusalem.

Zarahemla: Literary and Historical Studies of the Book of Mormon (Provo, UT: Religious Studies Center, Brigham Young University, 1998), 75–98.

32   David R. Seely, "Abinadi, Moses, Isaiah, and Christ: O How Beautiful upon the Mountains Are Their Feet," in *The Book of Mormon: The Foundation of Our Faith: the 28th Annual Sidney B. Sperry Symposium* (Salt Lake City: Deseret Book, 1999), 201–16.

33   Not only did the early saints refer to Brigham Young as Moses, but Brigham Young also referred to himself as Moses. Willard Richard's Journal contains a quote by Brigham Young, "I feel all the time like Moses." "Unlike the original Moses though Young would reach what Clayton termed, 'the place which God for us prepared." (Willard Richard's Journal 14 March 1847). Quoted from John G. Turner, *Brigham Young: Pioneer Prophet* (Cambridge, MA: Harvard University Press, 2012), 148, 443 n. 8.

CHRISTMAS AS DEVOTIONAL:
A TIME OF COMMITMENT

Cherry B. Silver

Abstract: *Christmas is more than a time for celebrations and traditions — it is an occasion to remember the blessings and miracles in our lives. From the joy of friends and family to the peace inspired by devotion and dedication Christmas offers us a time to marvel at the mercies of God; let us remember the holier anthems of the season.*

When asked, "What Christmas do you remember best," we often think of times when celebrations were beyond the ordinary. In normal times, fulfilling Christmas traditions is hard work, and results are often transient. We dive into our eight areas of celebration, driven by visions of Christmas past: 1) decorations, 2) food, 3) music, 4) cards and letters, 5) gifts, 6) charity, 7) gatherings and friendship, and 8) religious services and special presentations.

People look forward to the holidays, expecting sentiment, sociability, and sensory experiences. Conversely, people suffer from disappointment and even depression when high expectations go unfulfilled. If Christmas is just lights and gifts, tearing off wrapping paper by the tree gets us through the externals very fast. Then comes the letdown. As Mary Ellen Edmunds philosophized, "You can never get enough of what you don't need."[1]

It is a serious task to draw from the well of life experience and express what matters at this season, to somehow blend ultimate hope and deep seeking with family and traditions, to probe beyond the popular and counter the commercial.

---

1. Mary Ellen Edmunds, *You Can Never Get Enough of What You Don't Need: The Quest for Contentment* (Salt Lake City: Deseret Book, 2005).

Create a Personal Message

In the Bushman home, my artist father created cards from Ted and Dorothy each year with a jazzy drawing and a friendly greeting to send to friends. As a graduate student in Boston, I decided to send out my first personal Christmas message. I began with a simple drawing, a line of scripture, and a meditative verse. It was a time when metaphysical poets earned my respect. If I could imitate their sincere praise of the child that became the Savior, I reasoned, I might make my greeting a message of devotion, not just celebration of a season.

Such verse is based on an idea or *conceit* that radiates meanings in several directions. The governing metaphor meshes present time with past and future, mortal life with the eternal, struggle with fulfilment, uncertainty with commitment. And all this makes sense through the mission of Jesus Christ.

My model was Edward Taylor (1642–1729), a Puritan minister in western Massachusetts. As he prepared to administer the sacrament of the Lord's supper at the high holiday in his simple meetinghouse, Taylor collected his thoughts in verse and created more than two hundred private poems. Through a startling yoking of dissimilar images, Taylor's raw lines convey his concern for man's fallen condition and his felt need for God's grace. In Meditation 8 on John 6:51, for example, Taylor treats "I am the Living Bread." Here is stanza four.

> In this sad state, Gods Tender Bowells run
> Out streams of Grace: And he to end all strife
> The Purest Wheate in Heaven, his deare-dear Son
> Grinds, and kneads up into this Bread of Life.
> Which Bread of Life from Heaven down came and stands
> Disht on thy Table up by Angells Hands.[2]

There is a tactile, kinetic power in the imagery of God grinding, kneading, and serving his Son as the bread of life to save us. The literalness shocks us into sensing God's sacrifice. The Father conveys unbounded mercy as He offers us a chance to partake of the Lord's supper.

I experimented with verse forms over the years, trying like Edward Taylor to prepare my mind for the season through a family Christmas message. After our daughter was born, for instance, my verse in the

---

2. Edward Taylor, "I am the Living Bread Meditation Eight: John 6:51," Poetry Foundation (website), https://www.poetryfoundation.org/poems/46135/i-am-the-living-bread-meditation-eight-john-651.

metaphysical tradition described God drawing us like fish into his basket through this infant:

> Her smiles and happy, noisy songs are bait
> > To catch our praise
> > For Him who saves
> By drawing us where holier anthems wait. ...

> The sweetness of her five months' life has set
> > Our purpose. God
> > Could find no rod
> To land us better in the gospel net.

Savor Times of Testimony

Twenty-four years later Barnard and I, as missionaries, celebrated Christmas with a small group of believers in Abidjan, Côte d'Ivoire, West Africa. That proved to be a special outreach event. Our daughter had flown in from Utah on her December break from medical school to join us. Côte d'Ivoire was a country where we had lived as a family when she and her brother were in grade school and this was her first time back. On Saturday, the group held a baptismal service at the lagoon. On Sunday, after services, Church members and investigators came to the missionary apartment for a light buffet and a spiritual feast. It turned out to be our last week in the country: due to security concerns, we were being transferred to the Democratic Republic of the Congo.

After the buffet, as we stood in a circle, Elder Silver asked each one — man, woman, school-aged child — to declare what Jesus meant to them. Each had something personal and sweet to say. I later tried to capture in free verse the feeling of that circle of faith:

> That hot Christmas day in Abidjan
> we celebrated after church by cooking rice and sauce
> for fifty-seven friends —
> Ivorians, some Zairoise, Americans, Ghanaians too —
> who crowded in our house and sang with us in French,
> "Venez, tous fideles."

> And when we told them we were leaving soon,
> some cried and pressed our hands
> and made us take their photos
> so that our comradery would not be lost.

So much is lost, if only mortal,
that we cannot love fully if we seize this day as all.
But when we shared our hope in Christ for life,
not just a village/city life,
but living on with Him in brotherhood, forever,
they understood, they smiled and waved us on.
Next Christmas, they will cook the rice and lead the hymn,
"Douce nuit, sainte nuit! ... C'est Jesus le Sauveur!"

And we will sing it here, a hemisphere away,
Silent night, holy night ... Jesus Lord at his birth ...
Christ the Savior is born.

Find the Miracles in Your Life

The spiritual highlight of the 2013 Christmas season began for our family in October. That was when a fierce microburst of wind in southeast Idaho blew two missionaries on a service project off a trailer and smashed them into the pavement. Our eighteen-year-old grandson, Stewart Silver, was one of the young elders. He hit the back of his head and began to convulse. From that point on, my husband Barnard registered thirty-six miracles that made possible Stewart's survival. Among those miracles was getting help immediately, being flown to a trauma hospital, having space cleared for an operation, lifting part of his skull as his brain swelled, surviving on a ventilator in a coma while his brain bled, regaining consciousness and then speech, mobility, and memory.

Grandfather Barnard Silver had the privilege of giving Stewart a priesthood blessing as he lay in the coma, assisted by the boy's uncle Drew Clark. He expressed confidence that the missionary would recover. His mother Ariel Clark Silver, who had flown in from Ohio, and I added our faith and fervent prayers. That evening Barnard consulted with the Intensive Care Unit physician who showed him the x-rays of the damage and confided there was very little chance the young man would come out of it. Which to believe — the physician with his tangible evidence, or the blessing from his grandfather with its spiritual insights? Despite the doctor's discouragement, Stewart's path turned into one of healing. In two and a half weeks instead of the six anticipated, he left the hospital supported by his father, still recovering balance and strength but walking and talking.

As his mother then his father returned to their work and other children in Ohio, it was decided to have Stewart recuperate at our home in Salt Lake City, where we as grandparents could drive him to appointments with his surgical team in Pocatello every few weeks. The end goal was to replace his own skull cap — kept frozen in the hospital's freezer — before Christmas.

All that fall, Stewart wore a black plastic protective helmet on his head to protect the area missing a skull piece. He attended Church and concerts and dinner meetings with us. He received an apostolic blessing from Elder Neil L. Andersen. He had an interview with Elder Russell M. Nelson, then responsible for all missionary service in the Church. When his surgeons checked him in November, they were encouraging: "We've never seen anyone recover so well from the craniectomy procedure." As we neared mid-December, he was hitting the markers in physical and occupational therapy sessions that would permit pre-Christmas restorative surgery. His mother, Ariel, flew to Utah to join us for the repair. Once again, he lay unconscious in bed with a drain line easing pressure and his head wrapped in white bandages. This time, he got up faster and was soon eating and walking.

While in the hospital, Stewart and Ariel sat beside the surgical assistant to examine the detailed CT scans taken shortly after the accident. Only then did they see the heart of the miracle — that the blow against the pavement fractured his skull in a curving pattern that missed the foramen magnum, the crucial area protecting the brain stem which controls life and thought processes, by a mere 0.42 cm. Death and disability were definitely possibilities, but they were avoided by a fraction of a centimeter.

I don't remember how our Christmas Day was spent in Salt Lake City that year. I do remember that Ariel and Stewart caught a December 21st flight from Utah to Ohio, permitting him to greet his father and five sisters again and accelerate his recovery during the holiday season. Our Christmas thoughts focused on their reunion. After New Year he enrolled in a college term. In June he received a recall to the Idaho Twin Falls Mission and successfully completed his two-year service. In 2018 a Church production crew interviewed Stewart and his former missionary companion at the scene of the accident to add their wisdom to a Church documentary film on safety. His black protective helmet now sits on our upper closet shelf as a memento of miracles.

Meditate on a Scripture Verse

Every Christmas, I have decided, invites fulfillment of warm traditions in many ways, but the season becomes truly memorable when we insert devotion and dedication, making it a time to marvel at the mercies of God and pledge to maintain a worthy way of life. The model I found years ago in Edward Taylor's poetic meditations encouraged my adaptation of the story of the tax collector Zacchaeus from Luke:

> Jesus once spied high in a tree
> A recalcitrant sinner,
> And stopped to abide with him that day.
> Elated, repentant,
> He descended, never to let free
> Of his Redeemer's
> Hand down the sacrificial way.
>
> We who keep watches in the fearsome night—
> Over a fretful child
> Or concerned for self and loved ones and the rest
> Of men — need
> Like Zacchaeus climb awhile for sight,
> And then rejoicing
> Haste down to serve in peace our princely guest.

Christmas 2020 for everyone is bound to be a notable one. May it be a holiday of commitment and dedication as well as celebration.

Cherry Bushman Silver *holds degrees in English and American literature from the University of Utah, Boston University, and Harvard. She has taught courses at BYU-Provo and colleges in Washington State and California. While serving on the General Board of the Relief Society from 1990 to 1997, she contributed chapters to* Knit Together in Love: A Focus for LDS Women in the 1990s *and wrote the* History of the Elaine Jack Administration. *For eighteen years she has focused on women's history and has served on the executive committee of the Mormon Women's History Initiative Team (MWHIT). With Carol Cornwall Madsen, she edited* New Scholarship on Latter-day Saint Women in the Twentieth Century *(2005). She is currently helping edit and annotate 47 years of diaries written by Emmeline B. Wells, editor, suffrage leader, and fifth general Relief Society president. The Wells diaries are being published online by the Church Historians Press. Cherry and her husband, Barnard Silver, served missions in Abidjan, Cote d'Ivoire, and in Kinshasa and Lubumbashi, Zaire, now the Democratic Republic of Congo. They live in Holladay, Utah, and have two children and ten grandchildren.*

Medieval Christian Views of Hebrew as the Language of Magic

Andrew C. Skinner

Abstract: *The view of Hebrew as a language of magic, for which precedents can be discerned in the Bible and in rabbinic tradition, spilled over into early and medieval Christianity. Andrew Skinner adroitly explores the material and theological history of this trajectory, showing how this contributed to the emergence of Christian Kabbalah in the sixteenth century.*

[**Editor's Note:** Part of our book chapter reprint series, this article is reprinted here as a service to the LDS community. Original pagination and page numbers have necessarily changed, otherwise the reprint has the same content as the original.

See Andrew C. Skinner, "Medieval Christian Views of Hebrew as the Language of Magic," in *"To Seek the Law of the Lord": Essays in Honor of John W. Welch,* ed. Paul Y. Hoskisson and Daniel C. Peterson (Orem, UT: The Interpreter Foundation, 2017), 375–412. Further information at https://interpreterfoundation.org/books/to-seek-the-law-of-the-lord-essays-in-honor-of-john-w-welch-2/.]

The study of the Hebrew language by Christians during the Middle Ages is a field yet to be fully explored.[1] One of the most fascinating

---

1 There has been a lot of work done on the Christian study of the Hebrew language after the Middle Ages, from the Renaissance onward, and a lot done on the study of Hebrew by Jews in the Middle Ages. But medieval Christian Hebraica from say AD 300 to 1300 (the dates usually regarded as encompassing the Middle Ages) is still a field not yet fully cultivated. Some scholars seem to conflate the study of Hebrew by Christians in different periods into a single topic.

aspects of medieval Christian Hebraism is the reputation Hebrew acquired as a preeminent language of magic in some circles. This brief essay seeks to survey this aspect of the history of the Hebrew language. We find that while most medieval Christians eschewed the Jews, some believed that their traditional language, Hebrew, possessed special power to manipulate cosmic or supernatural forces to bring about desired personal results. The medieval Christian belief in the supernatural power of the Hebrew language itself led directly to the study of Kabbalah by Christians in the Renaissance and beyond.

The Historical Setting

Undoubtedly, the greatest name associated with early medieval Christian Hebrew studies is Eusebius Hieronymus Sophronius — St. Jerome (circa 340–420 CE).[2] Between AD 390 and 406 he produced the *Vulgate*, introductory prefaces to biblical books and explanatory notes on Hebrew, two works on Hebrew etymologies, and numerous other commentaries and treatises.[3] Jerome indicates he gave himself over to the study of Hebrew unrelentingly. His initial contribution to the study of Hebrew among Christians is not easily overstated. He spoke often of the *Veritas Hebraica* — "Hebrew truth" — and earned for himself the epithet *Doctor Maximus sacris Scripturis explanandis*, "supreme doctor in interpretation of sacred scripture."[4]

Jerome's own description of his initial motivation for undertaking the study of Hebrew is a bit surprising, perhaps even titillating, and, for our purposes, quite telling. From a passage in his *Letters*[5] we read:

---

2 See practically any one of the studies on medieval Christian Hebraists, especially Raphael Lowe, "The Medieval Christian Hebraists of England: Herbert of Bosham and Earlier Scholars," *Transactions of the Jewish Historical Society of England* 17 (1953): 226. He says that if it were not for the writings of St. Jerome, "one might well wonder whether any knowledge of Hebraica and Judaica would have existed in Western Christendom at all."

3 Francis X. Murphy, ed., *A Monument to Saint Jerome* (New York: Sheed and Ward, 1952), 43 notes: "…from 391 to 406, formed the most productive period in the industrious life of Jerome." For a sampling of some of Jerome's most important works from this period see J.P. Migne, ed., *Patrologiae cursus completes, Series latina*, 221 vols. (Paris: 1844–1864) 23:771–928, 935–1010 which comprises his *Liber Hebraicarum Quaestionum in Genesim*, *Liber de Nominibus Hebraica*, and *Liber de Situ et Nominibus Locorum Hebraicorum*.

4 Murphy, *A Monument to Saint Jerome*, 37.

5 Jerome's Letters are collected in Migne, *Patrologia latina* vol. 22. Selected letters are found in *A Select Library of Nicene and Post-Nicene Fathers of the Christian Church*, vol. VI: *St. Jerome: Letters and Select Works*, Philip Schaff and Henry Wace, eds.,W. H. Fremantle, trans. (New York: The Christian Literature Company, 1893).

As a youth, even while I was hemmed in by the solitude of the desert, I could not bear the stimulation of the passions and nature's ardor. Though I tried to overcome it by frequent fasts, my imagination was still aflame with impure thoughts. So, in order to bring my mind into control, I made myself the pupil of a certain fellow monk who had been converted from Judaism to Christianity. And thus, after studying the acumen of Quintilian, the eloquence of Cicero, the majesty of Fronto, and the suavity of Pliny, I learnt the Hebrew alphabet and exercised myself in its hissing and aspirate words. What labor I then underwent! What difficulties I had to bear! How often I quit in despair, and how often I began again through my ambition to learn!...But I thank the Lord that from this bitter seed of study I can now gather the sweet fruits.[6]

Whether or not Jerome was here given to hyperbole makes little difference for our purpose. This autobiographical note still tells us something of the early medieval Christian attitude toward Hebrew. It was thought to be a most difficult language to learn, requiring so much concentration in Jerome's view as to be able to rid the mind of all other thoughts.

The study of Hebrew was looked upon as a true test of one's ability. It seems almost as though a medieval scholar's reputation was at once confirmed if he could be linked to that language. For example, Cassiodorus—himself no mean intellectual—described Jerome as "a most outstanding propagandist of the Latin tongue, who so greatly excelled us in the translation of the divine Scripture since we could scarcely approach the Hebrew source...it is well known that he overwhelmed us with the great richness of his learning."[7] Even Augustine, whose preference for the Greek text of the Old Testament is manifest,[8] indicates his admiration for Jerome's erudition, based in large

---

6   Murphy, *A Monument to Saint Jerome*, 56. See also Schaff and Wace, eds., *St. Jerome: Letters and Select Works*, 248.

7   Cassiodorus, *Divine Lectures*, 21 "...latinae linguae dilatator eximius, qui nobis in translatione divinae Scripturae tantum praestitit, ut ad Hebraium fontem pene non egeamus accedere, quando nos facuundiae suae multa cognoscitur ubertate satiasse, plurimis libris copiosis epistolis fecit beatos..."

8   "Even as late as the time of the *De Civitate Dei*, St. Augustine still maintained his position as to the primary authority of the Septuagint." Herman Hailperin's review of Beryl Smalley, "Hebrew Scholarship Among Christians in XIIIth Century England as Illustrated by Some Hebrew Latin Psalters" in *Historia Judaica* II (1940): 124.

measure on his facility with Hebrew: "for [he was] well versed in Greek and Latin, and above all in Hebrew eloquence."[9]

The view that Hebrew study was an arduous task, that it was a difficult language to learn for Christians with no Jewish background, was prevalent in the early Middle Ages. It is a view that continued to exist through the end of the medieval period, but it is not the only view.

Conditions requisite for serious scholarship of any kind in Christian Europe during the Middle Ages could only be found in monasteries.[10] Serious study of the Hebrew language was fairly well relegated to the purview of churchmen — and not great numbers of them at that. But interest in Hebrew among Christians was spreading. There were increasing attempts by scholars to learn at least some elements of the Hebrew alphabet[11] even though, for the most part, that alphabet and the language itself "stood for something odd, strange, and difficult."[12] Alongside those interested in Hebrew scholarship were scholars who chose not to study Hebrew at all for the very reason that it was odd, strange and difficult. But by the same token, some people, not motivated by serious scholarship, had been attracted to Hebrew precisely because it was strange and mysterious and generated a perceived connection with what has been termed "white magic."[13]

It should be acknowledged, as scholars have pointed out, that relatively little effort has been expended in formulating a clear definition of the term magic.[14] The study of medieval Christian Hebraica highlights the challenge in defining magic in contradistinction to religion. However, it may be said that many scholars seem to agree that magic is not different in essence from religion. Rather, magic is a "form of religious deviance...alternate to those [activities] normally sanctioned by the

---

9   St. Augustine, Contra *Julianum* I, 7, 34, cited in Murphy, *A Monument to Saint Jerome*, vi. "...qui Graeco et Latino insuper et Hebraeo eruditus eloquio..."

10   Beryl Smalley, *The Study of the Bible in the Middle Ages* (Notre Dame: University of Notre Dame Press, 1978), 29.

11   Ibid., 43.

12   Charles Singer, "Hebrew Scholarship in the Middle Ages Among Latin Christians," in *The Legacy of Israel*, ed. Edwyn R. Brevan and Charles Singer (Oxford: Clarendon Press, 1927), 287.

13   See Theodore Schrire, *Hebrew Magic Amulets* (New York: Behrman House, 1983); see also, *The Catholic Encyclopedia*, ed. Charles Hebermann et al. (1911), v. s.v. "Occult Art, Occultism."

14   Stephen D. Ricks and Daniel C. Peterson, "Joseph Smith and 'Magic': Methodological Reflections on the Use of a Term," in *To Be Learned Is Good If...*, ed. Robert L. Millet (Salt Lake City: Bookcraft, 1987), 130.

dominant religious institution."[15] To members of the dominant religious institution—the "insiders"—their sanctioned beliefs and practices constituted religion. Magic was what was practiced by "outsiders"; it was unsanctioned but not ineffective.[16]

Most people in the Middle Ages generally differentiated between mischievous, evil, destructive black magic, and beneficent, acceptable white magic, whose purpose was to protect against the harm of evil magic and the powers of darkness it employed. White magic often made use of objects or amulets which possessed or invoked special protective powers. But, at the heart of the matter was the power inherent in certain words and special verbal formulas which could be and often were inscribed on objects or amulets, or which might be used in independent oaths.[17] The belief in the power of language — or more particularly the Hebrew language — to create or destroy, to help or hinder, even to shape life or change history, dates back to ancient biblical times.[18]

Israelite and Rabbinic Backgrounds

From certain prohibitions found in the Bible (see for example Exod. 22:18, Deut. 18:10–11; 2 Kings 21:1–2, 6) it may be inferred that magic of various types had gained a foothold in ancient Israel early on. In a famous episode, Israel's first king, Saul, consulted the witch of Endor toward the end of his life (1 Sam. 28:5–20). Repeated bans testify to how deeply-rooted was the belief in the efficacy of magical practices, separate and distinct from Yahweh worship. When, for example, the prophet Isaiah[19] placed the "diviner," the "smart magician," and the "wise charmer" on a par with "the mighty man, the man of war, the judge, and the prophet," he was testifying to the recognized existence of all these professions in the life of Israel's people. Despite the continued denigration of magic (and its practitioners) throughout the biblical period by religious leaders,[20] the practice persisted.

---

15 David Aune quoted in Ricks and Peterson, "Joseph Smith and 'Magic'," 130.

16 Ricks and Peterson, "Joseph Smith and 'Magic'," 129-47.

17 Schrire, *Hebrew Magic Amulets*, v.

18 See, for example, Gerhard von Rad, *Old Testament Theology*, 2 vols. (New York: Harper and Row, Publishers, 1965), 2:81–82. See also *Interpreter's Dictionary of the Bible*, 1962 ed., s.v. "Name" by R. Abba, and "God, Names of" by B. W. Anderson.

19 Isa. 3:2–3.

20 See *Interpreter's Dictionary of the Bible*, 1962 ed., s.v. "Magic" by I. Mendelsohn which contains a substantial list of passages. See, for example, Exod. 22:18; Lev. 19:26; Isa. 44:25; Zech. 10:2, etc.

By the post-biblical period, Israelite religion had become Judaism, per se. The kind of magic emphasized during this period was "defensive," which sought to protect one against evil and sickness, and was, with some exceptions, generally intended not to harm persons but, rather, demonic forces — so called "white magic."[21] By the Talmudic age (AD 200–500) this same kind of magic was employed not only for the benefit and protection of people against demonic powers but also against destructive illnesses. The Talmudic tractate Pesahim 112a, for instance, recommends reducing the force or severity of an ailment by a verbal formula which subdues the invoked spirit of the ailment. Joshua Trachtenberg believes that by the Middle Ages (roughly AD 330 to 1300) Jewish magic was entirely free of Satanic elements, and demons appear as evil influences to be fought off, not as agents of magicians.[22]

Protective magical powers are often described in the Talmud.[23] One of the most interesting and instructive statements is found in the tractate Sabbath 61 and concerns amulets (Hebrew *qemī 'ot*, קמיעות). We are told that a person is not to go forth carrying an amulet that is not obtained from an expert. Such an amulet is one that has cured on three occasions or has been issued by an expert magician. Hence, proven performance is an important key and one which presupposes widespread use of the magical art.

As to why the rabbis permitted such activity to exist when it had been so resoundingly forbidden in the Torah, Saul Liebermann has said: "The Babylonian Rabbis...kept the rule that there is no need to fight the superstition of the people when it is possible to transform it into true religion...The Rabbis did their utmost to combat superstitions which were forbidden by the Written Law, to eliminate the magic which smacked of idolatry, but they had to accept those charms which were sanctioned by the 'scientists' of that time."[24]

Furthermore, the rabbis well understood the basic human need for any little bit of psychological security — especially in particularly oppressive times, as the years following AD 70 proved to be. This is confirmed in an insightful statement found in the Babylonian Talmud, tractate Pesahim 110b: "When one is concerned about demons, the demons concern themselves with that person, but if one is not concerned

---

21 *The Catholic Encyclopedia*, s.v. "Occult Art, Occultism."

22 Joshua Trachtenberg, *The Devil and the Jews* (Philadelphia: The Jewish Publication Society of America, 1983), 59.

23 See Rabbi Manual Gold in Schrire, *Hebrew Magic Amulets*, v.

24 Saul Liebermann, *Greek in Jewish Palestine* (New York: Jewish Theological Seminary, 1941), 103, 110.

about demons, then the demons are not concerned with that person. In any event one must be cautious."

Among almost all Jews, Hebrew carried special power and thus gave extra authority to magic formulae. The Talmud speaks of the special status of Hebrew. It was the original language of sacred scripture. It was God's language (a concept accepted by many Christians as well). It was the holy tongue. Tractate Abodah Zarah 44b reports: "Abaye said 'It is permitted to discuss secular subjects in the holy tongue but it is forbidden to discuss holy subjects in the vernacular.'"

Talmudic rabbis used the Hebrew language as a device by which to compare humankind to heavenly beings. Hebrew was believed to be the sole language understood by angels (see Sotah 33a). Hagigah 16a tells us that one of the three ways men and angels are alike is the capacity of both to speak "the holy tongue."

The belief in the monolingual nature of angels was used to explain why Aramaic prayers are found in Jewish ritual; namely, rituals were couched in Aramaic so as to remain purposely unintelligible to angels and not annoy or arouse them.[25] More importantly, the belief in Hebrew as the official language of God, Heaven, and angels "made necessary the bestowal of a Hebrew name upon every Jew, in addition to his secular name, and the use exclusively of the Hebrew name in the course of a religious rite, for the angels certainly could not be expected to recognize an individual by any other."[26] By extension, to call upon the celestial court (especially angels) for special help — healing, protection, or whatever — by any means other than Hebrew would be futile.

The rabbinic approach to supernatural protection centered on the power of language. The magic described in the Talmud depended largely upon the potency possessed by the words of an incantation or phrase.[27] The forces inherent in written words — particularly *shemoth* or names — was especially powerful.[28] Eventually even the individual letters of the Hebrew alphabet came to be regarded as possessing viable, creative power. This principle is confirmed in the *Zohar*: "The world was created by the help of the Hebrew letters." A similar thought is expressed in the Jewish text, *Sefer Yetzirah*: "He [God] created His Universe by three

---

25 Joshua Trachtenberg, *Jewish Magic and Superstition* (New York: Behrman's Jewish Book House Publishers, 1939), 74.

26 Ibid.

27 Ibid., 88.

28 Schrire, *Hebrew Magic Amulets*, 9.

forms of expression, numbers, letters, and words."[29] It is little wonder then that the Hebrew language was considered an especially effective magical medium.

The popularity of Hebrew as the prime language for supernatural rites can be seen among almost all non-Jewish sorcerers from late antiquity through Talmudic times. Because Hebrew was an exotic and unintelligible tongue it was capable of lending extra power and effectiveness to existing religious devotions.[30] This is apparent from a variety of sources. For example, magicians of the synchronistic Hellenistic period favored words and names from the Hebrew language, as is evident from magical papyri dated to this period.[31] This tradition was even manifest later among Moslem magicians and practitioners in an interesting way. "Since the Jewish population in Arab lands have resided there for many centuries and since the Arabs themselves are known to be great believers in the efficacy of amulets, this characteristic being known from time immemorial, it is not surprising that amulets with inscriptions both in Arabic and in Hebrew should be found."[32]

Christian Veneration of Hebrew

Against the backdrop of this environment we may now consider in greater detail Christian use of Hebrew as the language of magic. From a very early time in their history many Christians believed that the Jews were, among other things, a people possessing special mystical or supernatural powers — especially the powers of healing and protection.[33] Goodenough and Simon indicate that Jewish magic is characterized by three features: first, a great respect for Hebrew phrases; second, a belief in the power of special names which, when invoked, would bring desired

---

29   Zohar 1:204, II:411; and in Rabbi Akiba ben Joseph, *The Book of Formation (Sepher Yetzirah)*, ed. and trans. Knut Stenring, (London, 1923), 21. This became a popular "handbook" for Jewish amulet makers.

30   Trachtenberg, *Devil and the Jews*, 61. For Coptic evidence see W. H. Worrell, "A Coptic Wizard's Hoard," *American Journal of Semitic Languages* 46 (1929–30): 239–62.

31   Karl L. Preisendanz, ed., *Papyri graecae magicae*, 2 vols. (Leipzig: B. G. Teubner, 1928). This point is also driven home by Thorndike, *History of Magic and Experimental Science* 1:450, "It is even possible for persons who are not true Christians to make use of the name of Jesus to work wonders just as magicians use the Hebrew names."

32   Schrire, *Hebrew Magic Amulets*, 72.

33   For instance, one Jewish sect during the intertestamental period, the Essenes living at Qumran (circa 140 BC – AD 68), were known for performing healings as part of their cadre of religious practices.

results; and third an overwhelming regard for angels and demons which could, respectively, intercede or interfere in one's life.[34]

All three of these features fit into the theological framework of early Christianity. Hence, while sorcery was condemned in the Apostolic and post-Apostolic Church,[35] some Christians perpetually turned to the magic of the Jews and held the Hebrew language in special repute as a key to unlock extraordinary powers of the supernatural world. Of this we have many interesting examples.

We read of those Christians in the second century who, submitting themselves "to the incantations of a Jew" to cure gout, were chided by Lucius of Samosate.[36] One is almost certainly correct in assuming that at least a share of such "incantations" were performed in Hebrew owing to the comments of Origen, as well as those found in the Talmud (to which we have made reference). Origen, who boasted a wide knowledge of Hebrew literature, testifies that this kind of adjuration of demons or spirits was specifically "Jewish" and that such adjurations and incantations *had to be made in Hebrew*.[37] Among some Christians it was believed that Hebrew words themselves conveyed power, and if they were "translated into another language they [would] lose their operative force."[38]

However this was not universally true. From documents of the late Roman world we learn that the power behind mere mention of the Hebrew language in general in demonic adjurations and incantations was recognized.[39] In other words, instead of performing elaborate

---

34   Erwin R. Goodenough, *Jewish Symbols in the Greco-Roman Period*, 13 vols. (Princeton: Princeton University Press, 1968), 2:161 ff. See also Marcel Simon, *Versus Israel, Etude sur les relations entre chrétiens et juifs dans l'empire romain* (Paris: E. De Boccard, 1964), 407.

35   See Acts, 13:10 (the magician Bar-Jesus is called an enemy of all righteousness); Gal. 5:19-21 and 2 Tim. 3:8 (sorcery is comparable to immorality and idolatry); and Rev. 9:21, 18:23, 21:8, 22:15 (sorcerers are on the same plane as liars and murderers).

36   Theodore Reinach, *Textes d'auteurs grecs et romains relatifs au Judaisme* (Paris: E. Leroux, 1895), 165.

37   J. P. Migne, ed., *Patrologiae cursus completes, Series graeca*, 161 vols. (Paris, 1844-1964), 13:1757. See Origen's "Commentary on Matthew," xxvi, 63. Also Lynn Thorndike, *A History of Magic and Experimental Science*, 1:437 and Trachtenberg, *Devil and the Jews*, 229 note 7.

38   Lynn Thorndike, *A History of Magic and Experimental Science*, 6 vols. (New York: Columbia University Press, 1964), 1:450.

39   Robert Wilken, *John Chrysostom and the Jews* (Berkeley: University of California Press, 1983), 85. Also Judah Goldin, "The Magic of Magic and Superstition," in *Aspects of Religious Propaganda in Judaism and Early Christianity*, ed. Elisabeth Schüssler Fiorenza (Notre Dame: University of Notre Dame Press, 1976), 123-24.

rites in Hebrew, sometimes simple reference to the language itself, as an independent force of great efficacy, was enough to accomplish the task. Hence, the phrase "I exorcise you in the Hebrew language,"[40] was a familiar magical formula of early medieval times.

A Coptic Text

One of the most interesting attestations of this theme is found among the magical papyri of what appears to have been "the humble literary stock of a Coptic magician."[41] The text is an apparent adaptation from Judaism made by a Coptic Christian, though it purports to have been made by Sethian Gnostics. It is preserved only in seventh century (or later) Coptic copies. Explicit stress is laid upon the special and potent power of the Hebrew language in general — "the language of heaven" — as a magical tool. The complete text is quite long. We quote several lines to present the context of the significant parts, noted in italics, relevant to our study:

> O God, O Lord, O Lord, O Omnipotent
>
> Whose body is the color of fire
>
> Who is light in the hidden
>
> Whose name no flesh-born man knoweth
>
> Save only himself...
>
> Perform for me every labor pertaining to this spell
>
> And every operation which I shall undertake...
>
> Give ear to our authority...
>
> All your ministrants who are proclaimed by those all above them
>
> And these great archangels which are great in their power
>
> These whose names were first announced to them
>
> Namely: the angels that call all the appellations that are *written in Hebrew, in the language of heaven*
>
> That they give ear to every man who shall perform in purity, and chastity of deed
>
> I am Seth the son of Adam
>
> I have purified myself forty days

---

40   Preisendanz, *Papyri graecae magicae*, 1:38.
41   Worrell, "A Coptic Wizard's Hoard," 239.

Till its power (i.e., the power of the spell) is manifest

And the *power of its Hebrew and all its executions*

That it may assist in every task which I shall undertake[42]

The text continues for many lines in the same general vein but finally ends with what the text's modern translator, W. H. Worell, calls "a terrible ragout of Gnostic invocation, no longer understood by anyone."[43] Though they are called Hebrew magic formulae in the text, Worrell believes they could not have been pronounced but were "pure hocus pocus to the magician [though] he calls it Hebrew."[44]

Actually, among this series of unusual "magic" syllables we find some genuinely Semitic terms (Hebrew and Aramaic).[45] For example, ΜΑΡ is probably from Aramaic *mār*, "lord." The syllable ΕΛ, *ēl*, is the common ending for names of angels and the general Hebrew (as well as Semitic) term for God. Likewise ΒΠΛ, *bēl*, is the Hebrew term for a foreign deity (see Isa. 46:1). Also included are ΡΑΒ, *rab*, Hebrew and Aramaic for "great"; ΙΑω, *Iaō*, is the shortened Hebrew form for Yahweh or Lord; ΑΔΟΝΠ ΕΛωΕΙ is the Hebrew *adōnāi elōhāi* for "my Lord, my God"; ΒΑCΠΜ represents the Hebrew *bash-shēm*, meaning "in the Name [of God]"; CΑΒΑωΘ is the translated Hebrew word, *saba'oth* meaning "[Lord of] hosts"; and ΑΒΟΥΠΛ, *Abouēl* represents the Hebrew word for "God-Father."[46] A series of other vowel combinations are found (ΙΠ, ΕΙΕ, ΑΙ, etc.) and look suspiciously like permutations of the Divine Name ΙΑω, *Iaō*, for Yahweh. Of significance is the fact that these terms were thought to convey extra special power in and of themselves, and add one more witness to the special place accorded Hebrew in magic spells.

This Coptic text harmonizes with other evidence that shows that several Hebrew words were regarded by Christians and Jews alike as effective purveyors of magical forces derived from the Bible. (Bibliomancy was a form of magic found among many people holding a belief in sacred scripture.)[47] This Coptic Text also shows that since traditional opinion among Jews and Christians held that because the Old Testament (Hebrew Bible) was God-given, and thus words and sentences

---

42 Ibid., 255, 256.

43 Ibid., 255.

44 Ibid.

45 Ibid., 262, a list made by Worrell. The Coptic terms have been copied in their own script.

46 Worrell sees ΑΟΥΗΛ as an Arabic-Hebrew combination, "A Coptic Wizard's Hoard," 262. Goodenough treats it as Hebrew in *Jewish Symbols*, 2:166.

47 Goldin, "Magic of Magic and Superstition," 123-24.

of scripture derived their magical power directly from the Divine Source, it was not even necessary to make use of whole sentences; abbreviations became common and were considered to be quite effective.[48]

In particular, the use of the terms *Iaō* and *Adōnāi* are noteworthy carriers of magical power, especially among certain Gnostic-like sects; *Iaō*, being a transliteration of the shortened form of the Hebrew Yahweh, and *Adōnāi* being the Hebrew word for Lord as we saw above. In his discussion on Christian magical charms Erwin Goodenough mentions this phenomenon, noting that where Christian elements in these medieval incantations are slight, such elements are recognizable intrusions or additions to formulas which "…appear to be very old Jewish forms."[49]

A Syriac Text

One such formula, written in Syriac (Eastern Aramaic), opens with an invocation of the Trinity, goes on to quote the introductory verses of the Gospel of John and then changes to what Goodenough calls "a purely Jewish invocation."[50] The last portion reads:

> By the power of those ten holy words of the Lord God, by the Name, I am that I am, God Almighty, Adonai, Lord of Hosts, I bind, excommunicate, and destroy, I ward off, cause to vanish, all evil, accursed, and maddening pains and sicknesses, adversaries, demons, rebellious devils, also the spirits of lunacy, the spirit of the stomach, the spirits of the heart, the spirits of the head, the spirits of the eyes, the ills of the stomach, the spirit of the teeth, also the evil and envious eye, the eye that smiteth and pitieth not, the green coloured eye, the eye of every kind, the eye of all spirits of pain in the head, pain on one side of the head, sweet and soft (doleful) pulsations, seventy-two such sweet and mournful noises, also the fever, cold and hot, visions fearful and false dreams, as are by night and by day also Lilith, Malvita, and Zarduch, the dissembling (or "compelling") demon, and all evil pains, sicknesses, and devils, bound by spell, from off the body and soul, the house, the sons and daughters of him who beareth these writs, Amen, Amen![51]

---

48 Schrire, *Hebrew Magic Amulets*, 100-03.
49 Goodenough, *Jewish Symbols*, 2:164.
50 Ibid.
51 Goodenough, *Jewish Symbols*, 2:164.

Some of the elements of this invocation are recognizable. The opening phrase, which summons the "power of those ten holy words of Lord God," possibly has reference to the ten commandments issued on Mount Sinai. However, it seems more likely that the phrase is alluding to the ten attributes of God or ten *sefiroth* (signs, manifestations) by which deity reveals himself and through which his creative power is manifest.[52] This is a mystical concept which plays a major role in Kabbalistic doctrine.

In Kabbalah the *sefiroth* are known as ten holy words of power, which are their names. They form layers of divine power[53] and are "the names which He [God] gave to himself."[54] By invoking them in his spell, the magician is simply adding one more set of divine names and words of power to his incantation in order to achieve his purposes. This is a standard principle of medieval Christian magic. One can and should use as many of the most effective words of power as possible. In this charm, of course, Christian forms are simply added to existing Jewish ones.

The next phrase "by the Name, I am that I am" simply denotes one of the divine names which God revealed to Moses as recorded in Exodus 3:13–15. We need to remember that from Old Testament times on, the names of God were thought to carry special power.[55] In the Middle Ages, out of concerns for brevity and the sanctity of the names of God, the abridged phrase "in the name" (Hebrew *bash-shēm*) or "by the name" was often used in texts to infer that the power of the divine name was being invoked without having to repeat the rest of the phrase "I am that I am." We see this formula, for example, in the list of those Hebrew magic terms at the end of the seventh century Coptic-Gnostic text discussed above. It is also typical of Jewish amulets which often begin with the invocation "in the name of...". In the present Syriac text, however, the entire phrase "in the name, I am that I am" is used.

Some of the most fascinating elements of this charm are those terms not so readily recognized, such as "Lilith," Malvita," and "Zarduk." These constitute specific Hebrew names of demons which sometimes appear in Jewish magical and healing texts and in Christian incantations

---

52 *Encyclopedia Judaica*, 1972 ed., s.v. "Kabbalah" by Gershom Scholem. See especially the section "Sefirot" cols. 563–79. For a more detailed discussion in the whole context of mysticism see Gershom G. Scholem, *Major Trends in Jewish Mysticism* (New York: Schocken Books, 1961), 212–22 and passim.

53 Scholem, *Jewish Mysticism*, 214.

54 Ibid., 215-16.

55 *Interpreter's Dictionary of the Bible*, 1962 ed., s.v. "God, Names of" by B. W. Anderson.

displaying heavy Jewish influence. They derive from Jewish Midrashic literature.[56]

Lilith (Hebrew, לילית) is one of the best known of these evil spirits. The popular derivation of the name, which gives us a clue as to the nature of this demon in Jewish tradition, held the term to be from the Hebrew root-word for night (*Layil*, ליל) with a feminine adjectival suffix *ith*. The concept of Lilith becomes more fully developed in post-biblical and medieval times. According to the later rabbis this "nocturnal spectre," in the form of a beautiful woman, lay in wait for victims (especially children) at night.[57] The Talmud (Sabbath 151b) issues a precaution that can be taken in order to deflect and obstruct the evil activities of Lilith: one is to refrain from sleeping in a house alone.

Lilith's connection to the night-time is further elaborated in the Zohar[58] where we learn that she is the mother of all demons and was Adam's first wife for 130 years. Because she demanded certain rights, was refused them by Adam, she pronounced God's Ineffable name and retreated to her own kingdom near the Dead Sea where she established her abode and mated with other demons. The creation of Eve and the happy union between her and Adam aroused in Lilith feelings of jealousy and spite and thus she has been plaguing Adam's posterity ever since. She appears to the sons of man in their dreams and causes them to have nocturnal emissions from which other spectres — *lillin* — are produced so that the propagation of the demonic species is continued and ensured by the union of spirits with mortal men while they are sleeping.[59] Since nocturnal emissions are a source of ritual or ceremonial defilement (according to rabbinic interpretation of Lev. 15:2) such tradition may be a way of obviating some of the personal responsibility and guilt felt by strict observers of Jewish ritual.

While it is unlikely that many Christians were familiar with the details of the Jewish traditions surrounding Lilith, it is certain that they knew of the numerous malevolent demons and spirits of Jewish tradition which were bent on afflicting and tormenting mankind. The overall

---

56   See Schrire, *Hebrew Magic Amulets*, 112-20, which is a concise discussion on Midrashic *Shemoth*.

57   For the popular etymology see Samuel P. Tregelles, trans., *Gesenius' Hebrew and Chaldee Lexicon* (Grand Rapids: Wm. B. Eerdman Publishing Co., 1974), 438. The more recent scholarly view is found in *Interpreter's Dictionary of the Bible*, 1962 ed. s.v. "Lilith" by T. H. Gaster.

58   The *Zohar* or "Book of Splendor" is the greatest thirteenth century work of Jewish mysticism and Kabbalistic doctrine written sometime after 1275.

59   See Schrire's discussion in *Hebrew Magic Amulets*, 114–17.

intent of this Syriac text which we have been discussing is quite clear. It aims at providing its owner or recipient with physical *and* psychological protection by warding off any and all dangers and banishing or even destroying those evil spirits and demonic forces which may be the cause of pains and bodily ills. It is only natural that they be intimately connected with magic texts using the special power of Hebrew words and phrases. After all, the Talmud itself explains to us that demons, like angels, speak Hebrew (see Hagigah 16a).

Christian Amulets

Syriac amulets used in protective and healing magic have been found in the Christian city of Antioch dating from the fifth and sixth centuries. In John Chrysostom's time (c.a. 347-407) we know that Christians were wearing gospel texts around their necks, encased in small boxes as good-luck charms. They used amulets and charms to ward off demons, to protect themselves from harm, and to heal their ills.[60] Chrysostom, church father and patriarch of Constantinople, held a strong disdain for Judaizing Christians as well as for Jewish magic and the Hebrew language due, in part, to its connection with that magic. Yet, the Christians of Antioch continued to visit the Jews and practice their magic because, as even Chrysostom admits, Christians were being healed.[61]

It may be added in passing that this same kind of circumstance (Christians putting more stock in Jewish healers than Christian ones) continued throughout the Middle Ages. A tale of Franco Sacchetti, a friend of Boccaccio (d. 1375), about two women swindled by a Jewish peddler of fertility potions, ends with the remark: "It is remarkable that Christians, men and women, will put more trust in one Jew than in one hundred Christians, yet will repose no trust at all in a single Christian."[62] In a similar story he repeats the claim: "It is something new, to seek healing in Jewish machinations. It happens quite often nowadays that one trusts a single Jew more than a thousand Christians."[63] In fact Sacchetti was wrong—it was nothing new at all, as Chrysostom would have told him.

An important example of Hebraic influence on Syriac Christian magic comes from a medieval charm which is clearly attributable to

---

60 Wilkin, *Chrysostom and the Jews*, 84.

61 They ran to the Jews to be healed by charms, incantations and amulets and were healed. Migne, *Patrologia graeca*, 47:935, 937–38.

62 Quoted in Trachtenberg, *Devil and the Jews*, 94.

63 Ibid.

Christian authorship.[64] It opens with an invocation of Christ and an appeal to the Trinity, but with Kabbalistic overtones: "Through the power of the Lord Jesus Christ....By the power of these ten holy words of the glorious Godhead..." The Jewish influence is unmistakable, as is the special role and influence of Hebrew in this magical text. It invites special power to attend the practitioner by invoking the "ten holy words," a Jewish Kabbalistic phrase we have encountered before, but not of God but of the Godhead. And something new is introduced—*Shaddai* or *El Shaddai* (Hebrew, "Almighty" or "God Almighty").[65] This is a common Hebrew epithet for deity and was thought to be especially effective in Jewish magic formulae, though here it is included with names of strictly Christian importance:

> By the power of these ten holy words of the glorious Godhead, and in the name [of] אהיה אשר אהיה ["I am that I am"], *El-Shaddai, Adonai,* Lord *Sabāôth* [and] by the power and by the command of the Lord Jesus Christ, I bind and I expel and I objurgate the evil and bewitching eye...and I bind wounds [?and] the stroke of rupture and all sicknesses, and all diseases and all plagues...of demons and of rebellious devils and satans...by the prayer of my lady, Mary the blessed, and of Mar John the Baptist, and of Rabban Phetion, greatest of masters, and of Mar Abd-Ishu'...[66]

Undoubtedly it was the author's intention to strengthen the force of this magic spell or incantation by connecting the godhead with those Hebrew names for deity found in the Old Testament as well as Kabbalah. A collection of similar magical texts shows a number of such phenomena.[67]

European Evidence

Christian interest in Hebrew as the language of magic was not localized nor was the Christian use of Hebrew words and expressions restricted to Syriac or Coptic texts. There exists a peculiar set of what has been termed

64   Willis H. Hazard, "A Syriac Charm," *Journal of the American Oriental Society* 15 (1893): 284–96.

65   Hazard, "A Syriac Charm," 285; See Trachtenberg, "Jewish Magic," 158.

66   Hazard, "A Syriac Charm," 285–86. Mar Abd-Ishu', "the anchorite and monk of God" was evidently the author of this charm. Several lines later he again testifies to how thoroughly Jewish tradition was bound up with magic when he says an evil spirit appeared to him by the name of *Lilitha*!

67   Goodenough, *Jewish Symbols*, 164.

"semi-magical documents" originating in the British Isles, written in Latin, and dating from the sixth and seventh centuries.[68] There are also a few magical formulae dating to about the ninth or tenth century from England which exhibit Hebrew elements. These compositions are referred to by scholars as "Hisperic Literature."[69] They tend to show us the rather widespread and continuing belief that Hebrew, above all others, was the language of magical power.

In the late eleventh to early twelfth century, Archbishop Gerard of York had a definite interest in Hebrew. He was found to be the owner of at least two Hebrew psalters. But the focus of his interest is fascinating. Aside from any theological concerns, Gerard enjoyed a reputation for the practice of magical arts, as well as for learning.[70] In the eleventh century it was established among churchmen that Hebrew letters might be used for casting spells.[71] It seems that the Archbishop's interest in the language was due to quasi-magical fascination rather than pure biblical studies.

Along these lines we have the curious confession of a Westphalian priest, Johannes of Scheven, who authored a manuscript entitled *Margarita exorcistarum*. Unfortunately the only copy of this was destroyed in World War II. However, Bernhard Bischoff has commented on part of its contents.[72] Johannes reported that he took some Hebrew lessons from a Jew in order to pronounce correctly—in his exorcisms— the names of the tormenting demons, that names mainly sounded Hebrew. Whether or not the names were, in fact, Hebrew is of little matter to us. What is significant is the association of the Hebrew language with demons and magical rites that was so prevalent in the Middle Ages.

Magic was a preoccupation of the age. "The revival of classical learning and of humanistic studies in the twelfth and thirteenth centuries were accompanied by an unparalleled and almost universal addiction to magic."[73] The fact that Hebrew was regarded by some Christians of the High Middle Ages (12th–14th centuries) as a key to unlocking the most potent forces and powers of magic is attested by a number of late

---

68   Singer, "Hebrew Scholarship in the Middle Ages," 286-87.

69   Ibid., 287.

70   Raphael Loewe, "The Medieval Christian Hebraists of England: Herbert of Basham and Earlier Scholars," *Transactions of the Jewish Historical Society of England* 17 (1953): 234.

71   Smalley, *Study of the Bible*, 81.

72   Bernhard Bischoff, "The Study of Foreign Languages in the Middle Ages," *Speculum* 36 (1961): 209.

73   Trachtenberg, *Devil and the Jews*, 59.

medieval amulets which were formerly thought to be of Jewish origin, for Jewish use, because of their Hebrew inscriptions, but which are now known to have been exclusively for and, in some cases, by Christians.[74]

Amulets, in general, have a long and varied history. They have been found in increasing numbers from Neolithic times on, and have always had as their primary objective the influencing of the course of events by the occult control of nature or the protection of the wearer against evil or the Evil Eye (a phenomenon going back to the Egyptians and Sumerians of the Bronze Age).[75]

During the later Middle Ages the reputation of Jews as manufacturers and peddlers of magic amulets was widespread, so much so that it had become satirized by the time of Martin Luther, as evidenced from an anecdote recounted by the Reformer himself: "A Jew brought to Count Albrecht of Saxony an amulet which would make him immune to all weapons of attack; Albrecht forced the Jew to take his own medicine: to test the efficacy of the amulet he hung it about his owner's neck and ran him through with his sword."[76] Such a story, whether true or not, implicitly testifies of the continued importance attached to the use of magic by Christians.

In the late medieval period the Jewish *mezuzah* (Hebrew, "doorpost") was regarded as a magical device by Christians — being both an object of suspicion and desire. The *mezuzah*, of course, is a small container holding four passages of the Hebrew Bible written on parchment and attached to the doorposts of Jewish dwellings.[77] Though many argue that to consider the mezuzah — an object of profound religious veneration — in the same breath with amulets and articles of magical potency is sacrilege, we have evidence that it was regarded as an object of supernatural power by both some medieval Jews and Christians.[78] In the thirteenth century Jews of the Rhineland had to cover or hide their *mezuzoth* because, as one contemporary writer reported, "The Christians out of malice and to annoy us stick knives into the *mezuzah* openings and cut up the parchment."[79] Though the author blames this action on the desires of Christians to annoy the Jews, one suspects that it was motivated, at least

---

74   Ibid., 61.

75   See the general discussion in E. A. Wallis Budge, *Amulets and Talismans* (New York: Collier Books, 1970), 1–27.

76   Martin Luther, *Werke* (Erlangen, 1854), LXII, 375.

77   *Encyclopedia Judaica*, 1972 ed., s.v. "Mezuzah" by Louis T. Rabinowitz.

78   Trachtenberg, *Jewish Magic*, 146.

79   Trachtenberg, *Devil and the Jews*, 91.

in part, by a desire to weaken or destroy the magical powers believed to be inherent in the *mezuzah* Hebrew texts, themselves.

On the other hand, some medieval Christians respected this Jewish symbol as a receptacle of desirable supernatural power, as attested by other evidence. For example, toward the end of the fourteenth century the Archbishop of Salzburg asked a Jew to give him a *mezuzah* to attach to the gate of his castle. Upon checking rabbinic authority, however, the request was refused by the Jew. In the fifteenth century Christians were encouraged by a certain writer to attach a *mezuzah* to their doorpost for magical protection.[80] The Hebrew writing contained within the *mezuzah* was in large part regarded as being responsible for this power. Among Jews the *mezuzah* was intended to be a constant reminder of the Divine Presence. This aspect of its usage was not lost on Christians seeking the protection and watchful care of forces from another world. Some Christians seem to have regarded the *mezuzah* as another kind of amulet.

The King Solomon Connection

Tradition reports that King Solomon himself was a powerful and wise magician who was in possession of the Ineffable Name—the single greatest Hebrew name of God.[81] In Jewish religious thought and lore the Ineffable Name held tremendous power, enabling its possessor (and utterer) to exercise great supernatural control over man and, indeed, all of creation. The general belief in the magical efficacy of that proper name became dominant as early as the first millennium BC in Canaan.[82] Layers of Jewish tradition strengthened and expanded this notion to include a firm belief in the tremendous power of all the written names of God, of angels, and of various biblical quotations. This formed the basis for the mystics' faith in the power of words and specific words of power.

According to Jewish mystical beliefs it was by means of the power of the Ineffable Name Solomon erected the Temple in Jerusalem, could understand the language of all animals, and acquired his all-comprehensive wisdom. This name was passed down as a secret rite to

---

80 These two episodes are from Moses ben Eliezer, *Sefer Hasidim Tinyana* (Piotrkov, 1910), 7a. Recounted in Schrire, *Hebrew Magic Amulets*, 71.

81 Thorndike, *Magic and Experimental Science*, 2:279–89; Trachtenberg, *Devil and the Jews*, 63–64; and Goodenough, *Jewish Symbols*, 2:227–35. Goodenough adds new insights.

82 For an excellent brief discussion on the Divine Name (יהוה), the loss of the correct pronunciation, and its relationship to magic, see Elias Bickerman, *From Ezra to the Last of the Maccabees* (New York: Schocken Books, 1975), 65–71.

those priests serving the Temple, but was uttered only once a year by the High Priest officiating in the Holy of Holies on *Yom Kippur* (the Day of Atonement). As the name was lost after AD 70 (the final destruction of the Second Temple), a meticulous and ongoing search of ancient literature and mystical tradition was carried out in order to re-capture the Ineffable name or at least find satisfactory substitutes to re-garner the greater powers and supernatural forces once held by Solomon and others. The Solomonic legends exerted a strong influence over the medieval Christian imagination precisely because the age seemed to be preoccupied with magical concerns and Solomon had been regarded as the archetypal magician since late Roman-Christian times, as artifacts and literature from late antiquity and the medieval period attest.[83]

We have already mentioned Origen who, in his "Commentary on Matthew," asserted that Jews were adept in the adjuration of demons and employed charms in the Hebrew language drawn from the books of Solomon.[84] Perhaps some of the more interesting evidence connecting King Solomon to magical power is found in the form of early medieval Christian amulets which either mention the name of Solomon or depict him as a warrior, sometimes mounted, sometimes without a horse. The inscription on one such amulet written in Hebrew reads: "Seal of the living God, guard him who wears this, Holy, holy, holy, Lord Sabaoth, heaven and earth are full of thy glory." On the reverse side, "Get out, hated one. Araaph the angel and Solomon drive you away from him who wears this."[85]

Often such amulets bear formulas which are entirely Hebraic except for square crosses commonly found on one side. Thus, "a new religion may take over the old magic, signs, names, mottoes; the Christian wanted to keep what was effective in the old age, but to add the new Christian potency to it."[86] Certainly this is true regarding special Hebrew words and names. In fact, the legends regarding Solomon as foremost magician seem to be a far more important feature of Christian rather than Jewish medieval magic.

Solomon played only a minor role in Jewish magic of the period. Certain conjuring books ascribed to Solomon by the church were condemned by the recognized authorities of rabbinic Judaism.[87] Hence,

---

83 Thorndike, *Magic and Experimental Science*, 2:279.

84 Migne, *Patrologia graeca*, 13:1757.

85 Goodenough, *Jewish Symbols*, 2:231.

86 Ibid.

87 Trachtenberg, *Devil and the Jews*, 231 note 16.

as the regard for "Solomon the Magician" seems to have decreased in Jewish thought his status increased in Christian thinking during the Middle Ages. Solomonic legends possessed two main elements: the wise monarch's dominion over devil and demons and his utilization of this power for magical ends. This latter theme was so highly developed with different kinds of variations that Solomon came to be regarded both as the archetypical sorcerer and the originator of occult science. "So deeply did the belief in [Solomon's] magical supremacy enter into medieval thought that nothing more was required to authenticate the worth of a formula or an amulet than to trace it to him, and the most popular magical works drew their authority from his reputation."[88]

In this regard Peter Comestor (d. 1179), biblical scholar, Dean of the Notre Dame Cathedral at Troyes, and teacher at the University of Paris, authored one of the most popular Christian books of the Middle Ages. Entitled *Historia Scholastica* (though the twelfth century masters called it simply *The Histories*), the work was a great "summary of biblical history."[89] In it Comestor ascribes *all* the magic and magical paraphernalia of his own time to Solomon. This is particularly significant in light of Comestor's own interest in Hebrew as well as the interest in biblical studies that his *Histories* helped to generate among Stephen Langton and others.[90]

Two Oxford manuscript copies of the work display a knowledge of Hebrew on the part of their owners and/or glossators. One of the copies, which early-on belonged to the Dominican Friars, had in it a Hebrew text of the description of the porch of Solomon's Temple.[91]

Other medieval Christian magical compositions also regarded King Solomon as the foremost magician of the ages. The "Golden Flowers of Apollonius," an early fourteenth century mystical work, for example, mentions Solomon in almost every other sentence.[92] A treatise on palmistry is attributed to him, as is a composition entitled "Philosophy of Solomon" in a late twelfth century text.[93] Certain other magical and semi-magical works are ascribed to Solomon in medieval manuscripts. By far the most interesting work of this category, which not only informs us about medieval magic but the use of Hebrew as a tool of that art, is the *Liber Sacratus*, as William of Auvergne (d. 1249) entitled it, or *Liber sacer*

88 Ibid., 63.
89 Smalley, *Study of the Bible*, 178–79.
90 Ibid., 178–82, 199.
91 Ibid., 339.
92 Thorndike, *Magic and Experimental Science*, 2:282.
93 Ibid.

or *Liber juratus* as it is also called in different manuscripts.[94] It is a work immediately associated with the name of Solomon.

The preface of *Liber Sacratus*, as it is found in a fourteenth century Latin edition, denigrates the pope and cardinals as themselves being under the influence of *evil* spirits when they passed a decree condemning the magic arts and magicians because magicians and necromancers injure everyone, transgress the statutes of the Holy Mother Church, and make innovations and sacrifices to demons. *Liber Sacratus* denies the latter charges, argues that only pure men can work by the magic arts and compel spirits against their will, and then recounts something of the story behind *Liber Sacratus*.[95]

Accordingly, an assembly of 89 masters of the magical arts from Naples, Athens, Toledo, and elsewhere chose one Honorius to reduce all their magic books (going all the way back to Solomon) to one volume, which could be more readily concealed and preserved. The followers of the magic arts then took an oath not to give this volume to anyone until its owner was on his death-bed, never to have more than three copies of it in existence at one time, and never allow it to pass into the hands of those who were not of proven maturity and fidelity. Each new recipient of the sacred volume was to take this oath; hence the name *juratus* (from the Latin *jurare* "to swear"). Its other titles *Sacer* or *Sacratus* most probably refer to the sacred names of God which make up a good portion of the actual text. After the presentation of introductory material, the work itself opens with the first statement of its author or editor: "In the name of almighty God and Jesus Christ, one and true God, I, Honorius, have thus ordered the works of Solomon in my book."[96]

Without question, *Liber Sacratus (Juratus)* is an important Christian work on medieval magic. A manuscript copy said to have belonged to Ben Jonson[97] has the term "Theurgia" written across the flyleaves before the beginning and after the close of the text.[98] ("Theurgia" is derived from a Greek word meaning "work of divination.") But, more significantly, the text itself is full of names of spirits, prayers in strange words, and a series of letters supposedly derived from Hebrew or Chaldaic (Aramaic), as well

---

94 Ibid., 2:283–84.

95 Ibid., 2:284–85. Thorndike quotes much of the introduction of the work.

96 Ibid., 2:285.

97 Ibid., 2:284. Sloane manuscript 313 in the British Library entitled *Opus de arte magica, ba Honorio ordinatum.*

98 Thorndike, *Magic and Experimental Science*, 2:286. The manuscript is also said to have Jonson's motto inscribed on it, "Tanquam Explorator."

as other gibberish. Indeed, the first chapter deals with the composition of what is called the great 72-syllable name of God.

This latter epithet consists of seventy-two syllables, each of three Hebrew letters. The construction is based on the three verses of Exodus 14:19–21, each of which is composed of seventy-two letters. In this regard one scholar has explained that,

> The first letter of the first verse, the last letter of the second verse and the first letter of the third verse constitute the first syllable of the name. The second letter of the first verse, the penultimate letter of the second verse and the second letter of the third verse constitute the second syllable and so on until 72 syllables, each consisting of three letters are formed. The total number of letters [216] makes this name a particularly bulky and difficult one.[99]

Other items of note in the *Liber Sacratus* include the names of important and well known angels including Raphael, Michael, and others, and the names of various spirits (especially those associated with the planet Saturn), all of which have the typical Hebrew ending *el* or *iel*. By contrast, very few of the names of demons in the work end in *el* or *iel*.[100] Hence, it seems that an important psychological principle is at work. The demons are viewed as pagans and damned, while all angels and spirits with Hebrew-sounding names are viewed as good!

It is well known that the pseudo-science of astrology—made up mostly of magic with some bit of true astronomy—was an important part of the medieval world, even "the fundamental doctrine of the medieval Weltanschauung."[101] It is, therefore, not surprising to find the Hebrew language connected with astrology, as we see demonstrated in *Liber Sacratus*.

Another example of Hebrew's connection with medieval astrology occurs in a tenth century Latin manuscript dealing with "the science of astronomy,"[102] and which is full of Hebrew words written in the Hebrew script. Entitled *Mathematica Alcandrii* the text purports to be the work of one Alcandrius or Alhandreus, supreme astrologer in ancient times, who aims at treating "the order of the planets according to nature and

---

99   Schrire, *Hebrew Magic Amulets*, 98.
100   For Saturn these include *Bohel, Casziel,* and *Daedel.* See Goodenough, *Jewish Symbols,* 2:233.
101   Trachtenberg, *Devil and the Jews,* 72.
102   Thorndike, *Magic and Experimental Science,* 1:710. Also Singer, "Hebrew Scholarship," 289.

their names according to the Hebrews."[103] The twelve signs of the zodiac are given by their Hebrew and Latin names as are the Hebrew names for certain planets and constellations known to the author. The author's astrological system is largely based on the numerical values of the letters of the Hebrew alphabet, a concept which became very important to later Kabbalists.[104]

Though angelology generally seems to have played a lesser role in medieval Christian thought than in Jewish theology (the Archangel Michael being the only individual angel honored in liturgical feasts in the Church before the ninth century),[105] nevertheless the names of angels appear in Christian magical texts often in borrowed form from Judaism, as in the *Liber Sacratus*. Yigael Yadin informs us that Jewish angelology emerged as a complete and complex doctrine in the Apocrypha and Pseudepigrapha (which is to say by circa 200 BC) and reached its climax in Jewish circles in later Kabbalistic writings.[106]

We know that more than a few Christians of the Middle Ages put great stock in the occult powers possessed by angels as taught in Hebrew magical works. An anonymous Hebrew book of magic, received as authentic by Christians as well as Jews, was mentioned in the thirteenth century with regard to a formula for exorcizing demons. William of Auvergne, for example, regarded it as authoritative and said that this Hebrew work expressly stated that "one of the holy angels said the top of the heart of a certain fish placed on live coals would drive out demons from men or women."[107]

Many names of angels consist of two parts: a word depicting a particular attribute (sometimes written in Hebrew, sometimes in Aramaic or another language), plus the theophoric Hebraic element *'el* as a suffix. (The two radicals *'l* comprise the general Semitic root meaning God.) Most angels were believed to have wide ranging powers and be able to protect against a variety of troubles and difficulties. Because a number of attributes could be depicted in Hebrew adjectival form and combined with the theophoric element *'el*, innumerable hosts of heaven and innumerable powers were available by name to the supplicant or practitioner and could be used on an amulet or in an incantation. Indeed,

---

103   Thorndike, *Magic and Experimental Science*, 1:711. Also Singer, "Hebrew Scholarship," 289.

104   Singer, "Hebrew Scholarship," 289-90.

105   *New Catholic Encyclopedia*, 2007 ed., s.v. "Angels" by A. A. Bialas.

106   Yigael Yadin, *The Scroll of the War of the Sons of Light Against the Sons of Darkness* (London: Oxford University Press, 1962), 229.

107   Thorndike, *Magic and Experimental Science*, 2:363.

Hebrew magic amulets often have the names of at least one or two angels inscribed on them, in addition to whatever else is found on them.

> This was the background of thirteenth-century Jewish name-magic, which improved upon its antecedents by multiplying the number of names, both of God and of the angels, available to the enterprising sorcerer...Medieval Christendom, under the influence of the same Gnostic and Hellenistic tendencies, was equally well acquainted with the virtues and effects of name-invocation. The Hebrew names of God and of the angels...proved especially popular, undoubtedly because of their strangeness.[108]

Provence Amulet

While many names of angelic ministrants were available for supernatural invocations it is more than likely that, by the later Middle Ages, the Hebrew names of certain angels became the somewhat stock-in-trade terms of Christian occult healers and practitioners of magic. One amulet excavated from Provence, France, made of cast lead, displays the image of a bearded Jesus, and is an excellent example of Christian occult use of Jewish angelology and recognizable Hebrew formulas. On the side opposite the one bearing the image of Christ we find Hebrew writing of a distinctive quality, including the twelve-letter name of God, as well as the names of the four most commonly implored angels on magic amulets: Michael, Raphael, Gabriel, and Uriel.

This selection of names is certainly influenced by Jewish tradition. The *Zohar* lists ten classes of angels in descending order of rank.[109] The first class consists of only two angels, Metatron — the translated Enoch — and Sandalphon, who is said to have been known on earth as Elijah of fiery chariot fame. In the next highest group we find none other than the four archangels whose names appear on the Provence amulet.

Michael is the greatest of these angels. He prays for the souls of the wicked and, like Gabriel, he is a guardian of Israel. Raphael is especially called upon when health is the object of concern. Gabriel is the angel of strength, and Uriel is an angel of light (knowledge?) who is supposed to have wrestled with Jacob in one strand of Jewish thought.[110] Such a list as this gives us an idea of the forces often sought after in medieval

---

108   Trachtenberg, *Jewish Magic*, 89.
109   Schrire, *Hebrew Magic Amulets*, 104. See *Zohar* Exodus 43a.
110   Schrire, *Hebrew Magic Amulets*, 108–09.

Christian magical texts. One assumes that some care was employed by Christian magicians as to which names from among all the heavenly hosts were desired on their amulets.

The Provence amulet is one of the most distinctive dating from the Middle Ages. The side holding the image of the face of Jesus is enclosed in a pentagon-shaped border with the various Hebrew forms of the name "Jesus" (יהשוע, ישוע, ישו) placed around the border. Other Hebrew writing is placed inside the border around the image of the bearded face, but is not legible.[111] The Christian character of the amulet is beyond question, but so is the great regard for Hebrew as a facilitator of magical power which it displays.

The names of the four archangels were placed on the amulet in a configuration around the outside edges of a square, which in turn circumscribed the twelve letter name of God plus four additional lines of Hebrew writing. These lines read:[112]

In the Name (Bash-shem) of He who lives forever

בשם ש חי לעולם

The Lord God of Hosts he is Shaddai

יהוה צבאות הוא שדי

(line three undecipherable)

Father God he is

אבי יהוה הוא

Again we note the similar formulas and invocations of god as found in previous magical texts: *Bash-shem, YHWH, Shaddai* and *Sabaoth.* They, too, have become standardized formulas for Christians as well as Jews. Even the square configuration, around which the angels' names appear and inside of which the invocation is written, is not an ordinary figure but a powerful traditional symbol of magical and mystical power as well.[113]

Evidence from Africa

Sometimes the content of the text of certain amulets is so typically Jewish that it would be impossible to designate them as being for Christian use

111   See Schrire's whole discussion on "Hebrew Christian Amulets," in *Hebrew Magic Amulets,* 69–132, 144–45, 165.

112   Schrire, *Hebrew Magic Amulets,* 165 and plate numbers 42 and 43. We are given both the photographs of the amulets and Shrire's transcription.

113   On the symbol of the square see Budge, *Amulets and Talismans,* 45-46.

were it not for some unusual configuration or symbol on the amulet. Such is the case with one interesting example from Morocco where the commonly found names of Gabriel and Michael appear, as do the names *Shaddai, Yah* (for Yahweh) and *Lillin*. What makes the amulet distinctive is the cruciform image on its obverse side which circumscribes part of the text.[114] During the Middle Ages the image of a cross was abhorrent to almost every Jew.

As usual, the purpose of the amulet was to provide a special mantle of safety for its owner. To this end it invokes God, by some of his various names, as well as the angels to "protect the wearer from demons, spirits, Lillin and everything evil."[115]

Amulets similar to this Moroccan one have been found in the region of Northeastern Africa, the area known as Abyssinia. Up to the beginning of the fourth century AD, the Ethiopians were pagans, even though Hebrew traders who settled in the country brought with them their language and their Yahwist religion. In the first half of the fourth century the famous king Ezana (Greek "Aizanes") renounced paganism and made Christianity the official religion of his empire. The crescent and the star, symbols of authority, were then replaced by the Christian cross at the beginning of all inscriptions. The cross also became the first and greatest of protective symbols and amulets.[116]

Most such amulets have inscriptions written in Ge'ez, the old Ethiopic literary language of the land. But their potency derives from the special letters of the inscriptions. Wallace Budge has categorized the types of inscriptions found on these amulets.[117] Often they reveal the same Hebrew words and names seen over and over in medieval magical texts. And as with other Christian amulets, the Hebrew words often have been mingled with specifically Christian magic formulae and words of power. This pattern displays the same kind of syncretistic arrangement seen in various magical texts of the Greco-Roman and early medieval periods. Hebrew formulae could be and often were consistently added to existing religious and magical rites (whether Christian, Greek, or Egyptian) in order to supply greater potency to charms and spells in various languages.

The general categories for terms found on the Ethiopian amulets include the various names of God, e.g., Adonai, Elohim, Yah, El-Shaddai;

---

114   Schrire, *Hebrew Magic Amulets*, 72 and 145 plus plate number 7.
115   Ibid., 145.
116   Budge, *Amulets and Talismans*, 178–79.
117   Ibid., 180–81.

the names of archangels, e.g., Michael and Gabriel; the magical names of Christ; the names of the fiends and devils (sometimes recognizable from Jewish tradition) which produce sicknesses and diseases in the human body; strings of letters arranged singly or in groups of three — spells which cannot be translated; words of power thought to be used by Christ, "Asparaspes" and "Askoraskis" and those by Solomon, "Lofham" and "Mahfelon."

Like others, the Ethiopians and their descendants wore amulets for the physical benefits which they believed would come to them. Women wore amulets with inscriptions of power to give fertility and immunity from miscarriage. They expected that amulets would protect their children from the Evil eye. Men wore them for virility and strength; and both men and women expected the amulets to preserve them from attacks of demons which cause sickness and disease.[118]

It is abundantly clear that the underlying principle of protection for every soul who believed in the efficacy of incantations and charms — both Jew and Christian alike — were those words of power found inscribed on the amulet. Moses Gaster has provided us with directions which were to be followed by makers of amulets when the texts of those amulets were written on parchment. The most important aspect of the ritual to be followed by the manufacturer was the utterance of a special blessing which focused on the power of the language displayed by the amulet. Since that language was invariably Hebrew, it is only natural that Christians would associate the real power behind the amulet with the power of the Hebrew language.

> When the writer dips his pen into properly prepared ink he must say: "In the Name of Shaddai who created Heaven and Earth, I, N the son of M writes this *Kamea* [amulet] for A the son of B to heal him of every kind of fever" and he must then say the blessing of the *Kamea* as follows "Blessed are Thou O Lord who hast sanctified Thy great Name and has revealed it to Thy pious ones to show its power and might in the language, in the writing of it, and in the utterance of the mouth."[119]

Theodore Schrire has further commented on the Christian desire for the great protection afforded by amulets of the later Middle Ages written in Hebrew. He says the demand for Hebrew inscriptions on Christian

---

118 Migne, *Patrologia graeca*, 47:935–38; as did most Christians.

119 *Encyclopedia of Religion and Ethics*, 1911 ed., s.v., "Amulets, Jewish" by E. von Dobschütz.

amulets was *so great* that "they were made in vast quantities and cast in lead so that numbers of them have been unearthed from time to time."[120] Amulets of this kind were particularly made for the protection of Christian travelers leaving Europe from the ports of Southern France as crusaders or pilgrims embarking on dangerous sea-journeys to the Holy Land and elsewhere.[121]

Vilification of the Jews

The foregoing is important testimony to the great respect accorded Hebrew as *the* language of beneficial magic and supernatural power in many quarters. But not everyone in medieval society, of course, held the Hebrew language in high esteem—precisely because it was regarded as the language of magic and supernatural power! Several bits of evidence show us that in some Christian circles Hebrew was closely allied with the Devil himself. This is an extension of the belief that the Jews were the Devil's offspring or henchmen, at the very least.[122] Consequently, their language—which was clearly presumed to be Hebrew—was closely connected with Satan.

We see this reflected in various types of literature from the early Christian age onward. Beginning with the founding documents of Christianity—the New Testament Gospels—Jews are portrayed as devilish and Satanic. The very words of Jesus promoted this perception: "Ye [Jews] are of your father the devil...*When he speaketh* a lie, he speaketh *of his own*: for he is a liar, and the father of it...He that is of God heareth God's words: ye therefore hear them not, because ye are not of God" (John 8:44, 47).

Taking their cue here from what they regarded as explicit statements of well deserved condemnation, some Christians no doubt began associating the language of the Jews with the speech of the Devil (the father of lies). After all, the Jews were the children of the Devil; and children naturally speak the language of their parents.

That this kind of reasoning is not hypothetical but was actually promulgated can be seen from the fact that there have come down to us several parodies from the Middle Ages originating from Christian sources, which purport to be Jewish prayers directed to the Devil and

---

120   Schrire, *Hebrew Magic Amulets*, 71.

121   Ibid.

122   This is well documented by Trachtenberg, *Devil and the Jews*, 11–31 and throughout the work.

which mimic the Hebrew words of those prayers.[123] Also, the Jews are portrayed in certain medieval mystery plays and religious dramas as summoning their demonic compatriots in some kind of unintelligible gibberish intended to represent Hebrew.[124] The French play *Le Miracle de Théophile*, composed around 1261 by the Parisian trouvère known simply as Rutebeuf, is a case in point. A Jewish magician named Salatin attempts his Satanic conjuration in the following words:

> Bagahi laca bachahe
>
> Lamac cahi achabahe
>
> Karrelyos
>
> Lamac lamec bachalyos
>
> Cabahagi sabalyos
>
> Baryolas
>
> Lagozatha cabyolas
>
> Samahac et famyolas
>
> Harrahya.[125]

The Devil, after he has been conjured, says to Salatin, "You spoke the proper formula well—Your teacher forgot no part of the spell."[126] Thus it is implied that this supposedly Hebrew spell had been passed down from one generation of Jewish magicians to the next; and though the influence of the Hebrew language on medieval drama as a whole may have been only slight,[127] the attitude projected by certain Christian samples of that drama toward Hebrew was enough to add to Christian repulsion of the Jews.

Even the great Dante, a liberal scholar who extolled the virtues of Hebrew, may have succumbed to these influences which promoted the magical and satanic basis of the language. A couple of passages of

---

123   Ibid., 26.

124   Ibid., 61. Also, so say Richard Axton and John Stevens, eds. and trans., *Medieval French Plays* (Oxford: Basic Blackwell, 1971), 309. Sometimes Arabic is intended, as in the play "Le Jeu De Saint Nicolas." But both Arabic and Hebrew are the languages of the enemies of Christendom!

125   Cited in Axton and Stevens, *Medieval French Plays*, 175.

126   Ibid.

127   M. J. Landa, *The Jew in Drama* (New York: William Morrow and Company, 1927), 23. The author says the influence of Hebrew literature on drama, as a whole was great, that "that of the language is slight."

mysterious gibberish in *The Inferno*, the first part of his trilogy, *The Divine Comedy*, are believed to have been intended to represent Hebrew.

Pape Satan, pape Satan Aleppe (*Inferno* 7:1)

Rafel mai amech zabi et almi (*Inferno* 31:67)

According to the Jewish historian Cecil Roth, these lines disclose no satisfactory interpretation when considered as Hebrew.[128]

Montague Summers aptly expressed one of the lamentable currents of the medieval Christian ethos when he said that the Jews were persecuted not so much for the observance of their rituals and ceremonies "but for the practice of the dark and hideous traditions of Hebrew magic."[129] This is all the more saddening and ironic because some Christians had no qualms about consulting their own magicians who used Hebrew, even for the express purpose of harming the Jews — the very ones from whom they learned Hebrew and whom they accused of black magic. The *Emek Habacha (Vale of Tears)* recounts such an episode in France under Henry I (1031-1060) when certain Christians of the realm consulted with a magician in order to drive the Jews from Normandy.[130]

So ingrained was the association between magic and the Hebrew language (or anything reported to have sounded like it) in the medieval mind that its usage in spells and charms was enough to brand the users as adept magicians; and mere attempts by Christians to learn any Hebrew were regarded with suspicion in certain circles, not to mention outright fear of cavorting with Satan. Guibert, Abbot of Nogent, was much concerned about the prevalence of sorcery among the clergy of his time and laid the blame for this condition at the feet of the Jews who were in company with the Devil, the villainous Prince.[131]

Unquestionably, the hatred of the Jews, the fear of Jewish magic as Satan's tool, and the perception that Hebrew was the medium of that magic all worked to dissuade some from studying the Hebrew language or having anything whatsoever to do with it. There is no better example of how these beliefs were combined and propagated in the anti-Jewish legends of Christendom than the tale about a locket-like amulet which

---

128   Cecil Roth, *The Jews in the Renaissance* (New York: Harper & Row, Publishers, 1965), 86.

129   Montague Summers, *The History of Witchcraft and Demonology* (London, 1926), 195.

130   Harry S. May, trans., *The Vale of Tears (Emek Habacha)* (The Hague: Martinus Nijhoff, 1971), 18–19.

131   Bernard Monod, "Juifs, sorciers et Hérétiques au moyen age," *Revue des Éstudes Juives* 46 (1903): 237–245.

a Jew had provided for a Christian to calm his troublesome horse. After having worked well for many years, the amulet was finally opened, and much to the horror of those present was found to contain the following inscription in Hebrew: "The master of the horse shall belong to the devil so long as the horse stand still when it is struck."[132]

One of the fascinating ironies connected with this attitude of "Hebrew-phobia" concerns the oaths Jews were required to take before civil authorities in certain areas of Europe (parts of what later became Germany and France) during the Middle Ages, which were intended to serve as sworn depositions regarding their own as well as others' activities and loyalties. These oaths, generally known under the rubric of *more Judaico*[133] ("Jewish custom"), were really conceived by Christians as magically coercive formulae put back on the heads of those who were perceived as being the masters of sorcery. They were designed to incorporate Jewish components of magic — among them being some of the most potent Hebrew words of power — so as to bind the Jew.

Generally the Jew was required to swear by the Hebrew term for God, *Adonai*, and sometimes by "the seventy names of God" or the names of angels plus other Hebrew epithets.[134] Of note is the late fourteenth century formula from Mainz wherein a Jewish attestant was also made to swear by the law which God himself created and wrote, all the while standing "on a sow's skin [with] the five books of Master Moses [lying] before him."[135] Thus magical formulae (especially Hebrew words of power) which originated with the presumed masters of magic (the Jews) in Europe were being used to disadvantage supposed sorcerers themselves.

In the late Middle Ages the connection between evil and Hebrew — as the language of the Father of Evil — may have been brought home to certain minds in another fascinating way. Fraudulent beggars, imposters, hucksters, and riff-raff who crowded around church porches and places of pilgrimage proved a tremendous nuisance in this period. One characteristic of the argot or special jargon of this group (as well as other

---

132   Johann Jacob Schudt, *Jüdische Merckwürdigkeiten*, 4 vols. (Frankfurt und Leipzig, 1714–1718), 2:393.

133   *The Jewish Encyclopedia*, 1971 ed., s.v. "Oath More Judaico." Also Jacob R. Marcus, *The Jews in the Medieval World, A Sourcebook: 315–1791* (New York: Atheneum, 1975), 49–50.

134   Trachtenberg, *Devil and the Jews*, 69.

135   Marcus, *Jew in the Medieval World*, 50. That the requirements of this oath varied from place to place is also seen in a law of Breslau which demanded that Jews stand bareheaded and swear by the Ineffable Name—YHWH!

criminals) appears to have been a strong mixture of words derived from Hebrew.[136] Such a circumstance can hardly have engendered favorable feelings toward the Hebrew language.

The indisputable tradition of Hebrew as the predominant language of the sorcerer may help to explain, in part, the well-known medieval Christian animosity toward the Jews and their principle text, the Talmud, since it was written in Hebrew and Aramaic (which, to most Europeans, looked and sounded like one and the same). Agobard of Lyons, in his work *De judaicis superstitionibus*, said the Talmud contained magical elements.[137] In the fourteenth century, a certain Bishop of Wurzburg and some of his Christian followers who had learned something of the Talmud and its teachings were condemned since its teachings were considered nothing less than necromancy—the study which Satan aids![138] In the sixteenth century the Roman Church took care of all the problems it felt were caused by the Talmud and other writings by simply proscribing Hebrew works.[139]

Conclusion: Moving to the Renaissance

In the Middle Ages the connection between the belief in the special and magical power inherent in the Hebrew language and those religious currents known collectively as mysticism was a close one. Medieval Jewish mysticism and medieval magic were allies. At the heart of both was a belief in the supernatural power of the Hebrew language — the official language of the celestial court, an idea at home in early Christian as well as Jewish theology. Medieval magic was intertwined with, and in some sense a catalyst spurring the development of, Jewish mysticism. Hebrew magic lore "involved a close acquaintance with…essentially beneficent magic…" whose "primary principle was an implicit reliance upon the powers of good: the angels and the manifold differentiated and personalized attributes of God, which were invoked by a complicated

---

136   In the German lands this type of language was called Rotwelsch. See Bishoff, "Foreign Languages in the Middle Ages," 36:222 who calls this a "bastard among languages."

137   Trachtenberg, *Devil*, 68.

138   Rochus von Liliencron, *Die historischen Volkslieder der Deutschen vom 13. bis 16. Jahrhundert*, 4 vols. (Leipzig: F. C. W. Vogel, 1965–1969), I:173. "Etliche mit grawen har lernten erst den talmut die heilig schrift ducht sie nit gut…Sie heten al gelernet wol, ir kunst heist nigromanci Satanas was auch darbi, wane sie die rede geteten."

139   The Talmud had already been condemned in the thirteenth century as well as burned publicly. See Marcus, *Jew in the Medieval Inquisition in the Middle Ages*, 3 vols. (New York: Harper and Brothers, 1888), 1:554.

technique or permutation and combination of the letters of the Hebrew alphabet."[140]

Beliefs about the special nature of Hebrew influenced not only medieval Christian magic (and ideas about magic) but also medieval Jewish mysticism. In Christian circles these streams of thought fully converged in the fifteenth and sixteenth centuries, culminating in a profound interest in Hebraica, generally, and Christian Kabbalah, specifically, after the centuries of medieval developments. The prime example of this convergence is to be found in the writings of Johannes Reuchlin (1455–1522), "father of Hebrew philology among Christians"[141] and a foremost exponent of Christian Kabbalah.

Kabbalism is distinguished by an unusually positive attitude toward the Hebrew language.[142] Indeed, Kabbalism was based on the belief that every Hebrew word, letter, number, and even accent contained mysteries interpretable by those who know their secrets. Kabbalists also believed the names of God contained miraculous power and that each letter was potent. Gershom Scholem has said that to the medieval Kabbalists Hebrew, the holy tongue, was not simply a means of expressing thoughts, but had mystical power and was a reflection of God's creative power. All life was an expression of God's language.[143]

In Reuchlin the beliefs of the magician and the mystic concerning Hebrew come together. He is the one in whom many of the salient features of Christian views about, and attitudes toward, the Hebrew language during the previous thousand years find their fullest expression. He took up the study of Kabbalah and published the first Latin works ever written by a non-Jew on the subject, *De Verbo Mirifico* ("On the Miracle-Working Word," 1494) and *De Arte Cabalistica* ("On the Science of Kabbalah," 1517).[144]

For Reuchlin, as for those before him (from Origen onward), Hebrew was God's language; and, like the medieval mystics who preceded him, he believed that Kabbalah was God's grammar. In 1508 Reuchlin wrote that Hebrew was important because "God wished His secrets to be

---

140   Trachtenberg, *Devil*, 59.

141   E. Kauzsch and A. E. Cowley, eds., *Gesenius' Hebrew Grammar* (Oxford: The Clarendon Press, 1976), 20.

142   Gershom Scholem, *Major Trends in Jewish Mysticism*, 17.

143   Ibid.

144   *Encyclopedia Judaica*, s.v. "Kabbalah." A new edition of *De Arte Cabalistica* has been published with Latin facsimiles and English translation: Johannes Reuchlin, *De Arte Cabalistica*, trans. Martin and Sarah Goodman (New York: Abaris Books, 1983). They translate "Arte" as "Art" as opposed to E. J. "science."

known to man through Hebrew."[145] Again, in 1510, he said, "For when reading Hebrew I seem to see God Himself speaking when I think that this is the language in which God and the angels have told their minds to man from on high."[146]

In his *De Arte* Cabbalistica, Reuchlin shows that his interest in Hebrew is mystical: "This alone is the field of true contemplation; the single words which are single mysteries, and the single utterances, syllables, the apexes of the letters and the vowels are full of secret meanings."[147] But like the magicians of the Middle Ages, who respected the power inherent in the Hebrew language, Reuchlin had a special interest in the power of Hebrew names, especially the varied names for God. In *De Verbo Mirifico* he wrote: "The holy names of the Hebrews are more sacred than those of the Egyptians both because they are older and because they apply to the worship of the one supreme God."[148] Even though other special names might bring some insight into magical power, "no names...have the same power as those in Hebrew or those closely derived from Hebrew because of them all, they are the first formed by God."[149]

In sum, when we trace the development of medieval Christian beliefs and views about Hebrew as the language of magic, we are led, eventually, to the emergence of Christian Kabbalah in the sixteenth century. Christian Kabbalah was the result of an evolutionary process involving the combination of an early belief in the special and supernatural power of Hebrew, which belief was held by Christians as well as Jews, with the principles of Jewish mysticism—which, itself, was influenced by medieval Hebrew magic.

Andrew C. Skinner *is an award-winning professor of Ancient Scripture and Near Eastern Studies at BYU. He is the author or co-author of 20 books, including* Discoveries in the Judaea Desert, Unidentified Fragments from Cave 4 *(Oxford), and most recently,* To Become Like God: Witnesses of our Divine Potential *(Deseret Book). He has also edited 6 books and published over 100 articles on religious and historical topics. He served as Dean of Religious Education and founding director of the*

---

145   A letter of 1508 translated in Jerome Friedman, *The Most Ancient Testimony* (Athens: Ohio University Press, 1983), 73. I prefer his translation over most others.
146   Friedman, *The Most Ancient Testimony*, 73.
147   Ibid.
148   Ibid., 74.
149   Ibid.

Neal A. Maxwell Institute for Religious Scholarship at BYU. He currently serves on the board of directors of the Dead Sea Scrolls Foundation. He is married to Janet Corbridge Skinner and they have 6 children and 9 grandchildren.

Made in the USA
Columbia, SC
22 March 2021